HIDDEN
WEAPONS

BASIL COLLIER

HIDDEN WEAPONS

ALLIED SECRET OR UNDERCOVER SERVICES IN WORLD WAR II

With a Foreword by
R. V. JONES C.B., C.B.E., F.R.S.

PEN & SWORD MILITARY CLASSICS

First published in Great Britain in 1982 by Hamish Hamilton Ltd

Published in this format in 2006 by
Pen & Sword Military Classics
An imprint of
Pen & Sword Books Ltd
47 Church Street
Barnsley
South Yorkshire
S70 2AS

ISBN 1 84415 367 3

The publishers have made every effort to trace the author, his estate and his
agent without success and they would be interested to hear from anyone who is
able to provide them with this information.

A CIP catalogue record for this book is
available from the British Library

Printed and bound in England By CPI UK

Pen & Sword Books Ltd incorporates the Imprints of Pen & Sword Aviation,
Pen & Sword Maritime, Pen & Sword Military, Wharncliffe Local history,
Pen & Sword Select, Pen & Sword Military Classics and Leo Cooper.

For a complete list of Pen & Sword titles please contact
PEN & SWORD BOOKS LIMITED
47 Church Street, Barnsley, South Yorkshire, S70 2AS, England
E-mail: enquiries@pen-and-sword.co.uk
Website: www.pen-and-sword.co.uk

Contents

Tables

Foreword

The Defence of the United Kingdom was the Volume of the Official History dealing with British air defence in the Second World War; and despite the books that have appeared on the same subject since its publication in 1957, it remains the standard authority. It was written by Basil Collier, who is the author of this book; as he explains in his Introduction, he was aware of the Ultra decrypts of Enigma messages when writing the Official History, so that nothing he wrote there was likely to need revision when what has been called the Ultra secret was revealed. Now, twenty-five years later, Mr Collier takes the opportunity to review the contributions of all forms of Intelligence, and the use and misuse that was made of them, in all the major phases of World War II.

His task has required very wide reading of the great volume of original documents and derivative literature that is now available; and I admire the judgement that is evident throughout the book. Even in the one instance where my own assessment would differ from Mr Collier's, I recognize the great care which he has taken to work only from authoritative sources. This concerns the raid on Coventry on 14/15 November 1940, where he states the we knew by 3 p.m. that the German beams were intersecting over Coventry. The authority for this is a single sentence in an Air Staff report written three days later; but not only do I myself have the positive recollection that by 6 p.m. I myself did not know where the beams were intersecting, despite a conversation with the operational unit concerned, but also this recollection is consistent with the fact the the Air Staff officer whose duty it was to warn our defences when the target had been identified never sent the warning telegram that he had been ordered to send, since the draft is still on his file with a blank left where the name of the target was to have been filled in. And clearly he did not know the target by 4.15 p.m., for he did not mention it in the alerting telegram which he sent at that time in accordance with his orders when we were aware that a major attack would take place somewhere that evening. All this, though, is a small point (in which, incidentally, the official historians of *British Intelligence in the Second World War* agree with Mr Collier rather than with me) which would only assume importance if any credence were to be given to the theory that Churchill sacrificed Coventry, a theory which Mr Collier rightly ignores; and he is equally judicial in his assessment of the part played by Enigma decrypts in the Battle of Britain.

His account of the weak state of British Intelligence between the wars leads me to recall a conversation that I had years later with Lord Vansittart. I had remarked to him that one weakness of an organization like MI6 was that since the work was so confidential you had to be very sure of the trustworthiness of any new recruit, and so you were likely to bring in men whom you already knew; and if they were trustworthy, you were likely to have already established friendships with them. This could easily drift into a practice where you recruited your friends more because of their friendship rather than of their competence. Lord Vansittart agreed, but promptly added, 'There is another point, though. The pay was so bad that it was only your friends that you could persuade to take the job!' And, as if in confirmation of this, Kim Philby has recounted how his first attempt to get into the Government Code and Cypher School, under MI6, failed because the recruiting officer told him that he was too good for the pay that MI6 could offer.

But the very weakness of MI6 that Philby could so ably exploit had its occasional compensations. Niels Bohr, the most eminent of nuclear physicists, told me after his escape from Denmark to Britain in 1943 that he now had no doubts about the morality of working with the British Secret Service because he had found that it was run by a gentleman.

Another echo from those prewar days recalls the notorious Air Staff overestimate of the casualties that would be caused by a German air attack on London. It happens that I subsequently knew the officer who made the estimate, Wing Commander, later Air Vice-Marshal, F. F. Inglis: he told me that he had been asked to produce the estimate at very short notice and the question had been put to him in such a way that he decided a silly question deserved a silly answer and he never expected the estimate to be taken seriously, because of the manifest unreality of its basic assumptions.

Moving to the far end of Mr Collier's narrative, I can endorse his account of our knowledge of the prospect of Japan suing for peace before the atomic bomb was dropped. This came from decrypts of signals from Tokyo to the Japanese ambassador in Moscow in, as far as I can recall, February 1945. In fact, one officer at Bletchley, discussing their import with me, commented that he would not be surprised if the war with Japan finished before Germany was defeated. Whether or not this evidence was appreciated at the operational levels is, as Mr Collier says, a factor to be mentioned in any discussion of the decision to drop the bomb.

Mr Collier is judicious not only in his critical assessment of contributions made by various forms of Intelligence, but also in giving credit to our enemies and to those of our prewar politicians whose actions have perhaps been subsequently criticized more than they deserve; and there is food for thought in his accounts of the various attempts to rationalize our Intelligence organizations, and of the attitudes of the Armed Services and Whitehall Ministries towards them. Not the least of these factors is the way in which doctrine can be developed in contradiction to observable facts.

Mr Collier's Introduction recounts that serving officers lecturing at the Imperial Defence College before the war were forbidden to say that they expected the Luftwaffe to be used mainly as an army-support weapon; and the staffs of Bomber Command and the Air Ministry itself were unwilling to admit the inability of our bombers to hit their targets until two years of war forced the evidence upon us. But this is a weakness of almost all organizations and of many individuals, for few are as courageous as Lyon Playfair, who when sent by Robert Peel in 1845 to investigate the effect of the potato disease on Ireland, reported frankly that the prospect for Ireland was starvation unless the Corn Laws, which were the creation of Peel's own party, were repealed. And still fewer are as great as Peel, who replied, 'I am indeed sorry that you have to make so unfavourable a report, but the knowledge of the whole truth is one element of security,' and turned on his party to repeal the Corn Laws.

Within the limits of treating the widest aspects of Intelligence in World War II in a small compass, Mr Collier has told the whole truth, fortunately without it turning out to be very unfavourable: and in the lessons to be drawn from it, we indeed have one element of security if properly applied.

R. V. JONES

Introduction

When Group Captain F. W. Winterbotham's book, *The Ultra Secret*, was published in 1974, a good many people learned for the first time that in World War II the Allies had access to a mass of information about Axis plans, dispositions and intentions, derived from the reading by the British Government Code and Cypher School at Bletchley of signals encyphered by advanced versions of the German Enigma machine.

Group Captain Winterbotham's disclosures were followed by a partial relaxation of security regulations and the appearance of a number of books about Bletchley's contributions to Allied knowledge and their application to strategy or tactics. Unlike Group Captain Winterbotham's, which was written without access to official records and is surprisingly inaccurate in view of his experience, these are generally well researched.

Some reviewers of such books appear to be under the impression that, until a few years ago, historians of World War II worked in the dark so far as the information furnished by Bletchley was concerned, that consequently the history of the war needs to be rewritten in the light of material newly transferred to the public domain. Some of them do not seem, if I may be allowed to say so, quite to have got hold of the right end of the stick. I was one of the officially-accredited historians of World War II, a contributor to the United Kingdom military series of official histories. Contributors to that series were under an obligation not to refer, in volumes published before about 1978, to the source of Bletchley's information or to mention Ultra. (This was the security classification applied from 1941 to decrypts or translations of high-grade cypher messages and – from 1942 in the form Top Secret U – to reports or appreciations which reflected knowledge derived from them.) That does not necessarily mean that they had no knowledge of information so classified. I cannot speak for others; I became an authorized recipient of Ultra material nearly fifteen years before my official history, *The Defence of the United Kingdom*, was published in 1957.

I have not tried in this book to rewrite the history of the war. I have aimed at making, in so far as it can be done within the limits of a fairly short book and with the means available, a critical assessment of the use made by the Allies in World War II of intelligence from all sources and of their secret services and other clandestine agencies.

The standpoint is that of a user and purveyor, not an originator, of information from secret sources. I joined the RAF as an intelligence officer in 1940. The only training I received consisted of a brief course of lectures on various aspects of intelligence. A lecturer on espionage told us that beautiful female spies were a myth. A lecturer on Nazi Germany, apparently considering me a suitable recipient of such an aside, caught my eye and broke off his set discourse to remark: 'You can't imagine what life in Nazi Germany is like; hardly anyone wears tails nowadays.'

As I worked during the latter part of the Battle of Britain and throughout the Blitz in the underground operations room at Headquarters, Fighter Command, the account I give in Chapter Five of its activities is based on first-hand knowledge as well as documentary evidence. In 1941 I graduated to the Intelligence Hut above ground, where my duties consisted largely of acting as a post office for information passed to me by Air Intelligence from its subterranean lair in London or, after I became an indoctrinated recipient of Ultra material sometimes directly from Bletchley.

In 1943 we began to be worried about the secret weapons the Germans were said to be developing. I was given the job of assembling all the information about the still-hypothetical long-range rocket which Air Intelligence was willing to impart. When the Vice-Chiefs of Staff declared on 6 September 1944 that in their opinion long-range rocket attacks on London need no longer be expected, it therefore fell to me to point out – although doubtless the same thought occurred to others – that London could still be reached by rockets launched from Western Holland. A few hours after the first rocket arrived in the United Kingdom, I was given authority to set up the special intelligence section mentioned on pages 291 and 292.

In the autumn and early winter of 1944 I made two visits to France and Belgium, the first to accompany my chief on a round of visits to captured sites and the headquarters of the Second Tactical Air Force, the second as one of six members of a mission sent by the Chiefs of Staff to advise

General Eisenhower about counter-measures to flying bombs and rockets aimed at Continental targets.

At the end of the war in Europe, after serving for about six months in the organization set up in the light of the mission's report, I returned to Fighter Command as Air Historical Officer. Most of my work was done in London, but one of my duties was to make periodical visits to Bentley Priory, go through stacks of files, and tell the Chief Clerk which to keep and which to throw away. A good deal of material which survived this winnowing would seem afterwards to have disappeared from the archives, presumably because it was pulped to make room for more recent acquisitions.

*

I think no one who undertook such a study as I have attempted could fail to be struck by the low priority given to intelligence by successive British governments during the greater part of the period between the wars. In the interests of economy, the armed forces were ruthlessly pruned after the armistice with Germany. To save the cost of an arms race with the United States, restrictions imposed by the Naval Treaty of Washington were accepted and the Japanese alliance was allowed to lapse. As espionage and signal intelligence are much cheaper than fleets and armies, one might have thought that in these circumstances expenditure on the secret services would be increased as at least a partial insurance against the unexpected. On the contrary, it was so drastically reduced that MI 6 was forced to abandon or curtail its activities in a number of countries. By 1936 it depended for much of its information about Germany on the French.*

The situation improved in some respects during the next three to four years. A fair amount of information about the Wehrmacht – some of it good and some not so good – was received from service attachés and in confidential disclosures by the Germans. Financial restrictions were eased to some extent after Munich. With the arrival of new blood from the universities, MI 6 ceased to be exposed to the reproach – if it is a reproach – that its headquarters was manned almost exclusively by members of White's and retired officers of the Indian Police. Reservists and newcomers recruited from a wide range of professions joined the intelligence branches of the service departments. Copious and highly circumstantial reports about the German Army's dispositions and mobilization plans were received from a well-placed agent employed by

* See Chapter Two.

the Czechoslovak intelligence service, based from the spring of 1939 in London.*

However, these improvements had little practical effect. Ministers and senior officials liked to be regaled with secret service reports, just as some of them liked reading thrillers. They did not take either reports or thrillers very seriously. When it came to choosing or recommending a course of action, they tended to rely on preconceptions or hunches, sometimes backed by unconfirmed rumours or private communications.

Much the same could be said of many regular officers of the armed forces. Regular officers put in charge of intelligence sections sometimes showed a strange contempt for their stock-in-trade, although they would stoutly defend themselves and their subordinates against external criticism. Army and RAF intelligence officers who thought in the second half of the 1930s that the Luftwaffe would be used in a European war mainly as an army-support weapon were forbidden to say so when lecturing at the Imperial Defence College or elsewhere.† As late as the spring of 1940 the General Staff preferred the Deuxième Bureau's estimates of the strength of the German Army to those made by their own intelligence officers, although there was good reason to believe that the French figures were inflated.

No evidence that Hitler was preparing to attack Britain or the British Empire prompted the Defence Requirements Committee's pronouncement in 1934 that Germany was the 'ultimate potential enemy'. Clearly his policy was to cultivate good relations with the British and expand eastwards. Germany was the potential enemy only inasmuch as adherence to that policy might precipitate a conflict from which an ill-armed and reluctant Britain would find it hard to hold aloof. In fairness to the Baldwin and Chamberlain governments, it must be borne in mind that not only the politicians but also the general public were dismayed by the prospect of another European war. The statesmen were haunted, too, by the knowledge that involvement in such a war would greatly increase the difficulty of discharging Britain's obligation to contribute to the security of Commonwealth countries and colonial possessions and dependencies.

For a time the most promising solution seemed to lie in the combination of a conciliatory attitude towards Germany with modest additions to the national and imperial defences and preparations for no

* See below, pp. 24–5, 29, 33, 41–2, 46.
† Strong, *Intelligence at the Top*, 18; Hinsley, *British Intelligence in the Second World War*, i, 78–79.

more than limited and contingent participation in a European war. But rearmament was hampered by budgetary considerations, reluctance to interfere with normal trade, and the fear that even modest programmes might seem to the Germans to threaten them with encirclement. Hitler could not be prevented from adopting an increasingly bellicose attitude towards countries allied with France, and eventually the concept of a war of limited liability had to be abandoned.

Other possibilities considered at various times between 1938 and the summer of 1940 were that Germany might be weakened by subsidized partisan activities in countries occupied by her troops, and that Hitler might be deposed by a *coup d'état*. SOE had its genesis in studies of methods of propaganda, sabotage and subversion begun in 1938;* the peace-loving Neville Chamberlain signed in the summer of 1939 the document afterwards regarded as its charter. There was no lack of Germans willing to conspire against Hitler, but pre-war discussions came to nothing. When the British tried after the outbreak of war to resume negotiations, they fell into a trap.†

In the meantime the British and French governments bought a year's respite from war by sacrificing Czechoslovakia. The rights and wrongs of their decision to do so have been much canvassed in the light of post-war statements by German generals and captured documents; but what did the intelligence agencies think and say at the time? This question is discussed on pages 32 to 40. A point which seems to me to deserve more emphasis than perhaps it has received in some accounts is that the British Foreign Policy Committee and the Cabinet decided little more than a week after the rape of Austria in the spring of 1938 that pressure should be put on Czechoslovakia to make concessions to the Sudeten Germans. They did not give themselves and their advisers much time to digest the lessons of the march to Vienna and assess the Wehrmacht's ability to sustain a two-front war against France in the West and Czechoslovakia in the East. Reliable intelligence about the German Army's plan for the invasion of Czechoslovakia did not reach London and Paris until the summer. By that time the British and French governments were too deeply committed to their policy of appeasing Hitler at Czechoslovakia's expense to pay heed to it.

I have done my best in Chapter Two to extract from conflicting accounts the truth about the parts played by Polish mathematicians and French spymasters in early attempts to break Enigma, and in later

* See pp. 12–13.
† See pp. 33–4, 55.

chapters to give a fair though necessarily much compressed account of contributions made by the reading of Enigma messages to Allied thought and action. Not the least important of these was that the copiousness and manifest authority of the decrypted traffic at last convinced commanders and staffs that intelligence had something to offer.

The evidence set out on pages 65 to 69 suggests to me that the German invasion of Norway in April 1940 ought to have been foreseen, and would have been foreseen if the Admiralty had not obstinately refused to shed a preconception. Some items of intelligence that might have led the French to expect a major thrust in the Ardennes in May are mentioned in Chapter Four. These were not conclusive; what is surprising is that reports received during the first few days and nights of the campaign failed to convince the High Command that far more than local attacks in the Sedan–Dinant sector were impending. Evidence which pointed to the postponement of Sea lion is summarized on pages 110 to 111.

As is shown in Chapter Five, Fighter Command received very little Enigma material of immediate operational significance during the daylight Battle of Britain, although some published accounts give the opposite impression. The arrangements for passing the material expeditiously to commands, on which Group Captain Winterbotham justly prides himself, were not made until long after the battle was over. The fighter groups relied for most, if not all, of their tactical intelligence on the radar chain and the Y-Service. Group Captain Winterbotham cannot have been gratified in the summer of 1940 by the sight of neat sheets of paper marked Ultra (*The Ultra Secret*, p. 61), because the term was not used before 1941.

Important intelligence contributions to defence against the night Blitz are described in Chapter Seven. Professor Hinsley interprets with admirable precision in his official history the surviving evidence that bears on what was thought at the Air Ministry before the Coventry raid about Moonlight Sonata, but I don't think Fighter Command ever expected Moonlight Sonata to take the form of attacks on any part of Southern England. I think Fighter Command expected, from the time when Moonlight Sonata was first mentioned, a new series of raids on the industrial Midlands. According to my recollection of a document apparently no longer extant, Wolverhampton and Birmingham, in that order, were considered the most likely targets for the first raid.

I discuss in Chapter Six some intelligence problems arising from

Italy's entry into the war, and some failures and successes. Matapan was a triumph for intelligence, but I can find no evidence for the belief that Italian cypher tables were borrowed for a night by a seductive female spy. Crete was the first major action of the war in which the evidence of Enigma traffic might have turned the scales in favour of the Allies. It just failed to do so, despite the great pains taken to ensure that the Allied commander was well briefed.

From the spring of 1942 commanders in the Middle East received a copious stream of intelligence derived from Enigma. It did not save them from some staggering reverses, but contributed to Montgomery's victory at Alam el Halfa, generally considered his most successful battle.

Allied foreknowledge of Barbarossa is discussed in Chapter Eight. A point overlooked in some accounts is that the Air Ministry asked Bomber, Fighter and Coastal Commands five days before the Germans opened their offensive to consider ways of helping Russia.* The sources of the remarkable information conveyed to the Russians during the campaign by the agent Lucy remain mysterious, although the Czechoslovak intelligence chief Frantisek Moravec claimed to know them. I have always supposed that Lucy received from the British the substance of Enigma decrypts, but this has been authoritatively denied. The Russians did, however, receive through the British Military Mission in Moscow the substance of some of Enigma decrypts in disguised form.

Two questions never likely to be answered to everyone's satisfaction are why the Americans went out of their way to precipitate hostilities in the Far East and the Pacific at a time when adroit diplomacy could surely have postponed them for at least some months; and why, although privy to some of Japan's most closely-guarded secrets and aware that the Japanese carrier fleet was unlocated, they allowed the Pearl Harbor attack to take them by surprise. I can throw no light on the first question; some aspects of the second are discussed in Chapter Nine. Signal intelligence made momentous contributions to the battles of the Coral Sea and Midway Island; thereafter intelligence was perhaps a less important factor for the Americans, because before long they possessed such overwhelming numerical superiority that they could afford to make mistakes. Not so the British, who could scarcely have hoped to escape defeat at Kohima and Imphal if they had not known what to expect. The book ends with a brief discussion of Allied knowledge, before the first atomic bomb was dropped, of Japan's earnest desire to make peace.

The late Sir Lewis Namier remarked long ago that there are very few
* See p. 202.

profound secrets to which one cannot find a reference somewhere in a printed book if one knows what to look for. Bearing that dictum in mind, I have drawn freely on official histories and other published works, using unpublished material chiefly to test their accuracy, or for the light it may throw on controversial issues. This procedure has enabled me to cite in support of most statements sources available to the general reader for whom this book is intended.

ONE

Cloaks and Daggers

Secret services and other clandestine agencies are generally held to have played a more important role in World War II than in any previous war. How big was the contribution made by such organizations to the military success of the uneasy coalition called by Churchill the Grand Alliance?

One of many factors which preclude a simple, clear-cut answer is that there was no Grand Alliance until the war was two years old. During those two years the secret armouries of its members reached different stages of development and were developed with different ends in view. When Britain committed herself to war in 1939 with France and Poland as allies, few things seemed less probable than a full-blown military alliance between the capitalist British Empire, the anti-capitalist Soviet Union and the anti-imperialist United States. An Anglo–Russian alliance had been mooted in the spring and early summer, but in August the Russians had thrown in their lot with Hitler by signing the Moscow Pact. We know that President Roosevelt and his naval and military advisers recognized in 1939 that eventually the national interest might require that United States forces should be sent to Europe or Africa to secure the defeat of the Axis powers.[1] We also know that they did not aim at committing the nation to a war in which it was not ready to play a major role. As for the British, the Chamberlain government was more interested in buying American machine-tools, aircraft, food and raw materials, and in securing some relaxation of restrictions on the supply of arms and credit to belligerents, than in persuading the Americans to take a course which would divert a great part of their industrial capacity to the expansion of their own armed forces.

*

On the outbreak of war the German section of the military intelligence branch of the British War Office predicted that Poland would be overrun in three weeks, that Hitler would then make overtures to France and Britain, and that he would launch an offensive on the Western Front in the early winter if these were rejected.[2]

These predictions were substantially correct. Much to the dismay of the German generals, Hitler insisted when Poland fell that an offensive on the Western Front should be launched in November. The generals were correspondingly relieved when an unfavourable weather forecast gave them a valid pretext for postponing the assault two days after the preliminary order was given.

Not all attempts by the British to divine the enemy's intentions or assess his resources were as close to the mark. None of the service departments knew on the outbreak of war that the Germans were equipped with radar, or that they were experimenting with long-range rockets as military weapons. The Admiralty suspected that the German Navy might use magnetic mines but received no warning from the Naval Intelligence Division, which had not been told that Britain had used a magnetic mine in 1918, or that an improved magnetic mine was under development in the United Kingdom.[3] The War Office was rather better informed than its French counterpart about the number of divisions the Germans could mobilize, but credited them with many more tanks than they possessed.[4] The Air Ministry grossly over-estimated the Luftwaffe's stored reserves, and its peacetime forecasts of the enemy's course of action in the early stages of a war between Britain and Germany were consistently tendentious and misleading.[5]

To understand how these and other mistakes arose, it is necessary to take a look at the peacetime structure of the British intelligence organization and to note its response, or lack of response, to some of the problems that confronted it between the wars.

*

Only a small proportion of the information about developments in foreign countries that was available to British governments between 1918 and 1939 came from intelligence agencies, and a still smaller proportion was processed by intelligence officers. The Foreign Office had no intelligence branch, and it did not apply the term intelligence to the material that reached it from British diplomatic missions abroad and foreign diplomatic missions in London. Other sources of information distinct from that furnished by intelligence agencies included consular reports, private communications from British subjects domiciled or travelling abroad, and statements made by immigrants and real or supposed defectors and dissidents. Some of this material was valuable, but inevitably it included a fairly high proportion of spurious information planted by counter-intelligence agencies or inspired by love of scandal or wishful thinking.

Peacetime sources of information that *was* classed as intelligence included reports from agents employed by the Secret Intelligence Service or by foreign secret services with which it was in contact; statements by informants in touch with the Security Service; reports from intelligence officers of the armed forces stationed abroad; clandestine aerial photography; and intercepted signals.

The Secret Intelligence Service could trace its origins at least as far back as the sixteenth century. It was remodelled in the first decade of the twentieth century to meet the situation arising from Britain's emergence from splendid isolation, her alliance with Japan, her new understandings with France and Russia about colonial, imperial and strategic questions, and a tentative decision to send to France, in the event of war with Germany, the expeditionary force hitherto intended for despatch to the North-West Frontier of India in the event of war with Russia. In 1909 Asquith's Liberal government set up a Secret Service Bureau which consisted essentially of a Foreign Section concerned with espionage in foreign countries, and a Home Section which replaced the Special Duties Division of the War Office (or MO 5) as the authority responsible for counter-intelligence and security. Initially both sections were administered by the War Office. They became separate though closely related entities when, in 1910, administrative control of the Foreign Section was transferred for the time being to the Admiralty. The Foreign Section was headed by Captain (afterwards Sir) Mansfield Cumming, the Home Section by Captain (afterwards Major-General Sir) Vernon Kell. By signing minutes and memoranda with the first letter of his surname, Cumming established the tradition that he and his successors should be known as C.

During World War I both the Admiralty and the War Office set up espionage organizations which were distinct from the Secret Intelligence Service and drew their information largely from sympathizers in territories occupied or infiltrated by the enemy. The War Office also regained administrative control, though only for a time, of C's organization, which became the MI 1(c) section of the Military Intelligence branch. It retained a military designation, as MI 6, when control was transferred later in the war to the Foreign Office. Kell's organization, already controlled administratively by the War Office, became MI 5.

At the end of the war the wartime espionage networks established by the Admiralty and the War Office since 1914 ceased to function. In 1919 a ministerial Secret Service Committee was appointed to consider the future of the permanent intelligence agencies. In the same year, government departments were instructed to review their estimates for the coming year on the assumption that there would be no great war involving the British Empire for at least ten years. C's budget was thereupon reduced from £240,000 to £125,000. A further reduction to £65,000 was proposed in 1920, but a strong protest from the War Office led to the adoption of a compromise figure of £100,000. A similar threat in 1922 was countered by the War Office with a demand for £150,000. The outcome was that a revived Secret Service Committee, reduced from ministerial to official status, set a figure of £90,000.[6]

These were dangerous economies at a time when the army could barely meet demands for garrisons at home and abroad and the partial or complete disintegration of the Hapsburg, Ottoman and Tsarist empires had created a host of new states which needed watching. Their effects were felt for many years, and were only partly mitigated by more generous treatment after Hitler's accession to power.[7] C complained as late as 1935 that his total budget did not exceed the normal cost of maintaining a single destroyer in home waters.[8]

On the advice of the ministerial Secret Service Committee, the Secret Intelligence Service was made in the meantime exclusively responsible for espionage on behalf of the Foreign Office, the Home Office, the India Office, the Colonial Office, the Admiralty, the War Office and the recently formed Air Ministry. The Foreign Office retained the ultimate responsibility for its administration which it had assumed before the end of the war. The War Office relinquished control of MI 5 to the Home Office, but remained responsible for security in the field. A civil Directorate of Intelligence formed by the Home Office in 1919 was disbanded in 1921. In effect, the mantle of the old Special Duties Division of the War Office descended upon MI 5 and the Special Branch of Scotland Yard.

Contributions to the intelligence picture by officers serving overseas included reports from intelligence officers of all three services at stations in various parts of the empire. The Admiralty maintained, in addition to Staff Officers (Intelligence) at the headquarters of naval commands at home and abroad, a world-wide network of Naval Reporting Officers to report shipping movements. An inter-service Far East Combined Bureau was formed in 1935 at Hong Kong and moved in

1939 to Singapore. A Middle East Intelligence Centre was established at Cairo in the summer of 1939.

Aerial photography for intelligence purposes was not regarded by the British as a necessary or desirable peacetime activity until, in 1935, the Abyssinian crisis prompted the RAF to take oblique photographs of Abyssinia, Eritrea, Cyrenaica and Sicily from positions outside Italian territorial limits. Some three years later Squadron-Leader F. W. Winterbotham, whose duties included liaison between Air Intelligence and the Secret Intelligence Service, discussed with the Deuxième Bureau of the French Armée de l'Air the taking of vertical photographs of potentially hostile territory. French reconnaissance aircraft had resumed flights over Germany, after a long interval, in 1936, but had covered only a small part of the country. The outcome of Winter-botham's conversations with the French was that the Secret Intelligence Service formed, in association with the Deuxième Bureau and under the cover-name of the Aeronautical Research and Sales Corporation, a Special Flight for the purpose of undertaking clandestine aerial photography on behalf of the intelligence services of both countries. Its leading figure was S. F. Cotton, an Australian businessman who had served in the RNAS in World War I and had afterwards become a pilot and navigator of exceptional skill by flying his own aircraft about Europe. Assisted by Flying-Officers R. H. Niven and M. V. Longbottom, Cotton developed a technique of high-altitude photography which set new standards of clarity and precision. Between 1935 and the outbreak of World War II the Air Ministry spent substantial sums on the training of aircrew for photographic reconnaissance and on photographic equip-ment and research, but formed no special photographic reconnaissance units. This was partly because the RAF had few aircraft to spare, partly because it regarded photographic reconnaissance as a task which could and should be undertaken in wartime by existing bomber and general-reconnaissance squadrons.

The Special Flight did not begin to function until the spring of 1939, and its resources were small. British officers stationed in the Mediterra-nean or east of Suez were not in a position to throw much light on German intentions or resources. It is therefore fair to say that, apart from diplomatic and other reports traditionally excluded from the intelligence category, agents' reports and signal intelligence were potentially, albeit not always actually, the best sources of information about developments in Germany available to British governments between the wars.

The British were well placed to make a success of signal intelligence. Besides sharing with the leading Continental powers an accumulated experience of code-breaking which went back to the sixteenth century or earlier, they were pioneers of wireless intelligence, of techniques which included the location of transmitters afloat or ashore by direction-finding, the study of call-signs and signal procedures, the decrypting of transmissions in high-grade or low-grade cyphers. Their overseas empire gave them exceptional facilities for the installation of listening-stations in most parts of the world.

During World War I the Admiralty established, and eventually located in Room 40 of the Old Admiralty Building, a cryptanalytical bureau which studied both naval and diplomatic traffic. Its best-known feat was the decypherment of the notorious Zimmermann telegram, which promised German support for Mexican claims to lost territories in Texas, New Mexico and Arizona if Mexico entered the war on the side of the Central Powers. A less widely publicized cryptanalytical bureau, which dealt mostly with tactical traffic, was established by the War Office and became the MI 1(b) section of the Military Intelligence Branch.

At the end of the war Room 40 and MI 1(b) were disbanded. Their place was taken in 1919 by a civilian organization, the Government Code and Cypher School. Although in practice chiefly concerned with signal intelligence, this organization was responsible not only for the study of codes and cyphers used by foreign powers, but also for advising on the security of those used by the British. For administrative purposes it was put in the first instance under the Admiralty, but control passed in 1922 to the Foreign Office. On the death of Sir Mansfield Cumming in 1923 his successor, Rear-Admiral 'Quex' Sinclair, was given the formal style of Chief of the Secret Service and Director of the Government Code and Cypher School, but the two organizations remained distinct although they were closely linked. The civilian cryptanalysts of the Government Code and Cypher School – most of them recruited from Room 40 or MI 1(b) – were paid by the Foreign Office not from its Secret Vote but from its ordinary vote.

During the greater part of the period between the wars the listening stations (called Y-Stations) which furnished the Government Code and Cypher School with its raw material were operated and administered solely by the fighting services. Responsibility for establishing and manning the Y-Stations was shared between the service departments in accordance with a series of *ad hoc* decisions intended to ensure that, although each had its own Y-Service, wasteful overlapping was avoided. Guidance was provided in theory by a Cryptography and Interception Committee established by the GC & CS in 1924, in practice usually by a standing sub-committee, the Y Sub-Committee. In 1937 the sub-committee, recognizing that in wartime the existing Y-Stations might be fully occupied with naval, military and air force traffic, made arrangements for the General Post Office to install, operate and administer additional Y-Stations to intercept Axis diplomatic traffic for the benefit of the Foreign Office.[9] In the following year the GC & CS set up a commercial section to glean from intercepted signals, mostly in plain language or published commercial codes, material of interest to the Industrial Intelligence Centre. This was an offshoot, formed in 1931, of an industrial intelligence sub-committee of the Committee of Imperial Defence.

The existence of the GC & CS was justified in the eyes of the service departments chiefly by its responsibility for the breaking of high-grade cyphers. To what extent it should concern itself with the reading of signals in plain language or low-grade cyphers and the study of call-signs, signal procedures and communication networks was debatable. In the opinion of the service departments these tasks, collectively called traffic analysis, could be adequately performed by their Y-Services. Nevertheless the Y Sub-Committee recommended in the spring of 1938 that traffic analysis should be centralized at the headquarters of the GC & CS – then in London but due to move on or shortly before the outbreak of war to Bletchley Park in Buckinghamshire – and that all interception and direction-finding stations in the United Kingdom should be linked with it, and with each other, by secure telephone and teleprinter networks.[10]

The service departments accepted the second proposal, but not the first. Eventually it was agreed that traffic analysis and direction-finding should not be centralized, but that the GC & CS would be free to undertake such duplication of work done by the service departments as was essential to its cryptanalytical functions, on the understanding that the service departments would not be responsible for finding or paying any additional staff required for the purpose. The service departments, which had hitherto reserved the right to withdraw their liaison sections on the outbreak of war or earlier, accepted compromise agreements which ensured that, to some extent at least, the GC & CS would continue to function in wartime on an inter-service basis.

The Foreign Office took no part in these discussions.[11] Its reluctance to become embroiled in a controversy touching on the domestic affairs of an organization whose activities could not be acknowledged was understandable, but scarcely made for harmonious relations with its unavowable dependent. Commander Alastair Denniston, the retired naval officer who headed the GC & CS from its formation until 1942, complained that his organization was relegated in peacetime to the status of an adopted child of the Foreign Office, without family rights, and a poor relation of the Secret Intelligence Service.[12]

The Secret Intelligence Service, too, was an adopted child of the Foreign Office. Here again the attitude of the Foreign Office to an unavowable but by no means disreputable protégé left something to be desired. The Foreign Office insisted that the Secret Intelligence Service, in so far as it concerned itself with political intelligence, should do so for its benefit and under its supervision. Nevertheless its officials showed little interest in the organization, methods or problems of the service for whose welfare and efficiency they were ultimately responsible.

A more serious reproach that must be levelled at the Foreign Office is that it yielded too readily to pressure from the Treasury to keep expenditure on the Secret Intelligence Service to a minimum at a time when the intentional running down of the national defences made an ample flow of reliable intelligence more important than ever. In 1920 the Foreign Office would have cut C's budget by nearly half if the War Office had not intervened. In 1922 it accepted the absurdly low figure proposed by a committee headed by a Treasury official. No serious attempt to improve matters was made before 1935. By that time Hitler had been in power for two years, Mussolini had embarked on a course destined to extinguish his power to oppose German designs on Austria, and there was an urgent demand for more information about Germany and Italy than an impoverished Secret Intelligence Service could supply.

Peacetime arrangements for the processing of information furnished by the intelligence agencies was far from satisfactory. Despite its lack of an intelligence branch, the Foreign Office claimed a monopoly of the interpretation and analysis of political intelligence. Agents' reports containing political intelligence were handled by officials likely to judge their reliability by the extent to which they were corroborated by the diplomatic information with which the Foreign Office was primarily concerned. Items of naval, military or air intelligence which came to their attention were passed to the appropriate service department without comment, but not necessarily before conclusions had been drawn which might differ from those drawn by the ultimate recipient. The service departments insisted that naval, military and air intelligence should be interpreted and analysed exclusively by their respective intelligence branches, but tended in peacetime to regard all but the most senior posts in those branches as havens for officers in poor health, on the eve of retirement, or judged temperamentally unfit for more active employment. Especially in the navy, service in the intelligence branch was a hindrance rather than a help to an officer's career.

These were not the only shortcomings of the system in force between the wars. Before the second half of the 1930s there was no regularly constituted forum, below the impractically high level of the Committee of Imperial Defence, for the discussion on an inter-departmental or supra-departmental basis of intelligence of interest to more than one department. The Chiefs of Staff were made formally responsible in 1926 for tendering advice to the government about matters of joint concern. They provided themselves with a Joint Planning Staff, but took no steps during the next nine years or so to set up a joint intelligence staff. They and the Joint Planners drew their information about developments in foreign countries from the intelligence branches of their respective departments, and from periodical summaries of the international outlook compiled by the Foreign Office. The consequences were not only that little attempt was made to collate information available in the different departments and arrive at joint interpretations, but also that the habit of not attempting joint interpretations persisted even after the means of consultation were provided.

The first attempt to create some kind of joint intelligence body – apart from abortive discussions in 1934 between the Director of Naval Intelligence and the Director of Military Operations and Intelligence – was an almost total failure. Early in 1936 the Committee of Imperial Defence set up, on the initiative of the Deputy Chiefs of Staff, an Inter-Service Intelligence Committee consisting of the Deputy Director of Naval Intelligence, the Deputy Director of Intelligence at the Air Ministry, and the head of the MI 1 branch at the War Office. It had no secretariat, no provision was made for it to meet regularly, and it appears to have left no record of its meetings, if indeed it held any.[13] In the following July it was replaced by a Joint Intelligence Committee intended by the Chiefs of Staff to provide a channel for the conveyance to the Joint Planners of material contributed by more than one department. Initially its composition was the same as that of its ill-starred predecessor, but it was empowered to co-opt a representative of the Industrial Intelligence Centre, and in fact did so. Until the summer of 1939, when it acquired a secretariat of its own, it shared a secretary with the Joint Planners.

The Joint Intelligence Committee proved not to be in peacetime, nor in the early stages of World War II, an effective instrument for the co-ordination of intelligence. With the benefit of hindsight, it is not difficult to see that what was really needed was a strong, independent, self-confident body of experts capable of putting its own interpretations on reports from all sources, and if necessary of challenging – perhaps even overriding – interpretations put upon them by individual departments. The Joint Intelligence Committee, as originally constituted, came far short of meeting that requirement. Largely preoccupied with administrative matters, it made few independent contributions to the intelligence picture before the outbreak of war, or indeed for some time afterwards. Nor was it in a position, until almost the eve of the war, to collate naval, military and air intelligence with political intelligence and information received by the Foreign Office from diplomatic or private sources. No representative of the Foreign Office attended a meeting of the committee until well after Munich, and the Foreign Office was not regularly represented at its meetings before the summer of 1939.[14]

The Chiefs of Staff and the intelligence branches, although anxious to safeguard the rights of the service departments, were by no means satisfied that a system from which the Foreign Office held aloof left no room for improvement. The Chiefs of Staff suggested in the spring of 1938 that the Joint Planners should be allowed to discuss the international outlook with the Foreign Office, instead of merely receiving summaries which they printed verbatim in their reports. The Deputy Director of Military Intelligence proposed early in 1939 that the Joint Intelligence Committee should be given a Foreign Office chairman and empowered to 'sift all political intelligence'.[15] The Foreign Office resisted all such proposals until, in the spring of 1939, the Chiefs of Staff gained the support of the Minister for the Co-Ordination of Defence and the Prime Minister for their demand that a Situation Report Centre, to which the Foreign Office would be required to appoint a representative, should be formed to deal on an inter-departmental basis, if not with all intelligence reports, at any rate with those which might seem to call for prompt decisions.

The Situation Report Centre consisted of representatives of the service departments and the Foreign Office, with the representative of the Foreign Office in the chair. Its functions were not unlike those of the watchmen at one time employed by owners of large country houses to perambulate the premises at night and announce at hourly intervals that all was well. For some two months it issued daily reports, irrespective of whether there was anything worth reporting. At the end of that time it was amalgamated, at its own request, with the Joint Intelligence Committee.

In consequence of the amalgamation the Joint Intelligence Committee acquired a new status and was given new terms of reference. Henceforward its meetings were attended, as a matter of course, by a representative of the Foreign Office, with the rank of counsellor, who in practice presided over them although nominally it had no chairman. It continued to issue the daily situation reports hitherto issued by the Situation Report Centre and the weekly commentaries on the international situation which the report centre had taken to distributing. In addition it was instructed to ensure that any action taken by the government in the light of intelligence received from abroad was based on the best and most carefully co-ordinated information obtainable, co-ordinate any intelligence data called for by the Chiefs of Staff or by the Joint Planners on their behalf, and consider any measures that might seem necessary for the improvement of the intelligence organization as a whole.[16]

In the event, the committee was largely concerned during the remaining months of peace with such matters as the supervision of arrangements for the exchange of intelligence with the French and the co-ordination of preparations for the establishment of military missions in Poland, Rumania and Turkey. Before 1940 the Directors of Intelligence seldom attended its meetings, at which they were represented, as a rule, by their deputies. The Chiefs of Staff continued to rely for their knowledge of foreign navies, armies and air forces on the intelligence branches of their respective departments, and these still suffered from weaknesses arising from the low priority accorded to intelligence in peacetime by the fighting services.

The intelligence branches were not, for example, well placed either to acquire or to interpret information about scientific and technical developments in foreign countries. The technical section of the Naval Intelligence Division consisted in peacetime of one officer.[17] The Military Intelligence and Air Intelligence branches of the War Office and the Air Ministry had no technical sections, but each employed one officer concerned with technical matters.[18] None of these officers was powerful enough to exert much influence on the briefing of agents by the

Secret Intelligence Service, and they were not expected to do much more than take note of such information as happened to come their way.

However, in the spring of 1939 the Chairman of the Air Ministry's Committee for the Scientific Survey of Air Defence, Sir Henry Tizard, proposed that a scientific officer should be attached to the staff of its Director of Scientific Research for liaison with Air Intelligence. The post was offered in May to Dr R. V. Jones, a twenty-seven-year-old physicist already employed by the Air Ministry but seconded to the Admiralty Research Laboratory adjoining the National Physical Laboratory at Teddington. Jones accepted the appointment with effect from 1 September.[19] As he was on leave on that day, he did not take up his new duties until a day or two after the outbreak of war. The original intention was not that he should take an active part in the assembly or interpretation of intelligence, but that he should report on the means employed by the intelligence branches to acquire, interpret and distribute information about technical and scientific developments in foreign countries, and should suggest improvements. This was expected to take him about six months. As things turned out, he stayed to become a full-time intelligence officer whose services to the Air Ministry, and indeed to the country, proved invaluable.

*

The British authorities gave some thought, before the outbreak of war, to the formation of clandestine agencies not primarily concerned with the gathering of information or with counter-intelligence. In the spring of 1938 the Foreign Office set up an organization – sometimes called CS because it was headed by Sir Campbell Stuart and sometimes EH because it was located at Electra House, on the Thames Embankment – for the purpose of investigating methods of influencing opinion in Germany.[20] At the same time an organization called Section D, also controlled ultimately by the Foreign Office, was formed to explore a field afterwards defined as 'every possibility of attacking potential enemies by means other than the operations of military forces'.[21] The most obvious of these means were sabotage and propaganda, but Section D did not have a monopoly of either. Propaganda was Sir Campbell Stuart's business. Sabotage soon became a matter of interest to the General Staff (Research) section of the War Office, commonly called GS (R).

GS (R) consisted initially of one typist and one General Staff Officer, Grade II, who reported directly to the Vice-Chief of the Imperial

General Staff. The post was what its holder and the VCIGS liked to make it. The officer who held it when Section D was formed was concerned with army education. He was succeeded towards the end of 1938 by Major J. C. F. Holland, an engineer officer who had served in Ireland during the troubles and had studied reports of partisan activities in Spain and China. Appointed on the understanding that he would be free to follow his own line, he negotiated with Section D an informal agreement by which Section D took for its province the study – but in peacetime not the practice – of unavowable forms of co-operation with dissidents or resistance groups, while GS (R) concerned itself mainly with the development of weapons and equipment suitable for irregular warfare but not necessarily or obviously intended only for such purposes.

In the light of a paper prepared jointly by Section D and GS (R), the Foreign Secretary and the Chief of the Imperial General Staff agreed shortly before the Germans marched into Bohemia and Moravia that, if the Prime Minister concurred, clandestine preparations should be made for the fostering of resistance to National Socialism in small countries overrun or about to be overrun by German troops. Soon afterwards an expanded GS (R) was incorporated in the Military Intelligence branch as MI (R). Holland was joined by Major Colin Gubbins, who shared his interests and his experience of service in Ireland. Before leaving MI (R) to become Chief of Staff of the British Military Mission in Warsaw, Gubbins compiled what was in effect a field service manual of irregular warfare by writing short pamphlets on guerilla tactics, the use of explosives for small-scale demolitions, and the leadership of partisan forces. He also made secret visits to Eastern Europe and the Baltic States. In the summer of 1939 Section D and MI (R) jointly organized courses attended by civilians chosen for their experience of exploration or mountaineering or their knowledge of foreign languages and foreign countries.[22]

TWO

Between the Wars

In the early years of the twentieth century the British Secret Service was regarded with considerable respect, and even awe, in foreign countries. Its reputation for discreet efficiency was by no means wholly unde-served, but rested largely on the success of the British in holding India with relatively small forces and in countering the activities of foreign agents in Central Asia and the Near and Middle East. The Foreign Office, which was not directly concerned with Indian or Colonial affairs, preferred diplomatic reports and private communications to secret intelligence, did not allow British agents abroad to communicate with London through diplomatic channels, and would gladly have seen the role of the Secret Service confined to the furnishing of naval and military intelligence to the service departments. Enquiries by the Committee of Imperial Defence revealed that in 1907 the Secret Service had no agents in Europe and had made no provision for the establishment of espionage networks in European countries in the event of war.[1] Notwithstanding the formation of the Secret Service Bureau some two years later, on the eve of World War I the British still depended largely on the French for information about the German Army.[2] During the war the navy and the army relied not only for tactical but also for strategic intelligence partly on their own resources.

The post-war reforms mentioned in the last chapter left Britain with a peacetime signal intelligence service which employed initially some twenty-five cryptanalysts drawn from Room 40 and MI 1(b), and a Secret Intelligence Service whose financial resources did not enable it to meet all the demands made upon it by the seven government departments for which it was expected to cater. Someone had therefore to decide which demands should be accepted and which rejected, and in what order of priority those accepted should be listed. Ideally, these decisions would have been made by an arbiter so well informed about all aspects of every question that he could strike a rational balance between the desirable and the feasible, and so powerful that his conclusions would not be challenged. In the absence of such a paragon, they had to be made by C himself. Ministers and officials to whom he had access could give him broad guidance about policy; at a lower level the service departments, in so far as they were able to formulate their demands without knowing in advance how much information about any particular matter was likely to be available, could make their wants known through liaison sections attached by each of them to C's headquarters. These arrangements left a good deal of room for misunderstanding and frustration. C's customers did not hold him in such awe that they hesitated to find fault with him; their dissatisfaction, sometimes openly expressed, did not increase his chances of receiving the additional funds which might have enabled him to provide a better service. At the same time, the work of the signal intelligence service became increasingly difficult as a result of the growing attention paid by foreign governments to security in the light of publicity given to Room 40's wartime achievements.

*

During the greater part of the period between the wars, the governments of the leading capitalist countries were much exercised by the problem of co-existence with the Soviet Union. In 1917 the leaders of the October Revolution in Russia demolished much of the Tsarist intelligence and counter-intelligence apparatus, but before the end of the year they established an Extraordinary Commission to Combat Counter-Revolution and Sabotage under Felix Dzherzhinsky, a Pole of aristocratic antecedents. This was known, from the initials of its Russian designation, as the CHEKA, but soon became the All-Russian Extraordinary Commission, or VECHEKA. Intended in the first instance as an instrument of counter-espionage and domestic surveillance, it acquired after a few years a foreign section which began by harrying expatriate dissidents in Paris and elsewhere but soon took to spying on foreigners as well as Russians. The People's Commissariat for War, under Leon Trotsky, also set up an espionage organization, headed in the first instance by Jan Berzin. Other bodies which sponsored clandestine activities in the early years of the Bolshevist régime included the People's Commissariat for Foreign Affairs (under George Chicherin and Maxim Litvinov); the People's Commissariat for Foreign Trade (under Leonid Krassin); the Communist International, or Comintern (under Grigori Zinoviev); and the Central Committee of the Soviet Communist Party in Moscow.[3]

Tasks undertaken by Soviet agents included not only the gathering of information about naval, military, political and industrial developments in capitalist countries, but also the dissemination of anti-capitalist propaganda and attempts to infiltrate politically oriented associations and to suborn journalists. Their efforts were a frequent source of embarrassment to statesmen torn between fear of Communism and awareness of the economic value of links with Russia. In Britain the short-lived Directorate of Intelligence administered by the Home Office drew attention in 1920 to such conclusive evidence of subversive activities by a Soviet trade delegation led by Krassin himself that Lloyd George, as Prime Minister in a coalition government supported by the Conservative Party, was obliged to concur in measures which cut across his attempts to improve relations with the Russians. More Reds were discovered under the government's bed in 1924 and 1927. On the last of these occasions such indiscreet references were made in the House of Commons to intercepted communications between London and Moscow that the Russians tightened up their signal security, with the result that thereafter their signals could not be read.

The Russians were not alone in paying special attention to signal security in the second half of the 1920s and the 1930s. A number of governments and governmental agencies introduced more complex hand-cyphers than those previously employed, or adopted modified versions of commercial cypher-machines on sale in various countries. Modified versions of the Enigma machine designed by Arthur Scherbius and marketed in Germany from 1923 were, for example, adopted in 1926 by the German Navy, in 1929 by the German Army, and in 1934 by the still-clandestine Luftwaffe. Other users in Germany included the state railways, the police and the SS. Advanced versions of the Enigma machine were considered by German cryptologists so secure that an unauthorized recipient would not be able to read messages encyphered by them even if he succeeded in capturing a machine complete in all its parts.

A further reminder of the importance of signal security was given by revelations made in 1931 by the American cryptanalyst Herbert Osborne Yardley. A former code-and-cypher clerk in the Department of State, Yardley took charge in 1917 of a wartime cryptanalytical bureau called MI-8 but largely concerned with diplomatic traffic, and in 1919 of a clandestine successor financed jointly by the Department of State and the Department of the Army. A small signal intelligence section was established independently by the Department of the Navy in 1924. In 1929 the Hoover administration disbanded Yardley's organization and ordered him to deliver his records and the unexpended balance of his funds to the Signal Corps of the United States Army. Thrown out of work at a time of mounting unemployment, Yardley decided after selling most of his possessions to rescue himself and his wife and child from penury by publishing an account of his experiences. In effect he revealed in his book, *The American Black Chamber*, and in articles based upon it which appeared in *The Saturday Evening Post*, that countries on whose diplomatic correspondence the Department of State had eavesdropped between 1917 and 1929 included Argentina, Brazil, Chile, China, Costa Rica, Cuba, France, Germany, Great Britain, Japan, Liberia, Mexico, Nicaragua, Panama, Peru, San Salvador, Santo Domingo, the Soviet Union and Spain.[4] He also revealed that packages had sometimes been opened and refastened with forged seals.

Writing in haste and without access to government records, Yardley made some mistakes and was guilty of some wild exaggerations, but these did not lessen the impact of his disclosures. Foreign rights in his book were bought by British, French, Japanese and Swedish publishers, and a pirated edition appeared in China.

The disclosure of official secrets was not an indictable offence in the United States, but the authorities were understandably displeased. Retrospective legislation was considered, but ultimately Congress contented itself with a measure which empowered the government to forbid publication of Yardley's next book and impound the manuscript. Yardley lived to make his peace with the authorities and re-enter government service as an official of the Office of Price Administration in World War II. He died in 1958 and was buried with military honours in Arlington National Cemetery.

An important consequence for the British of the increased attention paid by governments to signal security after World War I was that the Government Code and Cypher School not only ceased in 1927 to be able to read the Soviet Union's diplomatic traffic, but was also unable in the early 1930s to read Germany's.[5] Such military traffic as could be intercepted and read in the United Kingdom during the next few years yielded nothing thought by the GC & CS worth passing to its customers.[6] Since the cover provided by the Secret Intelligence Service was far from complete and there was still no effective machinery for the discussion and co-ordination on an inter-departmental basis of reports from all sources, the inevitable result was that important decisions bearing on relations with Germany were sometimes made in the light of inaccurate or imperfectly co-ordinated information.

*

As an island power largely dependent on imports to feed her population, and on visible and invisible exports to provide the means of paying for them, Britain had a strong interest after World War I in the avoidance throughout the world of conflicts inimical to international trade. The British delegation at the Preliminary Peace Conference of Paris in 1919 aimed at disarming Germany; discouraging the French from taking advantage of German weakness to establish a dominant position in Europe; and, as far as possible, resisting an American challenge to British command of the sea without entering into a prohibitively expensive arms-race with the United States. The French were induced by an Anglo-American guarantee of support against renewed aggression to renounce their claim to a permanent strategic frontier on the Rhine; in return for British support of proposals for a League of Nations, the Americans agreed to defer the discussion of naval questions until after the peace treaties were signed. The British recognized that the disarmament clauses of the Treaty of Versailles bore hardly on Germany, but hoped to reconcile the Germans to these restrictions by persuading the French to relinquish their conscript army and join Britain, Germany and the United States in a general scaling-down of armaments.

The refusal of the United States Senate to ratify the Treaty of Versailles was therefore an immense setback for the British, although it was not one which ought to have surprised them since their delegates had been warned by American colleagues at the peace conference that President Wilson had no mandate to commit his country to a foreign alliance and could not count on the support of Congress. In view of the consequent nullification of the Anglo-American guarantee, the French insisted on retaining their large standing army and provided themselves with the strongest military air force in the world. Despite a temporary improvement in Franco-German relations during the Locarno era in the mid-twenties, they began in 1927 to build along their frontier with Germany the chain of fortified positions afterwards called the Maginot Line.

Chiefly in deference to American wishes but also in the light of opinions held by some of the self-governing dominions, the British allowed their alliance with Japan to lapse when its renewal came up for discussion in 1921. At the Washington Conference in the following winter they agreed, in effect, to share command of the sea with the United States. The Japanese accepted naval inferiority to the Anglo-Saxon powers, but even so the Washington treaties left them in a better position to attack American possessions in the South-West Pacific than the Americans were to defend them. The Americans had the stronger navy, but no first-class naval base nearer to the Philippines than Pearl Harbor, far away in the Central Pacific. The British established at Singapore a base to which they hoped to send, in the event of trouble with Japan, a fleet capable of dominating the seaward approaches to Malaya, British Borneo, Australia, New Zealand, India and Burma.

Before the outbreak of World War II the Japanese were interested, however, not in attacking British or American possessions but in extending their power and influence on the mainland of East Asia and in countering Soviet influence in that area. Despite the shortcomings of their intelligence organization the British were, in general, well informed about Japanese aspirations and the extent to which they constituted a threat to British and other foreign interests in China.

In September 1931 the wrecking of a short stretch of the South Manchurian Railway by a mysterious explosion led to a clash between Chinese troops and the force, called the Kwantung Army, which the Japanese were allowed to maintain in Manchuria to protect their economic interests there. The Kwantung Army went on to seize strategic points throughout Manchuria and establish the puppet-state of Manchukuo. The Chinese appealed to the League of Nations and instituted a boycott of Japanese goods at Shanghai. The Japanese responded to the boycott by presenting an ultimatum whose acceptance failed to avert an exchange of shots between Chinese soldiers and Japanese marines in the vicinity of the International Settlement. The Japanese then disembarked an expeditionary force which advanced about twelve miles before neutral mediators persuaded its commander and the Chinese authorities to come to terms. Meanwhile the authority of the Japanese government was eroded both by its manifest inability to restrain the Kwantung Army and by its failure to prevent acts of terrorism by self-styled patriots. When these culminated in the assassination of the Prime Minister, the Emperor appointed a non-party government which took Japan out of the League of Nations, extended formal recognition to Manchukuo, and embarked on an ambitious programme of rearmament.

The beginnings of this new trend in Far Eastern affairs coincided with a marked drift towards extremism in Germany. The British Chiefs of Staff urged the government in 1932 to abandon the long-standing assumption that there would be no great war involving the British Empire for at least ten years, and to start plugging gaps in the national and imperial defences. The government suspended the ten-year rule and sanctioned completion of the naval base at Singapore and its fixed defences by 1936, but declined to do much more before it could see the outcome of a full-scale disarmament conference about to assemble at Geneva.

By the early winter of 1933 it was clear that British attempts to reconcile German aspirations with French fears for their security had failed. The government then appointed a Defence Requirements Committee to advise it how to repair 'the worst deficiencies' in the defences. In the meantime Hitler's accession to power gave rise to a stream of reports about conditions in Germany from refugees, opponents of the National Socialist régime still resident in Germany, and other private informants. These far outnumbered reports from accredited agents whose reliability could be tested.

The Chairman of the Defence Requirements Committee was Sir Maurice (afterwards Lord) Hankey, the vastly experienced Secretary of the Cabinet and former Secretary of the Committee of Imperial Defence. Its members included the three Chiefs of Staff; the Secretary of the Treasury, Sir Warren Fisher; and the Permanent Under-Secretary of State for Foreign Affairs, Sir Robert Vansittart.

In its first report, completed on 28 February 1934, the committee expressed the view that, although the immediate danger lay in the Far East, the 'ultimate potential enemy' was Germany.[7] This pronouncement accurately reflected Vansittart's opinion of National Socialism, but it was not based on evidence from intelligence sources, or indeed on evidence from any source, that the Germans were contemplating an attack on Britain or on any part of the British Empire. On the other hand, the Germans had made it clear at Geneva that, in the absence of an international arms convention to which they could adhere, they would rearm at their own pace. Hitler had openly expressed the view that Germany needed additional living-space in Eastern Europe. It was not unreasonable to suppose that, if attempts to find it at the expense of countries allied with France brought him into conflict with the French, Britain would find it hard to stay out of the struggle.

The committee also drew attention to the danger of air attack, 'especially in the early stages of a war'.[8] Again, there was no evidence that the military air force with which the Germans proposed to provide themselves was intended for attacks on the United Kingdom. The committee's warning was based on the British Air Staff's conviction that strategic bombing, rather than direct co-operation with naval or land forces, ought to be the primary function of an air force. Whether the Germans held similar views was debatable. Nevertheless the belief that a war between Britain and Germany was almost sure to start with heavy air attacks on the United Kingdom came to be widely accepted during the next few years in British governmental and official circles. The doctrine of the knock-out blow from the air, propounded in the first instance by the Air Staff, was warmly championed in Whitehall by Sir Warren Fisher.[9] Newspaper articles and speeches which reflected it commanded ready attention from members of the public who remembered that Stanley Baldwin had said in 1932, when proposals for the abolition or restriction of air forces were being ventilated in London and at Geneva, that 'the bomber would always get through'. They were not to know that an early-warning system based on radar would soon transform the outlook, and security regulations prevented them from being told so.

In the spring of 1934 the Secret Intelligence Service reported that the Germans were building warships at Kiel in contravention of the Treaty of Versailles.[10] They were known to be spending large sums on airfields and other military installations, intensifying military training, and laying the foundations of an air force due to attain a first-line strength of 576 aircraft in the autumn of 1935.[11] In the spring of that year they came into the open by publicly announcing the revival of the Luftwaffe. From that time until 1938 the German authorities allowed and encouraged visits to aircraft factories by British aeronautical engineers and test-pilots, and on a number of occasions they made confidential disclosures about the progress of their air expansion schemes. Tactical traffic intercepted and decyphered in the United Kingdom during training exercises suggested that the Luftwaffe's target for the autumn of 1935 would be attained without much difficulty and that the Germans should not have much difficulty, either, in completing a second-stage programme designed to give them 1,368 first-line aircraft by the autumn of 1936.[12] There was still no evidence that any of these aircraft were intended for attacks on the United Kingdom or that Germany was contemplating war with Britain.

The crux of the problem for the British was that, notwithstanding the lack of any positive evidence of German hostility, no one could predict the use that Hitler might make of his growing air power if he were thwarted. Neither the Secret Intelligence Service nor the Government Code and Cypher School could throw much light on the matter, nor could they reasonably have been expected to do so. In the absence of reliable information about Germany's economy, the effectiveness of the control exercised by the German government over production and distribution and the extent to which its actions would be determined by economic factors, the Foreign Office and the service departments were not well placed to say what might befall if Hitler took the bit between his teeth.

Even so, the British can scarcely be said to have made good use of such information as they did possess. At best, their performance was uneven. For example, in the autumn of 1936 the Air Staff made what turned out to be an accurate forecast of the Luftwaffe's first-line strength on the outbreak of war by predicting a progressive increase 'up to a figure of not less than 4,000 first-line aircraft'.[13] On the other hand, when asked what weight of bombs the Luftwaffe could be expected to drop on the United Kingdom, they produced grossly exaggerated estimates based on rule-of-thumb calculations which took no account of the practical difficulties the Germans could be expected to encounter in mounting an attack from distant bases.[14] No serious attempt was made to assess the feasibility of the much-discussed knock-out blow. Had such a study been made by an impartial body, it could scarcely have failed to lead to the conclusion that heavy and sustained attacks on the United Kingdom from bases in Germany would be almost impossible with the aircraft likely to be at the Luftwaffe's disposal in 1939. It might also have shown that the Air Staff's own plans for the bombing of Germany in the event of war were hopelessly unrealistic.

The Air Staff were not, however, the only offenders. If they sinned, as indeed they did, they were also sinned against. During a debate on the service estimates in the House of Commons in November 1934, Winston Churchill supported an attack on the government's current air expansion scheme by asserting that the still-clandestine Luftwaffe was already nearly as strong as the RAF, and that it would be nearly half as strong again by the end of 1936 and nearly twice as strong in 1937. Stanley Baldwin, replying for the government, said that in twelve months' time the RAF would have a numerical superiority over the Luftwaffe 'in Europe alone' of nearly fifty per cent, but that he could not 'look more than two years ahead'. This disclaimer could have been interpreted as merely an imprecise way of saying that, although Baldwin knew that Britain would still be on the right side of the ledger in 1935, he was not prepared to say what would happen in 1936 or 1937. It was, however, taken to mean that he *could* look two years ahead but no more, and to imply that the RAF would still have a margin of superiority in November 1936. At any rate in retrospect, Baldwin himself accepted that interpretation, for he afterwards apologized for misleading the House and complained privately that an official who was not an intelligence officer or a member of the Air Staff had given him a defective brief. His public statement gave the impression that he had been misled by Air Intelligence, which he had not. He had been warned in ample time for the debate that the Luftwaffe was expected to overtake the RAF before November 1936.[15]

In the following March the Foreign Secretary, Sir John Simon, visited Hitler in Berlin. He was accompanied by Anthony Eden, a member of the government with special responsibility for League of Nations affairs and destined to follow Simon's successor, Sir Samuel Hoare, as Foreign Secretary. Hitler told Simon and Eden that the Luftwaffe was already as strong as the RAF. The German Air Ministry knew, and the British Air Ministry believed it knew, that this was untrue, but the Foreign Office was not easily convinced that the Air Ministry was right and the Führer wrong. Eden confessed many years later that Hitler's claim filled his heart with 'grim foreboding'.[16] It ought not to have done so.

As a result of these and other incidents, the Air Ministry's intelligence officers were more than once compelled in later years to defend themselves against the charge that their figures could not be right because they differed from those adduced by Churchill or the Foreign Office. Moreover, a tendency to give undue weight to uncorroborated reports or *ex parte* statements was not confined to Ministers of the Crown. Sir Robert Vansittart, both as Permanent Under-Secretary of State for Foreign Affairs and (from 1938) as the government's Chief Diplomatic Adviser, made such frequent use of unofficial communications to buttress his opinions about Germany and German rearmament that eventually a good deal of what he had to say was discounted as likely to have been inspired by his 'private detective agency'.

The Defence Requirements Committee made three reports. Its second report led the ministerial committee which examined it to conclude in the summer of 1935 that preparations ought to be made to meet a German attack at any time after the early part of 1939. Its third

consisted largely of detailed proposals for the improvement of the
defences and an account of what was known about foreign rearmament
programmes, with special reference to naval programmes.

The government's response to the committee's recommendations
was conditioned both by fear of the Luftwaffe and by financial
considerations. Neville Chamberlain, as Chancellor of the Exchequer in
Stanley Baldwin's government, pronounced the capital expenditure of
roughly seventy-one million pounds proposed by the committee beyond
the nation's means. The government lopped about a third from the total,
reduced the army's share by roughly a half, and increased the RAF's
allotment. In accordance with the Air Staff's theory that, in the long run,
the best defence was the power to hit back, the Air Ministry did not
concentrate exclusively on the improvement of the air defences but
devoted considerable sums to the development of a bomber force which
proved unsuitable for most of its intended tasks.[17]

The committee drew attention in its third report to the importance of
obtaining more and better information about Germany's industrial
potential as a basis for the estimation of her future striking-power. It
recommended greatly increased expenditure on the Secret Intelligence
Service, mentioning half a million pounds as the smallest sum that
would be 'really adequate'.[18] This recommendation was accepted in
principle by the ministerial Defence Policy and Requirements Committee early in 1936 and afterwards approved by the Cabinet. How much
money C actually received between that time and the outbreak of war
has not been revealed, but he is known to have felt that it was not
enough.[19]

Nevertheless the performance of the Secret Intelligence Service
improved considerably during the last few years of peace. C complained
after German troops marched into the demilitarized Rhineland in 1936
that lack of funds compelled him to rely largely on the French for
information about Germany; but contact with the Deuxième Bureau
proved beneficial at least inasmuch as it led ultimately to the formation
of Cotton's Special Flight.

Another foreign contact provided information of great value,
although little positive use was made of it. In the spring of 1937 a
correspondent who identified himself only as Karl but was obviously
well acquainted with military matters and intelligence procedure offered
his services as a secret agent to Colonel Frantisek Moravec of the
Czechoslovak Intelligence Service.[20] As the sequel to a nocturnal
rendezvous at which he arrived carrying two suitcases full of documents

and went through the prescribed recognition procedure by pretending to set his watch by a clock that in fact had stopped, he was duly enrolled as agent A-54. Karl was Paul Thümmel, an officer of the German military intelligence and counter-intelligence service, the Abwehr. In addition to copious and detailed information about the order of battle and mobilization plans of the German Army and some information about the equipment of both the army and the Luftwaffe, he gave accurate and timely warnings of German plans for the dismemberment and subjugation of Czechoslovakia and the invasion of Poland.[21] The substance of his reports was passed to the British and French intelligence services by Moravec, who received the impression that the French were not much interested but formed a high opinion of the local representative of MI 6, Major Harold Gibson. With Gibson's help, Moravec moved his headquarters to London when German troops moved into Prague in the spring of 1939. He maintained contact with espionage networks organized from Paris, Warsaw, Stockholm, Belgrade, Zurich and The Hague, and with a valuable stay-behind network in his own country.

Exchanges of information between British and American officers about defence plans and programmes began early in 1937, soon after President Roosevelt's election for a second term and Japan's conclusion of an Anti-Comintern Pact with Germany. In the following summer an undeclared war between Japan and China was sparked off by a clash between Chinese troops and the Japanese North China Garrison Army, stationed near Tientsin under the terms of the Boxer Protocol of 1901. At the beginning of 1938 Captain R. E. Ingersoll, of the War Plans Division of the United States Department of the Navy, visited London on the initiative of the President for talks with the Foreign Office and the Admiralty. Thereafter the Admiralty regularly supplied the United States Naval Attaché in London with intelligence about the Japanese Navy.[22] The Department of State was able in 1939 to throw some light on the Kremlin's attitude to German overtures which led to the Moscow Pact, but in general the Americans were not in a position, until well after the oubreak of World War II, to make any significant contribution to British knowledge of developments in Germany, Italy or Japan.

This was true both of the American espionage organization and of American signal intelligence. Early in 1939 the Department of the Army and the Navy agreed on a division of responsibilities which enabled the head of the Intelligence section of the Signal Corps, Walter F. Friedman, to give priority during the next eighteen months or so to attempts to break the machine-cypher adopted by the Japanese in 1937 for their most secret diplomatic communications.[23] Despite efforts which took him to the verge of a nervous breakdown, Friedman scored no success before the second half of 1940. He read his first complete message on 25 September, two days before Japan's Tripartite Pact with Germany and Italy was signed in Berlin.[24]

British cryptanalysts found the machine-cyphers used by Germany's armed forces no less baffling. They recognized by 1937 that the German Army, the German Navy, and probably also the Luftwaffe, the German railways and the SS, were all using versions of the Enigma machine whose mysteries they could not fathom and saw no immediate prospect of fathoming.[25] Even so, considerable progress was made in a number of directions during the second half of the 1930s. From 1935 some of the service sections of the Government Code and Cypher School received additional staff. By the time of the Abyssinian crisis a number of high-grade cyphers used by Italy's armed forces and the Italian colonial authorities in East Africa could be read; by the summer of 1939 the Italian diplomatic cypher had been broken and most naval, military and air force traffic relating to events in the Italian overseas empire and the Mediterranean was readable. Japanese naval and army cyphers were unreadable from 1937 until after the outbreak of World War II, but traffic analysis enabled the Admiralty to keep track of important naval movements. From 1937 the GC & CS was able, too, to read messages encyphered by a relatively simple version of the Enigma machine used by German, Italian and Spanish Nationalist forces in Spain.[26]

Valuable though little-regarded information about German and Italian operations in Spain was also received from other sources. The Spanish Civil War gave the world a preview of most of the aircraft which formed the backbone of the Luftwaffe on the outbreak of World War II. These included versions of the Me 109 fighter, the Ju 87 dive-bomber and, among long-range bombers, the He 111 and the Do 17 but not the Ju 88. Sub-committees appointed by the Joint Intelligence Committee reported that both in Spain and in China air forces were being used largely to support land forces. Although this was manifestly true of the German air contingent which supported Franco's troops, senior members of the British Air Staff refused to believe that more than a small proportion of the Luftwaffe would be so employed in a major war.[27] Admittedly their German counterparts were themselves rather slow to apply the lesson. The fact remains that no serious attempt was made in Britain to correlate reports of German air operations in Spain with information that was available in London about the organization of Germany's armoured forces. The British failed, therefore, to understand that what they had to fear in the early stages of a war with Germany was not so much an air offensive against their centres of production or population as penetration of the Allied line in France and the Low Countries by armoured columns with powerful air support. They went to war in 1939 still believing that the French, with some help from their allies, could hold a continuous front from the North Sea to the Alps. Any attempts made by the enemy to breach it by means of frontal assaults preceded by tell-tale artillery bombardments would, they hoped, merely hasten the hour when economic stresses forced Germany to give up the struggle.

It was not, however, until early in 1939 that the British committed themselves to direct participation in a land campaign. Until that time they intended to limit their contribution to operations by naval and air forces and economic pressure. Heavy demands were made, therefore, on the intelligence services for information about Germany's naval and air resources and her economic and industrial potential, although this does not mean that they were not also asked to provide information about other matters. Their inability to meet all these demands, and above all the lack of effective machinery for the co-ordination and interpretation of information from all sources, contributed to a climate of doubt and apprehension in which ministers and officials sometimes based decisions or advice on unreliable reports. The government tacitly recognized the existence of this state of affairs when, some two months before the outbreak of war, it instructed the reorganized Joint Intelligence Committee to ensure that in future information on which it might have to act was the best obtainable.

*

Until well into the 1930s, the Soviet leaders regarded Germany as their most promising ally in a hypothetical war with France and her allies in Eastern Europe. Hitler's advent to power compelled them to reverse their foreign policy. Once convinced that National Socialism was not a passing phenomenon but had come to stay, they approached the French with proposals for an alliance directed against Germany, joined the League of Nations and became enthusiastic champions of collective security.

The Franco-Soviet Pact soon ceased, however, to have much value in Soviet eyes. The standing of the French was irretrievably weakened by their failure either to offer any resistance, or to make the best of a bad job by negotiating in advance of the event, when Hitler responded to their ratification of the pact in the early part of 1936 by marching troops into the demilitarized Rhineland. In the following summer the refusal of Léon Blum's Popular Front government to commit the country to active support of the Republican cause in the Spanish Civil War led to political and industrial strife which made havoc of plans for the re-equipment of the Armée de l'Air. Strikes which brought the aircraft industry almost to a standstill were the direct cause of the appalling shortage of modern bombers from which the French were to suffer in 1940.

The British were not much more than spectators of these events. If their intelligence services had been able to tell them that Hitler proposed to move into the Rhineland no more than 30,000 troops with orders to withdraw at the slightest sign of opposition, they might have given the French more robust advice than they were able to offer when the outlook was discussed in London some weeks before he made his gesture.[28] But they could not in any case have saved France from the consequences of many years of Soviet-inspired anti-capitalist propaganda which reduced her to impotence at the very moment when Soviet interests required that she should be strong.

In circumstances on which neither the Secret Intelligence Service nor the British Embassy in Moscow could throw much light, Stalin went on to weaken his own army by purging it of many of its ablest officers, apparently in the belief that some or all of them were conspiring with the German General Staff to overthrow him. The logical outcome was the Moscow Pact, with its aftermath of repeated attempts made by Stalin between 1939 and 1941 to appease Hitler at almost any cost.

The headquarters staffs of the Soviet intelligence agencies did not escape the Stalinist terror. Dzerzhinsky – whose organization became in 1922 the GPU, in 1924 the OGPU and in 1934 the State Security Department of the People's Commissariat for Internal Affairs, or NKVD – had died in 1926, allegedly of heart-failure. His successor, Vyacheslav Menzhinsky, was murdered (or perhaps executed) in 1934. The next incumbent, Genrik Yagoda, was arrested in 1936 and executed two years later. Nicolai Yezhev, who followed him, was removed to a lunatic asylum in the year of Yagoda's execution and succeeded by Stalin's fellow-Georgian and trusted henchman, Lavrenti Beria. The veteran chief of Military Intelligence, Jan Berzin, was replaced by General Semyon Petrovich Uritsky before the alleged plot against Stalin was uncovered, but he too was arrested, tried, and executed in 1938.

In 1937 the British received incomplete accounts of some of these events. They also received warnings that Hitler intended to seize Austria and possibly Czechoslovakia. These came mostly, but not entirely, from diplomatic sources. According to Moravec, Thümmel produced at his first interview with the Czechoslovak authorities evidence of the German Army's intention of stirring up dissent among the German-speaking inhabitants of the Sudetenland as the prelude to an invasion of Bohemia and Moravia from Saxony.[29] He afterwards gave a more detailed account of the German plan. Confirmation – again according to Moravec – was received from another agent, A-53, who was also a German officer.[30]

In the early stages these warnings of impending trouble in Central Europe were not taken very seriously in London, or indeed elsewhere. No one doubted that Hitler would like to absorb Austria, or that complaints made by the Sudeten Germans owed something to promptings from Berlin. Whether Germany would risk a European war in the uncertain hope of incorporating Austria and part or even the whole of Czechoslovakia in the Reich was another matter. Even if Thümmel's reports were accurate, the existence of a military plan for the seizure of Bohemia and Moravia was not proof of a firm intention to give effect to it. The Foreign Office did not regard the evidence which pointed to operations against Austria or Czechoslovakia as very strong.[31] Sir Nevile Henderson, who had succeeded Sir Eric Phipps in the spring of 1937 as British Ambassador in Berlin, regarded reports of Germany's hostile intentions as far-fetched.[32] Austria had signed in the summer of 1936 an agreement with Germany which purported to safeguard her rights as an independent though 'Germanic' state. President Eduard Benes of Czechoslovakia, when warned by Moravec in the spring of 1937 of indications that Germany was preparing for military action of some kind, expressed the opinion that Hitler would not succeed in imposing his will on Central Europe by force of arms.[33] Some two years earlier, when Benes was Foreign Minister, he had told the British that he did not expect a conflict with Germany.[34]

In May 1937 Neville Chamberlain succeeded Stanley Baldwin as Prime Minister. From that time the difficulty experienced by members of the government in knowing what to make of the international outlook was increased by differences of opinion between Chamberlain and Eden. Chamberlain was one of a number of Cabinet ministers who regarded both Eden and Vansittart as too inflexible in their attitude to Germany and Italy. He believed that ultimately Hitler would prove amenable to the argument that he could do more for Germany by negotiation than by military means. Chamberlain also believed that, although relations with Italy had been severely strained by the Abyssinian affair and Italian contributions to the Spanish Civil War, Mussolini might still be able and willing to exert a restraining influence on Hitler. He was therefore anxious that high-level conversations with the Italian government should start without delay. Eden insisted that the Italians should first demonstrate their good faith by redeeming promises to reduce the number of their volunteers in Spain and abstain from anti-British propaganda. Chamberlain, undeterred by intelligence reports which showed that Italian volunteers were still active in Spain, conducted a clandestine correspondence with the Italian Ambassador in London through Sir Joseph Ball of the Conservative Central Office and a junior member of the staff of the Italian embassy.[35] The Italian government also corresponded with Downing Street through Wladimir Poliakoff, an intermediary to whom the author of this book was introduced in the 1930s by a friend who remarked afterwards that Poliakoff was almost certainly a secret agent of some kind.[36] In addition, Chamberlain received occasional communications from the Italian Foreign Minister through Lady Chamberlain, the widow of his half-brother Sir Austen Chamberlain. Of these, however, he made no secret.

Towards the end of 1937 Vansittart, who had been Permanent Under-Secretary for nearly seven years, was offered but declined the important post of Ambassador in Paris. The hitherto unknown post of Chief Diplomatic Adviser to His Majesty's Government was then specially created for him. Eden himself resigned in February 1938 and was succeeded by Lord Halifax, whose views were rather closer than his to Chamberlain's. One of Eden's last acts was to press for the resumption of staff talks with the French. The Chiefs of Staff at first objected to a move which they thought would be resented by the Germans, but eventually the talks were sanctioned with the proviso that they should take place at a level not higher than that of the service attachés.

From the time of Eden's resignation, the policy of the British government with respect to Germany was to cultivate good relations with the National Socialist authorities but at the same time make it clear to them that they would, in the opinion of the British, be ill-advised to press their revisionist claims to a point that might involve them in a European war from which Britain would find it difficult to stand aside.

Sir Nevile Henderson's efforts in that direction did not, however, prevent the Foreign Office from attaching some importance to reports which suggested that the National Socialist régime might be overthrown by a *coup d'état*.[37] Attempts by the Secret Intelligence Service to assess the chances of such a reversal were resented by the War Office and the Air Ministry as a diversion from what they judged to be its more important task of providing factual information about Germany's armed forces.[38] At the same time, the slow progress of British rearmament did not make for harmonious relations in Whitehall, or between Whitehall and the headquarters of the Secret Intelligence Service in Broadway, Westminster. Officials of the Foreign Office who chafed under the necessity of placating National Socialist Germany reproached the service departments with the poor state of the national defences; the service departments reproached the Treasury with providing inadequate funds; and everyone reproached the Secret Intelligence Service with its inability to say what Hitler would do next.

On 3 March 1938 Henderson discussed the international outlook with Hitler at an interview planned before Eden's resignation, but postponed as a result of Hitler's preoccupation in February with other matters. These included the dismissal of his Minister of War, Field-Marshal Werner von Blomberg; his own assumption of the post of Supreme Commander of the Armed Forces, with General Wilhelm Keitel as his Chief of Staff; the replacement of General Werner von Fritsch as Commander-in-Chief of the German Army by General Walther von Brauchitsch; and the replacement of Baron von Neurath as Foreign Minister by the inexperienced and truculent Joachim von Ribbentrop. We now know that in the previous November Blomberg, Fritsch and Neurath had all responded to an exposition of Hitler's Central European policy by warning him against any action that might involve a risk of conflict with France and Britain.

At the interview with Henderson, Hitler accused the British of intervening in matters which were not their business. He asserted that millions of Germans in Central Europe were being unjustly treated, and that this was a situation which concerned Germany but not Britain. If the British opposed a just settlement of the Austrian problem Germany would have to fight, and if Hitler did intervene in Austria he would act like lightning. He did not claim any Czechoslovak territory, but said that the Sudeten Germans must have autonomy in cultural and other matters. He declared that only fifteen per cent of the population of Austria supported the existing régime in that country and that Austria must be allowed to vote, but declined to say whether this meant that he thought the future of Austria should be decided by a plebiscite.[39]

The Austrian Chancellor, Dr Kurt von Schuschnigg, was already under pressure from Hitler to endorse a settlement accepted in principle by his colleagues and by the President, but from which he recoiled. On 9 March Schuschnigg made a desperate bid for independence by announcing that a plebiscite would be held on Sunday, 13 March, to decide for or against union with Germany.

Reports that German troops were moving towards the Austrian frontier reached the British Embassy in Berlin early on 11 March. Although their accuracy was at first denied by the Ministry of War, they were soon confirmed by direct observation. The British Secret Intelligence Service, however, gave no warning. Indeed, it was itself taken by surprise, with the result that the head of its Austrian espionage network was arrested when the Germans reached Vienna on 12 March.[40]

The British government responded to the rape of Austria with unwonted swiftness. On 19 March the Joint Planners prepared a draft which formed the basis of a paper on the military implications of German aggression against Czechoslovakia, submitted by the Chiefs of Staff to the Foreign Policy Committee two days later. The substance of its conclusions was that incautious handling of the Czechoslovak problem could lead to a world war for which Britain was unprepared, and that hostilities against Britain might take the form of an attempted knock-out blow from the air. In the light of this essay in defeatism the Foreign Policy Committee recommended on 22 March, and the Cabinet agreed, that pressure should be put on the Czechoslovak government to make concessions to the Sudeten Germans.[41] The outcome was that, although Chamberlain made a public announcement on 24 March to the effect that Britain might not stand aside if Czechoslovakia were attacked, the British and French governments agreed at the end of April to make diplomatic representations in Prague with a view to persuading the Czechoslovak government to grant the Sudeten Germans at least a substantial measure of autonomy.

Since only a week divided the crossing of the Austrian frontier from the drafting by the Joint Planners of their review, the intelligence staffs did not have much time in which to receive and digest reports of the German Army's not very impressive performance during its unopposed march to Vienna and beyond, or to inform themselves of the effects of the Anschluss on its plans. At a moment when the Secret Intelligence Service was handicapped by the collapse of its Austrian network, they were not well placed to contradict the assumption that access to Austrian territory had put Czechoslovakia at Hitler's mercy. Evidence that Hitler's military advisers were far from satisfied that Czechoslovakia could be overrun before the French fell with overwhelming numerical superiority on Germany's Western Frontier was forthcoming later in the year; but by that time the British government had already begun to implement its policy of putting pressure on the Czechs to make concessions, and in effect discouraging the French from honouring their treaty obligations.

Early in May Czechoslovak agents reported exceptional concentrations of German troops in Saxony and Silesia. According to Moravec, the Czechoslovak signal intelligence service provided partial corroboration by intercepting and reading orders to SS regiments to move towards the Czechoslovak frontier.[42] Thümmel reported on 12 May that an uprising in the Sudetenland was planned for 22 May, when municipal elections were to be held, and that the German-based Sudeten German Legion was then to march into Czechoslovakia with support from the SS.[43] Diplomatic enquiries in Berlin brought denials that any invasion of Czechoslovakia was in prospect, and the British Military Attaché and his assistant motored many miles through Saxony and Silesia without finding evidence that German troops were about to cross the frontier. Nevertheless the Czechoslovak government ordered a partial mobilization and strengthened its garrisons in areas where trouble was expected. The elections passed off without any major disturbance, but the Czechs were not convinced that no major disturbance had been planned. They believed that a crisis had been averted only by their prompt action and the diplomatic support given to them by the British and the French.

In July Thümmel confirmed reports that a new series of demonstrations in the Sudetenland was in prospect and described the plan for a two-pronged invasion of Bohemia and Moravia from north and south which the German Supreme Command had adopted at Hitler's behest at the end of May.[44] Moravec concluded in the light of Thümmel's figures that the plan would leave the Germans with too few battleworthy divisions to defend their Western frontier, and would therefore be feasible only if the French refused to fight. Hitler's military advisers were of the same opinion.[45] He countered their objections by asserting that neither the French nor the British had any real intention of fighting for Czechoslovakia, but failed to stifle opposition to his policy of smashing the Czechs at the risk of precipitating a European war. In August his critics sent an emissary, Ewald von Kleist-Schmenzin, to

London with instructions to warn the British not to be deceived by Hitler's claim that he was interested only in the fate of the Sudeten Germans. He was to say that Hitler's directive envisaged the subjugation of the whole of Czechoslovakia and that 'all the German generals' were against it. The German generals asked for an unequivocal public announcement that Britain would fight if Czechoslovakia were invaded. If that failed to deter Hitler, they would depose him as soon as he gave the executive order for invasion. Alternatively, they were prepared to act on the strength of a private assurance to the same effect.

Kleist-Schmenzin was interviewed by Vansittart, among others, but he failed either to convince Chamberlain and his colleagues that the conspirators were capable of unseating Hitler, or to persuade them to stop putting pressure on the Czechs to make concessions and start putting pressure on the French to honour their obligations. He took back to Germany only a reminder that Chamberlain had already said, on 24 March, that participation in a war arising from aggression against Czechoslovakia would probably not be confined to powers with direct obligations to the Czechs.

In the meantime a British emissary, Lord Runciman, arrived in Prague with instructions to impress upon the Czechs the importance of coming to terms with the enemy within their gates lest worse befall. The Chamberlain government was afterwards bitterly reproached by historians with the policy of appeasement of which the Runciman mission was a sample. The government did not, however, adopt that policy because Chamberlain had any particular desire to gratify Hitler. An uneasy feeling that the Sudeten Germans had something of a case did play some part in its thinking, but the decisive factor was fear of the Luftwaffe. The crucial question for the British was what the Luftwaffe might do to the United Kingdom if they provoked Hitler by making common cause with the French and the Czechs against him.

This was the kind of question to which the Air Ministry had been giving mind-boggling answers ever since it came into existence in 1918. In the early twenties, when the future of the RAF as an independent service was in jeopardy and British and French diplomacy were out of step, the Air Staff had prompted the veteran statesman A. J. Balfour, as Chairman of a Standing Sub-Committee of the Committee of Imperial Defence, to declare that three hundred French bombers could render London uninhabitable by delivering 'a continuous torrent of high explosives at the rate of 75 tons a day for an indefinite period'.[46] Their successors had now to consider what the Germans might be capable of doing.

In some respects the outlook had, of course, changed for the better since Balfour's day. His pronouncement was made at a time when the wartime air defences had been demolished and the country was wide open to attack. Since that time successive governments, besides sponsoring the study of passive air defence, had sanctioned air expansion programmes which raised the number of fighter squadrons eventually to be made available for home defence from nine in 1922 to thirty-eight in 1937. During the same period approval had been given to a series of plans for the deployment of fighter squadrons, counter-bombardment squadrons, anti-aircraft guns, searchlights, observer posts and early-warning devices. The most recent of these, adopted by the Chamberlain government in 1937, was intended to provide a continuous defended zone covering the eastern and south-eastern approaches to London and the industrial north and Midlands and also to provide some local protection for the Clyde, the Firth of Forth, the Tyne and Tees, the Humber, Harwich, Dover, Portsmouth, Leeds, Manchester, Sheffield, Birmingham and Bristol. A chain of twenty radar stations would give continuous cover of the East and South coasts from Lowestoft to the Isle of Wight, and partial cover of the East Coast between Lowestoft and a point north of St Andrews. The plan called for seven more fighter squadrons than were envisaged in the current air expansion programme, and many more anti-aircraft guns and searchlights than were likely to be available for a long time to come.

The actual situation in 1938 was that the plan was still far from completion. The radar chain gave partial cover of the vital stretch of coast from The Wash to Dungeness, though its stations were not yet equipped to detect low-flying aircraft, such as might be used for tip-and-run attacks or minelaying. The British, like the French, were still extremely short of modern anti-aircraft guns. In September Fighter Command had only twenty-nine mobilizable fighter squadrons. Five of these were equipped with an up-to-date monoplane fighter, the 325-mile-an-hour eight-gun Hurricane, but the guns of the Hurricanes had yet to be modified to work satisfactorily at heights above 15,000 feet. The remaining squadrons were equipped with biplanes of which the fastest were the 250-mile-an-hour four-gun Gladiator and the 230-mile-an-hour two-gun Gauntlet. There were no mobilizable Spitfire squadrons and no stored reserves of fighter aircraft. Immediate reserves with squadrons or in workshops totalled about two-fifths of first-line strength.[47]

The Air Staff were therefore justified in concluding that the air defences were in no position to parry a knock-out blow which might take the form either of repeated heavy attacks extending over a considerable period, or of an all-out effort lasting only a few days. Whether the Luftwaffe was capable of delivering such a blow was another matter. Other pertinent questions were whether the Luftwaffe had made any plans for an air offensive against the United Kingdom, or any preparations such as the assembly of target data and the accumulation of substantial quantities of bombs, fuel and spares at appropriate bases. These were just such questions as a competent intelligence service might have been expected to answer, but little attention appears to have been paid to them.[48]

The Air Staff credited the Luftwaffe in 1938 with 2,640 first-line aircraft.[49] In fact, it had 2,847 on the eve of Runciman's arrival in Prague in August, and 2,999 when the Czechoslovak crisis reached a climax in September, although only 1,646 and 2,805 respectively were service-able.* From a breakdown of their figure, and after deducting short-range fighters, dive-bombers and tactical reconnaissance aircraft incapable of reaching the United Kingdom from German bases, the Air Staff calculated that the Luftwaffe might be able to drop six or seven hundred tons of bombs a day on the United Kingdom for weeks on end. They also calculated that it might be able to drop 3,500 tons in the first twenty-four hours of an all-out offensive.

A better example of the danger of rule-of-thumb scale-of-effort calculations would be hard to find. The first of the Air Staff's tonnage figures was about three times the nightly average achieved by the Luftwaffe during its offensive against London between September and November 1940, when it was not confined to bases in Germany but had access to airfields in France, Belgium, the Netherlands, Denmark and Norway. The second figure was about five times the tonnage dropped by day and night in the first twenty-four hours of that offensive. Moreover, even if all the serviceable bombers the Germans possessed on 26 September 1938 had been concentrated against the United Kingdom, to drop 3,500 tons of bombs in twenty-four hours its bomber-crews (including those whose operational training was not yet complete) would have had to make an average of something like three sorties each within that period.

* See Table I (page 37).

TABLE I

FIRST-LINE STRENGTH OF THE LUFTWAFFE
BEFORE MUNICH

(Figures in brackets denote serviceable aircraft)

	1 August		*26 September*	
Long-range bombers	1,157	(582)	1,128	(1,040)
Dive-bombers	207	(159)	226	(220)
Ground-attack aircraft	173	(1)	195	(182)
Fighters	643	(453)	773	(738)
Strategic reconnaissance aircraft	197	(136)	222	(206)
Tactical reconnaissance aircraft	285	(164)	291	(270)
Coastal or naval aircraft	185	(151)	164	(149)
	2,847	(1,646)	2,999	(2,805)
Transport aircraft	81	(23)	308	(299)
	2,928	(1,669)	3,307	(3,108)

Source: Records of the Quartermaster-General's Department of the German Air Ministry.

The British Air Staff did not know in 1938 that the Luftwaffe had only 378 fully-trained bomber-crews on 1 August and 744 on 26 September.[*] They cannot be blamed for assuming that the Germans would find crews for all their serviceable bombers, as indeed they could have done in September by using a proportion of crews not yet fully operational. The Air Staff's failure to make good use of information they did possess is harder to excuse. The German bombers of 1938 were the Do 17, the He III and the obsolescent Ju 86. (The Germans also had the Ju 88, but it was not yet in squadron service.) All these aircraft had been seen in Spain and at international air shows; their performance and characteristics were matters of everyday comment in aviation circles. The Ju 86 (from which a moderately successful high-altitude reconnaissance aircraft was afterwards developed) had a maximum speed of less than 200 miles an hour and its record in the Spanish Civil War was poor. It should have made an easy prey even for Gladiators and Gauntlets. The

[*] See Table II (page 38).

TABLE II

CREWS AVAILABLE FOR GERMAN FIRST-LINE AIRCRAFT BEFORE MUNICH

(Fully-trained crews were those which had completed operational-training courses with the aircraft they would use in war. All crews can be assumed to have completed flying-training courses)

| | *1 August* | | *26 September* | |
	Fully Trained	*Partly Trained*	*Fully Trained*	*Partly Trained*
Long-range bombers	378	411	744	427
Dive-bombers	80	123	118	133
Ground-attack aircraft	89	11	185	7
Fighters	537	364	705	178
Strategic reconnaissance aircraft	84	57	145	61
Tactical reconnaissance aircraft	183	128	184	127
Coastal or naval aircraft	71	34	74	64
	1,422	1,128	2,155	997
Transport aircraft	10	17	289	67
	1,432	1,145	2,444	1,064

Source: Records of the Quartermaster-General's Department of the German Air Ministry.

relatively fast Do 17 had a normal range of approximately 750 miles with a one-ton bomb-load, but its range could be substantially increased by reduction of the bomb-load to half a ton or so. Versions of the still faster He III in service in 1938 could carry about two tons of bombs to the same radius of action as the Do 17, or one ton to a substantially greater one. The crews of Do 17s and He IIIs, if ordered to make the round trip from Germany to the United Kingdom and back without flying over neutral territory, would have been forced either to operate uncomfortably close to their effective radius of action, or to secure a margin of safety by carrying reduced bomb-loads. In any case the Luftwaffe could not, at one and the same time, have provided cover for a two-pronged invasion of Czechoslovakia, supported defensive operations on the Western Front and mounted heavy attacks on Britain.

Nevertheless the Air Staff's figures were not seriously challenged. By extrapolation from data derived from a limited experience of bombing in World War I, estimates of casualties were produced which subsequent experience showed to be fantastically exaggerated. Fear of the Luftwaffe was assiduously fostered by its administrative and operational chief, Reichsmarschall Göring, and by the German Ministry of Propaganda. Göring told Sir Nevile Henderson that, while no one could predict the final outcome of a war between Britain and Germany, one thing certain was that very little of London would be left standing at the end of it.[50] The American airman Colonel Lindbergh was primed with accounts of the Luftwaffe's capacity for destruction which duly found their way to the British through diplomatic channels.

Against this background of misinformation and information misinterpreted or disregarded, Chamberlain flew to Germany on 15 September to ask Hitler what price he proposed to exact from the Czechs for letting France and Britain off the hook. Hitler insisted that the Sudeten Germans must be allowed to determine their own future. The British and French governments then persuaded the Czechs, with great difficulty, to accept the principle that limitrophe areas of which more than half the population was German should be ceded to Germany. On returning to Germany to discuss ways and means, Chamberlain found that Hitler had raised his terms on the pretext that Poland and Hungary had claims on Czechoslovakia which could not be denied. As the sequel to an unsatisfactory meeting on 22 September, the British government informed the Czechs that it could no longer take the responsibility of advising them not to mobilize, but did not abandon its attempts at mediation. In a memorandum completed late on the following day, Hitler insisted that the Czechs should begin the evacuation of predominantly German areas of the Sudetenland at 8 a.m. on 26 September and complete the process by 28 September. The Czechs ordered general mobilization, the French called up half a million reservists, and the British mobilized the fleet and informed Berlin that Britain would feel obliged to support France if conformity with her treaty obligations involved her in hostilities against Germany. In a speech on 26 September, Hitler said that the German Army would march into the Sudetenland if the Czechs did not comply with his demands by 1 October.

Such was the state of affairs when, on 28 September, the British government received a warning that the Luftwaffe would launch an immediate attack on London if Britain declared war on Germany.[51] This came not from the Secret Intelligence Service but from a source in touch with the Security Service, MI 5. At the same time, the government was aware of indications that, although Hitler was eager to smash the Czechs, his military advisers were still opposed to any course of action that carried a risk of war with France and Britain. Göring's demeanour, on that day of diplomatic comings and goings in Berlin, convinced Henderson that he was against war.[52] As the better part of the Luftwaffe was at bases suitable for operations against Czechoslovakia and an immediate attack on London was therefore out of the question, Göring's attitude is understandable.

The immediate crisis was resolved when Mussolini responded favourably to a British proposal that Italy should join France and Britain in urging Germany to accept a negotiated settlement of the Sudeten problem. The German Army was already poised for action against the Czechs, but a telephone call from Rome gave Hitler a face-saving pretext for postponing the formal mobilization order which would otherwise have gone out at 2 p.m. on 28 September. The outcome was the Munich Conference, at which Britain, France and Italy agreed in effect to present Czechoslovakia with an ultimatum on Germany's behalf. Benes was replaced as President of Czechoslovakia by the ailing Dr Emil Hacha, who appointed a government which favoured friendly relations with Germany. Dissension between Czechs and Slovaks soon threatened to provide Hitler with a new pretext for intervention.

*

Despite promises made by Hitler to Chamberlain, the Munich agreement was not regarded in either diplomatic or intelligence circles as giving Europe much more than a breathing-space. The question was whether Hitler's next objective would be what was left of Czechoslovakia after the cession of the Sudetenland to Germany; Memel (in Lithuania but with 150,000 German inhabitants); Danzig (with 400,000); the Polish Corridor dividing East Prussia from the rest of Germany; or Poland proper. He was also thought for a time to have designs on the German-speaking cantons of Switzerland. One consequence was that the Swiss military intelligence service stepped up its watch on Germany, and in doing so acquired the services of Rudolf Rössler, a publisher who had moved from Germany to Switzerland in 1933 and had been deprived by the National Socialist régime of his German nationality. Rössler was afterwards to achieve pseudonymous fame as Lucy, the Soviet Union's most reliable source of information about the German Army's dispositions on the Eastern Front.

During the winter of 1938–39 the British government considered other possibilities. In November, and again in January, Halifax gave the Foreign Policy Committee the substance of reports received by the Foreign Office to the effect that Germany was contemplating an offensive in the West.[53] Some of these came from confidential informants in touch with the German Foreign Minister or the President of the Reichsbank, others from MI 5 sources who had contacts with the German Ministry of Propaganda or German agencies in London.[54] Their provenance might perhaps have suggested to an independent assessor that they should be regarded with suspicion as likely to have been planted by the German government to divert attention from other projects; the Foreign Office thought they rang true because it suspected Hitler of harbouring a grudge against the British in consequence of the praise heaped on Chamberlain for his peace-making efforts in the previous September.[55] There were also persistent rumours during the winter of German preparations for the bombing of London. The Foreign Office concluded that, since Hitler now seemed bent on attacking Britain but not France, the blow he was expected to deliver in March or later might take the form either of an air attack on the United Kingdom, or of an invasion of the Netherlands as a suitable base for operations against Britain.[56] The Chiefs of Staff, when asked by the Foreign Policy Committee to report on the military implications of a German occupation of the Netherlands, replied that it would present a direct threat to British security and must be resisted.

The reports on which the Foreign Office based its assessment were not shown to the Cabinet, and they do not appear to have been seen by the Chiefs of Staff.[57] On the strength of the assessment and a brief oral summary of the reports, the Cabinet decided in principle on 25 January to reverse its policy of only limited participation in a European war, should that course be proposed by its advisers.[58] On the following day, at a meeting attended for the first time by the service ministers and representatives of the Chiefs of Staff, the Foreign Policy Committee recommended, and in effect decided, that high-level staff conversations should be opened with the French and that an expeditionary force should be sent to the mainland of Europe in the event of war. The Cabinet reluctantly confirmed these momentous decisions on 25 February.

Not much more than a week later, Thümmel warned Moravec that

Bohemia and Moravia were to be occupied by German troops on 15 March.[59] The Germans expected no opposition, and hoped to pass off their move as a contribution to the restoration of law and order. Thümmel produced a list of major formations assigned to the enterprise, with names of commanders, routes and time-tables. He added that all Czechoslovak intelligence officers on whom the Germans could lay their hands were to be arrested and interrogated. He advised Moravec not to go to France if he decided to take refuge in a Western European country.

The Czechoslovak government received the warning with incredulity. Frantisek Chvalkovsky, the new Foreign Minister, assured Moravec that Germany had no hostile intentions towards Czechoslovakia. He said that relations between Berlin and Prague were excellent and that reports of an impending occupation of Bohemia and Moravia were baseless rumours.

Moravec decided that the time had come for his departure. His immediate superior agreed. Documents he could not afford to destroy were surreptitiously transferred to British custody. Discreet arrangements were made to fly Moravec and some of his staff in a Dutch civilian aircraft to Croydon, where the arrival of eleven mysterious Czechoslovaks at a moment when a crisis was clearly impending in Central Europe gave rise to much speculation.

On 11 March the government-inspired German press began to pave the way for the next move by coming down heavily on the Slovak side in the current dispute between Czechs and Slovaks. It also carried the news that Father Tiso, dismissed as Prime Minister of Slovakia by President Hacha on the previous day, had appealed to Germany for protection against the Czechs.

Henderson had returned to Berlin in February after an illness which kept him out of circulation for four months. According to his subsequent account, he felt fairly sure that the rumours which had been circulating while he was ill about an impending invasion of the Netherlands or Switzerland, or air attacks on Britain, originated with the Germans themselves.[60] Nor did he believe that Hitler would try to seize the Romanian oil-wells, as was also alleged. On the assumption that Danzig, the Polish Corridor and the future of Czechoslovakia were questions that governments apparently bent on cultivating good relations with Germany should be able to settle by negotiation, Memel seemed likely to be Germany's next objective.

However, by the middle of the second week in March, at the latest, the evidence that German troops were ready to enter Czechoslovakia was unmistakable. The British Embassy also received the disquieting news that Vojtech Mastny, the Czechoslovak Minister in Berlin, was being kept at arm's length by the German Foreign Ministry. On 13 March Henderson still hoped – though he scarcely expected – that Chvalkovsky might yet be able to strike an acceptable bargain with the Germans. He warned the Foreign Ministry that any contravention by Germany of the Munich agreement was bound to have an adverse effect on Anglo-German relations, but decided not to ask London for instructions to deliver a formal protest which he thought would arrive too late and in any case was unlikely to be effective.[61] He then advised Mastny, not for the first time, to ask Chvalkovsky to pocket his pride and come to Berlin without delay.

On the following day Henderson learned to his dismay that not only Chvalkovsky but also President Hacha were already on their way to Berlin. This seemed to him a serious tactical error, and so it proved. At a nightmare interview with Hitler in the small hours of 15 March, when German tanks were already rumbling across Czechoslovakia's post-Munich frontier, the unfortunate Hacha was bullied into giving a semblance of legality to the dismemberment of his country by signing a request for German intervention. He was also forced to warn his government by telephone that Prague would be bombed if the invaders were fired upon. The German Army occupied Bohemia and Moravia without firing a shot, but under cover of a demonstration by the Luftwaffe. The western provinces were declared a German protectorate, while Slovakia – already shorn by Hungary of a substantial strip of territory – became a separate state, nominally independent. Benes, who had fled to the United States after Munich, denounced these arrangements and proclaimed the existence of an independent sovereign Republic of Czechoslovakia, whose territory was occupied for the time being by an aggressor. In the following July Benes arrived in London, was received by Moravec, and established his headquarters at a villa in Putney.

Attitudes to the rape of Czechoslovakia revealed differences of outlook which made a genuine understanding between Britain and National Socialist Germany impossible. The British regarded the occupation of Bohemia and Moravia as a gross breach of the Munich agreement and a crime against humanity. They also regarded it as a blunder, since it gave Germany a protectorate seething with discontent in place of a prosperous trading-partner. The Germans found this attitude incomprehensible. Nearly always great sticklers for correctness even when they were behaving badly, they considered that they had acted with praiseworthy moderation and complete propriety. They could have conquered Czechoslovakia by fire and sword. In deference to British and French opinion, they had preferred a peaceful occupation for which they could produce written authority, signed by the Czechoslovak head of state. They were genuinely astonished when the British cancelled a projected visit to Germany by two members of the government. They protested that they had made repeated attempts to establish friendly relations with Britain and that all their overtures had been rebuffed. The view taken by the British was that, although nothing would have pleased them more than to get on good terms with Germany, the National Socialist government had made friendship impossible by doing everything the wrong way and by committing senseless acts of violence against Czechs and Jews.

Thereafter the Germans repeatedly accused the British of preparing for a preventive war against Germany, although they also said that Britain was decadent and would not fight for anyone or anything in any circumstances. The British clung as obstinately to the equally mistaken view that Germany was preparing to take the offensive against Britain. Neither side was right, and neither could point to any evidence from a reliable intelligence source to justify its fear of an unprovoked act of aggression by the other.

However, war between Britain and Germany was soon to become almost inevitable. The Germans followed up their bloodless conquest of Czechoslovakia by pressing the Polish government to accept a dictated settlement of outstanding issues. Thereupon the Poles suspended diplomatic conversations with Germany about Danzig and the Polish Corridor, but offered to resume them if the Germans would abstain from threats and inflammatory articles and speeches. In the meantime the British government called Henderson to London to report. During his absence from Berlin rumours began to circulate among diplomats and press correspondents to the effect that Germany was threatening Rumania as well as Poland and that a crisis was imminent. In the light of these alarms and of a recommendation from the Chiefs of Staff that plans should be concerted with both the Poles and the Rumanians, the Cabinet agreed on 18 March – only three days after the fall of Prague – to make approaches not only to Poland and Rumania but also to the Soviet Union.[62] Ten days later the Foreign Office was told by the British Embassy in Berlin and a British journalist who had contacts with the

German General Staff of a rumour that Germany would launch an immediate attack on Poland unless Britain and France made it clear that they would fight.[63] At a special meeting of the Cabinet on 30 March the Foreign Secretary informed his colleagues that there was now enough evidence to warrant a declaration in that sense.[64] Accordingly, the Prime Minister announced in the House of Commons on the following day that Britain and France would support Poland against any action that clearly threatened her independence. Similar guarantees were given a fortnight later to Rumania and Greece.

In fact, Halifax seems to have received no evidence apart from the rumour that reached London on 28 March.[65] When evidence of Germany's intentions did arrive later from secret intelligence sources, it pointed not to an imminent attack on Poland but to one to be launched after the middle of August.

The government's gesture created a difficult situation. The Poles were known to be doughty fighters, but their armed forces were substantially outnumbered by Germany's. They had no strong defensive positions covering their centres of production in Western Poland. At best, they might be able to hold a line from Bydgoszcz to Katowice for a limited period before retreating to the line of the Vistula and the San. Their ability to withstand a German assault for any considerable length of time would depend, therefore, on their receiving supplies from the east. In the east they had a long frontier with the Soviet Union and a short frontier with Rumania. Any supplies sent to them in wartime from Britain or France would have to travel by a long route through the Mediterranean, the Dardanelles, the Sea of Marmara, the Bosphorus and the Black Sea. Supplies sent directly from the Soviet Union, on the other hand, could reach them quickly. Although unwilling to admit Soviet troops to their territory, they were willing to receive supplies from the Soviet Union, and indeed counted on doing so. A firm understanding about these matters with the Soviet Union, and preferably also with Rumania and Turkey, ought surely to have preceded the Anglo-French offer of support. By offering support before coming to terms with the Soviet Union, the British and the French not only encouraged the Poles to entertain false hopes, but also deprived the Russians of any inducement to strike a bargain with them without first seeing whether the Germans had anything better to offer. In fact, the Germans were prepared to offer acquiescence in Soviet penetration of the Baltic States, which the British and the French were not. In May the Russians took their first overt step towards the Moscow Pact by dismissing the pro-Western Maxim Litvinov and replacing him as Commissar for Foreign Affairs by the enigmatic Vyacheslav Molotov.

In the meantime the collapse of the British Secret Intelligence Service's network in Czechoslovakia was partly offset – perhaps even more than offset – by the arrival of Moravec and members of his staff on British soil. Thümmel – still known to the Czechoslovak intelligence service only as A-54 or Karl – had assured Moravec at their meeting in March that he would get in touch with him again, and had been given addresses in Switzerland and the Netherlands. In June he established contact through Zurich, and arrangements were made for Moravec's deputy to meet him at The Hague. When told that the Czechoslovak intelligence service could no longer afford to pay him at the old rate, he offered to work for nothing. He reported the existence of a German plan for the conquest of Poland, promised to give details later, and added that the Germans now had nine armoured divisions.[66] Moravec passed this information to the British and the French. He also resumed a long-interrupted correspondence with the Polish intelligence service by passing it to Warsaw.

During the summer of 1939 the British and the French received reports in the same sense from other agents, but Thümmel remained an exceptionally valuable source. As a senior officer of the Abwehr, now stationed in Berlin, he had direct access to a wide range of classified material, could travel freely outside Germany, and was sometimes able to carry with him documentary evidence to support his statements. Early in August he brought to The Hague a detailed account of the German Army's plan for the invasion of Poland, with designations of most major formations and names of commanders down to divisional level.[67] He added that his chief, Admiral Wilhelm Canaris, had recently been asked by the SS for 150 Polish uniforms, with appropriate small arms. Thümmel guessed, correctly, that these were to be used for a ruse designed to give the impression that hostilities had been provoked or even started by the Poles. Finally, he arranged to notify Moravec of the dates fixed for the mobilization of the German Army and the invasion of Poland by transmitting warnings disguised as messages about deliveries of goods to the shop which served as cover for the local headquarters of the Czechoslovak intelligence service.

Thümmel reported in due course that Poland was to be invaded on 26 August, and later that the date had been put back to 1 September.[68] This information might have proved valuable to the Poles and their allies if the French had followed it up by preparing to attack the weak German forces in the West as soon as the first German soldier set foot on Polish soil or the first German aircraft violated Polish air-space. As things were, Britain and France did not declare war on Germany until 3 September. After learning late on 21 August that a non-aggression pact between Germany and the Soviet Union was to be signed in Moscow on the next day but one, the British and French governments made strenuous attempts to avert a European war by reaffirming their determination to honour their pledges and by urging moderation on both sides. These efforts, reinforced by Italy's refusal to go to war except on terms regarded by the Germans as prohibitive, contributed to the six-day postponement of the invasion. They did not prevent the German Army and the Luftwaffe from delivering a massive onslaught on Poland while the Poles were still struggling to concentrate their forces.

*

We have seen that by 1937 the British Government Code and Cypher School came to the conclusion that the German Army, the German Navy, and probably also the Luftwaffe and other government agencies, were all using versions of the Enigma machine to encypher messages which it could not read.* On the outbreak of war in 1939 signals encyphered by these machines could still not be read currently in Britain, but in the meantime discussions between the British, French and Polish signal intelligence services fostered the hope that eventually the problem might be solved.

To understand why a concerted effort to plumb the mysteries of Enigma was not made at an early stage by all the powers threatened or thought to be threatened by German expansionism, it is necessary to bear in mind that, although both the Czechoslovak and the Polish intelligence services were in regular contact with the French Deuxième Bureau during the greater part of the period between the wars, they were not on particularly good terms with each other, and that after Munich the attitude of the French to the Czechs was coloured by the belief that the Czechoslovak General Staff was likely to have been penetrated by the Abwehr.[69] Contact between the Czechoslovak intelligence service and Soviet Military Intelligence was established in 1936, and a fresh approach was made by the Russians in 1939, after Moravec had moved to

* See page 26.

London; but the Czechs received the impression that the Russians were more interested in receiving than in imparting information.[70] British relations with the French and Czechoslovak intelligence services, and eventually also with the Polish intelligence service, were generally good, but until well into 1939 British cryptanalysts were debarred by security regulations from disclosing their secrets to anyone outside their immediate circle.

In the autumn of 1931 Captain Gustave Bertrand of the signal intelligence section of the Deuxième Bureau was introduced by a colleague to an agent named Hans-Thilo Schmidt (but code-named Asché) who was employed in the cypher branch of the German Army.[71] Between that time and the date in 1934 when he was transferred to the signal intelligence section of the Luftwaffe, Schmidt furnished Bertrand with a mass of documentary information about the version of the Enigma machine then used by the German Army. This included detailed instructions for its use, and clear-text and encyphered versions of a long message. By 1932 Bertrand was in possession of tables showing the keys to be used in September and October of that year, and Schmidt seems later to have provided similar information for the whole of the period up to the middle of 1934.[72] He was, however, unable to throw any light on the internal wiring of the machine.

Almost from the beginning, Bertrand envisaged a joint effort by the British, the Czechs, the French and the Poles to exploit the material obtained from Schmidt. He presented the British in 1931 with photographic copies of two of the documents, but they had little or nothing to offer in exchange, and the Czechs seem to have been equally unresponsive.

With the Poles he was much more successful. On the initiative of the Polish intelligence service, a two-year course in cryptology for advanced students of mathematics had been started in 1929 at the University of Poznan, where nearly all the students spoke fluent German. Of some twenty students who attended the course, the most promising were Marian Rejewski, Jerzy Rozycki and Henryk Zygalski. When the course ended in the summer of 1931, all three were persuaded to join the signal intelligence branch of the Military Intelligence Department under a German-speaking former officer of the Austrian Army, Major Gwido Langer. The Poles knew by 1931 that both the German Navy and the German Army were using cypher machines, and their agents had reported that these were versions of the Enigma machine then still available on the open market. A commercial Enigma machine had been bought in 1930, and had turned out to be very similar to a machine briefly detained by the customs authorities in 1929 and covertly examined by intelligence officers.[73] Assuming that Germany's armed forces would not use machines that anyone could buy, the Polish cryptanalysts very much wanted to know to what extent, and in what respects, their machines differed from the commercial model.

Documents furnished by Schmidt and carried by Bertrand to Warsaw in December 1931 and later went some way to answer these questions. The instruction manual showed that the model described did differ from the commercial version, notably in having an external plugboard, but was not so radically different from it that the machine bought in 1930 could not be used as the point of departure for a reconstruction.[74]

The first problem was to establish the internal electrical connections. Here the Poles were helped by the fact that the enciphering rotors of all Enigma machines were geared to each other in such a way that the middle rotor of a three-rotor machine did not begin to turn until the right-hand rotor had made a complete revolution, the left-hand rotor not until the middle rotor had done the same. Until twenty-six characters had been enciphered, the middle and left-hand rotors and the reflector on the extreme left could therefore be treated as a fixed system. Furthermore, the order of the rotors on the shaft was changed at fixed intervals. It followed that each rotor in turn came eventually to occupy the right-hand position, and that therefore each could be considered separately.

Their familiarity with mathematical disciplines enabled the Polish cryptanalysts to take full advantage of this state of affairs. Their calculations were much helped by the fact that the clear-text versions of many enciphered messages began with the same stereotyped designation.[75] Using a mathematical process devised by Rejewski, they succeeded by November 1932 in establishing the internal wiring of all three enciphering rotors and the reflector. Knowledge of the daily keys for September and October then enabled them to work out the connections between the keyboard and the entry rotor.[76] By the end of the year they were thus in possession of the theoretical knowledge needed to reconstruct the machine used at that time (with different keys and important differences of procedure) by the German Army and the German Navy, and afterwards adopted (again with different keys) by the Luftwaffe.

This knowledge did not, of itself, enable them to read messages enciphered by the machine. They still had to cope with problems arising from changes in the order of the rotors and, in the case of the naval machine, the replacement of up to two of them by spares; from variations in the settings of the plugboard and of the rings attached to the rotors; and from the random choice by operators of the three-letter groups – called by the Poles the telegram-keys – which determined the final positions of the rotors immediately before encypherment began. In the early stages their task was eased not only by Schmidt's contributions but also by the tendency of operators to choose easily-typed groups such as AAA or SSS, and by the fact that each telegram-key was encyphered twice in succession. The double encypherment of repetitive groups gave rise to patterns, or cycles, which the Poles had many opportunities of studying before the Germans forbade their operators to choose such groups. Later, groups composed of letters next to each other on the keyboard were also banned.

The Polish cryptanalysts recognized from the outset that they could not expect to be provided for an indefinite period with tables showing the basic settings to be used on a particular day. Besides establishing the data which enabled their technologists to reconstruct the military version of the machine, they developed a number of devices for the rapid testing of possible settings. The most elaborate of these was an electro-mechanical scanner invented by Rejewski and known to him and his colleagues as a Bomby or Bombe. Although sometimes called the first computer, it used no electronics and had no memory. It might therefore be more aptly described as a lightning calculator. An alternative method devised by Zygalski employed large numbers of perforated sheets, each with about a thousand perforations.[77]

According to statements made on their behalf in 1939 and subsequent accounts by Polish writers, the Polish cryptanalysts were able by the early part of 1938 to read a high proportion of army and Luftwaffe signals within two hours.[78] On the other hand, they achieved only a very limited success with naval signals encyphered after the spring of 1937.[79] At the height of the Sudeten crisis the Germans dealt them a severe blow by furnishing each military Enigma machine with two spare rotors interchangeable with the existing rotors, and by making other changes.[80] The Poles were able to work out the internal connections of the additional rotors, but by the end of 1938 they could no longer read any naval, military or Luftwaffe signals currently. The few signals encyphered in recent months which they did manage to decypher were read only after long delays.[81]

The French were in no better case. In December Bertrand proposed a conference of British, French and Polish cryptanalysts.[82]

A three-day conference was duly held in Paris in January 1939. Except that Bertrand's organization and the British Government Code and Cypher School agreed to exchange liaison officers and establish a teleprinter link, no great progress was made. Regard for security prevented the British from saying much; the French had little to add to their earlier disclosures. The Polish cryptanalysts, having been told not to disclose their secrets unless the other delegates had something substantial to offer, were not forthcoming.[83]

The outlook changed considerably during the next six months. The British and French governments committed themselves to military intervention on Poland's behalf in the event of war, and to staff talks at the highest planning level. At the same time, an almost total lack of progress since January convinced the Poles that they had reached the limit of their achievement with their existing resources and without spending more than they could afford on new equipment. In these circumstances the Chief of the Polish General Staff ruled in July that the cypher branch should make a full disclosure of its problems, methods and achievements.

The outcome was another conference, held this time on Polish soil. Colonel S. A. Mayer, the Polish Chief of Intelligence, presided over the first meeting in Warsaw on 24 July; at subsequent technical discussions at a government communication centre in the outer suburbs the Poles were represented by Langer, his second-in-command and the three mathematicians. The French delegates were Bertrand and Captain Henri Bracquenié. The Government Code and Cypher School was represented by Denniston and 'Dilly' Knox, both veterans of Room 40; Admiral Sinclair, as its titular chief, by his deputy and eventual successor, Colonel Stewart Menzies. In accordance with the cloak-and-dagger tradition established by Cumming and followed by Sinclair, Menzies did not disclose his identity, although it was doubtless known to Colonel Mayer.

The Poles gave an account of their progress since 1932 and demonstrated their devices. They promised the British and the French each a copy of their reconstruction of the military version of the Enigma machine and a set of blueprints of their Bombe.

These gifts duly arrived. On 16 August Bertrand, with two companions, took the machine consigned to the British to London and delivered it at Victoria Station to a recipient whom he described as dressed *en smoking* and wearing the rosette of the Legion of Honour in his buttonhole.[84] This was apparently not Admiral Sinclair, who died some three months later, but Menzies in his capacity as Acting Chief of the Secret Service and Acting Director of the Government Code and Cypher School.

With the help of the Polish material, the British gained useful background knowledge during the next few weeks by reading old signals for which the keys had already been broken by the Poles. They were still unable on the outbreak of war to read current traffic encyphered by naval, military or Luftwaffe versions of the machine.[85]

THREE

The Phoney War and After

On the outbreak of World War II the British added to their rather ramshackle intelligence apparatus an organization for the overt censorship of posts and telegraphs, and a Combined Services Detailed Interrogation Centre intended primarily for the further questioning of prisoners-of-war already interrogated in the field. Control of Cotton's Special Flight passed on 23 September from the Secret Intelligence Service to the Air Ministry, but Cotton remained in charge and was commissioned as a Wing Commander. In December an inter-service Balkan Intelligence Centre opened at Istanbul for the purpose of collating information received by the service attachés in the Balkans and the Near East from a variety of sources. Cotton would have preferred the Special Flight to remain independent of the RAF until it could be put effectively on a war footing and equipped with new aircraft which he thought should include Spitfires, but he was overruled.[1]

The intelligence agencies also added to their resources the first of a number of wartime double agents whose co-operation enabled the British to penetrate, and ultimately to control, the German espionage network in the United Kingdom. This was a British electrical engineer who had contacts in Germany and had worked at one time for a firm under contract to the Admiralty. He had been employed for a short time in 1936 as a British agent, but had become suspect when he was found to be in touch with the local headquarters of the Abwehr at Hamburg. Towards the end of that year he had made a voluntary statement to the effect that he had accepted employment by the Abwehr with the intention of penetrating it in the interests of the British.[2] In 1939 he was known to have been furnishing the Germans for the past two years or more with information about naval and air matters, but during the same period he had communicated from time to time with MI 6 or the Special Branch, and had given them some account of his dealings with the Abwehr and the material he was asked to provide.

On the second day of hostilities between Britain and Germany, this man telephoned Scotland Yard and made an appointment to meet an inspector of the Special Branch at Waterloo Station. On arrival at the rendezvous he was served with a detention order under Section 18B of the Defence Regulations and taken into custody. He continued to proclaim his loyalty to Britain, and accepted a proposal that he should set a trap for the enemy by communicating with the Abwehr under British supervision. A wireless transmitter and receiver with which the Germans had provided him was installed in his cell at Wandsworth Prison and used to send a message in which he asked for an early meeting in the Netherlands with his principal Abwehr contact, Major Ritter.[3] He received in return a series of orders and requests for information. Released from prison, he met Ritter later in the month at Rotterdam, and returned with fresh instructions. He was accompanied on his next visit to the Netherlands by a retired inspector of police whom he introduced to his Abwehr contacts as a member of the Welsh Nationalist Party and a suitable organizer of a projected insurrection in South Wales. This was to be accomplished with the aid of weapons and explosives which the sabotage department of the Abwehr (Abt II) proposed to deliver by submarine. He returned from this further visit with a sum of money thoughtfully provided by the Germans; the promise of regular payments to be made in future by a woman living near Bournemouth; and some microphotographed material which included a letter to a British-domiciled Abwehr agent whom he was instructed to contact with a view to employing him to microphotograph his reports. The woman was duly traced, arrested and imprisoned. The man, although of German origin, turned out to be a loyal British subject, recruited by the Abwehr under duress.[4]

Besides leading more or less directly to the discovery of a number of German agents in Britain and providing the British with a means of planting false information on the enemy, this fortunate stroke gave MI 5 a valuable insight into the Abwehr's methods and the means by which it communicated with its agents. Moreover, it was to be expected that sooner or later questions put to supposedly loyal agents would throw a useful light on Germany's intentions. At a fairly early stage, some of the questions put to Britain's first wartime double agent did in fact suggest that airfields and aircraft factories were likely to be high on the Luftwaffe's list of targets in the event of a major air offensive against the United Kingdom. That could, however, in any case be inferred from experience in Poland.[5]

MI 6 was not so lucky. It still did not know that its organization in the Netherlands had been penetrated by the Abwehr. In the spring of 1939 the British had been asked on what terms they would recognize and support a resistance movement capable of establishing an alternative government in Germany. With the knowledge and approval of the Foreign Office, negotiations with Germans who claimed to speak for such a movement were handled on its behalf by MI 6. This meant that after the outbreak of war they were handled by MI 6's representatives at The Hague. On 24 October the Prime Minister authorized the Foreign Office to draw up a statement for submission to the Germans.[6] On 6 November, after consulting the War Cabinet and after a request for a more detailed statement had been received, he and the Foreign Secretary approved the terms of a further communication.[7] On the following day Halifax gave the French Ambassador an account of what was being done, adding that he doubted whether the approach made by the Germans would lead to anything, or was even genuine.[8] The outcome was that on 9 November Major Stevens and Captain G. Payne Best of MI 6 allowed themselves to be lured into an ambush at Venlo by their German contact, who was not the emissary of a resistance movement but an Abwehr officer. Both survived imprisonment in Germany, but their loss was a serious blow to MI 6 at a time when various agencies were competing for the services of linguists with a taste for clandestine pursuits. Best, in particular, was not only an exceptionally good linguist, but also a veteran intelligence officer whose experience as an organizer of espionage networks for the War Office and the Secret Intelligence Service went back to World War I. He was not easily replaced.

Not surprisingly, a big expansion of Section D between the outbreak of war and the spring of 1940 was regarded by the established intelligence agencies as a shocking waste of skilled manpower. MI (R) also branched out to some extent, but on a more modest scale. Section D established small dumps of sabotage material at ten places in northern France, but these proved virtually useless because the men left in charge of them when France fell were not told what to do with the material, and had no means of obtaining fresh supplies.[9] MI (R) dissociated itself to an increasing extent from the rival organization, whose plans for large-scale sabotage and subversion Holland thought far-fetched.[10] It was destined to make some useful contributions to the development of unorthodox weapons and the denial to the enemy of reserves of raw materials.

The performance of the information-gathering intelligence agencies in the early months of the war was not very impressive. The first-line strength of the Luftwaffe was considerably and its reserves were grossly over-estimated.[11] Substitution of a newly formed Ministry of Economic Warfare for the Industrial Intelligence Centre as the authority which shared with the Air Ministry responsibility for studying German aircraft production made matters worse rather than better.[12] The Admiralty's naval reporting network gave good warning of most sailings of merchant vessels for German ports, but little reliable information about German naval movements was received from any intelligence source. Surface warships employed as commerce raiders came and went without detection by reconnoitring aircraft and submarines.[13] Routes used by U-boats on passage to and from the Atlantic were only slowly and laboriously established from occasional sightings. Unlike the Luftwaffe, which made considerable use of low-grade cyphers for tactical traffic, the German Navy used for most of its signals a high-grade machine-cypher which was not broken until the spring of 1941.[14] The RAF's employment of ordinary bomber or bomber-reconnaissance aircraft for photographic reconnaissance led to heavy losses; these, and unfavourable weather, ruled out regular cover of German bases during the winter of 1939–40. The situation improved only when the Special Flight (renamed the Photographic Development Unit) at last received its specially modified, unarmed Spitfires. Emden and Wilhelmshaven were photographed by a Spitfire Type B in February 1940; Kiel could not be covered until a long-range Spitfire Type C became available in April. Bases east of Kiel were still out of range. The Naval Intelligence Division made no contribution to the cornering of the *Graf Spee* in the River Plate in December 1939.[15] No warning was received from any source of the penetration of the fleet base at Scapa Flow by the U-47 in October.[16] The Air Ministry's Y-Service did give warning of the Luftwaffe's raid on the Firth of Forth on 16 October, but no special precautions were taken in the absence of corroboration. The radar chain, still incomplete, worked unsatisfactorily, and the defences were taken by surprise.[17] A gross over-estimate by Air Intelligence of the number of German bombers within striking-distance of Scapa Flow was the immediate cause of the Admiralty's decision to relegate the main body of the Home Fleet to inconvenient anchorages on the West Coast of Scotland during the first winter of the war.[18]

However, in some respects the performance of the intelligence agencies was a good deal better than it looked. The Luftwaffe, besides making frequent use of low-grade cyphers for such purposes as the transmission of weather and reconnaissance reports, employed in peace and war a variety of radio aids to navigation. These were distinct from the very-high-frequency radio beams afterwards used in attacks on British cities. An Air Safety Service used medium-frequency transmissions to give directions to aircraft in flight. Call-signs were changed shortly before the outbreak of war, but the new call-signs of most operational units were known to the British by the end of 1939.[19] Medium-frequency transmissions from navigational beacons – of which the Luftwaffe had about fifty by the spring of 1940 – yielded valuable information well before Enigma traffic could be read currently. High-frequency transmissions used by operational crews for air-to-ground communication first came to the attention of the British towards the end of 1938, although it was not until much later that the coded call-signs used for this traffic were understood.[20] In the light of information from the Air Ministry's Y-Service, centred at Cheadle, Air Intelligence was able in the autumn of 1939 to trace the return of some Luftwaffe units from Poland to their home bases, and thereafter to identify and locate many units with which contact had been lost on the eve of the war. Moreover, on a number of occasions liaison officers attached from Cheadle to operational formations were able to give warning of air attacks before approaching aircraft were picked up by the radar chain. Fighter Command, profiting from the lesson of the October raid on the Firth of Forth, found such warnings particularly useful in view of its responsibility for the safeguarding of coastal convoys to which it could not afford to give continuous fighter protection by standing patrols.[21]

The cracking of Enigma traffic – and later the interpretation and secure distribution of the information it provided – posed more formidable problems. In the second half of September 1939 the Polish mathematicians obeyed orders to retreat to Rumania. They escaped internment by taking refuge in the French Embassy at Bucharest, and eventually found themselves drafted into Bertrand's organization, where they were joined by Langer and other colleagues. By October Bertrand's team comprised about fifty Frenchmen, fifteen Poles, and seven Spanish refugees working on Spanish and Italian cyphers, in addition to a British liaison officer.[22] Soon after the middle of December an emissary arrived from Bletchley Park with one of two sets of perforated sheets completed by the Government Code and Cypher School.[23] These differed from those prepared earlier by the Poles in lending themselves more readily to rapid large-scale production because the perforations were punched, not cut by hand.

At the end of the year the emissary returned with the heart-warming news that, soon after his arrival in France, a signal encyphered by the German Army on 28 October had been read with the aid of the sheets delivered to Bertrand's organization. The Government Code and Cypher School then used the sheets it had retained to read a signal encyphered on 25 October, also by the German Army.[24] This was the first wartime Enigma message read in Britain. A number of other signals encyphered in 1939 were read while the British cryptanalysts awaited a favourable opportunity of discovering whether signals encyphered after the end of the year would respond to the same treatment. Their doubts were resolved when a signal encyphered by the Luftwaffe on 6 January was read.[25]

During the next two to three months the Government Code and Cypher School solved, by similar methods, about fifty Enigma settings belonging to the series used by the German Army in Germany's twenty military districts (called by the British the Green Key); the series used by the Luftwaffe for administrative and later also for operational traffic (the Red Key); and the series used by the Luftwaffe for practice purposes (the Blue Key).[26] According to a quasi-official but not always accurate Polish account, the British solved about four-fifths of all keys broken by the Allies during that period.[27] This was to be expected, because Bertrand, Denniston and Langer had agreed that the traditionally pragmatic British should concentrate on the breaking of current keys while the French and the Poles continued their theoretical work with long-term ends in view. The British also assumed responsibility for the development of an improved Bombe.

In consequence of the Luftwaffe's responsibility for army support and its contributions to the war at sea, some Luftwaffe traffic was of interest to the War Office and the Admiralty as well as the Air Ministry. Naval Enigma, however, remained inscrutable. One reason was that – as the British learned by the end of the year – the German Navy's Enigma operators were able in 1940 to ring the changes on up to eight rotors.[28] Three rotors were captured from the crew of the submarine U-33 when she was sunk by a minesweeper on 12 February while trying to lay mines in the Clyde, but her machine was not recovered.[29]

The Allied espionage organizations were unlucky, inasmuch as their agents more than once gave a well-founded warning of an operation afterwards countermanded or postponed in circumstances no agent could be expected to foresee. Thümmel, for example, reported about the time when the German campaign in Poland was drawing to a close that an offensive in the West was due to start on 12 November.[30] We now know that readiness for an assault to be delivered on that date was duly ordered by the German High Command on 5 November, but counter-manded on 7 November.* A similar warning, conveyed through the Vatican and the Netherlands Military Attaché in Berlin, was received from the second-in-command of the Abwehr, General Hans Oster, who was not an Allied agent and seems to have been actuated by humanitarian motives.[31] At the end of November Thümmel told his Czechoslovak secret service contacts at The Hague that the postponed offensive on the Western Front was now due to start in the middle of December but was unlikely, in his opinion, to be launched before January.[32]

On 10 January a German aircraft carrying two staff officers made a forced landing in Belgium. A Luftwaffe instruction retrieved from it pointed to a thrust by the German forces in the West across Central Belgium.[33] On the same day – as we now know – Hitler issued orders for an offensive to begin on 17 January, but they were rescinded three days later. Almost simultaneously a member of the staff of the United States Embassy in Moscow heard in Berlin that Germany's offensive in the West was due to start on 13 January.[34] His report was conveyed to the British and the French through diplomatic channels. Again a warning was received from Oster.[35] Warnings not followed by attacks were received on a number of subsequent occasions. As neither intercepted signals nor such reconnaissance photographs as could be taken in unfavourable conditions threw any further light on the matter, the Allied military authorities scarcely knew what to expect. In the light of warnings from such well-placed sources as Thümmel and Oster, and of circumstantial reports of the German build-up in the West, they could scarcely doubt that an offensive of some kind was in prospect. At the same time, they could not exclude the possibility that the document retrieved on 10 January had been planted on them. If it had not been planted, would the Germans persist with a plan they must know was likely to have been compromised? Did they still intend to advance through Central Belgium towards North-East France and the Channel coast? Or would they content themselves with the capture of the Netherlands as a base for operations against Britain, or launch an offensive further south?

* See page 2.

Although unable to answer these questions to their satisfaction – and although they still imputed to the Germans many more tanks and far larger stored reserves of aircraft than they really had – the British were by no means badly informed in the early part of 1940 about the composition and location of the enemy's land and air forces. Some of their information came, as we have seen, from signal intelligence. Some came from neutral diplomatic sources and the German press and radio. There was also a steady flow of reports, not all of them accurate, from British and Allied agents. According to Moravec, the Czechoslovak intelligence service was in touch, as early as 1939, with Rudolf Rössler, to whom its representative at Zurich, Captain Karel Sedlacek, was introduced by a Swiss officer, Major Hans Hausamann.[36] Rössler would seem, from the account given by Moravec, to have furnished from the outset useful information, supposedly derived from sources in Berlin, not only about army and air but also sometimes about naval matters. Again according to Moravec, it was at this early stage of the war that the code-names Werther, Olga and Anna – afterwards familiar to the Russians – were first prefixed to messages referring respectively to the German Army, the Luftwaffe and the German Navy.[37]

The British also received, at an early stage of the war, a windfall in the shape of an unsolicited contribution to their knowledge of technical and scientific developments in Germany. Soon after the outbreak of war the British Naval Attaché in Oslo was asked by an anonymous correspondent whether the British were interested in receiving a report on such matters. If they were, they were to notify their assent by causing a slight change to be made in the preamble to the BBC's German-language news-broadcast on a particular evening. The change was made, and early in November 1939 the report arrived.[38] It opened with a brief and superficial account of the Luftwaffe's latest bomber, the Ju 88, followed by an unconvincingly high estimate of the rate at which it was being produced, but continued with impressively detailed descriptions of a number of sophisticated technical devices. These included remotely controlled anti-shipping missiles, two kinds of radar, torpedoes with acoustic and magnetic warheads, gyroscopically stabilized rockets, electrical contact and time fuses for bombs and shells, a radio navigational aid described as an 'aircraft range-finder', and a pilotless aircraft, or stand-off missile, intended for such purposes as the destruction of barrage-balloons. It said that the Germans had experimental establishments at Rechlin (which was already known) and at Peenemünde (which was not). Some of the British scientists and intelligence officers who examined the report believed it to be a hoax, but its authenticity became increasingly apparent when the existence of one after another of the devices described in it was confirmed.

The British were also helped, albeit indirectly, by a speech made by Hitler at Danzig on 19 September 1939. After referring in uncomplimentary terms to the use made by the British of the weapon of naval power to coerce neutrals, Hitler said that Germany, too, had a weapon with which she could not be attacked. The passage was rendered by a Foreign Office translator as 'a weapon against which no defence would avail'. The mistranslation came to light when the BBC's record of the speech was played back to a German-language expert, Professor Frederick Norman, who pointed out that Hitler had referred merely to the Luftwaffe, or Air Weapon.[39] In the meantime the Air Ministry instructed the newly joined Dr R. V. Jones to search the records of the Secret Intelligence Service for possible references to novel weapons. The pre-war files of MI 6 had been removed to the wartime quarters of the Government Code and Cypher School at Bletchley Park, officially known as Station X. After spending a few days at the headquarters of MI 6 at Broadway, Westminster, Jones was therefore sent to Bletchley. He thus gained, almost before his wartime career as a user and evaluator of intelligence had begun, a sound working knowledge of two of the principal sources of information. This proved extremely valuable when, later in the war, prompt answers had to be found to crucial questions about German navigational beams and other arcane matters. Jones also became thoroughly familiar with the Oslo report, and he did not share the low opinion of its credibility held by some of his fellow-academics.

Such strokes of luck went some way to offset the shortcomings from which the intelligence organization as a whole still suffered. The outbreak of war brought numerous demands for photographic reconnaissance from the service departments and other government agencies. There was as yet no machinery for the co-ordination of these demands and the allotment of priorities. The service departments were far from satisfied with the quality of the information supplied by MI 6. There was still no effective means of co-ordinating the work of the various bodies concerned with the interpretation of intelligence. The Joint Intelligence Committee continued to be too much preoccupied with administrative tasks and the preparation of routine reports to give much time to the drafting of independent appreciations, and such appreciations as it did attempt in the early months of the war were not very impressive.[40]

The Joint Intelligence Committee was not alone in having to devote a good many man-hours to the compilation of reports of little value, or of material for inclusion in such reports. The Chamberlain government was determined not to repeat the mistakes of 1914, when an unwieldy Cabinet found itself unable to exert much influence on the conduct of the war and was kept by Kitchener in almost total ignorance of the needs and problems of the Expeditionary Force. On the outbreak of war Chamberlain set up a small War Cabinet and insisted on its being furnished with an ample flow of documentary material. This included daily reports and weekly summaries from the Joint Intelligence Committee, a weekly résumé from the Chiefs of Staff, twice-daily reports from the Cabinet War Room, weekly reports from each of the service departments, monthly intelligence reports from the Ministry of Economic Warfare, occasional political intelligence reports from the Foreign Office, and (from October) a daily weather forecast. In addition it received oral reports from representatives of the service departments, and often also from the Foreign Secretary, at each of the meetings which it held at least once a day.[41] Except that the Admiralty rendered only one weekly report before dropping out of the system, this procedure remained in force until February 1940, when the War Cabinet decided to dispense with all routine reports except the daily situation report from the Joint Intelligence Committee and the weekly résumé from the Chiefs of Staff.[42]

Not surprisingly, the outbreak of war brought demands both from C and from the service departments for increased expenditure on the gathering of information. In December 1939 Chamberlain asked Lord Hankey, who had joined the government as Minister without Portfolio, to investigate the working of the intelligence system and suggest improvements. Hankey's enquiry extended not only to MI 6 and the Government Code and Cypher School, but also to MI 5 and agencies concerned with sabotage and propaganda in foreign countries. He had not yet completed his task when, on 10 May 1940, the Chamberlain government fell from office, but on the following day he produced an interim report. The gist of his findings was that a strengthened Y Sub-Committee should be given a full-time secretary and an independent full-time chairman and that liaison between the Secret Intelligence Service and the service departments should be improved, in so far as this had not already been done under his supervision while the enquiry was in progress.[43] He recorded the opinion that, on the whole (and with certain reservations), the Foreign Office and the Ministry of Economic Warfare were satisfied with the performance of the Secret Intelligence

Service but that the service departments were not. The Admiralty doubted whether the Secret Intelligence Service knew enough about the needs of its customers, and all three departments wanted more and better information.

*

Germany's invasion of Norway and Denmark in the spring of 1940, and the events that led up to it, confronted the British intelligence organization with its first big test. The invasion also exposed the Chamberlain government to stresses which resulted in its downfall. It seems fair to say, with the benefit of hindsight, that the government's failure to insure against the situation that arose in April was due not so much to the shortcomings of the intelligence agencies as to the failure of intelligence officers and others to make good use of the information they provided, and to the weaknesses of the intelligence complex as a whole.

We now know that the seizure of Norway was first proposed in October 1939 by the German Chief of Naval Operations, Admiral Erich Räder. Preliminary studies were sanctioned in December; detailed planning began in January. Hitler seems to have begun by regarding the plan as a precaution against Allied intervention, but his attitude changed when, on 16 February, a British destroyer followed the German supply-ship *Altmark* into Norwegian waters and rescued British merchant seamen who had fallen into German hands as a result of the *Graf Spee*'s attacks on ocean trade. This incident appears to have convinced him that the British would not shrink from invading Norway if it suited them to do so, and that he had better be ready to get his blow in first. On 1 March he ruled that preparations for landings in Norway and Denmark should be completed by 20 March. Two days later, having decided that the Scandinavian venture should precede his assault on France and the Low Countries, he ordered his armed forces to be ready by 10 March to launch it at four days' notice. In the event it could not be launched before April because the Great Belt was still blocked by ice at the end of March.

In reality the British did not intend to put troops ashore in Norway, except at the invitation of the Norwegian government, unless the Germans did so or were clearly about to do so. They did intend to lay mines off the Norwegian coast in order to make it difficult for the Germans to receive Swedish iron-ore shipped from the Norwegian port of Narvik when the Swedish port of Lulea, in the Gulf of Bothnia, was icebound. They also had a contingent plan which envisaged landings in

Norway and an advance through Swedish territory to Finland for the twofold purpose of securing the Swedish ironfields against German or Russian aggression and helping the Finns to resist an invasion launched by the Soviet Union in December.

On 5 February the Allied Supreme War Council accepted the British proposals with the proviso that effect should be given to them only if the Scandinavian governments were willing. But the Scandinavian governments were not willing, and in March the Finns and the Russians came to terms. The British then decided, in consultation with the French, to go ahead with the minelaying operation, even though the time was not far off when the Gulf of Bothnia would be free of ice. The Germans, it was thought, might retaliate by invading Norway, thus giving the Allies a legitimate pretext to disembark troops at Norwegian ports before the enemy could arrive in strength. The date finally fixed for the minelaying operation was 8 April. On 7 April troops to be carried to Bergen and Stavanger, if and when the British government received clear evidence that a German invasion of Norway was imminent, embarked in four cruisers at Rosyth. Transports which would carry troops to Narvik and Trondheim in that event assembled in the Clyde.[45] The troops were not intended or equipped to land in face of serious opposition.

In the context of any attempt to fix responsibility for the mistakes of April 1940, it must be borne in mind that there was never any doubt about the strategic advantages the Germans might hope to derive from access to Norwegian ports and airfields. Some of them were set out in a book by a German admiral, to which Vansittart had drawn the Admiralty's attention in the spring of 1939.[46] In any case they were fairly obvious. Whether the Germans would in fact try to establish themselves in Norway, except perhaps on a limited scale and in response to the minelaying operation, and whether if they did they would be successful, was another matter. Each of the departments concerned had its own opinions about these questions, and inevitably these opinions coloured their attitudes to reports and predictions received from the intelligence agencies and from diplomatic sources. The Foreign Office was anxious that Britain should not imperil her relations with a friendly neutral power by putting troops ashore in Norway without at least the tacit consent of the Norwegian government. At the same time, it was not in a position to rebut the argument that Allied intervention was strategically desirable and that consequently any German move which gave the Allies good reason to intervene would be beneficial to the Allied cause. It tended, therefore, to view forecasts of imminent German intervention in

Norway with scepticism because they seemed to good to be true.[47] The War Office admitted that reports that the Germans were preparing for a seaborne expedition might have some substance, but it could trace only six divisions – about the normal peacetime strength – in the area in which troops were said to be assembling. This was the number of divisions eventually used by the Germans in Norway, but it was less than a quarter of the number the War Office thought they would need to tackle the Norwegians and the Swedes.[48] Moreover, Military Intelligence could not exclude the possibility that the troops were intended not for an invasion of Norway but for some other purpose, such as a series of seaborne raids on the United Kingdom.[49] The Admiralty was troubled by the fear that German surface raiders might break into the Atlantic, as had happened at the beginning of the war. It was determined, therefore, not to commit the Home Fleet to a wild-goose-chase on the strength of rumours. It was all the more disposed to assign reports about German intentions towards Norway to that category because the First Lord, Winston Churchill, believed that invasion of Norway was beyond Germany's powers.[50] The Air Ministry was in some respects less sceptical about such reports than the other service departments. Even so, it tended to interpret them in the light of its preoccupations with the danger of a major air offensive against the United Kingdom.[51]

Information with a possible bearing on German intentions towards Norway which reached the Foreign Office or one or more of the service departments before the Germans landed in Norway and Denmark on 9 April 1940 can be summarized as follows.[52] The author's comments and explanations are in brackets.

1 Agents reported in December 1939 that an expeditionary force was assembling and undergoing combined training in Germany's Baltic ports, and that merchant vessels there had been modified to carry troops and vehicles.

2 Similar reports were received in January. Paratroops and transport aircraft were mentioned.

3 Early in February the British Military Attaché, Stockholm, passed on a message from his Rumanian colleague to the effect that the Germans were preparing to occupy the Swedish ironfields, and seize naval and air bases in Southern Norway, as a contribution to the encirclement of Britain. (The Rumanian attaché was not, however, considered a very reliable source. He was said to have given inaccurate information when serving in another post.)

4 The War Office was aware by early March that the Germans were

said to be paying attention to their defences on the frontier between Germany and Denmark.

5 A German informant (apparently an official who had been in touch with the Permanent Under-Secretary before the war) told the Foreign Office by 11 March that action was being planned against Denmark and Norway. (This accurate warning from an apparently well-placed source seems to have been disregarded by the Foreign Office, presumably because its origin suggested a plant by the German government. So far as is known, it was not brought to the attention of any of the service departments.)

6 An agent reported by 13 March that German firms working on government account had been told to complete their contracts by the middle of the month.

7 A neutral informant said about the same time that he had found on a recent visit to Germany that military action of some kind was widely expected.

8 The naval air station at Hatston, in Orkney, was attacked by the Luftwaffe on 16 March. (Besides being close to Scapa Flow, Hatston was the nearest British air base to Central Norway.)

9 On 20 March the Luftwaffe began a series of attacks on convoys moving between British and Norwegian ports. (This new departure had been predicted by the Air Ministry's Y-Service. Air Intelligence informed the Chiefs of Staff that it regarded these attacks, and also the attack on Hatston, as marking a change in German policy.)

10 The Admiralty's Operational Intelligence Centre noted (without comment) on 24 March that U-boat attacks on merchant shipping had ceased for the time being, and that the Germans were no longer using U-boats or destroyers for minelaying. (U-boats withdrew from the Western Approaches by 13 March, but remained active in the North Sea for another week. Mines were laid in the first half of the month both by U-boats and by a German merchant vessel in neutral guise.)

11 The British Air Attaché, Stockholm, reported on 26 March that the Swedish Naval Staff believed the Germans to be ready to seize Norwegian ports and airfields on the pretext of responding to Allied intervention.

12 The Assistant Naval Attaché, Stockholm, reported on the same day that ships concentrated at Kiel included fast merchant vessels with anti-aircraft guns and 'flying personnel' aboard. (German anti-aircraft guns, except in warships, were manned by airmen, but not by airmen who could be accurately described as flying personnel.)

13 A report received about the same time from the Military Attaché, Stockholm, stated that German officers there had hinted that the Swedish government was free to negotiate with the Finns, but should leave the Norwegians alone because Germany would soon be taking care of Norway.

14 On 27 March Military Intelligence noted that Germany had called up Danish-speaking reservists of six different classes (i.e., age-groups).

15 Military Intelligence noted on the following day that leave had been stopped in the German Army. (Leave had also been stopped on the eve of the abortive offensives on the Western Front in December and January.)

16 The Director of Naval Intelligence told the Naval Staff on 30 March that in recent weeks a German spy-ship had been active in Norwegian territorial waters. He recommended that she should be left unmolested because of the value of her transmissions to Signal Intelligence. (She had come to the attention of MI 5 as a result of information furnished by the double agent recruited at the beginning of the war. Her transmissions to the Abwehr were monitored by MI 5's Radio Security Service. The double agent's knowledge of Abwehr cyphers enabled the Government Code and Cypher School to read them.)

17 On 2 April the British Naval Attaché, Oslo, sent a report, graded A1, to the effect that large numbers of troops were concentrating at Rostock.

18 Information received from the Swedish government by 3 April indicated that troops and shipping were concentrating at Stettin and Swinemünde and that, according to unconfirmed reports, ships were embarking tanks and other war material at Hamburg.

19 A report that 117 German aircraft (the equivalent of one complete Geschwader and an additional Gruppe) had arrived in North-West Germany after undergoing navigational and night-flying training in the Baltic area was received by 4 April.

20 A British bomber crew saw at Wihelmshaven on 4 April 'two enemy capital ships of the *Gneisenau* class'.

21 The British Military Attaché, Copenhagen, reported on 4 and 5 April that precedence on the railway between Hamburg and Bremen was being given to military traffic, which included sealed trains, and that large numbers of transports were assembling at Kiel, Stettin and Swinemünde.

22 The news that a German aircraft, believed to be on photographic

reconnaissance, had flown over the West Coast of Norway on 4 April reached the Admiralty by 6 April.

23 At 12.25 a.m. on 6 April the British Minister, Copenhagen, reported that his American colleague had been told by a well-placed source that Hitler had given definite orders for a division carried in ten ships to land at Narvik on 8 April. Jutland was to be occupied on the same day, but Sweden was not to be invaded. German moderates were said to be opposing the plan. (Ten destroyers carrying 2,000 troops of the 3rd Mountain Division were in fact due to arrive near the entrance to the fjord leading to Narvik on 8 April, but were not to enter the fjord and disembark the troops until the following morning. Seaborne troops were to land on the same day at Trondheim, Bergen, Kristiansand, Arendal and Oslo, airborne troops at Oslo and Stavanger. Key-points in Denmark were also to be seized.)

24 At 2.17 p.m. the British Minister, Copenhagen, sent a further telegram. It said that the United States Minister considered the report about Narvik 'in principle fantastic', but felt it could not be disregarded. According to his information, the troops had embarked on 4 April but the German military authorities hoped to have the order rescinded. (In fact the troops began to embark on 6 April.)

25 A photographic reconnaissance of Wilhelmshaven on 6 April confirmed that the capital ships there were the battlecruisers *Scharnhorst* and *Gneisenau*. Other warships were present.

26 During the night of 6/7 April the Government Code and Cypher School noted German naval wireless activity of unprecedented intensity in the area Heligoland Bight – Jutland – Skagerak. The Naval Section reported this by telephone to the Admiralty's Operational Intelligence Centre, but could not say what it portended.

27 British bomber crews reported on their return from leaflet-dropping raids over Germany on the night of 6/7 April that they had seen intense activity in dockside areas at Kiel, Eckenförde, Hamburg and Lübeck, and on roads leading to them. A stationary warship had been seen in the Jade Roads and a large ship twenty miles north of Heligoland, heading north.

28 Photographs taken when Kiel was covered for the first time by the Photographic Development Unit on 7 April revealed a large concentration of shipping there.

29 The crew of a Coastal Command aircraft sent to reconnoitre the Heligoland Bight on 7 April reported seeing about 9 a.m. what they took

to be a cruiser and six destroyers north-bound off the Horn Reefs (East Coast of Jutland).

30 Another visual reconnaissance report, received later on the same day, stated that three German destroyers had been seen east of Jutland at 1.15 p.m. heading south. (These, it was thought, might be returning to base after some minor operation.)

31 At 1.25 p.m., again on 7 April, part of a bomber force sent to look for the ships seen in the forenoon found and attacked them, but scored no hits. The leader of the striking-force said later that he transmitted a wireless report soon after the attack, but it was not heard. Crews reported on their return to base that they had sighted the enemy squadron off the entrance to the Skagerak, that it was steering north-west, and that it consisted of possibly one battlecruiser, two cruisers and ten destroyers. (In fact the two German battlecruisers, with ten destroyers, and the cruiser *Hipper*, with four, were in the area at the time, and were bound in an approximately north-westerly direction.)

32 The Admiralty learned in the early afternoon of 8 April that German soldiers rescued by a Norwegian destroyer and Norwegian fishing-vessels after the sinking of a transport by a Polish submarine off Kristiansand (South) had said that they were to have landed at Bergen to protect it from the British. (Notwithstanding its impeccable source, this report seems to have been regarded at first with some scepticism. The Admiralty did not pass it to the Commander-in-Chief, Home Fleet, until the late evening, after it had been circulated by a press agency in Oslo. The Norwegian authorities alerted the coast defences, but withheld sanction for the completion of some defensive minefields on the ground that they might endanger friendly ships.)

33 During the afternoon of 8 April reports of the northward passage of German ships were received in London from agents of MI 6, the British Naval Attaché, Copenhagen, and the commanders of British submarines. Oster gave his customary eleventh-hour warning to the Vatican and the Netherlands Military Attaché, Berlin (but no attacks had followed his earlier warnings of impending offensives on the Western Front. No warning was received from Thümmel.)

Thus the British received, in addition to reports not incompatible with the Admiralty's belief that a break-out of the German battlecruisers to the High Seas was in prospect, a good deal of information which seemed at first sight open to more than one of the following interpretations:

1 That the Germans were assembling and training forces for a seaborne expedition whose most probable objective was Norway.

2 That they were assembling and training an expeditionary force not for immediate use, but to hide their true intentions.

3 That, in order to hide their true intentions, they were simulating the assembly and training of an expeditionary force by means which included not merely the spreading of false reports but the actual assembly of troops and shipping.

Examination of the evidence by a body of experts not wedded to the preconceptions of any particular department could scarcely have failed to lead to the conclusion that the second and third interpretations were too far-fetched to be accepted. If the enemy was aiming merely at passing a few heavy ships into the Atlantic without detection, as he had already done on a number of occasions, he would scarcely have recourse to an elaborate cover-plan which could serve no useful purpose unless it came to the attention of the Allies and which, if it did come to their attention, would cause then to become not less but more vigilant.

But the evidence was not examined by independent experts. The Joint Intelligence Committee was not yet an effective body. It provided intermittent contact between Directors of Intelligence or their deputies, and between them and the Foreign Office; there was little or no contact between departments at the level at which reports were scrutinized by specialists. Inevitably, interpretations put upon reports by naval, army or air intelligence officers were influenced to some extent by opinions current in the higher echelons of the departments they served. Also, there was a good deal of fragmentation within departments. Military intelligence officers concerned with Scandinavian affairs did not receive reports about events in Germany.[53] In the Admiralty, the section of the Naval Intelligence Division concerned with Scandinavian affairs did receive such reports, but some reports from MI 6 or diplomatic sources were withheld from the Operational Intelligence Centre, which dealt with movements of German shipping and other day-to-day events.[54] In both cases, provision was made for contributions from different sections to be co-ordinated at a higher level or by a section to which the task was delegated. But these arrangements did not work very well, because the co-ordinators lacked the detailed background knowledge needed to grasp the connections between two or more apparently unrelated sets of facts.

Despite these shortcomings, Military Intelligence made some praise-worthy attempts to assess the enemy's intentions in the light of information supplied by more than one department; but it was handicapped by its initial overestimation of the number of divisions the Germans would think necessary for a full-blooded Scandinavian expedition. The Air Staff suspected the Luftwaffe of working up for a major air assault on the United Kingdom, and Air Intelligence saw the attack on Hatston in that light. [55] The Naval Staff and the Foreign Office shared the opinion that the Germans would not dare to launch a full-scale invasion of Norway in face of Allied naval superiority. That would not have been an unreasonable view if the evidence had not contradicted it. We now know that Admiral Raeder's verdict on the German plan was that the operation was contrary to all the theoretical principles of naval warfare, but that nevertheless the troops could be carried successfully to Norway if complete surprise was achieved.[56]

Surprise was achieved because the Allies allowed themselves to be surprised. In the words of the British official historian of the war at sea, 'There was . . . a complete failure to realize the significance of the available intelligence'.[57] Admiral Sir Charles Forbes, Commander-in-Chief of the Home Fleet, had recently completed the reassembly of the main body of his fleet at Scapa Flow. At 11.20 a.m. on 7 April he learned of the sighting more than two hours earlier of the supposed cruiser and six destroyers. Soon afterwards he was told that bombers had been sent to attack them. He was also told, about 2 p.m., of the three destroyers seen on a southward course. At 2.20 p.m. the Admiralty sent him the gist of the telegram received early on 6 April from Copenhagen, but robbed the warning of most of its force by adding: 'All these reports are of doubtful value and may well be only a further move in the war of nerves'.[58] The Director of Naval Intelligence knew, when this message was drafted, of the abnormal wireless activity noted during the previous night, and perceived that it was consistent with the belief that the enemy had only a purely naval operation in view. He seems not to have been aware of the activity seen in dockside areas at Kiel and elsewhere, which was not consistent with that belief.[59]

Admiral Forbes did not learn until 5.27 p.m. that the German naval force believed in the forenoon to consist of a cruiser and six destroyers was now thought to be much larger and that it might include at least one battlecruiser.[60] At 8.15 p.m. he took his fleet to sea and set a course which would put him in a good position to intercept the force if it made for the Atlantic, but which left the central part of the North Sea uncovered. Admiral Sir Dudley Pound, the First Sea Lord, gave orders after Forbes had left that the cruisers which had embarked troops at Rosyth should disembark them and join the fleet at sea.[61] A cruiser and six destroyers which were to have escorted and covered the transports assembled in the Clyde were also ordered to rejoin the Home Fleet.[62] Thus the plan to forestall the enemy at Narvik, Trondheim, Bergen and Stavanger was abandoned at the very moment when the circumstances arose which it was designed to meet.

At 11.15 a.m. on 8 April the Admiralty sent Forbes a signal to the effect that the report received from Copenhagen early on 6 April might after all be true.[63] The Naval Staff continued in the meantime to act on the assumption that the Germans were trying to pass their heavy ships into the Atlantic. Indeed, they did not fully relinquish that assumption until the following day. Pound's order to the cruisers at Rosyth to disembark their troops was not rescinded. Orders given by the Admiralty, without the Commander-in-Chief's concurrence, to destroyers at sea in connection with the minelaying operation removed them from the approaches to Narvik some hours before the German troop-carrying destroyers, no longer accompanied by the battlecruisers, arrived there.[64]

The War Office was equally reluctant to discard the view that Germany did not have enough uncommitted troops for major operations away from the Western Front. A Military Intelligence appreciation of 8 April recorded the opinion that the disposition of her forces made an invasion of Scandinavia improbable, but conceded that limited operations on the West Norwegian coast were possible.[65] About 5 a.m. on the following day the news arrived that German warships were approaching Oslo, Bergen and Trondheim. At Narvik the ten destroyers disembarked their troops at dawn, but an Admiralty signal despatched at noon mentioned only 'indications' that the Germans had landed there.[66]

*

On the day after their invasion of Norway and Denmark, the Germans began transmitting signals encyphered in an unfamiliar Enigma key which the British called the Yellow Key. The Yellow Key was not only new, it was also relatively simple. The Government Code and Cypher School succeeded in breaking it on 15 April. From that date until its use was discontinued in the middle of May, signals encyphered in it were read daily, and in most cases promptly. Some were read within an hour of their transmission and interception.[67]

The Yellow Key was used, for the special purpose of the campaign in Norway, by both the German Army and the Luftwaffe. Signals encyphered in it referred not only to army and air matters, but also to naval movements of which the army and the Luftwaffe needed to be told. The British were thus presented, for a time, with a good deal of information about the organization and disposition of the enemy's forces, the state of their supplies and even their intentions.

For a number of reasons, they were able to make only a very limited use of this windfall. One was that the Government Code and Cypher School was not yet equipped to deal promptly and effectively with a copious influx of unfamiliar traffic, much of it bristling with obscurities. Hitherto the Germans had been thought likely, on security grounds, to avoid an uninhibited use of wireless for high-level communications about operational as distinct from administrative matters. Offensives on the Western Front or elsewhere were expected to bring large increases in the amount of tactical traffic transmitted in plain language or low-grade cyphers; the considerable volume of Enigma traffic generated by the Scandinavian expedition came as a surprise. Additional naval, military and air experts had to be posted to Bletchley before all the decrypted material became intelligible; additional teleprinters to be installed before the results could be communicated to Whitehall without unacceptable delays.[68]

Another reason was that most of the intelligence officers to whom the information could have brought enlightenment were unaware of its value, while some did not receive it at all. This came about as a result of steps taken to protect the source. Arrangements were made in January, when wartime Enigma messages were first decrypted, for translations to be passed to the War Office and the Air Ministry, through MI 6, in the guise of agents' reports. This fiction was maintained when the translated decrypts began to be passed directly to the departments by teleprinter. At first the information was represented as coming from an agent or espionage circuit with the code-name Boniface; later the teleprinted signals were prefixed CX, presumably to invite the inference that Station X was using its teleprinters to transmit reports from C's organization. The result was that military and air intelligence officers, other than the very few who had been indoctrinated, viewed the information with the scepticism normally accorded to agents' reports.[69] The Naval Intelligence Division worked on a different plan, but this proved even more unsatisfactory. The Admiralty insisted that translations of Enigma decrypts bearing on naval matters should be passed directly to the Operational Intelligence Centre, without disguise. As the signals did not conceal the true source of the information, they were considered too compromising to be shown to the officers of the Naval

Intelligence Division between whom responsibility for studying the world's navies was shared on a geographical basis.[70] Officers of the Operational Intelligence Centre who did see the reports worked on a watchkeeping basis and had little time for research. As a source of background knowledge, material obtained from the breaking of the Yellow Key was therefore not as useful to the service departments as it could have been if security precautions had been less stringent.

The use that could be made of it as a guide to the conduct of operations was limited by two factors. The first was the absence of a means by which the authorities in Whitehall could communicate the translated decrypts to potential users in a form that was intelligible to them, and which emphasized their peculiar value yet concealed the source. The only way out of this conundrum was not to conceal the source, but that was a course the authorities were not yet prepared to take. In the context of the January arrangements, the Naval Staff had told Admiral Forbes and a few other very senior officers that information of exceptional value might in future be forthcoming from high-grade signal intelligence and that it would be communicated to them in signals prefixed Hydro, transmitted in a supposedly secure cypher.[71] As the War Office and the Air Ministry exercised no command functions comparable with those exercised by the Admiralty, the General and Air Staffs made no such provision, but appear to have briefed a very few senior officers based in the United Kingdom when the Yellow Key was broken.[72] Dissemination of information from Enigma to commanders in the field was considered safe only where it could be plausibly represented as coming from a source other than signal intelligence.

The other limiting factor was the shortness of the period for which information obtained from the breaking of the Yellow Key was available. Such information would have been invaluable if it had been forthcoming before Norway and Denmark were invaded. It might also have been useful immediately after the landings in Norway, when some of the German warships were returning to their bases, although as it happened fairly good information about their movements on the return journey was received from sightings. But the Yellow Key was not broken until 15 April. By that time the Germans were able to supply their troops advancing towards Central Norway by a safe route through Oslo. The state of the German forces at Narvik was precarious, but no foreknowledge of the enemy's intentions could have enabled the British to prevent them from receiving the small quantities of supplies which, on humanitarian grounds and under diplomatic pressure, the Swedish authorities allowed to pass by rail through Swedish territory. Nor is it probable that information from signal intelligence or any other secret source could have put the Allies in a position to deny them occasional air-drops.

Admiral Forbes did receive some Hydro signals between 15 April and 14 May, although apparently no record of them has survived.[73] He does not appear to have found them very helpful, for he complained afterwards that the Germans always seemed to know more about the movements of his ships than he did about theirs.[74] The disposition of U-boats assigned to the Scandinavian expedition was revealed not by signal intelligence but by a captured document.[75] For tactical intelligence, British troops ashore in Norway relied during their brief campaigns largely on the Norwegians, since their own facilities for the gathering of information in the field were poor.[76] Furthermore, no provision had been made for them to receive promptly such information as was obtained from tactical traffic intercepted and read in the United Kingdom.[77] MI 6 appears to have had no espionage organization in Norway when the campaign began, although the nucleus of a stay-behind network was established before it ended.[78]

On 14 May the Germans used the Yellow Key for the last time. Documents recovered on 26 April from a captured patrol boat enabled the Government Code and Cypher School to read, in May, naval Enigma traffic for six days in April. Otherwise this traffic was still unreadable. Extension of the German Navy's communication system to parts of Norway did, however, somewhat enlarge the scope of traffic analysis. During the last ten days of May the Naval Section of the Government Code and Cypher School warned the Operational Intelligence Centre of indications from this source that German warships were preparing to move from the Baltic up the coast of Norway. On 29 May, and again on 7 June, the Operational Intelligence Centre referred in its daily reports, but in guarded and somewhat obscure terms, to the possibility of offensive action by German naval units in the North Sea.[79]

Tentative though these warnings were, at any rate the last of them might have been expected to attract some attention in the Admiralty, because important Allied moves were in progress. In accordance with a decision made at the highest level, the Allies had captured Narvik on 28 May and carried out some rather ineffective demolitions as the prelude to withdrawal of all their forces from Northern Norway. The embarkation and return to the United Kingdom in large troopships of some

25,000 troops from the Allied base at Harstad was due for completion on 8 June. But in fact the reports went unheeded. Not even a qualified warning was passed to the Home Fleet.[80] No special reconnaissance patrols were flown over the area through which the troopships were to pass.[81] This was partly because the reports were not very strongly worded, partly because hitherto transports and storeships had come and gone between Norway and the United Kingdom with very little interference, partly because the operation was so shrouded in secrecy that intelligence officers and others who might with advantage have been told what was going on were kept in the dark. Coastal Command – the RAF command responsible for maritime reconnaissance – was not formally cognizant of the withdrawal, although the Air Officer Commanding-in-Chief was informed of it.[82]

We now know that the *Scharnhorst*, the *Gneisenau*, the *Hipper* and four destroyers, under the command of Vice-Admiral Marschall, left Kiel on 4 June for the purpose of attacking any shipping found at Harstad on the night of 8/9 June. On 7 June Admiral Marschall learned from air reconaissance reports that two groups of Allied shipping were at sea. He decided to attack the more southerly group. Early on 8 June he sank a tanker, a trawler which was escorting her, and an unladen troopship, but respected the immunity of an accompanying hospital ship. Disregarding orders from his shore command to leave attacks on convoys to the *Hipper* and the destroyers and proceed to Harstad, he continued to search with the battlecruisers for transports which he rightly believed to be bringing Allied troops away from Narvik, but sent the *Hipper* and the destroyers to Trondheim to refuel. About 4 p.m. he sighted the carrier *Glorious*. Because she was short of fuel, she was proceeding independently of the troopships and their escort, but had her own escort of two destroyers. In addition to her normal complement of naval aircraft, she was carrying RAF fighters which had taken part in the operations at Narvik. Within just two hours of the first sighting, Marschall sank the *Glorious* and both destroyers. The *Scharnhorst* having been damaged by a torpedo fired by one of the destroyers, he then turned away from an area afterwards traversed by lightly-escorted transports carrying 10,000 Allied troops.[83]

For reasons which will never be known, the *Glorious* did not use her naval aircraft to reconnoitre ahead of her, and was caught almost wholly unprepared. Her wireless equipment was wrecked early in the action. She sent a signal reporting the proximity of two German capital ships, but it was very faint and was not heard by any shore station. It was received, in garbled form, aboard a cruiser carrying the King of Norway from Tromsö to the United Kingdom.[84] The commander of the cruiser could not know that his ship was the sole Allied recipient of the signal. In view of the importance of his mission, he did not repeat it at the cost of revealing his own position to the enemy. The fate of the *Glorious* remained unknown until the following day.

However, soon after the time when the *Glorious* was afterwards known to have sunk, four signals were intercepted in the United Kingdom which could only have come from a German source. They could not be read, but one contained a group which was known to stand for 'Immediate'. Poor DF fixes suggested that the originator was a ship off the Norwegian coast. The matter was reported to the Operational Intelligence Centre. The Duty Officer attached no particular importance to the signals and took no action.[85] Afterwards it became clear that they must have reported Marschall's encounter with the *Glorious* and its outcome. An investigation then revealed that the Duty Officer had not been told of the withdrawal from Norway.[86] So far as the Operational Intelligence Centre was concerned, knowledge of it was confined to senior members of the staff.[87]

These experiences led the Admiralty to recognize that watchkeeping officers who did not know what to watch for were at a disadvantage. Although matters had improved since the chance of a Nelsonian victory at Jutland was lost because protocol prevented Room 40 from giving information for which it was not asked, there was still room for improvement. Steps were taken to establish closer relations between the operational and intelligence staffs and between the Operational Intelligence Centre and the Naval Section of the Government Code and Cypher School. A representative of the Naval Section visited Scapa to explain to the Home Fleet what signal intelligence could do for it.[88] Meanwhile, in May, the Government Code and Cypher School took delivery of the first British Bombe.[89] This was the 'Bronze Goddess' designed by Alan Turing, a pioneer of the analogue computer.

FOUR

France and the Low Countries: 1940

After the mishap of 10 January 1940, the German military authorities came to the conclusion that their plan for an offensive in the West had not only been compromised, but left a lot to be desired. As it stood at the beginning of 1940, the plan envisaged a thrust across the Belgian plain and into North-Eastern France by 43 divisions under Army Group B (General Fedor von Bock), for the twofold purpose of defeating as many Allied troops as possible and seizing a broad tract of country as a base for further operations and a defensive belt for the Ruhr. The Netherlands as well as Belgium were to be occupied in order to prevent the British from establishing bases there, and a supporting thrust in the Ardennes was to be made by 22 divisions under Army Group A (General Gerd von Rundstedt).

This plan, first adopted in October 1939 in deference to Hitler's wishes but twice modified in November, attracted a good deal of criticism, especially from Rundstedt and his staff. Its critics pointed out that, although it bore a superficial resemblance to the Schlieffen plan of 1905, it did not promise a decision because, unlike the Schlieffen plan, it did not provide for encirclement of the French Army. It would merely push the Allied armies back towards the Somme, where they could be expected to make a stand. In the light of arguments adduced by General Erich von Manstein, Rundstedt's Chief of Staff, the High Command of the German Army (OKH) agreed in principle that Army Group A should be given additional forces for the purpose of attempting a surprise crossing of the Meuse in the neighbourhood of Sedan, but still refused in January to shift the main weight of the attack to the Ardennes, as Manstein wished. OKH conceded that such a change of emphasis might be desirable, but insisted that it could only be made after the offensive had begun.

At the end of January Manstein was promoted to a corps command at Stettin, but an audience with the Führer on 17 February gave him an opportunity of expounding his plan. By that time war games and discussions had gone far to convince both OKH and the Supreme Command of the Armed Forces (OKW) that Army Group A must be considerably strengthened if it was to achieve anything worth-while. The outcome was that, in substance, Manstein's proposals were adopted. Army Group A was given 44 (afterwards 45) divisions, including most of the armour, with which to thrust across the Meuse between Sedan and Dinant. With the proviso that sanction must first be obtained from OKH, it was then to advance westwards, seize the crossings of the Lower Somme, and cut off Allied forces north of the line Sedan–Abbeville. Army Group B would have to make do with 29 (afterwards 28) divisions for the invasion of the Low Countries which was now its primary task, but was given virtually all the available airborne forces to enable it to seize key-points in the Netherlands and secure the crossings of the principal waterways. If all went well, it would provide the anvil against which Allied forces north of the Sedan–Abbeville line were to be hammered by Army Group A. On Rundstedt's left, 17 divisions under Army Group C (General Ritter von Leeb) would contain the Allied forces in the Maginot Line, and 46 divisions would remain for the time being in OKH Reserve. All possible steps would be taken to convince the Allies that the main assault was still to be made through Central Belgium, and thus to lure them into a trap.

The Allied military authorities arrived by the end of April at a reasonably accurate estimate of the number of German divisions on the Western Front or close behind it, but based their plans largely on the assumption the Germans wanted them to make. The following summary lists their chief sources of information, gives a broad account of the nature and scope of the material these provided, and draws attention (in the light of hindsight) to some items of special interest:

1 *Interrogation of Prisoners, Captured Documents, Observation on the Ground*
During the phoney war Allied troops between the Moselle and the North Sea were separated from the Germans by neutral territory (i.e., Luxembourg and Belgium). Between the Moselle and Basle the belligerents confronted each other across a common frontier, but there was very little fighting. The French made a limited advance on a front of sixteen miles in the Saar in the first month of the war; in the following month the Germans delivered a counter-attack with equally limited objectives. From that time until the following May there was little

contact between Allied and German troops. Patrols for the purpose of reconnaissance or the capture of prisoners or documents were not expressly forbidden by the French High Command, but were discouraged by insistence on meticulous form-filling after every patrol.[1] In any case, field intelligence was not likely to throw much light on the enemy's long-term plans. The recovery of an important document from the aircraft which landed in Belgium on 10 January 1940 was an exceptional occurrence.

2 *Aerial Reconnaissance*

Reconnaissance by the Armée de l'Air was restricted to some extent by bad weather, fear of reprisals by the numerically stronger Luftwaffe, and reluctance to affront neutral opinion by flagrant violations of Belgian air-space. Even so, it made some useful contributions to Allied knowledge of the enemy's dispositions; but such knowledge did not enable the Allies to judge whether troops concentrated in, for example, the Rhineland would move westwards into Central Belgium or south-westwards in the direction of Sedan. Blenheims of the Air Component of the British Expeditionary Force made 82 reconnaissance sorties, but the result were disappointing and eighteen aircraft were lost.[2] One squadron of the Photographic Development Unit was based in France, but it was largely employed on clandestine photography of Belgium for the purpose of providing information withheld by the still-resolutely neutral Belgian authorities, and an aerial survey of the Ruhr for the benefit of Bomber Command. However, according to Cotton the squadron photographed German armour on 6 May near the frontier between Germany and Luxembourg, and a low-level sortie on the following day revealed 400 tanks there.[3] The Air Ministry's alleged lack of interest in this discovery is said to have prompted Cotton to fly home for the purpose of bringing it to the attention of Bomber Command. Surviving records do not appear to confirm Cotton's account, but the lack of such corroboration is not conclusive. Most of the records of the British Air Forces in France (BAFF) were lost or destroyed during the subsequent retreat, and one would not expect Cotton's visit to Bomber Command to be recorded in the command's War Diary.

3 *Signal Intelligence*

Neither tactical traffic, nor such Enigma messages as could be read before the summer of 1940, revealed the adoption by the Germans of a new plan for their offensive in the West. On 1 May the indicators for all Enigma keys except the Yellow were changed. This does not seem to have appeared as significant at the time as it does in retrospect. Information from Abwehr traffic is discussed in paragraph 6, below.

4 *Agents' Reports*

The Allies continued after 10 January 1940 to receive many warnings from secret agents that an offensive on the Western Front was imminent. A high proportion of these referred to forthcoming attacks on the Low Countries. As Germany was already at war with France but not yet with Belgium or the Netherlands, the emphasis on projected violations of Belgian or Dutch neutrality does not seem surprising. Nor does it seem to justify the inference that the Germans still intended to make their main attack through Central Belgium. An advance through the Belgian Ardennes towards Sedan would be just as much a violation of Belgian neutrality as an advance to Brussels. According to Moravec, the Zurich headquarters of the Czechoslovak intelligence service received on 25 March a report from Thümmel, written in water between the lines of a letter ostensibly addressed by a young German to an uncle in Switzerland.[4] It stated that the Germans would launch their main attack through the Ardennes with the intention of crossing the Meuse north of Sedan and driving towards the Channel. Moravec quotes Menzies as greeting this forecast with the remark: 'A-54 is an agent at whose word armies march.' The French, who perhaps suspected A-54 of being a double agent, were sceptical. Moravec adds that Thümmel reported on 1 May, in a coded telegram to The Hague, that the offensive would be launched on 10 May.[5]

5 *Warnings Received through Diplomatic Channels*

The Allies also received many warnings from neutral diplomats or conveyed through diplomatic channels. Many of these stressed the imminence of attacks on the Low Countries without necessarily implying that the plan compromised in January still held good. The British Military Attaché, Berne, submitted on 4 May a report from a Polish intelligence officer to the effect that an offensive somewhere on the Western Front was imminent and that members of Göring's circle were confident that France could be overrun in four weeks.[6] Oster appears to have warned both the Vatican and the Netherlands Military Attaché, Berlin, on or about 3 May that an offensive on the Western Front would be launched in the following week. The attaché did not pass the warnings to The Hague because earlier warnings had been received with incredulity.[7] A further warning from Oster, given on the eve of the offensive, does not seem to have been taken very seriously.

6 *Counter-Intelligence, Double Agents and Defectors*

The French learned on 7 April from a German who had defected to Luxembourg that an attack on the Grand Duchy was planned for 14 and 15 April and that maps had been distributed to German formations.[8] His dates were wrong, but he may have been right about the maps. Wireless signals transmitted in the spring of 1940 by the local headquarters of the Abwehr at Wiesbaden were intercepted by MI 5's Radio Security Service. In the light of knowledge derived from the double agent recruited at the beginning of the war, the signals could be read. They included questions to agents about troop dispositions, road-blocks and other field works in the area afterwards traversed by Army Group A.[9] Similar questions, relating to troop dispositions, depots, bridges, road-blocks and other obstructions on the axis Sedan–Charleville–Saint Quentin–Amiens, were put to a double agent working for the French.[10] The head of the Service de Renseignements – a wartime offshoot of the Deuxième Bureau – conveyed this information in person to General Alphonse Georges, Commander-in-Chief of the Allied Land Forces on the North-East Front, and his Chief of Operations. He was told that it contradicted reports which led to the conclusion that the Germans would make their main thrust against Belgium and the Netherlands.[11]

*

The Deuxième Bureau is known to have regarded double agents as a particularly valuable source of information about an enemy's intentions.[12] The British, too, were well aware of the value of knowing what questions a hostile power was putting to its agents. One might therefore expect the evidence of the Abwehr traffic and its corroboration by the French double agent to have aroused keen interest in Allied intelligence circles. These disclosures did not prove that the enemy would try to cross the Meuse in the neighbourhood of Sedan and thrust westwards from that point; they did show that any rate he was interested in the possibility of doing so. Yet they seem to have attracted little attention outside the intelligence agencies immediately involved. So far as the British are concerned there is scarcely anything in the various reports and appreciations prepared by the War Office, the Joint

Intelligence Committee and the Chiefs of Staff to suggest that a serious objective study of the evidence furnished by intelligence and diplomatic sources was attempted. All these bodies seem to have taken as their point of departure the assumption that, because the supposedly precarious state of Germany's economy compelled her to seek a quick end to the war, she would aim at seizing the Low Countries in order to provide herself with bases for naval and air operations against the United Kingdom and its seaborne trade.[13] Items of information from intelligence or diplomatic sources which appeared, however superficially, to support that conclusion were seized upon; those that did not, if they were considered at all, were dismissed as lacking corroboration or as not coming from completely reliable sources. The Chiefs of Staff conceded early in May that a major attack on France was possible, but did not dissent from the view commonly accepted in Whitehall that the enemy's most probable objectives were the Netherlands and Belgium, in that order.[14] That Germany might aim, as in 1914, at inflicting a decisive defeat on the French Army in a matter of weeks was a possibility not seriously considered.

However, it is unlikely that a more realistic attitude on the part of the British would have made any difference to the outcome. Their expeditionary force was so much smaller than the French Army that the disposition of the Allied land forces was essentially a matter for the French.

Unlike the Joint Intelligence Committee and the Military Intelligence Branch of the British War Office, the Deuxième Bureau did not commit itself wholeheartedly to the view that either the Netherlands or Belgium, or the Low Countries as a whole, would be the enemy's main objective. It was confident by the spring of 1940 that surprise attacks on the Maginot Line or through Switzerland could be ruled out and that the main attack would be delivered somewhere north of the Moselle. It was not prepared, however, to say exactly where the blow would fall.[15] But these cautious prognostications had no appreciable effect on Allied strategy. The plan put into execution by the French High Command in May 1940 had been drawn up in the previous November. Except that provision was made in March for the French Seventh Army, hitherto in reserve, to move to the neighbourhood of Breda should the Netherlands be invaded, it remained substantially unchanged throughout the intervening months. Known as Plan D or the Dyle Plan, it was founded on the assumption that the Allies could best counter a threat to Central Belgium by standing on a line from Antwerp to the bend of the Meuse at

Namur, with the Belgians on the left, the British on the River Dyle in the centre, and the French First Army on the right. The framers of the plan did not exclude the possibility that the Germans might try to cross the Meuse upstream from Namur, but believed that they would not make the attempt without first pausing to bring up large quantities of artillery and repair or replace demolished bridges.

A striking feature of the Dyle Plan was the attention lavished on the Maginot Line. Despite the assurance given by the Deuxième Bureau that the Germans did not have enough troops south of the Moselle to attack the Maginot Line without warning, about forty per cent of the available Allied troops were still stationed in the first week of May between the northern terminus of the Maginot Line near Longuyon and the Swiss frontier.[16] The French believed that, if the Germans did break through on the Meuse between Namur and Sedan, they might try to roll up the Maginot Line from the north. But if that was their problem, they would surely have been well advised to make the Namur–Sedan sector stronger. As things were, on a front of 95 miles between Namur and Longuyon they had only twelve divisions, not all of the best quality.[17] Moreover, the overcrowding of the Maginot Line left them with only 29 divisions in GHQ Reserve, or 22 if the Seventh Army moved to Breda. Seven of these (the *Lot belge*) were earmarked for reinforcement of the First Army. Five (the *Lot suisse*) were held ready to counter an outflanking movement through Switzerland which the Deuxième Bureau said could not be made without ample warning.

The outlook for the Allies was not improved by a change in the command structure which contravened the well-established military axiom that the officer responsible for the adoption of a plan should also be responsible for its execution. When the Dyle Plan was accepted in principle by the Allied Supreme War Council as one to be put into effect if the Germans threatened Central Belgium and the Belgians asked for help in time, the French had only one GHQ under a Chief of Staff directly responsible to General Maurice Gamelin as Commander-in-Chief of the Land Forces in all theatres. As there were no hostilities on the Alpine front or in North Africa or the Middle East, Gamelin and the Chief of Staff were free to give most of their attention to the front from the North Sea coast to Switzerland, called by the French the North-East Front. General Alphonse Georges was Deputy Commander for the North-East Front, and worked immediately under Gamelin. But in January 1940 Gamelin persuaded the government to make Georges Commander-in-Chief of the North-East Front. Gamelin remained responsible for the allocation of troops and supplies, and in theory for the co-ordination of operations in all theatres. In practice, he forfeited strategic control in the only active theatre by setting up a separate GHQ Land Forces and becoming dependent for his knowledge of events on such reports as Georges thought fit to send him. To make matters worse, he took to spending most of his time at an underground command post at Vincennes, where he saw only staff officers, lost touch with the troops and was easily short-circuited.[18]

This was a pity. As a comparatively youthful staff officer, Gamelin had played a leading part in drafting Joffre's orders for the Battle of the Marne. He was a far more experienced strategist than Georges. He believed Georges to be thoroughly conversant with the Dyle Plan. Events were to show that Georges did not understand it well enough to know when to scrap it.

*

Despite the numerous warnings received by the High Command, the launching of the German offensive on 10 May came as an almost complete surprise to the Allied armies.[19] Gamelin explained afterwards that they had not been alerted because the offensive had long been expected and the troops could not be kept indefinitely in the highest state of readiness. Even so, one might have expected the High Command at least to suspend leave and urge commanders to keep their forces concentrated. As it was, thousands of Frenchmen of all ranks, including some generals, were on leave when the blow fell. Their attempts to rejoin their units when they were hastily recalled on 10 May put an additional strain on the railways at a time when every hour counted. The Second Army, responsible for the Sedan sector, had rejected a proposal from the Deuxième Bureau that everyone on leave should be recalled on the previous evening.[20] In the mechanized Cavalry Corps training proceeded as usual on 9 May, with the result that some units were far from their normal quarters. The corps commander had no idea that within a few hours he would be assembling his force for its allotted task of preceding the main body of the First Army into Central Belgium.[21] The British received their first warning that the offensive had begun when their airfields in France were bombed.

Bock and Rundstedt had orders to start crossing the frontiers of the Netherlands, Belgium and Luxembourg at 5.35 a.m. by German time. The first moves were made by small bodies of men wearing mechanics' overalls or Dutch greatcoats over their German uniforms, and by parachutists and glider-borne troops who landed near Fort Eben Emael, in Belgian territory. Their attempts to seize bridges across the Maas and the Albert Canal were preceded by numerous reports from diplomatic sources and secret agents of troop movements towards the Low Countries and in the Rhineland.[22] Soon after 5 a.m. by Western European time the air-raid sirens at Vincennes began to wail. At 5.20 a.m. the Ministry of Marine reported that Calais and Dunkirk were being bombed. Reports that German troops had entered the Netherlands and that bombs were falling on airfields in Northern France arrived soon afterwards. At 5.30 a.m. Georges alerted the First Army Group, which comprised (from left to right) the Seventh Army, the British Expeditionary Force and the First, Ninth and Second Armies. Requests from the Netherlands and Belgian governments for British and French help, although made in the early hours of the morning, seem not to have reached Gamelin at Vincennes until about 6.30 a.m.[23] He and Georges then agreed that the Dyle Plan should be put into effect and that the Seventh Army should move on Breda. Forward elements of the mechanized Cavalry Corps began crossing the Belgian frontier at 10.30 a.m., some five hours after receipt of the news that German troops were entering the Low Countries.

Reports received in the early hours of the morning indicated that German columns were moving not only towards the Maas and the Albert Canal but also towards the Belgian Ardennes and Luxembourg.[24] It followed that at least a diversionary thrust towards the Meuse upstream from Namur could be expected. In that sector the Second Army was already established on the line of the Meuse and the Chiers, with its right near Longuyon and its left beyond Sedan. On the Second Army's left, the Ninth Army had its right-hand corps already on the Meuse in French territory; its two left-hand corps had to move up to forty-five miles through Belgian territory to reach their positions on the left bank between Givet and Namur. They had only just begun to settle into their new positions when, on 12 May, German armour approached the right bank of the river at Sedan in the sector held by the Second Army, and at Monthermé and Dinant in the Ninth Army's sector. Belgian light infantry and partly mechanized French cavalry had been expected to delay the enemy's approach march through the wooded hills of the Ardennes, but they were not equipped to deal with armoured columns.

We now know that the German troops which appeared on the right bank of the Meuse on 12 and 13 May belonged to the three armoured divisions of the 19th Panzer Corps at Sedan; the two armoured divisions of the 41st Panzer Corps at Monthermé; and the two armoured divisions of the 15th Panzer Corps at Dinant. In Army Group B there were only the three armoured divisions of the 16th Panzer Corps. This detailed knowledge was not, of course, available to Georges or his staff. Nevertheless the appearance of German armour at three different places on a front of some fifty miles might have been expected to convince them that rather more than a diversionary thrust was in prospect. During the night of 12/13 May large numbers of vehicles, rightly thought to belong to a German motorized infantry formation, were seen by crews of French reconnaissance aircraft streaming through the Ardennes towards Bastogne and Sedan.[25] Next morning about 400 German tanks were visible on the right bank of the Meuse at Sedan alone.[26]

However, according to the commander of the First Army Group, the French High Command still did not believe that the thrust towards Sedan was the main effort.[27] As the light mechanized units and mounted troops sent to the far side of the river were known to have fared badly, two divisions from the GHQ Reserve were ordered to reinforce the Second Army, and a division from Lorraine was directed towards the rear of the Ninth Army; but GHQ North-East Front continued to give most of its attention to Central Belgium. There the commander of the Cavalry Corps found on reaching the positions to be held by the main body of the First Army that little had been done by the Belgians to prepare them for defence. He suggested to the commander of the First Army Group that the Seventh Army should be recalled and that the Dyle Plan should be discarded in favour of the alternative Escaut Plan, which called for a shorter advance to a longer line. His proposals were rejected, but the First Army was ordered to speed up the advance of its main body and was strongly reinforced. By 14 May it had thirteen divisions and some 800 tanks with which to fight a defensive battle on a twenty-two-mile front.[28]

Meanwhile dire events were occurring on its right. At Sedan elements of two of the three armoured divisions of the 19th Panzer Corps, without vehicles or supporting arms, crossed the river in collapsible boats in the afternoon of 13 May and scrambled ashore without effective opposition from defenders dazed and cowed by five hours of almost continuous air bombardment. Two rifle battalions of the 10th Panzer Division seized a small bridgehead to which they were pinned by artillery fire from the flanks. A larger force from the 1st Panzer Division occupied a bridgehead about four miles wide by four miles deep. Wild rumours to the effect that German tanks were already on the left bank had such demoralizing effects on the French troops in the immediate neighbour-hood that no resolute attempt was made to round up this force while it was still weak and unsupported. At Monthermé riflemen of the 6th Panzer Division, also using collapsible boats, gained access to a small area on the left bank which was swept by fire from the right bank, but for forty-eight hours made no further progress in face of machine-gun fire from two half-brigades of French colonial troops. At Dinant, where only a covering attack was intended, motor-cyclists crossed the river during the night of 12/13 May by an undemolished footbridge temporarily left unguarded. Riflemen of the 7th Panzer Division succeeded on the following day in reaching the left bank in collapsible boats at the second attempt. By midday they and the motor-cyclists held a bridgehead about three miles wide by two miles deep. They were greatly outnumbered by French troops in the immediate vicinity and had no artillery, tanks or anti-tank guns. Infantry supported by mechanized units might therefore have been expected to round them up without much difficulty. Two attempts by mixed forces on 13 May were, however, unsuccessful, because on each occasion the infantry component was either dispersed or fatally delayed by air attacks. A thrust by motorized cavalry and a divisional reconnaissance group on the following morning began well, but achieved only a fleeting success because the troops were ordered back to a specified containment line instead of being allowed to continue their advance. Meanwhile the Germans enlarged their bridgehead by making further crossings north and south of the town.

The methods by which the Panzer formations secured these gains ought not to have caught the French military authorities unprepared. Admittedly they could not have been expected to foresee that their gunners on the heights above the Meuse at Sedan would be so foolish as to start a panic by reporting that German armour had reached the left bank when only unarmoured elements of armoured divisions had done so, or that virtually an entire division would collapse in consequence. But they ought not to have been surprised that the Germans attacked in considerable strength with little support except from their tank guns and from aircraft. The French authorities were familiar with the arguments for and against the dive-bomber.[29] They were aware that the Germans had studied the use of dive-bombers and level bombers for close support of troops. They knew what co-operation between troops and aircraft had achieved in Spain and Poland. Their intelligence and counter-intelligence services had drawn attention to German interest in the Ardennes and the area between the Meuse and the Somme. Their mechanized and mounted troops sent to the right bank of the Meuse had reported the south-westerly movement of numerous armoured columns through the Ardennes. German tanks had duly debouched from the woods on the right bank in the Sedan sector on 12 May. Lorries carrying the motorized infantry which was to support the Panzer formations had been seen speeding through the Ardennes with headlights blazing on the following night.

The fact remains that the arrival of German troops on the left bank of the Meuse at Sedan and Dinant found the commander and staff of the North-East Front without a comprehensive plan for dealing with such a situation. Heroic but unsuccessful attempts were made by British and French bomber crews to prevent the Panzer formations from building or reconstructing bridges and passing tanks and wheeled vehicles across the river. What the enemy would do next Georges was unable to divine, although some of the intelligence he had received might have enabled him to make a good guess if he had thought it worth attention. As late as 5 p.m. on 15 May he still feared an attempt to roll up the Maginot Line from the north. He therefore ordered the right-hand corps of the Second Army to resist such a movement at all costs.[30] Less than five hours later, his staff were dumbfounded by the news that about a hundred German tanks had already reached Montcornet, forty miles due west of Sedan.[31]

By that time the Ninth Army was known to be in difficulties, although the full extent of the disaster that had overtaken it was not yet apparent. To understand how these troubles came about, it is necessary to go back to the evening of 14 May. At 7 p.m. on that day the commander of the corps responsible for the Dinant sector decided to form a barrier-line about fifteen miles west of the Meuse, from which a counter-attack could be launched by an armoured division transferred from the First to the Ninth Army and assembling in his rear. Appropriate orders were issued about an hour later. However, at 2 a.m. on 15 May the army commander told the commander of the First Army Group that he was contemplating a general withdrawal to the frontier positions from which his two left-hand corps had set out on 10 May. The army group commander made no objection, but insisted that an intermediate stop-line should be set up.[32] The consequent issue of conflicting orders at different levels of command helped to turn the Ninth Army's retreat into a rout. Some units went to the corps commander's line, some to the intermediate stop-line, some to the frontier positions. Others were overrun by the enemy or, having received no orders at all, disbanded when they reached French territory, with the result that nothing more was heard of them until stragglers turned up at base depots in the rear. Within seventy-two hours of the first attack on its positions, the Ninth Army fell to pieces without ever having fought a battle to which more than a few battalions or squadrons were committed. By the morning of 16 May its headquarters staff no longer had more than a vague and incomplete knowledge of the state of its formations or the whereabouts and effective strength of its units.[33]

The collapse of the Ninth Army and the left-hand corps of the Second Army opened a gap about sixty miles wide through which the Panzer formations poured towards the sea. To picture them as coming forward in a solid phalanx on a sixty-mile front would, however, be quite wrong. What happened was that in the north, as a result of the unexpected success of the covering attack, the 15th (afterwards the 39th) Panzer Corps pushed forward from Dinant to the neighbourhood of Arras by way of Philippeville, Solre-le-Château, Avesnes, Landrecies and Cambrai. In the south the 19th Panzer Corps, with the 41st Panzer Corps on its right, advanced along the Sedan–Amiens–Abbeville axis envisaged in the Manstein Plan. Between Arras and Bray-sur-Somme, where the routes of all the Panzer formations converged, the so-called Panzer Corridor was not sixty but only about twenty-five miles wide.

The Panzer divisions, despite attempts by OKH and the commander of the Panzer Group to curb their impetuosity, moved so rapidly that considerable gaps opened between them and the motorized infantry coming up behind them, still wider gaps between the motorized infantry and the ordinary infantry divisions toiling in the rear. Air reconnaissance revealed these gaps to the Allied High Command, but most of the troops that might have been used to exploit them were otherwise employed or, in the case of the three complete armoured divisions available to the French at the outset of the campaign, had been frittered away in premature and ill-co-ordinated counter-attacks during the first few days. Georges aimed at forming defensive fronts north and south of the corridor and at stopping the enemy in his tracks by interposing troops in front of him. He succeeded in his first aim because the Panzer formations were not interested in diverging to left or right; he failed in the second because they were too quick for him. On 20 May the 1st Panzer Division captured Amiens, the 2nd Panzer Division seized Abbeville without much difficulty, and one battalion of the 2nd Panzers reached the Channel coast at Noyelles. The rupture between the Allied armies north and south of the corridor was complete.

That Georges would have done better to aim at cutting the Panzer formations off by striking at their rear communications is not merely obvious in retrospect; it was apparent at the time to observers not bemused by preoccupation with linear defence and the mirage of containment. Gamelin, studying the reconnaissance reports in the monastic calm of his command post, deplored the failure of his ill-starred subordinate to seize his opportunities. He formed the impression that Georges, who had been severely wounded when King Alexander I of Yugoslavia was assassinated at Marseilles in 1934, was not physically equal to his task, but took no steps to replace him. Although urged by the Deputy Commander to assume direct control of the North-East Front, he did nothing until 19 May apart from asking the British for more aircraft. He then wrote out an instruction so tactfully worded that Georges did not regard it as an order. A few hours later, he was himself relieved of his command.[34]

The veteran General Maxime Weygand was summoned from Syria to replace Gamelin. On 21 May he flew across the corridor for the purpose of urging the British to join the First Army in attacking southwards with all available forces, and the Belgians to take up defensive positions on the flank. He conferred separately with the King of the Belgians and the commander of the First Army Group, but was unable to find the British Commander-in-Chief, Lord Gort, who had not been warned of his arrival. Weygand had just made up his mind to spend the night at Ypres and fly back to Paris on the following day in time for a conference in Paris rather than miss Gort altogether, when he was told that the airfield from which he was to fly was being bombed. To spare the pilots of his aircraft and its escort, he released them and accepted a proposal that he should return by sea and rail at the cost of leaving his mission uncompleted. The commander of the First Army Group was involved in a road accident on the way to his command post, and died two days later without regaining consciousness or leaving any record of his conversation with Weygand. In the absence of a secure means of communication across the corridor, Weygand's plan for the northern group of armies had to be pieced together from the recollections of an officer who had attended his conference with the Belgians. Moreover, as no successor was appointed until 25 May, the Belgian Army received no orders for four days.[35]

*

Apart from reconnaissance reports, the British Expeditionary Force
received very little intelligence during the first fortnight of the battle.[36]
Its field intelligence organization, built up to a strength of some 200 of all
ranks during the phoney war, was suddenly confronted with manifold
tasks which included not only the interception and interpretation of a
large volume of Luftwaffe tactical traffic in plain language or self-
evident codes, but also attempts to decypher and interpret a great deal of
army tactical traffic in codes and cyphers with which it was not familiar.
At the same time, it was handicapped by the splitting of its staff between
the British GHQ and Gort's command post fifty miles away, difficulties
of communication during the retreat from the Dyle, and the transfer of
some of its most experienced officers to *ad hoc* appointments in the field.

An epoch-making breakthrough by the Government Code and
Cypher School, although immensely valuable in the long run, did less
than might have been expected to help the immediate situation. Partly as
a result of mistakes made by German operators after the introduction of
the new Enigma indicators on 1 May, partly because from 10 May there
was much more material to work upon, Bletchley succeeded on 22 May
in breaking the new Red key for 20 May.[37] With few intermissions,
Luftwaffe traffic was read daily thereafter until the end of the war. From
the third week in May until the middle of June, translations of selected
decrypts were transmitted in a special cypher to a Secret Intelligence
Service mobile unit which passed them on to the British GHQ and
AHQ and helped commanders and staffs to interpret them. They were
also passed to the French. But the Government Code and Cypher
School was now handling about a thousand Enigma messages a day.[38]
Many of them were crammed with service jargon, technical terms,
code-names, personal names, unfamiliar map-references and other
obscurities, all of which had to be elucidated before the messages could
be safely used as a guide to operational decisions.

In any case, only a small proportion of the information obtained either
from Enigma or from low-grade traffic applied to the relatively small
sector with which the British were concerned. But air reconnaissance
continued, albeit in conditions of increasing difficulty, to provide useful
information, and easily read bomb-line signals broadcast by the
Luftwaffe enabled commanders and staffs to draw reliable inferences
about the positions reached by the enemy's forward troops.

What the enemy would do next was another matter. We now know
that the Panzer formations arrived at Amiens and Abbeville and in the
neighbourhood of Arras on 20 May with their strength much depleted

by casualties and mechanical breakdowns, but that many of their damaged or temporarily abandoned tanks were repairable. We also know that OKH and OKW were anxious about the weakness of their southern flank. Nevertheless they were ordered on 21 May to start wheeling to the north-east on the following day, seize Calais and Boulogne, and drive the northern group of Allied armies in the general direction of Dunkirk. After giving Major-General Erwin Rommel's 7th Panzer Division a shaking on 21 May, Gort withdrew from his salient at Arras, but still contemplated using at least two divisions in an offensive role if anything came of Weygand's proposals. Weygand, recognizing by 24 May that the British withdrawal might rule out an offensive in the immediate future, tentatively proposed on that day that the First Army should form in the neighbourhood of Dunkirk a quasi-permanent bridgehead from which an offensive could eventually be launched. But Gort's Chief of Staff had warned the War Office as early as 19 May that the British Expeditionary Force might have to be withdrawn to the United Kingdom, in which case Dunkirk would be its only port of embarkation.

On 23 May elements of two Panzer corps reached the line of rivers and canals that formed the western perimeter of the Dunkirk bridgehead. That evening Rundstedt ordered all his Panzer formations to stay where they were on the following day, 'to allow the situation to clarify itself and to keep our forces concentrated'. Hitler visited Rundstedt's command post on 24 May and approved of this decision. The policy then adopted by OKW (but challenged by OKH) was to use Army Group A to contain the Allied armies on the west, Army Group B to hammer at them from the east, and the Luftwaffe to prevent them from escaping by sea. Whether Hitler really believed the Luftwaffe could do this, or whether he thought it more politic to drive the British from the Continent than to destroy their army, remains debatable. There is no doubt that the Panzer divisions could have reached Dunkirk if they had been allowed to do so. It is equally certain that OKW foresaw that they would soon be needed for the thrust towards the Seine on which Hitler relied to knock France out of the war.

Enigma threw no light on these transactions. The Y-Service, however, intercepted on 24 May a plain-language message which announced that for the time being Army Group A's attack towards Dunkirk, Hazebrouck and Merville would be suspended.[39]

On the following day the British captured two documents of inestimable value from the staff car of the OKH liaison officer with

Army Group B.[40] One of them gave the War Office its first comprehensive picture of the German Army. The other told Gort that Army Group B was about to attack towards an alarming gap which had opened between the BEF and the Belgian Army. Gort then took a step which, according to the British official historian Major Ellis, saved the British Army.[41] He plugged the gap with the two divisions hitherto earmmarked for Weygand's offensive.

Meanwhile the Belgians were under severe pressure from Army Group B. As a Belgian officer afterwards pointed out, they not only received no orders from the Allied High Command for four days, but were not even asked how long they could hold the positions assigned to them in Weygand's plan.[42] When an emissary did arrive on 27 May, he was given a strong hint that the Belgian Army was near breaking-point. That evening the King of the Belgians agreed to surrender his forces to the Germans without terms.

The British withdrawal from Dunkirk began on the previous day. From the intelligence aspect its most significant feature was the ability of the Y-Service to predict movements of German aircraft in areas beyond the range of the radar chain. Information from this source was used not only by the RAF, but also to some extent by the navy as a guide to the timing of embarkations.

The Germans had already noticed, during their advance to the canal-line, that the British fighter force was more than able to hold its own.[43] Over Dunkirk and the neighbouring beaches the Luftwaffe met Spitfires as well as Hurricanes.[44] Its losses were greatly over-estimated by the British, but so were its reserves. As the Luftwaffe was unable to prevent well over a third of a million Allied troops from escaping to the United Kingdom, the British were not wrong in thinking at the end of the fighting that it had suffered its first serious setback since the beginning of the war.

Operation Dynamo was brought to a formal close by an Admiralty signal on 4 June. On the following day the Germans began their drive towards the Seine. In the light of the first of the documents captured on 25 May and recent Enigma traffic, the British knew that the French were heavily outnumbered.[45] A plan was made to form an Allied stronghold in Brittany, and two British divisions disembarked at Nantes. A retreat to North Africa was considered, and an 'indissoluble union' between France and the British Empire was discussed. But all these projects came to nothing when German forces fanned out towards the Atlantic coast and Marshal Pétain came to power with the avowed intention of concluding an armistice with Germany. On 10 June the sole remaining representative of MI 6 with the French intelligence agencies transmitted his last report on French plans and the progress of the German armies.[46] Enigma continued, however, to enable the British to keep track of the enemy's advance.

FIVE

Britain: 1940

One consequence of the fall of the Chamberlain government in May 1940 was a considerable shake-up of the British intelligence organization. As First Lord of the Admiralty and Chairman of the Military Co-Ordination Committee in the outgoing government, the new Prime Minister was at least as much responsible as any of its members for its failure to heed warnings that Norway was about to be invaded. That made Churchill all the more determined that, so far as it lay in his power to mend matters, henceforward the intelligence trumpet should not speak with an uncertain sound.

In April the Military Co-Ordination Committee had wanted to make the War Office, not the Joint Intelligence Committee, responsible for issuing daily Scandinavian intelligence summaries and reviewing the system by which intelligence was brought to the government's attention. In practice, the Joint Intelligence Committee had assumed those responsiblities and had arranged special meetings of representatives of the service departments, MI 6 and, in appropriate cases, the Foreign Office, for the purpose of collating information needed for the preparation of the summaries.[1] Furthermore, on the initiative of the Joint Planners, the Chiefs of Staff had asked the Joint Intelligence Committee to include in its daily reports brief appreciations of the enemy's probable intentions.[2] On becoming Prime Minister and assuming the additional post of Minister of Defence, Churchill instructed the Chiefs of Staff to take a fresh look at the relations between the authorities responsible for providing information and those responsible for operational decisions. Their response was to give the Joint Intelligence Committee a stronger secretariat and direct it to bring to their attention and to the attention of the Prime Minister and the War Cabinet, at any hour of the day or night, reports on any strategic development which any of its members thought they ought to know about without delay.[3] To ensure that bodies accustomed to report directly at the highest level were not short-circuited, the Joint Intelligence Committee arranged on 24 May that in future MI 5, MI 6 and the Ministry of Economic Warfare, as well as the service departments and the Foreign Office, should be fully represented at its meetings.[4]

This was a step in the right direction. However, the ability of the Joint Intelligence Committee to keep the Chiefs of Staff, the Prime Minister and the War Cabinet duly informed still depended largely on the extent to which the departments were able to furnish it promptly with adequately-processed information. In any case the value of its reports was governed ultimately by the quality of the raw material provided by the information-gathering agencies.

From that point of view the outlook in the early summer was not very promising. MI 6, hitherto dependent on the French for much of its information about Germany, had to rely after the fall of France largely on hastily improved stay-behind networks. These were supplemented to some extent by networks maintained by exiled governments or quasi-governmental agencies, but not all organizers of such networks were as co-operative as the Czechs. Both the volume and the operational content of German signals traffic intercepted and read in the United Kingdom declined sharply when the campaign in France and the Low Countries was over, and they could be expected to decline still further once the enemy was firmly established in the occupied countries and in a position to substitute landline for wireless communications. Except in so far as occasional raids on occupied territory might be possible, prisoners-of-war would be limited to survivors from wrecked aircraft or sunk or damaged vessels, captured documents to those recovered from them. Reconnaissance photographs remained an invaluable source, but experience had shown that only the specially-modified Spitfires recommended by Cotton could be relied upon to provide them. In the middle of May the Photographic Development Unit had only eight of these aircraft, those in France included.[5] As late as the end of July only eleven were available and only three of these were of the long-range type capable of reaching places as far away as Kiel.[6]

The severance of communications with Continental Europe, except by roundabout routes through Spain, Portugal or Northern Russia, did, however, have the advantage for the British of making the unobserved arrival of German agents in the United Kingdom rather difficult. Some weeks before the invasion of France and the Low Countries, the Abwehr officer Major Ritter proposed to the double agent recruited by the

British in 1939 (and called SNOW by the British quasi-official historian Sir John Masterman) a rendezvous in the North Sea. SNOW was to arrive in a trawler which Ritter thought he would have no great difficulty in obtaining, and to bring with him a sub-agent who would be trained in Germany and afterwards return to the United Kingdom. Ritter would come by aircraft or submarine. When this far-fetched project came to a head in May, the British provided both the trawler and the ostensible sub-agent, a reformed criminal called by Masterman BISCUIT.[7] As a result of misunderstandings between SNOW and BISCUIT, each of whom suspected the other of being a genuine German agent, and also of the premature arrival of an aircraft which displayed the agreed recognistion signal, no contact was made with Ritter. SNOW was afterwards able to convince the British that BISCUIT's aspersions were unwarranted. He also managed to persuade Ritter that the Abwehr could still rely on him. BISCUIT returned in August from a meeting with Ritter in Lisbon with fresh instructions, a new wireless set, and a substantial sum in dollars which MI 5 received as a welcome addition to its funds. The confidence still reposed by the Abwehr in SNOW proved extremely helpful to the British when, later in the year, a fresh batch of German agents arrived in the United Kingdom with identity cards and ration cards prepared in accordance with the misleading instructions he provided.

Churchill was keenly interested not only in the intelligence organization but also in subversion, partisan activities and what were afterwards called commando raids. The Chiefs of Staff thought on the eve of Dunkirk that, if France collapsed, Germany might still be defeated by a combination of air attacks, economic pressure, and the fostering of discontent in occupied countries.[8] By the early summer of 1940 Section D had to its credit the rescue of a substantial quantity of industrial diamonds from Amsterdam under the noses of the Germans.[9] MI (R) was responsible for setting fire, at a refinery in Normandy, to some 200,000 tons of oil which would otherwise have fallen into German hands.[10] As the outcome of discussions in which both sections were involved, a Directorate of Combined Operations was set up within the Admiralty to take charge of seaborne raids, and an organization was formed under the Minister of Economic Warfare, Hugh Dalton, 'to co-ordinate all action, by way of subversion and sabotage, against the enemy overseas'.[11] This organization, the Special Operations Executive, was called into being by a paper signed by Neville Chamberlain, the man of peace, a few days before he went into hospital to die. Section D was forthwith transferred to Dalton's control, but MI (R) remained for the time being under the War Office.

Not surprisingly, there was fierce opposition to a step which Dalton sought to justify by citing such dubious precedents as the Sinn Fein movement in Ireland and National Socialist penetration of foreign countries – though he also cited the more respectable example of guerilla activities in the Peninsular War.[12] By listing the methods he proposed to use as 'industrial and military sabotage, labour agitation and strikes, continuous propaganda, terrorist acts against traitors and German leaders, boycotts and riots',[13] he invited the rejoinder that Britain was fighting to rescue Europe from a tyranny imposed by licensed gangsters, not to promote anarchy.

Apart from the moral aspect, Dalton's proposals were open to the twofold objection that they would divert men and women with special qualifications from more constructive tasks, and that they ran counter to the accepted military doctrine that partisan activities were most useful when they paved the way for regular forces which alone could occupy territory and secure decisive results. The British Army would not be ready to return to the Continent before 1942, at the earliest. So what could Britain hope to gain by subjecting the unfortunate inhabitants of occupied countries in 1940 or 1941 to the all-too-predictable consequences of riots, boycotts, labour agitation, industrial sabotage and strikes?

The controversy dragged on for more than a year. At last, in August 1941, warring departments agreed that a clear distinction should be drawn between Dalton's propagandist and his subversive activities. Of the two sections into which the existing Special Operations Executive was divided, SO 1 became the Political Warfare Executive, charged with the tasks originally entrusted to the old EH or CS department; SO 2, responsible for sabotage and subversion was formed by the fusion of Section D with MI (R), became a separate organization and inherited the designation which had hitherto covered both sections.[14] Thus a new Special Operations Executive or SOE was born. But meanwhile Hitler's invasion of Russia, by transforming the political and strategic outlook, had raised yet another awkward issue which the British were reluctant to face. In seeking to overthrow National Socialism, did they intend to invoke the principle of legitimacy, as in the Napoleonic Wars, or would they be content to see capitalist governments replaced in Continental countries by Communist régimes?

In the spring and summer of 1940 the British were, however, more concerned with the immediate problem of survival than with long-term problems.

As early as October 1939, alarmist reports from agents and diplomatic sources led the Chamberlain government to ask the Chiefs of Staff to assess the chances of a descent on the United Kingdom by seaborne and airborne troops. The conclusion reached was that, while raids were possible and attempts at a full-scale invasion not inconceivable, the risk was not so great that the War Office would be justified in holding back troops ready to go overseas. A proportion of such troops as were not ready to go overseas, or were not required for that purpose, would be made available to resist seaborne landings or round up airborne forces.[15]

Hitler's Norwegian expedition gave a sharp jolt to preconceptions about what the Germans might be able to do and the risks they might be willing to take. Thereafter, when considering the chances of invasion, both the intelligence and the operational staffs were so determined not to repeat mistakes arising from past scepticism that they tended to err in the opposite direction.

We now know that Hitler was slow to believe that the British would carry on the war after France was defeated. Germany's armed forces received no instructions until 2 July to prepare plans for an invasion of the United Kingdom.[16] In the same month Hitler made it clear to his service advisers that he had not made up his mind that the invasion should be launched, and would give an affirmative decision only if the Luftwaffe gained air superiority over the landing area. Göring believed that the air defences of southern England could be knocked out in four days, the RAF as a whole reduced to impotence in four weeks. As naval preparations for Operation Sea Lion could not be completed before the middle of September, he decided in consultation with the Fuhrer to begin his battle for air supremacy on 10 August. In the meantime the Luftwaffe would test Britain's air defences by attacking ports and shipping.

All this is clear enough in retrospect. At the time, the British did not know what to expect. As the Germans did not begin their preparations until July, such obvious signs of readiness to invade as the assembly of large numbers of troops, transports and barges at ports within reach of reconnaissance aircraft were not forthcoming until the summer was well advanced. But that did not necessarily mean that the Germans were not making preparations at Baltic or Norwegian ports, or in South-West France. In any case the intelligence staffs were not prepared to make reassuring statements on the strength of negative evidence.

Moreover, not all the evidence was negative. Warnings were received from diplomatic sources before the end of May that a major assault on the United Kingdom was likely to follow, or might even precede, the fall of France. Agents reported about the same time that barges were being prepared at German ports.[17] Prince Bernhard of the Netherlands believed that the Germans were capable of mounting an airborne invasion while the campaign in France and Flanders was still in progress.[18] The Japanese Minister in Budapest reported to Tokyo that the Prime Minister of Hungary thought the Germans had a plan for invading Britain, and his message was intercepted and decrypted.

Not surprisingly, the British thought so too. On the first day of the campaign in France and the Low Countries, the Chiefs of Staff set up a new organization, the Home Defence Executive, to co-ordinate military and civil measures to resist invasion.[20] They believed when they took this step that invasion would be preceded by a major air offensive and that this would give time for the defences to be alerted; before long they managed to persuade themselves that, by using '200 fast motor boats, each carrying 100 men', the Germans might be able to deliver, without warning, a large-scale raid which might pave the way for invasion proper.[21] Although there was no evidence that the enemy possessed such craft, which would in any case be very unsuitable for the purpose, the Chiefs of Staff warned the War Cabinet on 29 May that a full-scale attack on the United Kingdom might be imminent, and recommended that the Commander-in-Chief, Home Forces, should be so informed.[22]

Within the next few days the military intelligence branch of the War Office concluded, in the light of the Luftwaffe Enigma traffic recently mastered by Bletchley and of other indications, that the Germans were unlikely to turn against Britain before finishing with France.[23] This conclusion was endorsed by the Joint Intelligence Committee, and on 3 June was accepted by the Chiefs of Staff with the reservation that the United Kingdom was none the less dangerously exposed to the risk of 'decisive' air attack or invasion, if not both.[24]

By that time a number of exceptional measures, some of them far-fetched, had been put in hand. Stretches of arterial road and open spaces were obstructed to prevent troop-carrying aircraft or gliders from landing on them. Place-names were removed from signposts, shop-fronts and tradesmen's vans. Milestones were defaced or uprooted. The sale of maps and guide-books was restricted. Large numbers of German refugees and about a thousand British eccentrics or members of extremist groups were interned in the belief that, if they were left at liberty, some of them might somehow manage to give aid and comfort to an enemy who was never to arrive and towards whom all but a few were far from well disposed.

In terms of its effect on the war effort, the worst consequence of the invasion scare was the diversion of warships and auxiliaries from convoy escort or service with the Home Fleet to sterile anti-invasion duties. If the intelligence organization had been able to promise even a brief warning of invasion or major raids, most of these ships could have been left to carry on as usual until the warning arrived.[25] As it could not, sinkings of merchant shipping rose sharply, the lives of many seamen were lost, and the activities of the Home Fleet were restricted by the transfer of cruisers and flotilla vessels to naval shore commands.[26] This was particularly galling for Admiral Forbes because he was confident that the Germans would not commit their slender naval resources to an attempt at invasion without first trying to win a major battle in the air. That was a sound inference from the known weakness of the German Navy, but the Admiralty declined to draw it in the absence of reliable information about the state of Germany's few heavy ships after the Norwegian campaign. Visual reconnaissance did not throw much light on the matter; the scope of photographic reconnaissance was limited by a dearth of long-range Spitfires.[27] The Admiralty based its plans to resist invasion on the belief that the enemy would be able to use the *Scharnhorst* and the *Gneisenau* to stage a diversion, and to employ two old battleships and about five cruisers in the southern part of the North Sea.[28] Its instructions to commanders stressed the importance of patrolling the whole of the coast from The Wash to Newhaven.[29] We now know that the two battlecruisers were not in an effective state, that only two German cruisers were ready for service, that no landings on the East Coast were intended. All the beaches finally chosen by the enemy for the disembarkation of his assault forces lay between Folkestone and Brighton.

By the early summer of 1940 the importance of improving reconnaissance cover in view of a real or supposed threat of invasion was clear not only to the Chiefs of Staff and their Joint Planning Committee but also to the service departments and the Joint Intelligence Committee. On 26 May the Joint Intelligence Committee recommended systematic and continuous air reconnaissance of all areas from which an invasion fleet might sail.[30] Although this was more easily said than done, the Joint Intelligence Committee went on to establish, within the Admiralty's Operational Intelligence Centre, an inter-service sub-committee charged with the collation and interpretation of information bearing on the invasion threat. This was the Combined Intelligence Committee, sometimes miscalled the Counter-Invasion Committee. The committee was given access to information from all sources, but was expected to find photographic reconnaissance and such Enigma material as might be forthcoming more useful than reports from agents or diplomatic sources, since these tended to be contradictory.[31] In view of the special importance attached to reconnaissance, representatives of the Admiralty and the Air Ministry recommended on 10 June that the Combined Intelligence Committee should assume exclusive responsibility for submitting requests for reconnaissance and establishing priorities. The Air Staff accepted these proposals, at the same time stipulating that the committee should also be exclusively responsible for collating information from air reconnaissance with information from other sources.[32] A logical corollary was that Coastal Command, as the RAF command responsible for maritime reconnaissance, assumed responsibility for photographic reconnaissance as well. On 18 June the Photographic Development Unit was transferred from the operational control of the Director of Air Intelligence at the Air Ministry to that of the Commander-in-Chief, Coastal Command, and was renamed the Photographic Reconnaissance Unit. Cotton's services were dispensed with when this change was made, but the soundness of the methods he had long advocated, sometimes in face of considerable opposition, was now recognized by all concerned.

Henceforward the procedure was that the Combined Intelligence Committee decided, in the light of the information it already had, what areas should be covered next. It then passed its requests to Coastal Command, which issued appropriate instructions. With almost unfailing regularity, the Photographic Reconnaissance Unit brought back the required photographs. The expert visual scrutiny called photographic interpretation was done until July by the Aircraft Operating Company, a private firm concerned in peacetime with aerial survey and equipped with a device of Swiss origin, the Wild machine, which enabled a trained operator to calculate the dimensions of ships, aircraft and buildings with considerable accuracy from high-altitude vertical photographs. The firm was then taken over by the Air Ministry and became the Photographic Interpretation Unit. More drastic changes, including removal from Wembley to Medmenham, followed in 1941, when the organization was renamed the Central Interpretation Unit. Thereafter it was allowed to employ only men and women who agreed to wear uniform and to draw service pay and allowances instead of salaries or wages.[33]

Throughout June, July and August the Photographic Reconnaissance Unit provided only negative evidence of German readiness to mount a seaborne expedition. No large concentrations of troops or shipping were photographed at the French Channel ports or at Belgian or Dutch North Sea ports.[34] When cover was extended to South-West Norway, Kiel and the estuary of the Gironde, no abnormal activity was photographed there either.[35] On the other hand, photographs did show that runways at airfields in France and the Low Countries were being extended. Enigma furnished incontrovertible evidence that some Luftwaffe units were resting and refitting in preparation for operations against the United Kingdom, that the aircraft used might include dive-bombers, that long-range guns were being installed at Cap Gris Nez. Air reconnaissance provided confirmation, but there was nothing to show whether the guns were intended to support a seaborne expedition or merely to attack shipping in the Dover Strait and lob an occasional shell at Dover. On 4 July the Combined Intelligence Committee reported, in the light of Enigma information, that most Luftwaffe units would have completed their refitting by the middle of the month, but it did not draw the inference that Germany's next move was more likely to be an air offensive than invasion. The Joint Intelligence Committee conceded that the evidence was open to that interpretation but concluded, on the principle that it was always wisest to assume the worst, that full-scale invasion might be expected by the middle of July and large-scale raids at almost any moment.[36] In view of the regularity with which the Photographic Reconnaissance Unit was able to cover French, Belgian and Dutch ports and harbours the Combined Intelligence Committee did, however, point out on 14 July, and again on 19 July, that a mass departure of barges from France or the Low Countries seemed unlikely to take place without some warning.[37]

By that time the preliminary phase of the Battle of Britain had begun. During the first nine days of July small formations of escorted bombers made daylight attacks on Falmouth, Plymouth, Portland, Weymouth and Dover, and seven attacks were made on Channel convoys. On 10 July – regarded by the British as the first day of the battle – about twenty bombers escorted and covered by some forty fighters approached a westbound convoy off Dover and were met by elements of five British fighter squadrons.[38]

Popular legend has depicted Air Chief Marshal Dowding as fighting the Battle of Britain from his headquarters at Bentley Priory with the aid of an encyclopaedic knowledge of the enemy's dispositions and intentions, derived from a source called Ultra. Apart from the fact that the term Ultra was not used before 1941 (and was not the name of a source but a security classification for material derived from Enigma), this is a highly misleading picture, for two reasons.

The first is that, except in a figurative sense, the Battle of Britain was not fought from Bentley Priory. Responsibility not only for the metropolitan fighter force, but also for the operational employment of anti-aircraft guns, searchlights and balloon barrages rested ultimately upon Dowding as Air Officer Commanding-in-Chief, Fighter Command. Tactical control was delegated to the fighter groups into which his command was divided on a geographical basis. Dowding and his staff concerned themselves with such broad issues of strategy and policy as the general disposition of the air defences and the rotation of units between active and quiet sectors; they gave no executive orders to fighter stations or squadrons, gun batteries, searchlight companies or balloon centres. Apart from the collation of information from the radar chain, which was done at the relevant time in a room adjacent to the underground operations room but afterwards decentralized, the only functions exercised at command headquarters that might be classed as tactical were the issue of orders for the dissemination and cancellation of air-raid warnings, and of instructions to the BBC to close or reopen specified transmitters which might be used by the enemy for navigation. Even the tactical reinforcement of one fighter group by another was left to group commanders or their duty controllers to arrange between themselves, although this was a matter in which, as things turned out, the Commander-in-Chief might with advantage have intervened. Movements of hostile or unidentified aircraft towards or across the United Kingdom were shown on the big table in the operations room, but not those of aircraft sent by sector stations to intercept them on orders from the appropriate group commander or controller. After the first few days of the war, when the appearance of a hostile or unidentified plot on the table was a novelty, Dowding seldom visited the operations room except to show it to a distinguished visitor. He said long afterwards that, once the daylight battle was launched, he trusted his group commanders and their staffs and watchkeeping officers to do what was expected of them, and gave most of his attention to preparations to meet the night attacks which he was sure would follow it.[39]

The second reason was that Enigma furnished very little material of immediate value as a guide to operational decisions. It helped the Air Ministry to predict the opening of the preliminary phase of the battle with considerable accuracy and to arrive at a sound estimate of the first-line strength of the German bomber force, but threw little light on the enemy's losses or the number of serviceable aircraft at his disposal on a given day.[40] Nor was it of much help to the Air Ministry or Fighter Command in forseeing changes in the Luftwaffe's strategy or policy.[41] In the later stages of the battle Enigma furnished some tactical intelligence, but little use could be made of it because this was an unexpected development and therefore no provision had been made for information of tactical value to be passed promptly to operational formations, either directly from Bletchley or through Cheadle.[42] The usefulness of Enigma decrypts as a guide to operational decisions was also limited by incompleteness. Plans revealed by Enigma might be modified by orders passed by landline and hence not intercepted. For example, Enigma showed that a big attack on London was planned for 6 p.m. on 13 September. The weather on that day was such that only minor raids were made. A later Enigma message indicated that the attack would be made on the following day. In the outcome it was made on 15 September without further warning.[43]

The radar chain and the Y-Service were the best sources of tactical intelligence. Since Dunkirk the Y-Service had provided itself with Home Defence Units, manned by German-speaking WAAFs or WRNS, to monitor voice transmissions. Originally these were intended mainly to listen to ground-to-ground or ground-to-air traffic in the event of invasion. As things turned out, their chief role was to monitor transmissions by Luftwaffe fighter pilots, although they could also hear transmissions from light naval craft. They were administered by a centre at Kingsdown and linked by landline with appropriate RAF headquarters and local naval commands. German bombers continued to use the methods with which the Y-Service had become familiar, and their crews did not always obey orders to observe wireless silence during active operations. By combining factual knowledge with reasoned guesswork, Cheadle was able on many occasions to give valuable information about impending raids or raids in progress.

Between 9 and 13 August the Enigma traffic carried references to *Adler Tag*. That this would inaugurate a new phase of the air offensive was fairly obvious, but neither the Government Code and Cypher School nor the Air Ministry could say when Eagle Day would come or what surprises it might bring. We now know that it was postponed for three days from 10 August in the light of unfavourable weather forecasts. We also know that misunderstandings and delays in the receipt of last-minute orders were responsible for the arrival over England early on 13 August of unescorted bomber formations and fighters without bombers. In the course of the day the Luftwaffe flew nearly fifteen hundred sorties and lost forty-five aircraft. Fighter Command lost thirteen aircraft but only seven pilots. Three airfields suffered considerable damage, but none was a fighter station although some fighters were temporarily based at one of them.[44]

After a day of relatively minor activity, the Luftwaffe made a vigorous attempt on 15 August to knock out fighter and bomber bases from Tyneside to Hampshire. For the first and last time in the daylight battle, aircraft of Luftflotte 5 from Denmark and Norway supplemented the efforts of the two Luftflotten based in France and the Low Countries. No warning of Luftflotte 5's contribution appears to have been received from signal intelligence, but its aircraft were detected by radar well before they reached the coast.[45] As the bombers from Denmark were unescorted and those from Norway accompanied only by heavy fighters which gave them no effective help, it is not surprising that Luftflotte 5 suffered prohibitive losses. Luftflotten 2 and 3 were more successful. Altogether the Luftwaffe flew nearly eighteen hundred sorties between dawn and dusk. It lost 75 aircraft to Fighter Command's 34, but fairly heavy damage was done to eight airfields, of which six were fighter stations. Hits were scored, too, on four aircraft factories at Rochester and Croydon. Further attempts to overwhelm the defences on 16 and 18 August, and six days of minor activity on 17 August and from 19 to 23 August, brought the first phase of the main offensive to a close.

We now know that the Luftwaffe lost 290 aircraft during that phase, 576 between 10 July and 23 August. Fighter Command believed at the time that its losses were much higher. The Air Ministry's· intelligence officers did not regard claims made by fighter pilots as reliable, but had little else on which to base calculations of the enemy's capacity to carry on the battle. They were hampered, too, by a continuing tendency to over-estimate the Luftwaffe's stored reserves. When major operations were resumed on 24 August, there was little to show that the Luftwaffe's effective strength was dwindling or was likely to dwindle within the next few days or weeks. Records now available disclose a substantial decline in its average daily effort during the phase that began on that day and ended on 6 September, but they also show that even at the end of August it could still fly about as many sorties in twenty-four hours as on Eagle

Day. It is therefore not surprising that, when asked at the beginning of September how long the Luftwaffe could keep up its effort, Air Intelligence made only the cautious prediction that the German fighter force would become ineffective in six weeks if losses continued at the current rate.[46] But no information from secret sources was needed to tell Fighter Command and its subordinate formations that the enemy had embarked on a policy of conserving his bombers by using them in daylight only when and where they could be strongly escorted and supported by single-seater fighters. This trend, and also a tendency to give priority to targets of cardinal importance to Fighter Command, were apparent in the pattern of his activities.

What information from intelligence sources did suggest was that, if the Germans regarded air superiority as a prerequisite of invasion, they still hoped to achieve it, and that they were making active preparations to land in Britain but that in August these had yet to be completed. Enigma showed towards the end of July that Luftwaffe crews had been ordered not to bomb harbour facilities at the British Channel ports.[47] On the eve of *Adler Tag* the same source revealed that units intended for a special task had been transferred to a Fliegerkorps associated with close support of troops, and that its commander had been promised thirty men with a perfect knowledge of English.[48] Thümmel reported on 12 August that there would be no invasion for at least two or three weeks.[49] Two days later the Combined Intelligence Committee, with Thümmel's report before it, expressed the opinion that no decision for or against invasion would be made 'pending the result of the present struggle for air superiority'.[50] In the meantime air photographs disclosed no abnormal activity at French, Belgian or Dutch ports, and an informant reported from Stettin that, notwithstanding rumours of secret preparations in the Baltic, all was quiet there.[51] The relevance to the invasion issue of a series of night attacks on Liverpool and Birkenhead by Luftflotte 3 in the last week in August was not apparent at the time; we now know that these raids were the outcome of a decision by Göring to limit Luftflotte 3 mainly to operations by unescorted bombers in order to provide as much fighter support as possible for Luftflotte 2's attacks on objectives in south-eastern England.

From the beginning of September marked changes were apparent. After concentrating its attacks since 24 August almost exclusively on airfields and especially fighter bases, on five of the first six days of the month Luftflotte 2 included in its target-list such objectives as Tilbury docks, aircraft factories in the Thames Valley and the Medway towns, and oil refineries at Thameshaven. Between 1 and 7 September photographic and visual reconaissance revealed striking increases in the numbers of barges at Flushing and Ostend, and a steady movement of barges, motor boats and larger vessels from the North Sea to the Channel ports.[52] Leave was reported to have been stopped in the German Army from 8 September; confirmation was received from signal intelligence that the moves of dive-bombers and long-range bombers ordered in August had been made.[53] At the same time, German agents began to arrive in the United Kingdom by such methods as parachuting from aircraft or rowing ashore from submarines or surface craft.[54] Most of them, if not arrested immediately after their arrival because Abwehr traffic had warned MI 5 that they were coming, soon gave themselves away by their obvious unfamiliarity with wartime Britain and their possession of documents which did not ring true. The fact that each had been given enough money to maintain himself for a month or two suggested that the Abwehr expected German troops to establish themselves on British soil within that time. Four of these men, caught landing from a rowing-boat, confessed that they were spies and that their mission was to report movements of reserves in the area London – Reading – Oxford – Ipswich – London.[55]

The arrival in Whitehall of a report to that effect on 7 September preceded by only a matter of hours the switching of the air offensive to round-the-clock attacks on Greater London. The Joint Intelligence Committee, bearing in mind that moon and tide would favour landings between 8 and 10 September and that these were dates mentioned in MI 6 and diplomatic reports, warned the Chiefs of Staff that invasion must be regarded as imminent.[56] At eight o'clock that evening GHQ, Home Forces, brought the troops to immediate readiness by issuing the code-word Cromwell.[57]

On the evidence available at the time, this move was justified. Only a few days had elapsed since Air Intelligence estimated that the Luftwaffe could continue operations at the current rate for six weeks. The Chiefs of Staff and the Joint Intelligence Committee could not know that on 7 September Luftflotte 2 was down to 533 serviceable single-seater fighters of its own and 63 shared with Luftflotte 3.[58] Nor did they know that the German Navy needed ten days' notice to mount Operation Sea Lion and that therefore the Luftwaffe had very little time left in which to gain air superiority if the order was to be given soon enough for landings to be made in September. They cannot be blamed for assuming that invasion would come soon if it came at all.

Whether the Chiefs of Staff were justified in continuing to believe in the invasion threat as long as they did is another matter. No intelligence source was able to tell them that on 17 September Hitler postponed Operation Sea Lion indefinitely and ordered a partial dispersion of the invasion fleet. On the other hand, the Joint Intelligence Committee did point out on 10 October that invasion had become for the enemy 'a hazardous undertaking'.[59] In any case one might have expected the Chiefs of Staff to conclude that the Germans, with an invasion fleet consisting largely of towed barges, would scarcely try to put troops ashore on open beaches unless they could count on almost perfect weather. Moreover, hints from intelligence sources were not altogether lacking. We now know that on 14 September Hitler announced that, in view of the uncertain state of the air battle, he did not propose to decide for or against invasion until 17 September. Next day an identical signal was transmitted on every German naval frequency.[60] This unique event was followed by a marked diminution of traffic in the frequency used in the Channel area. Between 18 and 30 September the number of barges photographed at the five main ports between Flushing and Boulogne fell from 1,004 to 691.[61] Photographs taken on 20 September showed that five destroyers and a torpedo-boat had left Cherbourg and that barges were dispersing. Thümmel reported on 30 September that invasion had been deferred until early in October; on 9 October that it had been put off until 1941.[62] Finally, Enigma revealed on 25 October that a special Luftwaffe unit attached to the invasion forces had been disbanded. There were also reports of the postponement of Sea Lion from other agents and from diplomatic sources.

The development of the air offensive, too, provided strong indications that by the latter part of September the invasion threat was a thing of the past, or at worst of the fairly distant future. Luftflotte 2 put substantial numbers of aircraft over Greater London during the daylight hours on five days between 7 and 15 September. On 7 September it sent more than 300 bombers, caught the defences at something of a disadvantage, but suffered fairly heavy losses. On 9 September it sent about two-thirds of that number. About a hundred were sent on 11 September and again on 14 September. On 15 September, by making a supreme effort, Luftflotte 2 succeeded in sending about two hundred bombers in two waves and in making about 700 fighter sorties, but it lost 60 aircraft and was believed by Fighter Command at the time to have lost 180. Thereafter the Luftwaffe put most of its efforts into night attacks. In addition, fighters flying without bombers or escorting only small bomber formations made periodical sweeps over London to test the defences. These tactics confronted Fighter Command with awkward problems, and the night bombing caused a good deal of damage and loss of life; but they could not give the Luftwaffe a decisive victory. They were interpreted by such experienced commanders as Dowding and Forbes as evidence that, at any rate for the time being, the Germans had relinquished the hope of achieving air superiority as a prelude to invasion.

The Chiefs of Staff were slow to accept that verdict. As late as 21 October they regarded such conclusions as premature.[63] It was not until the last day of the month that the Defence Committee conceded that the danger of invasion had become 'relatively remote'. A number of vessels diverted to anti-invasion duties then returned to their normal work, but the watch for an invader who never came continued until long afterwards to absorb a considerable proportion of Britain's war effort.[64]

SIX

The Mediterranean and the Near and Middle East: 1939–1941

One of many factors which bedevilled British preparations for war with Germany and Italy was that, apart from her concern with home defence and the defence of ocean trade and her obligations towards France and Poland, Britain was responsible in the Mediterranean area and in areas bordering on Italian possessions in North and East Africa for the defence of Gibraltar, Malta, Cyprus, Egypt and the Suez Canal, the Sudan, Palestine, Iraq, British Somaliland and Kenya. At the same time treaty obligations and the dependence of the United Kingdom on imported oil made the security of the Persian Gulf a vital British interest. The British also had contingent liabilities with respect to Greece and Turkey, and an interest in restoring Abyssinia to the exiled Emperor Haile Selassie.

The processing – to say nothing for the moment of the procurement – of intelligence covering so vast and heterogeneous an area called for a complex organization which operated at two levels. At the inter-service level, the Middle East Intelligence Centre was established at Cairo in the summer of 1939 for the threefold purpose of furnishing commanders-in-chief and representatives of civil departments in the Middle East with co-ordinated intelligence; providing the Joint Planning Staff in the Middle East with intelligence needed for the preparation of strategic plans; and supplying the Joint Intelligence Committee in London with processed information about Middle Eastern affairs.[1] At the service level, each service had its own intelligence staff. A Naval Operational Intelligence Centre, Mediterranean, was established at Malta in the spring of 1939 and moved to Alexandria in May 1940.[2] The Air Officer Commanding-in-Chief was served, from the time when he opened his headquarters at Cairo in March 1939, by an air intelligence staff responsible for co-ordinating operational intelligence for the benefit of all air forces in the Mediterranean and the Middle Eastern theatre.[3] The needs of the commander of the land forces were met by a section of the staff of Headquarters, British Troops, Egypt, from the summer of 1939 until, in February 1940, Lieutenant-General Sir Archibald Wavell became Commander-in-Chief and acquired a military intelligence staff which formed part of the staff of GHQ, Middle East.[4]

When the Middle East Intelligence Centre was set up, the Foreign Office expressed the hope that it would not concern itself with the assessment of political intelligence, and the Joint Intelligence Committee in London excluded the Balkans from its province. Although its staff consisted exclusively of naval, army and air force officers, it nevertheless set up a foreign affairs section, and in May 1940 the Joint Intelligence Committee yielded to its insistence that the ban on extension of its sphere of interest to the Balkans should be lifted. By that time it was regularly issuing both strategic appreciations and background studies covering some twenty countries. Its sources included not only agents' reports, high-grade and low-grade signal intelligence, photographic and visual reconnaissance and – when this became available – information from prisoners of war and captured material, but also appreciations made by intelligence organizations in the Middle East or sent to it from Whitehall, and material from British diplomatic, consular and colonial authorities. As its methods attracted a good deal of adverse comment in Whitehall, its replacement by a small committee consisting of one representative of each of the services and a secretary was mooted. Wavell scotched this proposal by pointing out that some seventy intelligence summaries circulated regularly in his theatre and that such a committee would be quite incapable of digesting them all and using them, as the Middle East Intelligence Centre did, as part of the raw material of broad applications which the operational and planning authorities could not afford to be without.[5] Once the navy's Operational Intelligence Centre had moved to Alexandria, the demand for a small inter-service intelligence committee was met to some extent by informal conferences between naval, army and air force intelligence officers.

A proposal made in the course of the discussions that led to the formation of the Middle East Intelligence Centre was that there should be an inter-service centre, on the lines of the Far East Combined Bureau, for the co-ordination of operational intelligence on behalf of all three services. This was defeated by the insistence of the services that each should have its own intelligence staff. The Government Code and

Cypher School continued to urge that they should at least pool their cryptanalytical resources in order to facilitate a mutually profitable exchange of material between Bletchley and some form of combined signal intelligence bureau in the Middle East. But the service authorities in Cairo and Alexandria made common cause against reforms which they regarded as a threat to their independence. They continued to resist them even when the Italians gave a new slant to the situation by entering the war and changing their cyphers. They argued that the new cyphers would be broken more rapidly, and with better results, if responsibility for the main crptanalytical effort passed to their separate organizations in the Middle East.[6] Eventually the Chiefs of Staff rejected that argument. After consulting the Directors of Intelligence in Whitehall, they ruled that a Combined Bureau staffed by cryptanalysts from Cairo and Bletchley should be established at Heliopolis. Bletchley would remain responsible for basic research and for the initial attack on Italian high-grade cyphers. The bureau would exploit the results and would also work on lower-grade cyphers, but would be controlled ultimately by the GC & CS.[7]

On the whole the authorities at home and in the Middle East were well supplied with information about Italy up to the time when she declared war on France and Britain, and not too badly supplied later. When the Chiefs of Staff concluded in February 1939 that in all probability Italy would be reluctant to commit herself to a European war as Germany's ally, they did so in the knowledge that the state of her armed forces was poor.[8] Her invasion of Albania in the following April came as a surprise to Whitehall and Downing Street, but they had at least received a general warning that some such move was possible.[9] In the spring and early summer of 1940 the service departments and the commanders in the Mediterranean and the Middle East had a good knowledge of the state of readiness of the Italian Navy and the Italian land and air forces in Libya and East Africa.[10]

The intelligence agencies also gave good warning of Mussolini's decision to hasten to the aid of the victors when the fall of France was imminent. We now know that he told Hitler on 18 March that he would be ready for war in three or four months. Nothing was known of this at the time, but in February and March decrypted signals showed that the rifle strength of the army in Libya was being increased, although it was still short of tanks, artillery and transport.[11] Information from the same source prompted the Commander-in-Chief of the Mediterranean Fleet to ask for reinforcements. In the light of rumours that Mussolini might be emboldened by the failure of the British to keep the Germans out of Norway, the Admiralty ordered precautionary measures.[12] Arrangements were concerted between the Photographic Development Unit and the Deuxième Bureau for a Spitfire of No. 212 Squadron to make clandestine flights from an airfield near Toulon over Bari, Milan, the Gulf of Genoa and the approaches to the Franco-Italian frontier.[13]

The Foreign Office and the War Cabinet were inclined to think early in May that these alarms were premature. But strong indications that Italy was preparing to take the plunge soon followed. On 22 May a decrypted signal revealed that the Italian Foreign Ministry was instructing its embassy in London to urge young Italians to return to Italy.[14] By the following day the Chiefs of Staff and the commanders in the Mediterranean and the Middle East were aware that a secret mobilization of Italian forces in Libya and East Africa had been ordered.[15] The Admiralty's Operational Intelligence Centre in Whitehall reported on 3 June that Italian consular officials in British colonies had been ordered to destroy their cyphers.[16] On 7 June the Italian Navy stopped using plain language in its W/T transmissions. Diplomatic sources and visitors to Italy reported that troops were moving towards the French and Yugoslav frontiers and that precautions against air attack and other defensive measures were being taken in Rome and elsewhere. Some of these reports wer confirmed by air reconnaissance. Thümmel appears to have reported on 7 June that hostilities would begin during the night of 10/11 June, but whether his report contributed to the Admiralty's prediction that they would start between 10 and 20 June is not known.[17]

So the Italian Foreign Minister's announcement on 10 June that Italy would be at war with France and Britain from the following day came as no surprise. Extension of the war to a new theatre in which naval power would play an important role did, however, throw a glaring light on past mistakes. In 1938 the Chamberlain government had authorized the Air Ministry to order virtually all the aircraft the British aircraft industry could produce.[18] Large sums had been spent on the development of a bomber force which was almost useless for its intended purpose of attacking industrial targets in Germany. Yet in 1940 the British were painfully short of high-performance aircraft with which to support their naval and land forces in the Mediterranean and the Middle East. The Spitfire which photographed parts of Italy between 12 and 14 May had to be withdrawn before its task was completed because it was needed elsewhere. Two more Spitfires were found, with difficulty, to finish the job between 28 May and 15 June. The air defences of Malta were pitifully inadequate. The RAF succeeded in mustering some 300 aircraft to support Wavell's offensive in December 1940 only at the cost of depleting its strength in the Sudan and at Alexandria and Aden. The navy's only dive-bomber in the Mediterranean theatre, or indeed in any theatre, was the Skua, a dual-purpose monoplane which served also as a fighter but was no faster than the Gauntlet. Its standard torpedo-bomber in all theatres was the Swordfish, a biplane with a maximum speed of 139 miles an hour.

How the Italians would start the war could only be surmised. Some intelligence material was available, but it was not conclusive. The Italian Navy was known from signal intelligence to have carried out in the summer of 1939 an exercise which simulated an attempt to intercept the Mediterranean Fleet in the Eastern Mediterranean with the help of submarines and aircraft.[19] A document obtained by the French before the outbreak of war with Germany indicated that Italy might aim at isolating Malta, severing the Eastern from the Western Mediterranean, and attacking the Suez Canal from Libya.[20] There was ample evidence that Marshal Rudolfo Graziani's army in Libya was too poorly equipped to launch an offensive towards the canal in the immediate future,[21] but Whitehall could not exclude the possibility of offensives by land forces against British Somaliland, France and Yugoslavia.[22] Admiral Sir Andrew Cunningham, C-in-C of the Mediterranean Fleet, expected the Italian Navy to go cautiously at first.[23] The RAF thought the Italians might begin by reinforcing the Regia Aeronautica in Libya and aiming knock-out blows at Malta and the Nile delta.[24]

*

On the day when Italy declared war, the Italian Army and the Regia Aeronautica changed the high-grade cyphers used by their forces in the Mediterranean theatre but not those used in East Africa, although later these too were changed. Lower-grade codes and cyphers were also changed, with the result that Italian tactical traffic became more difficult to read, though not unreadable. The prospect of a complete blackout of signal intelligence cost the British some anxious moments, especially as little information was forthcoming from MI 6. C had complained as long ago as 1935 that lack of money had compelled him to curtail his activites in countries from which good information about Italy might have been obtained.[25] The situation had not improved a great deal since that time, despite eleventh-hour attempts to establish networks in Italy and the Italian empire in North and East Africa.

To make matters worse, regular photographic cover of a vast new theatre of war seemed at first an unattainable ideal. At the height of the invasion scare at home, the Air Ministry was not prepared to station reconnaissance Spitfires more or less permanently outside the United Kingdom. Flying-boats working from Gibraltar, Alexandria and some-times Malta were fitted with cameras and their crews were told to seize such opportunities of taking photographs as came their way, but the primary role of these aircraft was visual reconnaissance over the sea. Malta-based Glenn Martin medium bombers (afterwards called Mary-land) proved more suitable. In the context of plans for the reorganization of the photographic reconnaissance system as a whole, the Air Ministry decided in October 1940 that a new photographic reconnaissance unit (No. 2 PRU) should be formed in the Middle East and equipped in the first instance with Marylands, and that the Marylands already working from Malta should be reinforced. Attempts made early in 1941 to implement these decisions were unsuccessful. A batch of Marylands consigned to No. 2 PRU in January was lost at sea. A second batch arrived safely in April but was pronounced unsatisfactory. As a stop-gap measure No. 1 PRU sent two Marylands from the United Kingdom to a forward base at Gibraltar, but reconnaissance of the Western Desert for the benefit of Wavell's land forces had to be done by Blenheims and Lysanders. To supplement these too-vulnerable aircraft three modified Hurricanes were sent to Egypt by way of the Gold Coast and French Equatorial Africa, but on arrival they were promptly restored to their original form and used as fighters.[26]

Photographic interpreters, too, were scarce outside the United Kingdom. Until 1941 the British Army and the RAF in the Middle East had only one trained interpretations officer between them.[27]

From the outset valuable information was, however, obtained from prisoners-of-war, captured documents, and censored or intercepted correspondence.[28] Moreover, before long both the Italian Army's and the Regia Aeronautica's new cyphers were broken by the Government Code and Cypher School. Problems of secure communication between Bletchley and Cairo were not overcome without some difficulty, but an accurate picture of the disposition of the enemy's land and air forces was available at GHQ and AHQ, Middle East, by the eve of Graziani's offensive in September 1940. A considerable over-assessment of his *effective* strength in the air was due chiefly to an inadequate allowance for unserviceable aircraft.[29]

Italian diplomatic traffic continued after the outbreak of war to be read without a break. The Royal Navy had the happy thought of cutting the cable between Genoa and Malaga. Urgent messages between Rome and Madrid – and most diplomatic messages seem urgent to their originators – had therefore to be put on the air. No revelations of outstanding strategic interest were forthcoming, but exchanges between the Foreign Ministry and various European capitals threw some light on economic affairs and the activities of the Italian secret service.[30]

Naval intelligence problems proved more recalcitrant. Until 5 July 1940 both the Italian surface fleet and Italian submarines used a general cypher which was largely readable. On that date the Italian Navy, having lost ten submarines of which at least one was known to have been captured more or less intact, introduced a separate system for underwater craft. On 17 July it adopted new tables for its general cypher, and on 1 October new tables for its most secret cypher. As a result of these changes comparatively little Italian naval traffic was read after the first few weeks of hostilities. From September 1940 the British were able to read signals encyphered by a version of the Enigma machine modified in the light of experience in the Spanish Civil War, but the machine was not used by the navy after the summer of 1941, and in the meantime was employed to encypher only one or two messages a day.[31]

Thus there was some ground for the complaint made afterwards by Admiral Cunningham that, at any rate in the early months of the war in the Mediterranean, he was rather sparsely furnished with information from intelligence sources and had 'no subterranean access to Italian secret documents or decisions'.[32] Like Vice-Admiral Sir James Somerville, who commanded from the end of June a detached squadron based on Gibraltar, Cunningham was conscious that he depended for his knowledge of the enemy's movements largely on reconnaissance aircraft of which there never seemed to be enough. The intelligence staffs were unable to predict sailings of Italian convoys to Libya; they gave no warning of the enemy's use of midget submarines and motor-boats carrying explosive charges. On the other hand it could be said that, in a sense, Cunningham did have some access to Italian secret documents, inasmuch as most of the Italian Navy's codes and cyphers had been read for months or years past when hostilities began. At that stage he was, in fact, fairly well provided with information about the strength and general characteristics of the Italian fleet. Moreover, he was by no means left wholly in the dark thereafter. On the first day of hostilities the Operational Intelligence Centre at Alexandria accurately reported the proximity of Italian warships to his fleet, although the warning did not reach him in time to be of use because its transmission was delayed.[33] Information from signal intelligence received during an encounter with the Italian fleet off the coast of Calabria on 9 July enabled him to avoid a trap that had been laid for him.[34] Reconnaissance aircraft were not so scarce that they failed to provide him with information needed for bombardments of the African coast and attacks by naval aircraft on objectives at Tobruk and Bomba in July and August. The success of an attack by aircraft from the carrier *Illustrious* on the Italian battlefleet at Taranto on 11 November was due largely to the excellence of the information furnished by Glenn Martin photographic reconnaissance aircraft from Malta.[35] The Glenn Martins also gave Cunningham his best material about the results of the attack, although some information was obtained, too, from a decrypted signal.[36]

Before and during the offensive launched by Wavell in December, the intelligence services provided a wealth of information about the strength and disposition of Graziani's forces and his logistic problems. Thereafter the limiting factor, both at home and in the field, was not so much the quantity or quality of the information received as the ability of intelligence officers to handle so much material and to draw conclusions which satisfied both themselves and the authorities they served. At the same time, increases in the amount of material received from signal intelligence and photographic reconnaissance tended to reduce the importance attached by the service departments and inter-service bodies to reports from agents, with the result that MI 6 had some difficulty in securing priority for its needs with respect to such matters as the provision of aircraft, submarines or surface vessels to carry its agents to foreign countries.[37] From the late summer of 1940 MI 6 had also to compete with the Special Operations Executive. This was unfortunate at a time when it was also competing with espionage organizations serving exiled Allied governments or quasi-governmental bodies operating from the United Kingdom. Its relations with such bodies were not improved by the failure of the attempt made in September 1940 to disembark an expeditionary force at Dakar for the purpose of persuading the French colonial authorities in Senegal to throw in their lot with General de Gaulle, or by its well-founded suspicion that one cause of this setback was that news of the expedition had been leaked to the Vichy government.[38]

Throughout this difficult period the Joint Intelligence Committee remained to a considerable extent a peripheral body, too heavily burdened with administrative responsibilities to give adequate attention to its primary tasks of warning the Chiefs of Staff and the War Cabinet about important strategic developments and predicting the future course of the war. From the autumn of 1940 prediction was, in any case, made difficult by the receipt of conflicting accounts of Axis intentions from intelligence and diplomatic sources. We now know that as early as the end of July OKH was trying to divert Hitler's attention from such dangerous courses as an invasion of the United Kingdom and an attack on the Soviet Union by advocating the despatch of armoured forces to Libya, an attack on Gibraltar through Spain, and an advance from the Balkans to the Suez Canal by way of Turkey and Syria. The British did not know that eventually all these proposals were to be rejected, although ultimately German armour *was* sent to Libya in circumstances rather different from those envisaged in 1940. The result was that, throughout the winter and early spring of 1940–41, their response to reports of Axis infiltration of the Balkans was coloured by the belief that a pincers movement against the Suez Canal from Libya and through Turkey and Syria was being seriously considered. The intelligence authorities and the Chiefs of Staff were all the readier to believe this because they considered that such a movement would give Hitler his best chance of ending the war quickly, especially if it preceded or accompanied an invasion of the United Kingdom. Largely because the Luftwaffe's first-line strength and reserves were still over-estimated, they were slow to recognize that invasion of the United Kingdom had ceased to be regarded by the Germans as a practical operation of war and that invasion preparations were being continued only as a blind.[39]

Evidence of Axis concern with the Balkans was not lacking. The Germans were known as early as the summer of 1940 to be actively interested in the security of the Rumanian oil-wells at Ploesti.[40] In the last week of September the imminent arrival of German anti-aircraft units at Ploesti was reported.[41] Presumably in the light of OKH proposals not accepted by OKW, Thümmel predicted on 29 September that German troops would enter Rumania early in October as the prelude to an attack on Turkey accompanied by an Italian offensive in Libya and a German advance through Spain.[42] As things turned out, all that happened in Rumania early in October was that German military and air force missions arrived there without concealment, ostensibly for the purpose of giving advice about the training of Rumanian troops and airmen. Soon afterwards the Italians were reliably reported to be reinforcing their troops in Albania with a view to the invasion of Greece which they duly but ineffectively launched on 28 October.[43] Almost simultaneously, Enigma traffic began to reveal the move to Rumania of Luftwaffe units formerly used against the United Kingdom, and to show that the Luftwaffe was interested not only in Rumania but also in Bulgaria. The Germans were known, too, to be forming new mechanized divisions and moving divisions from Western Europe to Poland.[44]

In the light of this and other evidence, the Joint Planning Staff in London concluded at the beginning of November that Italy's invasion of Greece was likely to be accompanied by a peaceful occupation of Bulgaria by German forces. These incursions, the Joint Planners thought, would be followed by a German advance into Turkey-in-Europe by the end of the year and a thrust into Syria and possibly Iraq in 1941.[45] With no dissent from the Joint Intelligence Committee or the service departments, they added that Germany's land and air forces were, in their opinion, quite strong enough for her to undertake such operations without ceasing to threaten Britain with invasion.[46]

As Hitler did not decide against the proposed attack on Gibraltar until December, and even then hoped to revive the project later, it is not surprising that this possibility, too, continued to receive attention in London and to figure in agents' reports and diplomatic warnings. The arrival in Sicily by the end of 1940 of Luftwaffe units and a Fliegerkorps headquarters associated with anti-shipping operations was duly noted by Air Intelligence, and by the third week in January the Germans were known to be using airfields not only there but also in Sardinia and North Africa.[47] The disembarkation of leading elements of the Afrika Korps in Libya in February 1941, on the other hand, came as a surprise so far as its timing was concerned, although the eventual arrival of German armour in the North African theatre had long been expected.[48]

In the meantime the Air Ministry's estimates of German air strength were sharply challenged by the Prime Minister's Scientific Adviser, Professor Lindemann, and by Churchill himself. Air Intelligence had credited the Luftwaffe in the early summer of 1940 with a first-line establishment of 5,000 or more aircraft, including 2,500 bombers, and 7,000 aircraft in reserve. On that basis the Joint Intelligence Committee had calculated that up to 4,800 tons of bombs a day might be dropped on the United Kingdom.[49] In July the Air Ministry submitted revised estimates of 1,250 effective long-range bombers and 1,800 bombs a day, but it continued to attribute to the Luftwaffe large stored reserves which could not be located, and a far greater first-line establishment than seemed compatible with its performance. In December Lindemann brought matters to a head by arranging conferences between representatives of the Air Ministry and the Ministry of Economic Warfare and their critics. At one such conference, on 7 December, Churchill and Lindemann discussed the problem with spokesmen for the departments for more than four hours without arriving at any firm conclusion.[50] Churchill then set out, in a carefully-considered memorandum, his reasons for thinking that the Luftwaffe's first-line strength could not exceed about 3,000 aircraft if the Ministry of Economic Warfare's production figures were correct. At the same time he proposed an enquiry by an independent investigator, Mr Justice Singleton.

By taking as his point of departure an arbitrary assumption about the size of the Luftwaffe's reserves on the outbreak of war, Singleton did not give himself much chance of ending the controversy. At highly secret Anglo-American staff conversations held soon after his enquiry was completed, the Americans were told that the Luftwaffe was believed to have a first-line establishment of 5,710 aircraft, an actual strength of 4,900 aircraft, about 3,230 serviceable aircraft and some 2,800 aircraft in reserve.[51] Figures which assumed such a low rate of serviceability for an air force believed to have such large reserves can scarcely have seemed convincing. Moreover, the estimate of first-line establishment did not meet Lindemann's objections. Singleton did, however, make a valuable contribution to the debate by drawing attention to the difficulty of reconciling the Air Ministry's establishment figure with the numbers of units and formations identified by signal intelligence.[52] In the light of a fresh examination of this evidence, Lindemann came to the conclusion that the reason why the Air Ministry's establishment figure was so high was that it included immediate reserves which, in his opinion, ought to be excluded. He pointed out that 134 German long-range bomber squadrons had been identified. Each was credited by Air Intelligence with a first-line establishment of twelve aircraft, but three of these were reserve aircraft intended to replace losses or stand in for aircraft undergoing repair or routine maintenance. If these were excluded, then the first-line establishment of the long-range bomber force would work out at some 1,200 to 1,300 aircraft.[53] On the assumption that long-range bombers accounted for about a third of the total strength, which was generally accepted, the first-line establishment of the Luftwaffe as a whole would be about 3,900 aircraft. These figures were consistent not only with the Air Ministry's recent estimate of 3,230 serviceable aircraft, but also with what was known or could be inferred about the scale of attack achieved by the Luftwaffe in the past. The only rational basis on which the first-line establishment of a squadron could be assessed was, in Lindemann's opinion, the number of aircraft it was expected to put in the air on active operations. In the case of a German bomber or fighter squadron, this was not twelve aircraft but nine.

Lindemann's argument was not accepted by Air Intelligence without demur, but eventually it was accepted. At a meeting on 20 February 1941 representatives of the planning and intelligence directorates of the Air Ministry agreed with Lindemann that, subject to further calculations by the Director of Intelligence, the basic unit of the Luftwaffe should henceforward be regarded as the squadron, or Staffel, of nine aircraft. The final outcome was that, after adjustments had been made for operational aircraft held on the establishments of higher formations than the Staffel, the Luftwaffe's first-line establishment was assessed on 24 March at 4,284 aircraft.[54] This was close to what we now know to have been, according to the German reckoning, the true figure of 4,508 aircraft.

Attempts to assess the strength of the German Army in terms of major formations formed or forming aroused far less controversy, but were by no means uniformly successful. The War Office was well informed about the numbers of armoured and motorized divisions, which it put in the autumn of 1940 at eleven and eight respectively.[55] Its estimates of the numbers of divisions of all categories available on various dates were less satisfactory. The disbandment of some divisions and the formation of new divisions after the fall of France made the document captured in May no longer valid, and lack of contact with German troops between the summer of 1940 and the arrival of the Afrika Korps in Libya in 1941 ruled out any immediate prospect of further captures. Army Enigma traffic could not yet be read, such tactical traffic as was intercepted while the German Army was regrouping was also unreadable, and Luftwaffe traffic did not throw much light on army matters until active operations in the Balkan theatre were imminent. Photographic reconnaissance continued to reveal apparent signs in France and the Low Countries of preparations for a deferred Operation Sea Lion, but made few contributions to the identification of units and formations. MI 6 was handicapped during much of 1940 by the after-effects of peacetime economies and the low priority accorded to its requests for the means of putting agents into occupied Europe. Towards the end of the year some good information was received from agents in the Scandinavian coun-tries, Poland, Rumania and the Protectorate of Bohemia and Moravia, but formations in France, Belgium, the Netherlands, Germany, Austria and Slovakia could seldom be identified with certainty.[56] In the absence of positive information, Military Intelligence tended to err on the safe side by assuming that sooner or later the Germans would manage to provide themselves with the 250 divisions which was believed to be the largest number their economy could support.[57] We now know that they were aiming in the autumn of 1940 at a total of 180 divisions by the spring of 1941 and that in the following June they had 208, SS divisions included. This figure included twenty armoured divisions, but the apparent doubling of Germany's armoured strength since the campaign in France and the Low Countries was achieved at the cost of a substantial reduction in the number of tanks held by each division. In general, the quality of the German tanks was, however, higher in 1941 than in 1940, when many units were equipped with the obsolescent PzKw I.

*

We have seen that in the autumn and early winter of 1940 evidence of Axis interest in the Balkans led the authorities in London to suspect that Germany was aiming at a thrust to the Middle East by way of Bulgaria and Turkey. These alarms were followed in the early part of December by something of a lull, but from the third week of that month there were many indications of an impending concentration of German land and air forces within striking distance of the frontier between Rumania and Bulgaria. In the light of reports that Germany intended to invade Greece in the near future by way of Bulgaria, the War Cabinet instructed the Commanders-in-Chief in the Middle East on 10 January 1941 to offer substantial aid to Greece. Wavell, preoccupied with his successful offensive in Cyrenaica, suggested that the Germans might be bluffing, but Churchill insisted that the evidence available in London did not support that conclusion. We now know that an advance into Thrace by three or four divisions about the middle of January was in fact tentatively proposed by OKH, but that Hitler stood out for a much larger force and that preparations which involved long-drawn negotiations with Bulgaria could not in any case have been completed within that time.

As the Greeks declined the British offer, and in view of further reports to the effect that the Bulgarians were still stalling, the Defence

Committee authorized Wavell to continue his advance to Benghazi, but stipulated that he should build up a mobile force in Egypt with a view to its possible use in Greece or Turkey within the next two months.

During the next few weeks the British received a great deal of evidence which pointed to German preparations for a southward move from Bulgaria but suggested that these were not likely to be completed before the beginning of March. Some of this evidence came from Luftwaffe Enigma, some from agents, some from other sources. German railway Enigma, which the Government Code and Cypher School was able to read from early February, revealed a massive movement of Luftwaffe stores to destinations in southern Bulgaria.[58] Abwehr traffic in a cypher distinct from that used for routine communications with agents, and not read before December 1940, showed that the main focus of interest for German military intelligence had shifted from Western to South-Eastern Europe and that the Abwehr counted on establishing in Greece an intelligence centre of a kind associated with occupied countries.[59] Information about the state of Bulgarian communications and the efforts that were being made by the Germans to repair roads and strengthen bridges supported the general impression that German troops were unlikely to enter Bulgaria in strength before the beginning of March.[60]

In the light of such evidence, the Director of Military Intelligence and his staff estimated in February that five German divisions might reach the frontier between Bulgaria and Greece shortly before the middle of March, and Salonika a week later. Assuming that the Greeks would fight, they calculated that ten German divisions might arrive in the neighbourhood of Athens some time between the middle of April and the middle of May.[61]

The Defence Committee considered the implications of this hypothetical time-table at a fateful meeting on 11 February. The Greek dictator General Metaxas had died a fortnight earlier. A new government was thought likely to take a more favourable view than Metaxas of British intervention. The committee noted that, if the Director of Military Intelligence was right, there would be time for British troops to reach northern Greece from Egypt before the Germans opened their attack. Churchill and the Chiefs of Staff were, however, unaware that forward elements of the Afrika Korps were already on their way to Libya.[62] They decided to order Wavell to give preparations for intervention in Greece priority over continuance of his advance to Tripoli. As they knew less about the military situation in Greece – or for that matter in Yugoslavia or Turkey – than they did about the state of German preparations, they also decided to send the Foreign Secretary and the Chief of the Imperial General Staff to Cairo and Athens to examine the political and strategic implications of British intervention.

In effect, the British government thus sacrificed the virtual certainty of a decisive victory in North Africa to the slender hope that the arrival of a few British divisions and air squadrons in Greece might induce the Greeks, the Turks and possibly the Yugoslavs to make common cause with Britain against Germany. Ironically, the military authorities in Cairo afterwards contributed to their own undoing by suggesting that the Germans were unlikely to reach the frontier between Bulgaria and Greece before 11 or 12 March.[63] After Rommel was known to have arrived in Libya as commander of the Afrika Korps, they also under-estimated the time that was likely to elapse before he launched a serious offensive.[64]

The British emissaries found on their arrival in Greece that the Greek Army was largely preoccupied with the Albanian front and was doing very little to guard against a thrust from Bulgaria. The Bulgarians openly threw in their lot with the Axis powers on 1 March, the Yugoslavs were known to be under strong pressure from the Germans to follow suit, and the Turks were not receptive to offers of British help. Nevertheless the British government persisted in its decision to intervene in Greece, although at one stage it came close to reversing it, and might perhaps have done so if Wavell had come down strongly against it. Convoys which left Alexandria at intervals of three days from 5 March carried some 60,000 British troops to the Piraeus, where they disembarked in full view of the German Military Attaché and the Luftwaffe's reconnaissance aircraft.[65] Attacks on the convoys by German and Italian aircraft were not very successful. Under pressure from the Germans, the Italians therefore agreed by 20 March to take naval action, with support from reconnaissance and striking aircraft to be provided by the Luftwaffe.

The British received warning of this intention – but not, as some writers have asserted, because the new cypher tables introduced by the Italian Navy in 1940 were stolen or borrowed on their behalf by a beautiful female spy. Luftwaffe Enigma traffic revealed on 25 March that German heavy fighters had been ordered on the previous day to move from Libya to Sicily for a special operation.[66] Signals encyphered on 25 and 26 March by the Italian Navy's little-used Enigma machine showed that something exceptional was to happen on 28 March, and that information was being sought about the movements of British convoys between Alexandria and the Piraeus.[67] In the light of these signals, which were correctly interpreted by the Admiralty as referring to the same operation, Admiral Cunningham cancelled a convoy which was due to leave the Piraeus late on 26 March, ordered a convoy moving in the opposite direction to turn back under cover of darkness, and arranged that four cruisers and four destroyers already at sea should arrive at dawn on 28 March at a position south of Crete, where they would be joined by five more destroyers. He also arranged to leave Alexandria after nightfall on 27 March with the battleships *Warspite*, *Barham* and *Valiant*, the carrier *Formidable* and nine destroyers.[68]

These arrangements were made during the evening of 26 March. At 12.30 p.m. on the following day the crew of a flying-boat from Malta sighted three Italian cruisers and a destroyer heading in the general direction of Crete from a position east of Sicily. That afternoon Cunningham presented himself with his clubs and an overnight bag at a golf-course frequented by the Japanese Consul-General, who was known to be in the habit of reporting the movements of the Mediterranean Fleet. After making sure that he had been seen, he returned to Alexandria and took his fleet to sea.

The outcome was the Battle of Cape Matapan. The Italians lost three heavy cruisers and two destroyers; the British no ships and only one aircraft. The battle was remarkable for the contrast between the excellence of the information furnished by signal intelligence and air reconnaissance, and the limited achievement of Cunningham's torpedo-bombers. The Italian battleship *Vittorio Veneto* was hit by only one torpedo in the course of numerous attacks.

We now know that Hitler's conception of the Greek campaign changed radically after British troops began to arrive in Greece. Hitherto he had intended to seize only Thrace and part of Macedonia in order to prevent the British from establishing air bases within striking-distance of the Rumanian oilfields. On 17 March he decided to occupy the whole country. OKH had therefore to allot a larger force to the enterprise and allow more time for its completion by advancing the target-date for the assault from 7 to 1 April. These changes of plan were not known to the British at the time, but Luftwaffe Enigma traffic decrypted on 23 March suggested that the Germans had either completed their preparations or would do so within the next few days.[69] As things turned out, the opening of the assault had to be postponed until 6 April in consequence of unexpected developments in Yugoslavia.

From the British point of view, the essence of the situation in Yugoslavia about the middle of March was that the Yugoslavs were believed to be fairly well armed by Balkan standards, but were known to be under strong pressure to join the Rome–Berlin Axis. As the line the British hoped to hold in Greece could be turned by an advance through Yugoslavia to the Monastir gap, the Foreign Office and the British Legation in Belgrade aimed at persuading the Regent Prince Paul and his ministers not to grant Germany the right of transit for her troops, even if they had to make other concessions. By 18 March that policy was deemed by the British Minister and his staff to have failed. Their opinion was shared by local representatives of MI 6 and by representatives of SOE who were using Yugoslavia as a base for attempts to organize resistance movements in the Balkans. On 20 March a majority of the Yugoslav Cabinet agreed in principle that Yugoslavia should adhere to the Tripartite Pact, but three ministers resigned in accordance with a plan preconcerted with the British.[70] On the following day the British Minister asked the Foreign Office whether the British government would approve of a *coup d'état* and support a new régime. On 23 March Anthony Eden, then in Cairo, gave him provisional authority to act as he thought fit; on 24 March he received full authority to do so. The sequel was that Yugoslavia's formal acceptance of the Tripartite Pact on 25 March was followed two days later by a *coup d'état* organized by army and air force officers with some help from the British service attachés and SOE.

Even though there would almost certainly have been a *coup d'état* in any case, this was SOE's first major intervention in European politics. The consequences from the British point of view were disappointing. For fear of provoking instant reprisals, Yugoslavia's new rulers refrained from immediately denouncing the Tripartite Pact and organizing defensive measures. The War Office thought Yugoslav resistance would force the Germans to move another thirty-two or thirty-three divisions to the Balkans; in fact they added only twelve to the seventeen already earmarked for the attack on Greece.[71] Greece and Yugoslavia were invaded simultaneously on 6 April; in a few weeks the British were driven from the mainland of Greece with substantial losses. In the meantime Rommel also belied British expectations by launching an offensive which drove Wavell's forces from practically the whole of Cyrenaica except a small bridgehead at Tobruk. These were disasters which the intelligence agencies were powerless to prevent, but which might have been averted if the authorities in London and Cairo had brought more realism to the study of the information they provided.

*

Of the attack on Crete which followed in May, the intelligence services had good warning. They also provided, a fortnight in advance, a detailed account of the enemy's plan, including an accurate list of his objectives.

From the last week f March, Luftwaffe Enigma traffic showed that the Germans were concentrating airborne forces in the Balkans for purposes which did not become clear until some weeks later.[72] Evidence from an undisclosed source led Military Intelligence to believe as early as 25 March that an expedition to Lemnos was intended.[73] The information was correct, but reports that transport aircraft were arriving in large numbers suggested that some more important objective was in view. Crete (where the Mediterranean Fleet had established an advanced fuelling base at Suda Bay) seemed an obvious choice. Alternatively, the Germans might aim at capturing Cyprus or gaining a foothold in Syria.

Before long the difficulty of deciding which of these objectives was the most probable was further increased by developments in Iraq. About the middle of April the Nationalist leader Rashid Ali, who had been put in power by officers of the Iraqi Army at the beginning of the month, was known from decrypted signals to be making urgent appeals to the Axis powers for support.[74] An airborne expedition to Iraq in one hop was not very probable, but Iraq might be the ultimate objective of an expedition to Syria.

We now know that an expedition to Crete was proposed in March by General Kurt Student of Fliegerkorps XI, and that his proposals were discussed at a Führer conference on 21 April. Hitler is said to have remarked: 'It sounds good, but it won't work.' Nevertheless he gave his approval four days later, after rejecting a landing in Malta on the ground that it could not be done unless the Italians were brought in. Student had directed airborne operations against the Low Countries in May 1940, and had commanded Fliegerkorps XI since its formation in December. He envisaged the operation – afterwards called Operation Mercury – as the first stage of a three-stage advance to the Suez Canal by way of Crete and Cyprus. The gist of the plan was that some 15,000 troops of Fliegerkorps XI were to be carried from the neighbourhood of Athens to Crete in 530 transport aircraft and 100 gliders. Heavy equipment, supplies, and some 7,000 troops of the 5th Mountain Division temporarily under Student's command were to follow by sea. About 650 long-range bombers, dive-bombers, single-seater fighters, heavy fighters and reconnaissance aircraft of Fliegerkorps VIII were to provide air support. D-day was to have been 17 May, but it had to be put back to 19 May, and finally to 20 May, because the arrival of fuel, bombs and ammunition was delayed by damage done to roads and railways during the fighting on the Greek mainland.

For the British the campaign on the mainland consisted largely of withdrawals by which they escaped encirclement, despite the turning of their forward positions by the advance through Monastir. The successful timing of these withdrawals owed a great deal to the decrypting and interpretation by the Government Code and Cypher School of Enigma messages in which Luftwaffe liaison officers reported the positions and immediate intentions of army formations to which they were attached.[75] As a result of the extension to Greece of the direct link with Cairo established in March, the GC & CS was able for the first time in the war to transmit up-to-date appreciations, based on the most recent decrypts, to commanders in the field. Another innovation was the use of the first fully mobile Y unit to reach the Middle East. It had been intended to handle mostly low-grade Italian traffic, but many of its officers had served in France and Belgium in 1940 and knew German as well as Italian. They had copies of Luftwaffe tactical codes and the Luftwaffe bomber-grid, and were therefore able to exploit the Luftwaffe's tactical traffic as well as the German Army's plain-language transmissions. The German Army's tactical codes and cyphers, on the other hand, remained unreadable, chiefly because scarcely any of its tactical traffic had been intercepted between the fall of France and the time when contact was renewed almost simultaneously in Greece and North Africa. The contribution made by field intelligence was limited, too, by difficulties of communication during the retreat, and by the very fact that – thanks largely to the Enigma decrypts – the heavily outnumbered British land forces were able to avoid a major clash with the main body of the enemy's troops. Some prisoners were taken and interrogated, and there was some visual but no photographic air reconnaissance.[76]

By the end of March forward elements of Fliegerkorps XI were known to have reached Plovdiv in Bulgaria. Enigma revealed by 18 April that 250 transport aircraft had been withdrawn from routine duties for Student's benefit, by 24 April that some of them were to be used for a special operation. This turned out to be an attempt to cut the British line of retreat by the dropping of paratroops near the Corinth Canal on 26 April. By that date Fliegerkorps XI was known to have been given priority for supplies of fuel, and mention had been made in the Enigma traffic of the importance of getting supplies to its area by 5 May. Moreover, a combination of railway and Luftwaffe Enigma showed that the transfer of part of Student's paratroop division to the Balkans was due to begin on 27 April, and references were made in the Luftwaffe Enigma on 26 April to 'Operation Crete' and to a request by Luftflotte 4 for maps and photographs of Crete.[77]

As late as the end of April, the Chiefs of Staff and the authorities in Cairo did not exclude the possibility that these references might be part of a cover-plan for an expedition to Cyprus and Syria.[78] In the meantime the direct link from the GC & CS had been extended to Crete. It was used on 16 and again on 21 April to warn the authorities there that preparations for an airborne expedition were being made in Bulgaria. On 18 April Wavell warned them that Crete was a possible objective.[79] On 22 April the link was used to urge them to burn all the signals they had received by it. As Churchill ruled that they were none the less to continue to receive the Enigma material, arrangements were made when Major-General Bernard Freyberg assumed command of the defences on 30 April for it to be passed to him in the guise of information from an agent in Athens. One of Freyberg's first acts was to warn his forces that they could expect an attack within the next two days.

Enigma soon showed that the assault was not as imminent as that, but confirmed that Crete was the objective. Signals decrypted between 1 and 5 May indicated that most of Fliegerkorps XI was still in Germany at the beginning of the month, that Student had been asked to say by 6 May when it could arrive in Greece, that Fliegerkorps VIII did not expect to move its headquarters from Plovdiv to Athens until 8 May. They also revealed that Fliegerkorps VIII had been ordered not to destroy Cretan ports and airfields, but to lay on extensive air reconnaissance and arrange for the preparation of a photographic mosaic of the island.[80]

On 6 May the Luftwaffe traffic yielded an even richer harvest. It showed that the Germans estimated that preparations would be completed on 17 May, and it carried detailed orders for the operation. Paratroops were to be dropped near Maleme, Canea (Khania), Retimo (Rethymnon) and Heraklion for the purpose of seizing airfields at the first, third and fourth of these places on the first day, occupying Canea and taking possession of the naval base at Suda Bay. Fighters and dive-bombers would move to Crete when the airfields were safely in

German hands; anti-aircraft units, heavy equipment, supplies and reinforcements were to follow by sea.[81]

General Freyberg would thus have at least ten or eleven days – and in the outcome had two weeks – in which to dispose his 40,000 British, British Commonwealth and Greek troops in such a manner as to make it unlikely that Maleme, Retimo and Heraklion would succumb to the largest force the enemy could bring to bear against them. How large that force would be the material decrypted on 6 May did not show. Freyberg was told ten days later that the Germans were expected to use 25,000 to 30,000 airborne troops – about twice the true figure – but clearly the strength of the first wave would depend on how many transport aircraft were available. The figure given to Freyberg was 600, which was about right if towed gliders are counted as transport aircraft. Whitehall estimated that 855 combat aircraft would support the landings. Cairo's estimate was 440, the true figure (reconnaissance aircraft excluded) about 600. The strength of the seaborne force was estimated at 10,000. The true figure was somewhere between 6,500 and 7,000, and in the outcome no troops arrived by sea while the battle was in progress.

Freyberg reported on 5 May that he was 'not in the least anxious' about the airborne assault.[82] He gave the impression that he regarded the seaborne expedition as a greater threat. However that may be, there is no doubt that the authorities in London and elsewhere went to a great deal of trouble to give him all the help they could, and to convince him of the importance of not allowing the airfields at Maleme, Retimo and Heraklion to be captured by airborne troops. Churchill wrote later of the pains he took to 'study and weigh the evidence' and to 'make sure that the magnitude of the impending assault was impressed upon the C-in-C and imparted to the General on the actual scene'.[83] A plan designed to ensure that maximum losses were inflicted on the enemy was drawn up by the Air Ministry after consultation with the Admiralty and the War Office and transmitted to Cairo.[84] Wavell sent an officer to Crete to bring home to Freyberg and his staff the relevance and importance of the information communicated to them.[85]

Decrypted signals continued between 7 and 19 May to provide useful information. They confirmed the arrival in the Athens area of Fliegerkorps XI and showed that the Germans were assembling shipping for the seaborne expedition. They reported German estimates of the results of softening-up attacks on Crete. They showed on 15 May that D-day had been postponed from 17 to 19 May. On 19 May they showed that German commanders were to meet that day with maps and photographs of Maleme, Canea, Retimon and Heraklion and that probably the assault would be launched on the following day. In the light of the decrypts the Defence Committee ruled on 14 and 15 May that the defence of Crete should take precedence over precautionary measures in Syria and Iraq and attempts to curb the flow of supplies to Rommel's forces in North Africa. By revealing the areas where German forces were assembling, the Enigma traffic also guided the RAF's choice of objectives for spoiling attacks.[86]

The outcome of the assault was awaited in London and Cairo with a confidence tempered by the knowledge that the Germans were superior in the air and that therefore a good deal might turn on the extent to which the defenders succeeded in rounding up the paratroops while the situation on the ground was still so confused that Fliegerkorps VIII would not dare to use its close-support units freely for fear of bombing its own side. At nightfall on 20 May all the objectives which were to have been captured on the first day were still untaken. On the following day, as a result of information from signal intelligence, the crew of an aircraft from Egypt sighted the first wave of the seaborne expedition. This was a convoy of caiques escorted by an Italian torpedo-boat. Shortly before midnight three cruisers and four destroyers of the Mediterranean Fleet sank about half the convoy, dispersed the rest and damaged the torpedo-boat. A second wave of caiques turned back but was caught and attacked at dawn on 22 May. The seaborne expedition was then abandoned. In the meantime Student made the bold decision to start landing troops of the 5th Mountain Division on the airfield at Maleme, which was more or less in German hands but swept by artillery fire. Their arrival turned the scale. The Mayor of Canea surrendered the town to a dishevelled paratroop commander on 27 May. Survivors of Freyberg's force began to embark at Heraklion and Sphakia on 28 May, and on 1 June a signal from Luftflotte 4 announced that Crete was clear of the enemy.[87] The British lost about 15,000 soldiers killed, wounded or captured and about 2,000 sailors killed or wounded, but Fliegerkorps XI's losses were so heavy that no large-scale airborne landings were attempted by the Germans throughout the rest of the war. Freyberg's failure to hold Crete was none the less a bitter disappointment to the cryptanalysts and intelligence officers who had kept him posted about the enemy's intentions and dispositions.

*

The intelligence organization made outstanding contributions to the defeat of the Italian forces in East Africa. Some information was obtained from captured documents, but signal intelligence was the main source. Soon after the opening of hostilities the Italians captured frontier posts at Kassala in the Sudan and Moyale in Kenya, and in August they entered British Somaliland. As the British continued to hold Egypt and the rest of the Sudan and to maintain a somewhat precarious grip on the Red Sea, Italy's East African empire was, however, completely cut off from metropolitan Italy so far as surface communications were concerned. The Italian authorities in Abyssinia, Eritrea and the Somalilands had therefore to put all their traffic with metropolitan Italy on the air. In November 1940 the GC & CS broke the new high-grade cypher used by the Italian Army in East Africa.[88] The Regia Aeronautica's East African high-grade cypher was changed in the same month, but the new cypher was soon broken by the Middle East Combined Bureau.[89] Lower-grade codes and cyphers used by the colonial authorities and the armed forces for local traffic were also broken. When the British turned to the offensive in East Africa in January 1941, they were therefore well informed about the strength and weakness of the enemy's forces and his difficulties of supply. From that time until the campaign ended with a formal surrender by the Duke of Aosta at Amba Alagi in the third week of May, the Middle East Combined Bureau or its outpost at Nairobi read as promptly as the authorized recipients – and sometimes more promptly – a stream of signals which ranged from the Viceroy's daily situation reports to returns made by the humblest unit in the field.[90]

In these circumstances the lack of a strong espionage network in Italian East Africa and a shortage of reconnaissance aircraft were not serious disadvantages. Apart from the enormous contribution made by signal intelligence, the British commanders received some help from partisans organized during the winter of 1940–41 by Brigadier D. A. Sandford, and later from Gideon Force. This was a body of irregular troops formed by Captain Orde C. Wingate round the nucleus of a Sudanese battalion. When Haile Selassie re-entered his capital a month before the surrender at Amba Alagi, he was accompanied by Wingate.

*

The intelligence organization did not show up so well before and during Rommel's offensive in Cyrenaica in the first half of 1941. The belief that sooner or later German armour would arrive in North Africa had led to the despatch of an armoured brigade from the United Kingdom to

Egypt in August 1940, when the outcome of the Battle of Britain was still uncertain. But German intervention was not then regarded as imminent. Some three months later the general opinion in intelligence circles was that German land forces were unlikely to appear on the battlefield before their introduction to the Mediterranean theatre was revealed by wireless traffic and the arrival of Luftwaffe units.[91]

However, when German aircraft did turn up in the Mediterranean theatre at the end of the year, they were correctly identified as belonging to units which specialized in attacks on shipping. Air Intelligence reported on 27 December that such aircraft had made wireless contact with controls in Italy, and the Luftwaffe was known by 4 January to have established bases in Sicily.[92] The fact remains that, although the Air Ministry knew by that date that attacks by German aircraft on the Mediterranean Fleet might be expected in the near future and the Chiefs of Staff referred in their résumé on 9 January to the arrival of Luftwaffe units in Sicily, attacks which severely damaged the *Illustrious* on 10 January and sank the cruiser *Southampton* two days later came as a surprise to the naval authorities at Alexandria and Gibraltar.[93]

The authorities were also rather slow to admit that the signs pointed to early intervention by German land forces. By the middle of January Luftwaffe tactical traffic revealed that German aircraft were operating over Libya.[94] At the same time, agents and diplomatic sources reported that the German Army was assembling equipment suitable for an African campaign and despatching troops and stores to Italy, but these warnings do not seem to have been taken very seriously either in London or in Cairo.[95] Even when air reconnaissance showed that by 3 February nearly half a million tons of shipping suitable for the transport of an expeditionary force was concentrated at Naples, neither the War Office nor the military intelligence staff in Cairo went so far as to say that the arrival of German troops in Libya was imminent.[96] Two days before the first Afrika Korps convoy left Naples for Tripoli on 8 February, the War Office conceded that an expedition of some kind was in prospect, but implied in its brief for the Chiefs of Staff résumé that Malta or Tunisia was at least as probable an objective as Libya.[97] The military intelligence staff in Cairo did not allow for German intervention when assessing the situation in Libya on 8 February.[98] The Air Ministry thought a week later that the Germans were not much concerned about the fate of the Italian empire in Africa and that even the Italians were more interested in saving what they could from the wreck of it than in restoring their ascendancy.[99]

On 9 February a signal transmitted by the Regia Aeronautica in its high-grade cypher referred to the escort by German and Italian aircraft of convoys between Naples and Tripoli. The GC & CS was not satisfied that its rendering of the signal was accurate in all respects, but was fairly sure that the convoys were German.[100] Whitehall was so reluctant to accept that interpretation that it was not until 12 February that the Admiralty passed the information to Cunningham, and not until 18 February that it warned him that the supposition that the convoys were German seemed to be correct.[101] Only four days later, German armoured cars were in contact with British troops at El Agheila and were seen elsewhere in Libya.

On 28 February the GC & CS broke a new Enigma key used by the Luftwaffe in the Mediterranean and North Africa until the end of 1941. By 3 March Rommel was identified as commander of the Afrika Korps and a good deal was learnt about the composition of his force and the disposition of its forward elements.[102] The gist of this and subsequent information was passed from the Air Ministry to Cairo by teleprinter until, on 13 March, the long-awaited direct link between the GC & CS and the Middle East came into use.

What the traffic did not show was how Rommel intended to use the resources he had and those whose arrival in the not-too-distant future it foreshadowed. Wavell suggested in an appreciation sent to Whitehall on the eve of a visit to Athens on 2 March that the newly arrived German force might make a limited advance to Agedabia, but was unlikely to try to reach Benghazi until it was built up to a strength of one infantry division and one or two armoured brigades, with transport to match.[103] His intelligence staff thought on 10 March that, even so, a thrust beyond Agedabia might be attempted, and a fortnight later that a limited offensive by one German light division and one Italian armoured division was possible, but that Rommel would scarcely try to capture Benghazi until he could bring up reinforcements unlikely to reach him before the middle of May.[104]

Views expressed by the authorities in Whitehall were not very different. The War Office did not believe that the Germans would be content with a purely defensive role. It referred early in March to indications that their strength might be built up to two armoured divisions as the prelude to a surprise attack, but could cite no convincing evidence that Rommel was likely to have such a force at his disposal within the next few weeks or even months.[105] The Joint Intelligence Committee felt that his troops would need time to acclimatize themselves.[106] The Chiefs of Staff in their corporate capacity stopped short of prognostication. The Chief of the Imperial General Staff agreed with Wavell that Rommel's offensive capacity might well be limited by difficulties of supply and maintenance.[107]

These conclusions were not unreasonable, inasmuch as Rommel had no authority from OKH to launch an offensive until the 15th Panzer Division reached him in May, or even then to advance in the first instance beyond Agedabia. The same can scarcely be said of Wavell's pronouncement on 27 March that the enemy's advanced forces near the border between Tripolitania and Cyrenaica were mainly Italian, with no more than a 'small stiffening' of German troops. He had been warned by his intelligence staff ten days earlier that Rommel had the best part of a light division or its equivalent.[108] That was surely a good deal more than a small stiffening.

How far Wavell can be held accountable for the Greek imbroglio is another question. The War Cabinet's decision to send British troops to Greece was made in principle on 24 February, two days after the first encounter with German mechanized units at El Agheila. When the matter was reconsidered in the first week of March, the government was influenced by Wavell's prediction that the Afrika Korps would not be ready for more than a limited offensive before the summer, and by his too-hopeful estimate of the minimum force needed to hold Cyrenaica. But the government's decision to go ahead with the Greek expedition was not based solely on Wavell's advice, nor was it influenced solely by considerations that came within his scope. Developments in Yugoslavia which transformed the outlook were not foreseen in the first week of March, and it was surely the business of the Foreign Office rather than the military authorities in Cairo to foresee them. The strategy to which Wavell assented was framed on the assumption that Greece would be attacked only through Bulgaria.

*

About a month after his arrival in Libya, Rommel flew to Rome and Berlin to propose an ambitious offensive and seek reinforcements for it. Enigma revealed to the British that he was going to Berlin, but not the purpose or outcome of his visit.[109] He was told not to count on receiving more than the 15th Panzer Division, already promised to him, and to confine himself to a vigorous defence of Tripolitania until it reached him about the middle of May.

After a preliminary skirmish on 22 March, forward elements of

Rommel's 5th Light Division captured the British outpost at El Agheila without much difficulty on 24 March. On the pretext that he envisaged only a reconnaissance in force, he proceeded on 31 March to tackle the main British position at Mersa Brega.

This was held by the support group of the one British armoured division in the forward area, with an armoured brigade to the rear of its left flank. After resisting a series of attacks supported by some fifty dive-bombers, the commander on the spot suggested that the armoured brigade should relieve the pressure on his front by attacking the German right. In effect, the battle for Cyrenaica was lost when, the divisional commander having refused this request on the ground that there were only a few hours of daylight left, the support group fell back along the coast road to escape encirclement and the armoured brigade conformed with its retreat. Having abandoned the Mersa Brega position, the British were powerless to prevent Axis forces from advancing along the coast road and fanning out to the east by desert tracks. Their armoured division, equipped largely with captured Italian tanks and British cruiser tanks in need of repair, lost so many vehicles from mechanical breakdowns that it was soon reduced to impotence. The 9th Australian Division had to be hastily pulled back from its stand-by position at Benghazi to Tobruk.

After launching an unsuccessful attack on Tobruk in the middle of April, Rommel stopped in the Egyptian frontier area, having outrun his supplies. On 27 April OKH sent General Friedrich Paulus to Libya to discover his intentions and warn him not to expect large reinforcements. Rommel persuaded him, with some difficulty, to sanction a fresh attack on Tobruk. When this failed, Paulus ordered him to concentrate on holding Cyrenaica with or without Tobruk, Sollum and Bardia and on reorganizing his forces, creating mobile reserves and establishing a secure line of communication with his base.

Wavell's prediction was thus fulfilled, but only after the British had lost the airfields of Western Cyrenaica, and with them any immediate prospect of gaining control of the Sicilian Narrows and relieving Malta. Inevitably, so serious a setback exposed the intelligence authorities to a good deal of criticism.

We have already seen that, in general, the authorities were slow to awake to the threat of intervention in Libya by German land forces and measure its extent, but that Wavell's intelligence staff did warn him on 17 March that Rommel had at his disposal the best part of a light division or its equivalent. No further warning was given by intelligence of

Rommel's attack on El Agheila or his offensive at the end of March, and the high quality of his equipment came as a surprise.[110]

The British commanders received very little tactical intelligence during the retreat from Mersa Brega to the Egyptian frontier. Their mobile signal intelligence unit, which had done well during the winter offensive, was handicapped by a tightening-up of Italian security since Rommel's arrival and its unfamiliarity with German traffic. Reconnaissance on the ground was made difficult by the speed of the German advance and the superior firepower of Rommel's armoured cars. Air reconnaissance, according to the army, was inadequate, but whether this was because the RAF did not understand the army's needs, or was due to circumstances beyond the RAF's control, remains to this day a controversial question. Enigma decrypts provided some tactical intelligence, but little use could be made of it. This was partly because the GC & CS did not always know which items would be useful to operational commanders, partly because, so far as North Africa was concerned, the direct link with the GC & CS stopped at Cairo. As the Germans were known to be reading the British field codes and cyphers, such decrypts as might interest operational commanders had to be carefully screened and paraphrased before they could be passed on, with the result that they seldom arrived in time to be of use.

The strategic value of the Enigma traffic, on the other hand, was considerable. It revealed on 2 April that Fliegerführer Afrika, commanding the Luftwaffe forces in Libya, was being denied reinforcements because operations elsewhere were more important.[111] It showed in the last week of April that, although he was still asking for more aircraft and claimed to be short of fuel, his superiors considered his resources adequate for tasks which they defined as the defence of Axis shipping at Benghazi and attacks on British shipping off Tobruk.[112] It furnished evidence on 5 April that Rommel was exceeding his instructions by advancing beyond Agedabia, on 14 April that most of his units were taking up defensive positions close to the Egyptian frontier.[113] Furthermore, the Luftwaffe Enigma was used to encypher a message in which Paulus reported to Berlin the instructions given to Rommel after the failure of his second attempt to take Tobruk. These showed that Paulus regarded Rommel's troops as exhausted and had forbidden him to make any major advance in the immediate future without express permission from OKH. They also showed that, although the 15th Panzer Division was known to the British to be on its way to Africa, the whole of it had yet to arrive.[114]

In the light of this disclosure, Wavell decided to counter-attack without waiting for a consignment of tanks which was being rushed to him by the hazardous Gibraltar–Alexandria route to offset the growth of Rommel's force. Operation Brevity was a limited offensive, undertaken in the belief that a scratch force which included two tank regiments brought up for the purpose could count on a substantial superiority in tanks in the forward area, and would be able to drive the Axis forces from the neighbourhood of the Egyptian frontier and perhaps beyond Tobruk. Air reconnaissance showed on the eve of the offensive that Rommel had some thirty to fifty tanks in the forward area and that most of his armour was seventy miles to the rear.[115] What it did not show was that he had been warned by his signal intelligence service of the impending attack, intended to move the main body of his armour forward, and would be able to do so without detection. With 29 medium and 26 heavy tanks, the British found themselves outnumbered. The attack was unsuccessful, and again inadequate knowledge of the enemy's dispositions and intentions had to bear some of the blame.

Operation Brevity almost coincided with the arrival at Alexandria on 12 May of Wavell's consignment of 82 medium, 135 heavy and 21 light tanks. Operation Battleaxe, which followed a month later, was a more ambitious affair. In the meantime Churchill and the Chiefs of Staff were worried by rumours of an impending German take-over of Syria. These arose from the presence of an Abwehr mission which had arrived early in 1941 and was making arrangements in the spring for the transit of small quantities of arms and a small number of aircraft consigned to Rashid Ali in Iraq.[116] When the Enigma traffic confirmed on 14 May that Luftwaffe aircraft had reached Syria and showed that the Vichy High Commissioner was providing landing facilities and conniving at the despatch of arms to Rashid Ali, the authorities in Whitehall became convinced that the Germans would soon arrive in strength if nothing was done to stop them.[117] So Wavell had once more to look over his shoulder. On 8 June a force which included French Gaullist troops entered Syria from Palestine with orders to take Beirut, Rayak and Damascus and afterwards advance to Palmyra and Homs and into Lebanon. Partly because the French colonial authorities were particularly incensed by the arrival of troops described as Free French, it met a good deal of resistance. Although Damascus fell on 21 June, hostilities were not brought to a formal close until July.

The chief contribution made by the intelligence agencies to the Syrian campaign was to show that it was unnecessary. Decrypted signals furnished ample evidence of German preparations for the attack on Crete. They revealed the modest provision made for the support of Rashid Ali. They furnished no evidence at all of preparations for military intervention in Syria.[118] Frequent air reconnaissance of Syrian airfields disclosed no signs of German activity not associated with the transit of war material to Iraq.[119] The obvious inference would seem to have been that the Germans reported to have arrived in Syria in the guise of tourists were Abwehr officers or agents, as indeed they were. But the authorities in Whitehall did not draw that inference. They declined to yield to negative evidence.

The gist of the plan for Operation Battleaxe was that, in the first stage, infantry columns supported by a brigade of heavy tanks were to attack the enemy's fortified positions on either side of the Egyptian frontier, while a brigade of cruiser tanks and the rest of the only available armoured division covered their desert flank. In the second stage, the whole of the armoured division was to advance on Tobruk. Thereafter, if all went well, the armoured division and the garrison of Tobruk would push on with the object of driving the enemy as far west as possible. An obvious shortcoming of the plan was that the pace of the whole operation would be keyed to that of the slow-moving heavy or 'infantry' tanks, but Wavell had no choice but to accept that disadvantage if the armoured division was to act as a whole after the first stage.

During the interval between Brevity and Battleaxe, decrypted signals showed that Fliegerführer Afrika had received no reinforcements and that the Luftwaffe's strength in Sicily had decreased.[120] Rommel was known to be strengthening his defences and appeared to have received no additional troops since the arrival of the main body of the 15th Panzer Division. Neither photographic nor visual reconnaissance could give a comprehensive account of the strength and disposition of his armour, but a substantial part of his force was known to be in the neighbourhood of Tobruk, some seventy to eighty miles from the forward area. It seemed safe to assume that not more than fifty to a hundred German tanks would be met in the first stage of the attack and that the British armoured division, with two hundred cruiser and heavy tanks, would not be seriously outnumbered later. Wavell's chief fear was not that his tanks would be outnumbered, but that Rommel's equipment might prove superior in quality.[121]

We now know that Rommel received from his signal intelligence service an accurate warning of the British offensive and the date when it would be launched. We also know that his defensive equipment included about fifty 50-millimetre anti-tank guns and a dozen 88-millimetre dual-purpose anti-tank and anti-aircraft guns. The 50-millimetre gun, although effective against heavy tanks only at close ranges, was a great improvement on the 37-millimetre gun which had hitherto been the standard German anti-tank weapon. The 88-millimetre gun, already used in an anti-tank role on the Western Front in 1940, could knock out any British tank at ranges up to 2,000 yards. As the British were met at two points by a devastating fire from these weapons, and were afterwards engaged successively by Rommel's tanks already in the forward area and those brought from Tobruk, it is not surprising that Battleaxe was an expensive failure. The British lost ninety-one tanks, the Germans only twelve.

This reverse was followed by a change of commanders. Air Chief Marshal Sir Arthur Longmore, called home for consultation on the eve of the attack on Crete, learned that he was to be replaced by his deputy, Air Marshal Tedder. A month later Wavell was replaced by General Sir Claude Auchinleck, whom he succeeded as Commander-in-Chief, India.

*

When Auchinleck arrived in Cairo at the beginning of July, the British had been driven from Greece and Crete with heavy losses. The Germans had begun their invasion of Russia with spectacular advances and were expected to defeat the Soviet Union in a matter of weeks, or at the most within three months.[122] On the assumption that they still aimed at knocking Britain out of the war as soon as possible, convergent thrusts towards the Suez Canal and the oil-producing regions of the Middle East seemed highly probable. In these circumstances, Auchinleck made it clear to the authorities in London that he had no intention of taking the offensive in the Western Desert until he was satisfied that his northern flank was as secure as he could make it. Even then he would need at least two armoured divisions and strong air support before he could think of trying to push Rommel out of Cyrenaica. Eventually it was agreed that he should launch an offensive at the beginning of November, but the date was afterwards put back to the middle of the month and finally to 18 November.

As Rommel, too, did not intend to go over to the offensive before November, both sides had five months in which to prepare for the next round. Rommel received very few reinforcements from Germany, but he did receive a valuable consignment of 50-millimetre anti-tank guns.

The only new division he was able to form during the summer and autumn was the Africa Division (afterwards the 90th Light Division) of motorized infantry. The 5th Light Division, with which he had begun his offensive in February, was renamed the 21st Panzer Division, but in November it had only 111 tanks, while the 15th Panzer Division had 133. The Italian Savona Division was put under his command, but it had no motor transport and could be used only in a static role. Six other Italian divisions, one of them armoured and one motorized, completed the Axis land forces in North Africa. Altogether the North Africa Command, commanded by General Ettore Bastico with Rommel as commander of an armoured group from which the Italian armoured and motorized divisions were excluded, had in the middle of November 552 tanks, of which 244 were German and the rest Italian. More than a third of them were Italian light tanks of little value, and virtually the only tanks in reserve were those under repair.

Auchinleck was more fortunate. As a result of the keen interest taken in the North African theatre by the authorities in London and especially by Churchill, by November his resources included, in addition to the Ninth Army in Palestine and Syria, a powerful Western Desert Force (renamed the Eighth Army) of six divisions and six independent brigades or brigade groups, with more than 700 tanks in active formations and 500 in reserve or in transit. He and his subordinate commanders also had the benefit of much-improved facilities for the acquisition, interpretation and dissemination of operational intelligence. The Eighth Army, with many more armoured cars than the old Western Desert Force, was in a far better position to send out patrols, including long-range patrols which covered the desert flank. It was supported by a tactical air force strong enough to reconnoitre freely, and served by a field intelligence organization no longer handicapped by unfamiliarity with German methods. By November the sections of the Government Code and Cypher School responsible for deciding which Enigma items were of operational significance in the context of the war in the Mediterranean and the Middle East had eight months' experience to draw upon. From August, Enigma decrypts passed to Cairo were handled by Special Communication Units and Special Liaison Units with facilities for dealing with them securely and promptly, and from September the system was extended to Alexandria, Malta and the headquarters of the Eighth and Ninth Armies. These reforms made it possible for the material to be passed to operational commanders and indoctrinated members of their staffs without disguise.[123]

Auchinleck chose as commander of the Eighth Army Lieutenant-General Sir Alan Cunningham, who had done extremely well in East Africa but had never commanded an armoured force. The principal formations at Cunningham's disposal on the eve of the November offensive (code-named Crusader) were the Tobruk Garrison, consisting of one infantry division, one infantry brigade group and one army tank brigade; an infantry corps (the 13th Corps) of two divisions, also supported by an army tank brigade; and a mobile corps (the 30th Corps) with the equivalent of three divisions and nearly 500 tanks. He launched his offensive on 18 November with a big preponderance over the Axis forces in armour, much stronger air support, and an excellent knowledge of the enemy's dispositions. Although ultimately some of the aims of Crusader were attained, he soon found that these advantages were not enough to ensure success.

In the middle of November the Axis command was making obvious preparations for a fresh assault on Tobruk. Most of its formations were either close to the Tobruk perimeter or in covering positions within thirty miles of it; but the frontier area in the neighbourhood of Bardia, Sollum and Sidi Omar was guarded by an Italian division augmented by Italian garrison troops and some German infantry. The 21st Panzer was in an immediate position about half-way between Sollum and Tobruk.[124]

Cunningham's plan was to use the 13th Corps to pin down the Axis forces in the enemy's forward area, and pass the 30th Corps across an unguarded stretch of frontier to the south of them. As soon as he was able to judge the enemy's response, he would decide whether the 30th Corps should go straight for Tobruk or wheel towards the coast. His intention was that in either case the 30th Corps should eventually make contact with the Tobruk Garrison, which was to break out of the perimeter to meet it, but that it should first seek out and destroy Rommel's armour. That intention was in line with current doctrine in the British Army, but it betrayed a certain confusion of thought arising from a false analogy with naval warfare. If Cunningham could relieve Tobruk and cut the enemy's communications so that no wheeled vehicles could reach him from his ports of supply at Benghazi and Tripoli, the 30th Corps would not need to seek out Rommel's armour. It would be at Cunningham's mercy, except in so far as it might subsist for a while on captured supplies.

On 14 November Rommel flew to Rome for a conference. On returning to his headquarters he found that the British were on the move. He came to the conclusion that only a reconnaissance in force was in prospect, and made no immediate change in his dispositions. Cunningham was therefore still in the dark when the time came for him to decide whether the 30th Corps should wheel to the right or continue towards Tobruk. Disregarding protests from his corps commanders, he proceeded to divide his force by ordering part of the 30th Corps to cover the left of the 13th Corps and sending the rest westwards. As a result of this decision and the determination of his subordinate commanders to lose no opportunity of engaging the enemy's armour even when the odds were against them, he gained little advantage from the overall numerical superiority in tanks which was his chief asset. As Rommel himself said later, it did not matter that the British had two tanks to his one if they used their armoured brigades piecemeal to attack his armoured divisions.[125]

Nor did Cunningham derive as much benefit as might have been expected from British superiority in the air. The fighting became so confused, so many British, German and Italian vehicles were moving in unexpected directions and turning up in unexpected places, that accurate observation from the air and helpful intervention by tactical bombers became extremely difficult. At the same time, field intelligence units on both sides were hampered by difficulties of communication and in some cases by the loss of wireless vehicles as a result of enemy action or mechanical or electrical breakdowns.

In the first five days Cunningham lost so many of his tanks that he suggested calling off the offensive while he still had some left for the defence of Egypt. Auchinleck's response was to fly to the forward area on 23 November and order him to maintain relentless pressure on the enemy, even if it cost him his last tank. About forty-eight hours later he decided to relieve Cunningham of his command and replace him by Neil Ritchie, hitherto Deputy Chief of the General Staff in Cairo. These decisions owed something to the light cast by signal intelligence on the enemy's lack of depth and problems of supply. They also reflected Auchinleck's knowledge that he had the means of replacing lost tanks from workshops and new arrivals.

In the last week of November Rommel made a bold attempt to envelop the Eighth Army by sending the 21st Panzer Division across the Egyptian frontier with orders to double back and attack westwards while the 15th Panzer Division attacked from south to north and the Italian Mobile Corps blocked the escape-routes to the west. When this failed as a result of breakdowns in communication, misunderstandings and shortages of fuel, water and ammunition, he was obliged to go over to the defensive. Early in December he proposed to the horrified Italians a general withdrawal from Cyrenaica. After a stormy discussion he agreed not to withdraw without first attempting a stand at Gazala, some thirty-five miles west of Tobruk. The British attacked the Gazala position in the middle of December, but could not prevent Rommel from extricating his force at the cost of leaving Axis troops in the frontier area to be rounded up by the British at their leisure. By the end of the year he was back in the bottleneck near the border between Cyrenaica and Tripolitania from which he had debouched in the spring.

Auchinleck's offensive had then to stop. Difficulties of supply would prevent him from maintaining more than about a division and a half in the forward area until the port of Benghazi could be restored to full working order. Such a force could not drive Rommel back to Tripoli. Nor would it suffice to repel a strong counter-offensive.

However, on the morrow of his retreat from Gazala, Rommel seemed unlikely to be in a position to attack before the end of February. A series of naval disasters then transformed the outlook. Already, in November, U-boats had sunk the carrier *Ark Royal* and the battleship *Barham*. On 19 December the *Queen Elizabeth* and the *Valiant* were severely damaged in harbour by mines clamped to their hulls by Italian frogmen. On the same day a cruiser force based on Malta, which had been harrying convoys carrying supplies to Rommel, ran into a minefield and was crippled. These calamities coincided with dire events in the Far East and the arrival of Luftwaffe reinforcements in Sicily. They tipped the scales in Rommel's favour.

SEVEN

Blitz and Blockade

Long before the daylight Battle of Britain was fought, the British were aware of indications that eventually the Germans might launch air attacks on the United Kingdom under cover of darkness or thick weather.

The Luftwaffe was known before the war to favour radio aids to navigation and to use a network of medium-frequency navigational beacons. Each beacon transmitted a call-sign followed by a brief continuous signal. By listening to two or more beacons, the navigator of an aircraft could obtain at least a rough idea of his position. The Air Ministry's Y-Service revealed when hostilities began that the Germans were making considerable use of the system, and after the fall of France that they were extending it to occupied countries. Although the British did not at first believe that the beacons would do much to help bomber-crews to find their targets at night, they provided themselves in the summer of 1940 with a counter-measure. This consisted of a number of masking beacons, or 'meacons', which re-radiated the German signals in such a way that a navigator who relied on the system would receive a false impression of his position. It worked so well that more than one German pilot made a forced landing in England in the belief that he had reached occupied territory.

Among technical devices mentioned in the Oslo report of November 1939 was one described as an 'aircraft range-finder'.* Eventually this turned out to be the blind-bombing device known to the Germans as the Y-Gerät, and in due course to the British as Benito. No more was heard of it for the time being, but early in 1940 a device called the X-Gerät, apparently intended for use in a bomber, was mentioned in the course of a bugged conversation between two prisoners-of-war.[1] Chiefly on the strength of this conversation, but guided to some extent by the answers to questions put to the prisoners at his suggestion, Dr R. V. Jones

* See page 60.

reported in the first week of March that apparently the X-Gerät was a bombing device which depended on the intersection over the target-area of beamed transmissions.[2]

In the same month a piece of paper was recovered from a crashed aircraft of the bomber formation KG 26. It carried what was evidently a summary of the navigational aids available to the crew. The summary ended:

Radio beacon Knickebein from 0600 hours on 315°[3]

This cryptic statement suggested that Knickebein, although described as a radio beacon, was no ordinary beacon. From an aircraft flying over England, the bearing of a beacon in Germany would be more like 45° to 135° than 315°. The figure would, however, be credible if the reference was to a station in Germany emitting a beamed transmission on a bearing of 315°, or in other words in a north-westerly direction. But whether the mysterious Knickebein had anything to do with the X-Gerät was not clear. A prisoner suggested that Knickebein was, in fact, something like the X-Gerät, adding that it had a very narrow beam.

A difficulty here was that a very narrow beam implied a short wave-length. Orthodox British scientists tended not to believe that signals transmitted on such a wave-length would follow the curvature of the earth to an extent which made it possible for a transmission from a station in Germany to be picked up over England. Jones was, however, shown a paper in which T. L. Eckersley of the Marconi company, who was the leading British expert on radio propagation, calculated the theoretical range of a transmitter on the top of the Brocken, in the Harz Mountains. Eckersley's figures suggested that there was no theoretical reason why high-frquency transmissions from Germany should not be receivable in an aircraft flying at 20,000 feet over England.[4]

By a curious chance, a diary was captured in May from the aircraft of KG 26 which had replaced the one lost two months earlier. It contained the entry for 5 March: 'We studied Knickebein'.[5]

The next reference to Knickebein was in an Enigma message sent by the Chief Signal Officer of Fliegerkorps IV on 5 June and decrypted four days later. As translated by the GC & CS, it read:

Knickebein at Kleve is confirmed (or established)
at point 33° 21'N, 1° W[6]

These co-ordinates indicated a position near Retford, in Nottinghamshire, where aircraft of Fliegerkorps IV were known to have been active. As no illicit beacon was found there, a reasonable assumption was that the reference was to the emission by a transmitter at Kleve, in the part of Germany nearest to England, of a beam which passed over that point.

This was not the only inference that could be drawn from the signal. Fliegerkorps IV was known to command two bomber formations, KG 4 and KG 27. Both were equipped with the He III. It seemed to follow that the device which picked up Knickebein transmissions must be capable of being carried in an He III.

Questions then put to prisoners elicited no information as to what the device was, but after interrogation one prisoner was heard to say to his room-mate that the British would never find what they were looking for, no matter how hard they looked.[7] This seemed to Jones to imply that the device was under the noses of the searchers but that they could not recognize it. He found in the technical report on an He III which had come down in the United Kingdom in October 1939 no reference to any equipment that could be used to receive high-frequency transmissions except the Lorenz blind-landing equipment normally carried by German bombers. He then asked the appropriate expert whether there was anything special about the Lorenz equipment carried by the aircraft in question. The expert replied that there was not, but added almost as an afterthought that it was more sensitive than it would need to be if it were used only for blind landings.[8] This was in fact true of the Lorenz equipment carried by all German bombers, all of which were therefore capable of receiving Knickebein transmissions.

On 14 June a detailed statement about Knickebein was at last received from a prisoner-of-war. He confirmed that it was a bombing device which depended on the intersection of two radio beams and that the transmissions were picked up by the Lorenz equipment.[9] Further confirmation came on 18 June from documents recovered from an aircraft which had crashed in France. These gave the precise locations of two Knickebein transmitters, one at Kleve and the other at Bredstedt, in Schleswig-Holstein.[10] Finally, a note taken on 20 June from a prisoner gave the same locations and revealed that the stations transmitted on frequencies of 31.5 and 30 megacycles a second respectively.[11]

In the meantime Jones found an opportunity of telling Lindemann that he had seen the signal decrypted on 9 June and was convinced that the Germans intended to use a system of intersecting beams for the bombing of Britain. He overcame Lindemann's predictable objection about the curvature of the earth by citing Eckersley's calculations. The outcome was that arrangements were made for a watch to be kept for beamed transmissions at five radar stations on the East Coast and from aircraft of a recently disbanded experimental unit with experience of flying along beams of the Lorenz type. This was reconstituted and renamed the Wireless Intelligence and Development Unit. The watch began on 19 June, but no transmissions were heard during the next forty-eight hours.

Jones found awaiting him at his office on 21 June a summons to a meeting in the Cabinet Room at 10 Downing Street. As he arrived at the office rather late and it took him some time to make sure that the message was not a hoax, he did not reach the Cabinet Room until about twenty-five minutes after the meeting had begun.[12] Called upon at the age of twenty-eight to expound the case for believing in the existence of Knickebein to the Prime Minister, the Chief of the Air Staff, their respective Scientific Advisers, the Commanders-in-Chief of Bomber and Fighter Commands and other dignitaries, he succeeded in convincing Churchill that the existence of Knickebein should be accepted. Churchill then ruled that attempts to locate and counter beamed transmissions should have 'absolute priority'.[13]

That afternoon both Jones and Eckersley attended a meeting called by the Director of Signals at the Air Ministry to discuss the use the Germans might make of beamed transmissions. To Jones's dismay, Eckersley said that he did not believe in the existence of Knickebein, that the signal decrypted on 9 June could not refer to a beam, and that the calculations used by Jones to demolish Lindemann's argument ought not to have been taken seriously. Jones countered this body-blow by suggesting that, as Eckersley had contradicted himself, his statements should be disregarded and the matter be considered solely in the light of the evidence from prisoners-of-war, captured documents and signal intelligence. He had great difficulty in persuading the Directorate of Signals that flights by the Wireless Intelligence and Development Unit should not be suspended. According to his subsequent account, he succeeded in doing so only by invoking Churchill's ruling.[14]

It was then agreed that the unit should search during the coming night on the assumption that Derby, where all the engines for Spitfires and Hurricanes were made, was the most probable target for the enemy's director-beam. An Anson piloted by Flight-Lieutenant H. E. Bufton, with Corporal Mackie as observer, duly took off from Wyton, in Huntingdonshire, and flew in a northerly direction so that it would cross beams laid from Kleve or Bredstedt over Derby. Bufton and Mackie were not told about Knickebein. Their orders were merely to search for, and investigate, transmissions with characteristics similar to those of the Lorenz blind-landing beam.

They picked up over Lincolnshire a narrow beam, some 400 to 500 yards wide, with such characteristics. At a point about ten miles east of Derby they found a second beam, with similar characteristics, whose bearing interesected that of the first beam. The frequencies were right, and the bearings were consistent with transmissions from Kleve and Bredstedt.[15]

Two days later Knickebein transmissions were intercepted for the first time on the ground. Documents recovered from crashed aircraft in July gave a general description of the system, confirmed what was already known or postulated, and showed that the width of the beam was about a third of a degree and that it could be aimed with an accuracy of one-tenth of a degree.[16] By the end of August the Germans were known to have set up at least two transmitters in occupied France, and in September a transmitter near Cherbourg was photographed.[17] Counter-measures, which included the 'meaconing' of transmissions from beacons and the distortion of Knickebein transmissions, were co-ordinated by a new formation No. 80 Wing, in which the Wireless Intelligence and Development Unit was formally incorporated in October.[18]

Little more was heard of the X-Gerät for some months after it was first mentioned in the early part of 1940. In August the Y-Service intercepted a series of beamed transmissions from the direction of France with characteristics not unlike those of Knickebein but frequencies of the order of 66.3 or 74 megacycles a second.[19] From the eve of Luftflotte 3's night attacks on Liverpool in the last week in August, many references were made in Luftwaffe Enigma traffic to beams from transmitters designated by the names of German rivers, and early in September specific mention was made of the X-Gerät in a context which indicated that the equipment was being installed in an aircraft of KGr 100 or KG 100.[20] Thereafter the activities of KGr 100 were closely studied not only at the Air Ministry but also at the headquarters of Fighter Command. As a matter of routine, the plots which appeared on the Operations Table at Bentley Priory were recorded on large sheets of squared paper. By collating these records with information from the Y-Service, Fighter Command's intelligence staff could sometimes draw valid inferences about the courses flown by aircraft of particular units or formations.[21]

About the middle of September, the GC & CS broke a new Enigma key. This turned out to be the key used for signals exchanged between the unit responsible for development of the X-Gerät and the advanced headquarters of KGr 100 at Vannes.[22] As the unit was not connected by landline with Vannes, returns and requests for new equipment had to be put on the air. Besides disclosing the precise whereabouts of some transmitters, the traffic showed that frequencies of the order of 65 to 75 megacycles a second were used. It also revealed the existence of a piece of equipment called Anna which appeared to be fitted with a graduated scale. At first suspected of being a wave-meter, Anna proved to be a complete VHF receiver. References in the traffic to 'Anna grads' were found to relate to settings which determined the frequencies used within the 65 to 75 megacycle range.

Jones reported on 11 September that the new series of beamed transmissions intercepted by the Y-Service could be tentatively associated with the X-Gerät and with KGr 100.[23] In a further report on 24 September he gave the precise locations of two X-Gerät transmitters near Cherbourg and the approximate locations of three near Calais and one in Brittany.[24] He also gave what proved to be a remarkably accurate account of the working of the system. The essence of it was that an aircraft of KGr 100 from Vannes flew along a director-beam laid over the target from a point near Cherbourg. This beam was intersected at two points short of the target by beams laid from transmitters near Calais. The time taken by the aircraft to cover the distance between the intersections gave its ground-speed, and from this the point at which its bombs should be released was computed.[25] Jones added that, although such a performance might seem incredible, theoretically the system should enable the Luftwaffe to place an aircraft within forty feet of a preselected position over London.[26] The positioning of the beams was in fact calculated by the Germans with an accuracy which required that allowance should be made for the fact that the earth is a spheroid, not a sphere.

In October KGr 100 began to drop flares over the United Kingdom. Jones thought this new departure might indicate that the Luftwaffe was preparing to use aircraft equipped to receive X-Gerät transmissions to mark a target for the benfit of aircraft not so equipped. At his suggestion, Lindemann gave Churchill a warning to that effect three weeks before the pathfinder technique developed by KGr 100 was first used.[27]

*

As a result of the warnings given by intelligence, Britain was fairly well provided with counter-measures to beacons and Knickebein when, on 7 September 1940, the Luftwaffe began the long-drawn series of night attacks on London which the British, with a characteristic blend of humour and contempt for foreign words and phrases, called the Blitz.

Their effectiveness is hard to measure. The bombing was much more widely dispersed than the Germans intended. This was not an unmixed benefit from the point of view of Londoners whose houses, shops or offices were blasted by bombs intended to hit docks, warehouses, power-plants or government buildings. Casualties were much lighter than had been expected. This was partly because successive governments since 1925 had paid far more attention than the public knew to measures of passive air defence, or ARP. We do know, however, that German bomber crews soon complained that their navigational aids were unsatisfactory. We also know that the leaders of the Luftwaffe recognized by the early part of 1941 that these complaints were justified, and that attempts to make Knickebein proof against interference were unsuccessful.

The performance of the air defences was disappointing. That was not the fault of the intelligence services. Despite Dowding's efforts in the summer to gird himself for a new encounter, Fighter Command was short of modern heavy fighters, reliable airborne radar, and upward-looking radar suitable for guiding night-fighters towards their targets. Priority had gone to aircraft and equipment needed for the daylight battle. The Blitz was an improvization, and so to some extent was the British response to it. Its paladins were not airmen but firemen, air-raid wardens, knights of the rescue-squad.

On 18 October Air Intelligence predicted that before long the Luftwaffe would concentrate on night attacks and might use as many as 600 bombers in a single raid. As it was already giving most of its attention to night attacks, had already used more than 400 bombers in a single raid and had attacked London with an average of 200 bombers a night on all but four of the last forty-one nights,[28] this could scarcely be called a startling forecast.

However, more was soon forthcoming. On 11 November Air Intelligence received from the GC & CS the translated decrypt of an Enigma message of 9 November which laid down the signal procedure for KGr 100 (called KG 100 in the GC & CS's version of the message) in connection with 'Moonshine Sonata' or 'Moonlight Sonata'.[29] On the following day Air Intelligence was told that a German pilot whose aircraft had been shot down on 9 November had confided to a stool-pigeon that a colossal raid was to be made between 15 and 20 November, that every bomber in the Luftwaffe would be used, and that the targets would be Coventry and Birmingham.[30] As there would be a full moon on 15 November, it seemed likely that he was referring to a night attack to be made by moonlight.

The salient features of the Enigma message of 9 November were as follows:

1 Call-signs were allotted to the Commander-in-Chief of the Luftwaffe, Luftflotte 2, Luftflotte 3 and KG (or KGr) 100.

2 A Hauptmann Aschenbrenner was mentioned by name in a context taken to imply that he was the commander of KG (or KGr) 100. A complete Kampfgeschwader would not, however, be commanded by a mere Hauptmann. Nevertheless the designation KG 100 continued to be used in British intelligence documents, although Air Intelligence was aware that the strength of the supposed KG 100 did not exceed that of a Kampfgruppe.

3 Knickebeins were mentioned. The X-Gerät was not mentioned by name, but there were indications that it would be used.

4 KG (or KGr) 100 was to transmit a tuning-signal at 1 p.m. on the day of the operation. This was to be repeated by Luftflotten 2 and 3.

5 Should the attack be called off 'on account of the weather-report from KG (or KGr) 100', the main W/T station of the Commander-in-Chief of the Luftwaffe would transmit a coded signal. This, with Item 1, was taken to imply that Göring would direct the operation in person.

6 The Knickebein 'beacons' would then be shifted to alternative targets.

7 The message included a list of fifteen signals, designated by numbers, which might have to be transmitted to cover such conditions or contingencies as 'Weather at target', 'Beam is to left of target', 'Beam interference', and so on. The list began with 'KORN' and ended with 'Target Area 1', 'Target Area 2', 'Target Area 3', 'Target Area 4'. No one

at the GC & CS or in Air Intelligence guessed that 'KORN' meant Coventry.

Early on 12 November Air Intelligence received from the GC & CS another Enigma decrypt. This was a message transmitted by KG (or KGr) 100 on 11 November. It began: 'Prepare for new targets as follows:'. It went on to give precise bearings for 'New target 51', 'New target 52', and 'New target 53' from five X-Gerät transmitters.[31] The precise locations of all five of these transmitters were known by 12 November to Air Intelligence. The bearings intersected at Wolverhampton (No. 51), Birmingham (No. 52) and Coventry (No. 53). The message did not mention Moonlight Sonata, and Air Intelligence may not have associated it with the message transmitted on 9 November. Raids on secondary targets in the Midlands or elsewhere had been made on many occasions during the Blitz on London, so the mere fact that additions were being made to the target-list would not necessarily have been surprising. 'New targets' could be targets which were to be attacked some time in the relatively distant future.

Surviving records do not show what action, if any, was taken by Air Intelligence on receipt of this decrypt. The author believes that a list of probable targets, in which other towns in the Midlands besides Wolverhampton, Birmingham and Coventry were included to protect the source, was teleprinted to Fighter Command and other recipients on or about 13 November, but can adduce no documentary evidence to support his recollection of such a signal. All copies of the signal, if indeed it existed, would seem to have disappeared.

What the records do show is that Air Intelligence attached great importance to the Enigma message transmitted on 9 November. On 12 November AI 1(w), a watchkeeping section of Air Intelligence, drew up for limited circulation a memorandum about Moonlight Sonata.[32] The memorandum predicted a big raid by moonlight on the night of 15 November or a suitable night thereafter. Luftflotten 2 and 3 and KG 100 would take part, and the operation would be controlled by the Commander-in-Chief of the Luftwaffe. The X-Gerät was not mentioned by name, but KG 100 could be expected to use 'the very accurate VHF beam, in the use of which it is specialized'. Its tasks might include the raising of fires on which other aircraft would bomb.

AI 1(w)'s attempt to predict the target were not very happy. On the strength of a captured map whose relevance to Moonlight Sonata had not been established, it thought Target Area 1 might be Central London, or possibly in the neighbourhood of Harwich or Ipswich, but confessed that it did not know. Target Area 2 it defined as Greater London and the area within the line Windsor–St Albans–Epping–Gravesend–Westerham–a little south of Leatherhead–Windsor. Target Area 3 was the triangle Farnborough–Reading–Maidenhead, Target Area 4 the neighbourhood of Faversham, Rochester and Sheerness.

This part of the memorandum can scarcely have carried much weight with anyone who had studied the recent operations of the Luftwaffe, and of KGr 100 in particular. It would be hard to imagine a more unsuitable objective for the kind of attack envisaged than the neighbourhood of Faversham, Rochester and Sheerness, or a vast area covering a great part of the Home Counties. The most convenient target for a joint attack by Luftflotten 2 and 3 would be one in a central position, close to the boundary between their respective spheres of interest. Wolverhampton, Birmingham and Coventry would all be suitable targets from that point of view.

By the evening of 13 November the Air Ministry was aware that the prisoner who had spoken of a colossal raid between 15 and 20 November had now said under interrogation that there were to be three attacks on consecutive nights, each using from 500 to 800 aircraft. He had also said that the targets would be 'in the industrial district of England'.[33]

In the early hours of the following morning the Air Staff drew up and circulated to the home commands of the RAF a counter-plan code-named Operation Cold Water. Its main features were:

1 A continuous watch on German signal activity in the widest sense.
2 Maximum interference with navigational beams and beacons.
3 Patrols by bomber aircraft over the bases of Luftflotten 2 and 3.
4 Air attacks on Vannes and on an airfield at Saint Leger believed to be an alternative base for KG (or KGr) 100.
5 Air attacks on Knickebein and X-Gerät transmitters near Cherbourg.
6 An air raid on 'a selected city in Germany' (in fact Berlin, where 30 bombers were sent with orders to attack military objectives).
7 A maximum effort by the air defences.

This plan was drawn up on the assumption that the target or targets would be in one or more of the areas mentioned in AI 1(w)'s memorandum, but that made little difference to the outcome. Most of the counter-measures were unaffected by doubts about the enemy's real objective, and in any case these doubts were soon resolved. The

gun-defences of Coventry had already been strengthened in consequence of a decision made before Moonlight Sonata was heard of.
Fighter Command's few night-fighter squadrons were so disposed that
most of them could operate equally well (or with equally poor chances of
success) against bombers flying either towards the Greater London area
or towards the Midlands.[34]

In the forenoon the Air Staff followed with a memorandum to the
Prime Minister. This, too, was based largely on AI 1(w)'s memorandum
and the Enigma message of 9 November, but it put some emphasis on
what the prisoner-of-war had said about Coventry and Birmingham.
The Air Staff said, in effect, that they expected the target areas to be
Central London, Greater London, the Farnborough–Maidenhead–
Reading area or the Rochester–Faversham–Sheppey area, but hoped
to get amended instructions out in time should further information point
to Coventry or Birmingham or elsewhere.[35]

Further information was both expected and forthcoming. About 1
p.m. a calibration signal received and acknowledged by Luftflotte 3 and
intercepted and read in the United Kingdom revealed that Moonlight
Sonata would be played during the coming night.[36] According to a
subsequent report, No. 80 Wing would seem to have been satisfied by 3
p.m. that the X-Gerät beams intersected over Coventry.[37] Within the
next hour or two the Directorate of Home Operations at the Air
Ministry telephoned the home commands of the RAF and warned them
and the civil and military authorities that Coventry was the target.[38]

Attempts to jam the X-Gerät during the Coventry raid were
unsuccessful. The equipment carried in KGr 100's aircraft included an
audio-filter tuned to a frequency of 2,000 cycles a second. For reasons
never established to the satisfaction of all parties, the jammers were set
that night to a frequency of 1,500 cycles a second.[39] What difference that
made to the outcome is hard to say. The moon was so bright and the
night so clear that KGr 100's crews might have been able to find
Coventry without any help from the X-Gerät. Against that it must be
admitted that the concentration achieved by the Luftwaffe in the
Coventry raid was well above its usual standard. On subsequent nights,
when the mistake was corrected, the results of jamming were usually
good and sometimes spectacular. They improved considerably when, in
the early part of 1941, enough equipment became available for
cross-beams as well as the main beam to be jammed. A crew of KGr 100
whose aircraft crashed in March admitted that interference with the

X-Gerät had been noticed as early as November, and by February had become serious.

*

From the time when Knickebein and the X-Gerät first came to his attention, Dr Jones kept watch for a navigational aid on the lines of the range-finding device described in the Oslo report. On 27 June 1940 Enigma revealed a proposal to set up Knickebein and Wotan installations near Cherbourg and Brest.[40] Professor Frederick Norman, who had exploded the 'secret weapon' myth in 1939, suggested that, as Wotan had only one eye, a Wotan installation might have something to do with a system which used only one beam.[41]

We now know that this ingenious guess was not quite on the mark. Wotan was the X-Gerät. The Y-Gerät was Wotan II. It was so called not because it used one beam and Wotan was a one-eyed god, but because it came after the X-Gerät and was a horse from the same stable.

The first authentic clue to the existence of the Y-Gerät, apart from the reference in the Oslo report to a device then still in the experimental stage, came from Enigma traffic in the key used for signals about the X-Gerät. A message addressed by KGr 100 on 6 October to Wotan II, near Cherbourg, gave the co-ordinates of 'Target 1'.[42] The fact that it was sent to a single station suggested a one-beam system. The co-ordinates were those of Bovington Camp, Dorset, which was attacked by two aircraft a few nights later.

Two practice messages were intercepted on 13 October. On 2 November reference was made to another target-number. By the end of November a link was established between beamed transmissions of an unusual character and the third Gruppe of Kampfgeschwader 26, known to be based at Poix.[43]

On the night of 19/20 January 1941 an aircraft of III/KG 26 was shot down during a raid on Southampton. It was so badly damaged that expert examiners could not say much more about a piece of equipment it carried than that it resembled, but was not the same as, the X-Gerät equipment carried by aircraft of KGr 100. All the crew were killed, but a notebook with charred edges was recovered. Its contents included some valuable information about frequencies and two handwritten tables. One of them was found to be a thinly-disguised list of six towns in England, with their distances and the reciprocals of their bearings from Poix. The other, when matched with the first, proved to be a series of bearings which intersected at a point near Cassel, in the Pas de Calais. Jones and his assistant, Charles Frank, concluded that crews of III/KG 26 were controlled during their outward but not their homeward flights from a ground-station, and that there was a ground-station near Cassel as well as one near Cherbourg.[44]

They also concluded that the system was vulnerable to interference. It depended on the reradiation from an aircraft of radiations from the ground-station, the time taken for the signal to return enabling the controller to calculate how far the aircraft was from him. The reradiated signals from the aircraft could be picked up even better in England than in France. They could then be radiated back to the aircraft, which in turn would feed them back to the ground-station, so that the controller would receive a false impression of the aircraft's position. Counter-measures on these lines were begun in February. Evidence was soon received that, as a result either of these measures or of technical hitches and the inexperience of controllers and crews, only a small proportion of aircraft equipped with the Y-Gerät were dropping their bombs in the right places. Crews were known to be troubled, too, by the fear that the British might give bogus orders, or even that this was already being done. Prisoners from three aircraft which crashed in May admitted that III/KG 26 was beginning to lose faith in the Y-Gerät, which no other unit was equipped to use. Moreover, examination of salvaged equipment showed that the system was even more susceptible to jamming than had been supposed.[45]

The transfer of Luftflotte 2 to the Eastern Front in the summer of 1941 left only weak bomber forces in the West. When major attacks on the United Kingdom were resumed with the Baedeker raids of 1942, the pathfinder group (now I/KG 100) was brought back. It used a variant of the X-Gerät with a supersonic modulation superimposed on the old frequency. Air Scientific Intelligence gave ample warning of this innovation, but in order to protect its sources asked that the appropriate counter-measure should not be brought into operation until the new variant was found to be actually in use. As the result of a slip-up at the technical level, the supersonic modulation was not detected until Bath, Norwich, York and Exeter had been bombed with disconcerting accuracy.[46] A much lower standard of accuracy was attained in most raids of the Baedeker series after the first few days of May, and in all but a few of the raids attempted in 1943.[47] Y-Gerät transmitters were switched on from time to time in 1942, but little use appeared to be made of them, and we now know that the system was afterwards abandoned on the ground that it was too susceptible to interference. During the Baby Blitz in 1944 the Luftwaffe was found to be using radar and voice transmissions to control its fighter-bombers over London.[48] Counter-measures were discussed, but the fighter-bomber offensive soon came to a standstill. In all but six of twenty-two major raids on English towns or cities attempted in 1944 fewer than half the bombs aimed at the target hit it, and on four occasions the target was not hit by any bombs at all.[49]

There is no doubt that Knickebein, the X-Gerät and the Y-Gerät could have become extremely potent aids to blind bombing if the Luftwaffe had been able to develop them at leisure and spring them on the British without warning. Their detection in time for counter-measures to be taken showed what could be done by a small, compact intelligence section able and willing to give time and thought to the fitting together of scraps of information from different sources.

*

During the winter of 1940–41 the Air Ministry acquired a new Chief of the Air Staff, reorganized its intelligence branch and committed itself to an attempt to wear the Germans down by the bombing of centres of industry and population under cover of darkness. One consequence was a keen demand from the Air Staff and Bomber Command for information about the means used by the Germans to obtain early warning of air attacks and direct fighters to their targets.

The Oslo report mentioned two kinds of German radar, one already in use and the other in preparation. In the summer of 1940 references were made in wireless traffic to 'Freya-reporting' as an aid to interception, and to something called a 'Freya-Gerät'.[50] A piece of equipment with that designation appeared to have been installed near Cherbourg within a few weeks of the fall of France, but it was not seen on air photographs taken at the height of the invasion scare. The presumption was that it was fairly small and easily transported.

On 29 July a British destroyer was sunk by German aircraft in the Channel, apparently after being detected at a range of sixty miles from a place called Auderville. In the following January a photographic interpreter, Claude Wavell, drew the attention of Air Scientific Intelligence to two small circles on a pair of stereo photographs of an area north-west of Cherbourg.[51] When Jones asked the name of a neighbouring village, Wavell said that it was Auderville. Close examina-tion of the photographs revealed shadows cast by some fairly tall structure at the centre of each circle. On the strength of this clue, Jones asked for a low oblique photograph. He knew that a pilot would have to risk his life to take one. In the outcome, two pilots did so. Two sorties had to be made before, on 22 February 1941, Flying Officer W. K. Manifould of PRU brought back a clear picture of what were undoubtedly two radar aerials mounted on turntables. Almost simultaneously, hitherto undetected radar transmissions from the neighbourhood of Cherbourg were picked up by D. J. Garrard, who had joined Air Scientific Intelligence from the Telecommunications Research Establishment and kept watch on his own initiative.[52]

Not the least of the benefits conferred by Manifould's photograph was that agents and resistance workers could now be told what to look for. Many descriptions of Freya installations, some accompanied by sketches, were received from such sources.

Further information about German radar was soon forthcoming from Enigma messages. These referred to deliveries to the Balkans of equipement apparently intended to cover the approaches to the Black Sea coast. Rumania was to receive a Freya and a piece of equipment called a Würzburg; two Würzburgs were allotted to Bulgaria. As the Bulgarians were unlikely to be given more equipment than they needed for their 150 kilometres of coastline, it seemed to follow that the all-round range of a Würzburg must be about 37.5 kilometres. This figure tallied fairly well with the reported existence of a circular night-fighting area in Western Europe with a radius of 40 kilometres. On the same principle, the Freya delivered to Rumania could be tentatively assumed to have an all-round range of the order of 90 to 100 kilometres. Such a performance would be consistent with what was known from intercepted transmissions of the technical characteristics of the equipment, and also with the detection of a destroyer by the Auderville Freya at a range of sixty miles.

A question that now arose was whether Würzburg was the second kind of radar mentioned in the Oslo report. The latter was described as working on a wavelength of 50 centimetres and transmitting short pulses 'narrowly directed by an electric dish'.[53] This description and an accompanying diagram suggested an installation with an aerial of paraboloid form and a general resemblance to an outsize electric bowl-fire. Transmissions on a wavelength of approximately 53 centimetres were detected, but many months elapsed before the first Würzburg was located. In the meantime there were indications that the Germans possessed an enlarged version of the Würzburg with a longer range. At last, in the autumn of 1941, Charles Frank drew attention to air photographs which showed two Freyas close to the village of Bruneval, near Le Havre, and a track apparently leading to some other object. Low-level obliques taken by Squadron-Leader A. E. Hill showed that the object was indeed a Würzburg and that it did look just like a large bowl-fire.

The sequel was the raid made on Bruneval on 27/28 February 1942 by troops of the 2nd Parachute Battalion for the purpose of capturing the Würzburg equipment and bringing it back to England. The set was dismantled by Flight Sergeant C. W. H. Cox, a radar mechanic who had never been in an aircraft or travelled outside England when he volunteered for a dangerous but unspecified task. The raid was organized by Combined Operations Headquarters, but SOE contributed special equipment and sent a Sudeten German prepared, if the need arose, to confuse the enemy by shouting orders and counter-orders.[54] Valuable information about the strength and disposition of German troops in the neighbourhood was furnished in advance of the raid by agents of General de Gaulle's Bureau Central de Renseignements et d'Action under the direction of Gilbert Renault-Roulier (Rémy).[55]

In the meantime a great deal was learnt about the air defences covering Germany's western frontier from a variety of sources. Agents of the Belgian resistance movement gave the locations of many radar stations. On a number of occasions in 1942 and 1943 carrier-pigeons dropped in containers from bombers brought home answers to such questions as: 'Are there any German radar stations in your neighbourhood with aerials which rotate?'[56] One Belgian resistance worker succeeded in stealing a map which showed the dispositions and chain of command of an entire searchlight regiment in southern Belgium. The searchlights had been withdrawn by the time the map turned up in London, but that did not matter because the map also showed the locations of radar stations which remained. Other agents managed to gain access to buildings and described the system by which the movements of British bombers and of fighters sent to intercept them were displayed on a ground-glass screen. Confirmation and additional information came from the interception of radar transmissions in the air and on the ground, photographic reconnaissance, intercepted orders given by controllers in plain-language or self-evident codes, and messages in which locations were only thinly disguised by the substitution of 'Hamster' for Hamstede, 'Tiger' for Terschelling, 'Zander' for Zandvoort, and so on. When new radar stations were established in

Denmark after Bomber Command's raids on Lübeck and Rostock in the spring of 1942, the Danish intelligence service communicated the positions of all of them to MI 6 through SOE before any of them came into operation.[57]

The knowledge of Germany's air defences gained by Air Scientific Intelligence made important contributions to the planning of raids by British and United States air forces. At any rate in the middle and later stages of the war, commanders, operational staffs and crews were also well provided with tactical target data such as lists of factories and power-stations, target maps and dossiers on individual targets.

Attempts to frame realistic strategic programmes for the bombing of Germany were not so successful. Reliable intelligence about Germany's war potential was hard to come by. Even where good information was available, the Western Allies tended to draw misleading conclusions from it because their calculations were based from the outset on false assumptions.

The British believed on the outbreak of war that the German economy was either already fully stretched, or would soon become so. They also believed that the National Socialist government had armed itself with dictatorial powers over virtually the whole of German industry, and that these powers were exercised with ruthless efficiency.

None of these assumptions was correct. There was a great deal of slack in the German economy. The National Socialist government did aim at a planned industrial output, but the means by which it sought to attain that aim were defective. The Minister of Economics, who from 1935 was also Plenipotentiary-General for the War Economy, was responsible in theory for steering production into the right channels by controlling allocations of raw materials, but he had no control over demands formulated by individual consumers or the placing of orders by the service departments. In theory the rearmamanent programmes of the three services were co-ordinated from 1934 by a branch of the Ministry of War with inter-service status, but in practice the departments retained control of current supplies and the development of new weapons. Nominally the Ministry of Labour was responsible for ensuring that the leading armament firms were adequately supplied with manpower, but it was powerless to move workers from one job to another without the consent of all parties. Nearly all industrial, commercial and agricultural undertakings, although grouped under the National Socialist régime in self-regulating associations, remained free of government interference except where allocations of raw materials were concerned. The 'ruthless efficiency' of Hitlerite Germany was largely mythical. Ruthless though party or governmental organizations might be in pursuit of their own interests, they were not necessarily efficient. The Directorate of Air Armaments of the German Air Ministry, to give only one example, was almost unbelievably inefficient.

Although largely ignorant of these matters, the British authorities made some creditable attempts to discern the weak spots in the German economy. From such information as they had they concluded, correctly, that Germany's reserves of certain materials would not suffice for a long war of attrition and that dependence on imported or synthetic oil was her Achilles' heel. They failed, however, to reckon with Blitzkreig tactics.

Nor had much thought been given to the probable effects on the German economy of a successful offensive in the West when, on 19 May 1940, the Chiefs of Staff were called upon to assess Britain's chances of carrying on the war if France fell. Their reply, drafted in great haste by the Joint Planners with help from a senior official of the Ministry of Economic Warfare, was to the effect that, if Britain received full economic and financial support from the United States, Germany might yet be defeated by a combination of blockade, air attacks on industrial targets and 'morale', and subversion in occupied countries.* Although much stress was laid on the economic factor, the compilers of the draft did not have time to make a considered assessment of the economic advantages the Germans might gain by conquering France and the Low Countries. According to a statement made afterwards by the official then in charge of the Enemy Branch of the Ministry of Economic Warfare, such an assessment could not have been completed in less than three months.[58]

Whether Britain was in a position to damage the German economy by bombing was a different question. The Air Staff had given much thought to attacks on industrial targets in the Ruhr, but until 15 May only the bombing of strictly military targets and the dropping of leaflets over Germany had been allowed. In the meantime losses incurred in attacks on warships and naval bases had forced them to discard the illusion that unescorted bombers flying in formation would be able to fight their way to their objectives in daylight with relative impunity. They hoped that crews would be able to locate industrial targets in Germany at night and bomb them with some approach to accuracy, but such evidence as was available up to the time when the Chiefs of Staff submitted their report did not go far to support that view. Crews sent to drop leaflets over

* See page 98.

Germany reported that in moonlight small towns were visible in favourable circumstances from heights of the order of 4,000 to 6,000 feet and individual buildings from 3,000 to 4,000 feet; at greater altitudes large rivers, lakes and canals could, as a rule, be made out if the moon was shining and the night was clear, but the only industrial objectives distinguishable were those that were either illuminated (such as marshalling-yards) or self-illuminating (such as coking-ovens). Moreover, although the crews of 41 out of 50 bombers sent on the night of 19/20 March to attack a seaplane base at Hörnum, on the island of Sylt in the Frisians, reported on their return to base that they had located the target without difficulty and that hangars and living-quarters had been hit and two hangars set on fire, no damage to buildings was visible on reconnaissance photographs taken on 6 April.[59]

Immediately after the lifting of the ban on raids which might endanger civilian life or property, Bomber Command began a series of attacks on industrial targets in the Ruhr. The intention was that these should be directed primarily against synthetic oil plants, but that crews who could not find their primary targets should attack coking-ovens and that 'harassing attacks' should be made on marshalling-yards. No reliable information about the results of these attacks was forthcoming from agents or signal intelligence, and such evidence as could be gleaned from reconnaissance photographs was not very encouraging. In any case the scale of attack was too small to be decisive. The intelligence case for a sustained offensive against oil targets remained strong, but the means were lacking.

However, not everyone was convinced that attacks on oil targets were the right answer. Churchill expressed the opinion early in July that only 'an absolutely devastating, exterminating attack ... upon the Nazi homeland' could make a major contribution to Germany's defeat.[60] Air Marshal Portal of Bomber Command was inclined to agree with this view, but the Air Staff were reluctant to order indiscriminate attacks on German towns as long as they continued to believe that precise objectives could be hit.[61]

On 24 August the Luftwaffe opened a new phase of the Battle of Britain. That night about 170 bombers attacked targets in various parts of the United Kingdom. About a dozen crews sent to bomb oil tanks at Thameshaven and aircraft factories at Rochester and Kingston-on-Thames went so far astray that bombs fell on the City of London and on districts of Greater London as far apart as Islington, Bethnal Green, Tottenham, Stepney, Finsbury, Millwall, Coulsdon, Leyton and East

Ham.[62] One consequence of what seemed an indiscriminate attack on the London area was that Churchill told Portal that he thought the time had come for Bomber Command to spread its bombs 'as widely as possible over the cities of Germany'.[63]

Just over a fortnight later the Luftwaffe began its Blitz on London. Although we know now that crews were given precise targets, the bombing was so inaccurate that it seemed indiscriminate. Even so, the Air Staff were not yet prepared to renounce attempts at precise bombing in favour of attacks on built-up areas. The basis of their long-term strategy, they told Portal on 21 September, was still disruption of the German oil industry.[64] They conceded that there were other target-systems whose disruption might help to undermine the German economy, and they did not forbid Portal to bomb Berlin for the twofold purpose of hampering industrial activity and harming the civil population. Whether Bomber Command had the slightest chance of sapping Germany's will to fight by harming the civil population of Berlin or any other German city is a question no intelligence officer seems to have been called upon to answer.

In October Portal was appointed Chief of the Air Staff. He failed to convince his successor at Bomber Command, Air Marshal Sir Richard Peirse, that attempts to disrupt the German oil industry and occasional attacks on marshalling-yards could be usefully combined with raids on twenty or thirty towns which Portal wished to include in Bomber Command's directive. Such a programme, Peirse thought, would lead to so wide a dispersal of his effort as to put satisfactory results out of the question.[65]

The outcome of prolonged and sometimes heated discussions in Whitehall and Downing Street was that the Chiefs of Staff, in their corporate capacity, expressed the view that Bomber Command should concentrate on disruption of the oil industry and not allow its effort to be diverted to other tasks. The Defence Committee accepted that conclusion, although Churchill still thought attention should be paid to attacks on German towns. Portal then agreed that Peirse should give priority to attacking seventeen synthetic oil plants whose destruction was calculated to do immense harm to the German economy, but suggested that he should consider attacking towns when conditions were such that oil targets could not be attacked with a reasonable prospect of success.[66]

There is no doubt that from the intelligence aspect, and in the light of the information available to the Ministry of Economic Warfare, the Air Ministry and the committee appointed by the Chamberlain government to keep the Axis oil situation under review, the decision to give priority to oil targets was a sound one, always provided that the plan was feasible. From the operational aspect, a fairly weighty objection to it was that the plan was *not* feasible. Bomber Command had not the slightest chance of destroying seventeen synthetic oil plants within the foreseeable future. Most of its crews were incapable of getting within miles of their targets at night, except by chance, with the equipment available in 1940 and 1941.

This drawback was not yet fully apparent to the Air Staff. Even so, there were already indications that relegation of the bomber force to indiscriminate attacks on towns might be the only alternative to abandonment of the whole concept of a strategic air offensive. On the night of 7 November 1940 twenty crews of Wellingtons sent to attack the Krupp works at Essen claimed on their return to base that they had attacked the target and started fires visible for miles. With one exception, crews of Hampdens and Blenheims who claimed to have reached the same target between one and four hours later saw no fires.[67] Again, on the night of 16 December, 134 Wellingtons, Whitleys, Hampdens and Blenheims were sent to Mannheim to make the first attack on a town as distinct from a precise objective. The most experienced crews were to drop incendiaries in order to start fires at which the less experienced would aim their bombs. More than a hundred crews reported on their return to base that Mannheim had been duly bombed, that most bombs had fallen in the target area and that the centre of the town had been left in flames. Reconnaissance photographs taken in daylight on 21 December showed that many bombs had fallen wide of the target and that the attack had failed.[68]

Reconnaissance photographs also showed that most of the 260 tons of bombs which nearly two hundred crews claimed to have aimed at two oil plants at Gelsenkirchen in December had fallen nowhere near them, but this evidence does not seem to have come to the attention of the oil committee until later.[69] A decision to make attacks on the seventeen crucial oil-plants the 'sole primary task' of the bomber force during the first half of 1941 was not rescinded. The new directive came into effect in the middle of January. Experts calculated that 3,420 sorties would be needed, that destruction of the seventeen plants might be completed in four months, but that further efforts on a similar scale would then be needed to prevent their recovery.[70]

But crews sent to attack oil plants needed good visibility. The weather in Western Europe in the late winter is seldom good. Only 211 sorties had been flown when, in March, the attempt to knock out the synthetic oil industry was called off and Bomber Command received a new directive.

This decision flowed partly from belated recognition of the fact that the number of nights in any month on which conditions suitable for attacks on precise objectives could be expected was fairly small; partly from intelligence which suggested that the enemy was about to step up his attacks on ocean trade. More than a year earlier a prisoner-of-war had reported that a new formation, KG 40, was being equipped with very-long-range aircraft and trained for anti-shipping operations. By the late summer of 1940 KG 40 was known from intercepted wireless traffic to be based at Merignac, near Bordeaux, and to be making frequent flights to and from Stavanger for the twofold purpose of observing the weather west of the British Isles and attacking shipping.[71] Later in the year it was found to be working from Merignac only and to be supplementing direct attacks on shipping by reporting shipping movements for the benefit of U-boats. An attack on Merignac by Bomber Command in November kept it quiet for a time, but in the first two months of 1941 it sank forty-seven ships and damaged another nineteen. Early in March it resumed its shuttle-service between Merignac and Stavanger.

In the same two months, submarines sank sixty British, Allied or neutral merchant vessels in various parts of the world, and 640,116 tons of shipping were lost from all causes in the North Atlantic and United Kingdom waters.[72] With these figures before him, and warned by Air Intelligence of indications that the Luftwaffe was preparing to extend its anti-shipping activities, Churchill decreed on 6 March that for the next four months attacks on U-boats and KG 40 and their bases should take precedence over all other tasks.[73]

Bomber Command's initial response was to send 54 Wellingtons on the night of 12 March to attack the factory at Bremen which made KG 40's Focke-Wulf 200 aircraft. Conditions were described as 'perfect'. Thirty-three Wellington crews claimed after the raid that they had found the target and attacked it with 132 high-explosive bombs and hundreds of incendiaries. Reconnaissance photographs showed that only twelve high-explosive bombs had hit the factory and only another twenty-eight fallen within 600 yards of it.[74]

In the light of this and other evidence, the authorities concluded that not more than three or four out of a hundred bombs aimed at a target such as an oil plant were likely to hit it even in the most favourable conditions, and that on dark nights only whole towns could be attacked with any prospect of success. A survey completed in the following

August by a member of the War Cabinet secretariat suggested that even this modest estimate was too sanguine. After more than 600 photographs taken while raids were in progress had been examined and compared with operational summaries and other evidence, he reported that in his estimation not more than one in five of the crews despatched on night operations in June and July had come within five miles of their targets. Of crews who claimed to have reached and attacked targets in Germany, probably not more than one in four had dropped their bombs within an area of 75 square miles round the intended point of aim. Where industrial haze and a dearth of landmarks made target-finding particularly difficult, as in the Ruhr, the proportion of crews who dropped their bombs anywhere near the places they thought they were attacking was probably much lower.[75]

The intelligence agencies, other than those concerned with the taking and interpretation of air photographs, were not in a position to throw much light on the material results of Bomber Command's offensive against German industry or their effect on the German economy. Good information about the physical effects of raids on targets in occupied territories was sometimes forthcoming from agents and resistance workers. Reliable reports from agents in Germany were rare. The best sources were photographs brought back by reconnaissance aircraft or taken from bombers during active operations.

*

The warning from Air Intelligence which contributed to Churchill's decision to issue his Battle of the Atlantic directive on 6 March 1941 was based largely on the inference that KG 40's resumption of its shuttle-service between Merignac and Stavanger boded no good for shipping off the West Coast of Ireland. It also reflected the knowledge, derived from low-grade signal intelligence, that the bomber formation III/KG 27, used during the Blitz for night attacks on British cities, had moved to Brest.[76] In March it carried out a series of attacks on shipping in the Irish Sea and the Bristol Channel. A combination of low-grade and Enigma traffic revealed by the end of the month that it was being reinforced by the first and second Gruppen of KG 27 and that a new Luftwaffe command, Fliegerführer Atlantik, was being set up to co-ordinate anti-shipping operations from bases in France and Norway.[77]

We now know that by April Fliegerführer Atlantik had about twenty very-long-range aircraft and about sixty long-range bombers, torpedo-bombers and reconnaissance aircraft. Although KG 27's aircraft had to be grounded for a time because of heavy losses, his strength was raised by the late summer to about twice that number. We also know that Air Intelligence was right in thinking that the Luftwaffe planned further additions to his force, but that its hopes were frustrated by inadequate reserves, mismanagement by the Directorate of Air Armaments of production and re-equipment programmes, and demands from other theatres. The volume of British, Allied or neutral merchant shipping sunk by aircraft rose alarmingly in March and April, remained disturbingly high in May, but thereafter fell off sharply.[78]

Sinkings by submarines, on the other hand, rose fairly steadily during the first half of the year. In addition, thirty-seven ships were sunk between January and March by surface warships, and twenty-five by merchant raiders. KG 40 was known to be reporting shipping movements for the benefit of the U-boat force. The Admiralty pressed for more frequent photographic reconnaissance, but there were still not enough suitable aircraft for German naval bases to be covered regularly. An espionage network organized by the Polish intelligence service furnished good information about sailings of U-boats from bases in Occupied France, but could not predict routes or patrol-areas. Luftwaffe Enigma and exceptional wireless activity sometimes gave indications that surface warships were about to leave the Baltic, but these were usually too slight to justify a sortie by the Home Fleet.

If the Enigma key used by the German Navy for nearly all communications between shore stations and submarines or surface vessels could be read, new prospects would open for the British. But by February 1941 traffic in this key had been read, as the result of chance captures, only for brief periods in the spring and early summer of 1940.

By that time the GC & CS had long been convinced that further progress was unlikely without the aid of additional material which could be obtained only from exceptionally well-informed prisoners-of-war or captured documents. A raid seemed the obvious solution, but finding a suitable objective was not easy.

The first step in that direction ws taken when the Admiralty and the GC & CS agreed that a special effort should be made to seize an Enigma machine and tables of settings during an impending expedition to the Lofoten Islands, south-west of Narvik.[79] The main purpose of the expedition, and the only one disclosed to most of those who took part in it, was to demolish fish-oil factories believed to be of considerable importance to the Germans. The operation was planned with the co-operation of the exiled Norwegian government and service authorities. British and Norwegian troops disembarked early on 4 March 1941 from two converted cross-Channel steamers escorted by destroyers and covered and supported by the Home Fleet. The factories ashore were duly demolished, a German factory-ship and some cargo vessels were sunk, and more than 200 prisoners and 300 volunteers for the Norwegian armed forces were brought back.[80]

More important than all this from the intelligence aspect was the capture of the German armed trawler *Krebs*. Her crew succeeded in throwing their Enigma machine overboard, but not in ridding themselves of spare rotors. The outcome was that the GC & CS was able to read retrospectively the whole of the naval Enigma traffic intercepted in February. By applying cryptanalytical disciplines, it went on to read the April traffic and most of the May traffic with delays of the order of three to seven days.[81]

This breakthrough opened the way to further progress. Examination of the decrypted February and April traffic convinced the GC & CS, and enabled it to prove to the satisfaction of the Admiralty, that the Germans were maintaining weather-ships north of Iceland and in mid-Atlantic, and that these ships carried naval Enigma machines. Because their routine reports were transmitted in a special weather-cypher, their signals differed outwardly from normal Enigma messages, but the evidence that they used Enigma was conclusive. A report submitted by the naval section of the GC & CS on 26 April showed that there were eight such ships, that all but two of them had been mentioned in a list issued by the German naval authorities in Norway in January, and that six of them were known to have been at sea in February and April. Besides the names of all eight ships and the tonnages of all but one of them, the naval section's report gave the two main areas in which they operated, positions from which they had transmitted reports on thirteen days in March and April, and some information about their activities and procedure. A further report, submitted on 19 June, gave positions from which one ship had transmitted reports on fourteen occasions during the past two and half weeks.[82]

In the light of this evidence the Admiralty mounted two cutting-out operations. The weather-ship *München* was captured on 7 May. Her Enigma machine was not recovered, but a table of settings enabled the

GC & CS to read the June traffic more or less currently. To take care of the settings for July, another weather-ship, the *Lauenberg*, was captured on 28 June.

A still more valuable catch was made on 9 May, when the U-110 attacked a convoy south of Greenland and was counter-attacked and seized by the convoy's escort. A boarding-party led by Sub-Lieutenant David Balme, R.N., recovered her Enigma machine, with ancillary material which included settings for April and June but not for May. Also included in the haul were the special settings used for 'officer-only' signals and the code used by U-boat commanders for brief sighting-reports.[83] These signals had not hitherto been read.

The broad effect of the capture of the *Krebs*, the *München*, the *Lauenburg* and the U-110, and of the acquisition by the GC & CS in the summer of 1941 of additional staff and more Bombes, was that the GC & CS was able not only to read the naval Enigma traffic for June and July more or less currently, but also to read the traffic for all but two days thereafter until the end of the war, usually although not invariably within thirty-six hours of the transmission of the signal.[84]

The Admiralty began in June to use Ultra instead of Hydro as the prefix to signals based on Enigma decrypts, and to employ for their encypherment a one-time-pad system which gave complete security. The term Ultra was afterwards generally adopted as a security classification for signals and reports incorporating information derived ffrom the reading of high-grade cyphers. By the latter part of 1941 the pretence that information from Enigma came from agents or prisoners-of-war was wearing thin. Thereafter the material was made available to a growing number of indoctrinated users who were told of the source and asked not to disclose it, or information derived from it, to the uninitiated.

*

The reading of naval Enigma made important contributions to the winning of the first round of the Battle of the Atlantic in the summer of 1941. It made only a single contribution to the events which led to the sinking of the new German battleship *Bismarck* in May, but that was an important one.

In the winter of 1940–41 the German naval authorities hoped to mount an ambitious series of raids by surface warships on ocean trade in the coming spring, using the *Bismarck* and the heavy cruiser *Prinz Eugen* from the Baltic and the battlecruisers *Scharnhorst* and *Gneisenau* from Brest.

When the time came the *Bismarck* and the *Prinz Eugen* were ready, but the *Scharnhorst* and the *Gneisenau* were not. The *Gneisenau* was severely damaged by a torpedo during a raid by torpedo-bombers of Coastal Command on 6 April, and on the night of 10/11 April received four hits during a raid on Brest by Bomber Command. The *Scharnhorst* was undergoing a refit not expected to be completed before June. After anxious debate, the German authorities decided that the *Bismarck* and the *Prinz Eugen* should not wait for her. The *Prinz Eugen*, with a limited endurance, was not an ideal commerce raider, but elaborate arrangements were made for surface raiders to be refuelled by supply-ships.

The Admiralty and Admiral Sir John Tovey, who had succeeded Admiral Forbes in command of the Home Fleet, expected a sortie by the *Bismarck* and possibly other heavy ships. On 19 April the *Bismarck* was wrongly reported to have entered the Skagerrak on the previous day, and on 22 April transports and patrol vessels at Narvik were mistaken for cruisers. But better intelligence was soon forthcoming. In the second week of May the Air Ministry's Y-Service reported exceptional activity by German reconnaissance aircraft in the neighbourhood of Scapa Flow and off the Norwegian coast. At the same time, Luftwaffe Enigma revealed that aircraft of KG 40 had reconnoitred the Denmark Strait (between Iceland and Greenland) for the purpose of reporting the limits of the ice-pack. On 18 May the Admiralty's Operational Intelligence Centre told Admiral Tovey that KG 40 had again been active in the Denmark Strait on the previous night.[85]

The *Bismarck* and the *Prinz Eugen* left Gdynia on that day. They were seen from the Swedish cruiser *Götland* in the Kattegat on 20 May. The *Götland*'s wirelessed report was seen by a senior officer of the Swedish Intelligence Service who passed the substance of it to the Norwegian Military Attaché in Stockholm without revealing the source. The Norwegian attaché, Colonel Roscher Lund, passed it to the British Naval Attaché, Captain Henry Denham. Accordingly, Denham informed the Admiralty during the night of 20/21 May that he had been told by a usually reliable source that two large warships, accompanied by destroyers, escort vessels and aircraft, had passed through the Kattegat that afternoon, steering north-west.[86] Confirmation was received soon afterwards from Norwegian resistance-workers.

At that point the Naval Enigma made its contribution. During the forenoon of 21 May decrypts of signals intercepted in April but only just read reached the Admiralty. Among them were messages which showed that the *Bismarck* had been exercising with the *Prinz Eugen* in the Baltic, and had embarked prize-crews and received charts suitable for a raiding expedition.[87] This information, none the less valuable for being belated, was followed in the afternoon by the news that at 1 p.m. a reconnaissance aircraft had photographed the *Bismarck* and the *Prinz Eugen* in Korsfiord, just south of Bergen. We now know that they had arrived less than two hours earlier and left in the early evening, after the *Prinz Eugen* had refuelled.

At 6.28 p.m. on 21 May the Operational Intelligence Centre passed the relevant Enigma decrypts to naval commands, adding a comment to the effect that one ship of the *Bismarck* class and one of the *Prinz Eugen* class had been reported by reconnaissance at Bergen, and that evidently the ships intended to raid trade-routes.[88] This was a great advance on the procedure in force at the time of the Battle of Jutland, when Room 40 was not allowed to communicate directly with commands, or to make unsolicited comments.

Admiral Tovey had already ordered a special watch on the Denmark Strait by the 1st Cruiser Squadron (Rear-Admiral W. F. Wake-Walker), and had two cruisers patrolling between Iceland and the Faeröes. He now sent the Battle Cruiser Squadron (consisting of the old battle-cruiser *Hood*, the battleship *Prince of Wales* and six destroyers, and commanded by Vice-Admiral L. E. Holland) to support the 1st Cruiser Squadron. He retained under his direct command at Scapa the battleship *King George V*, five cruisers and five destroyers. To these the Admiralty added the battle-cruiser *Repulse* and the new carrier *Victorious*, recalled from escort duty.

No further intelligence was received for more than twenty-four hours. Attempts by reconnaissance crews of Coastal Command to discover on 22 May whether the German squadron was still at Bergen were defeated by fog and low cloud. It was not until the evening that, on the initiative of the station commander, an old Maryland normally used for target-towing made a hazardous but successful flight below cloud from Hatston to Bergen and back. The aircraft carried a very experienced naval observer, Commander Geoffrey Rotherham, who was the station's executive officer. He reported that there were no heavy ships at Bergen or in the neighbouring fiords.[89]

On receiving Rotherham's report about 8 p.m., Tovey decided to proceed on the assumption that the *Bismarck* and the *Prinz Eugen* would head for the Atlantic. He ordered the cruisers already at sea to concentrate on the passages north and south of Iceland by which the enemy might break out. At 10.45 p.m. he took the main fleet to sea with the intention of covering the cruisers and taking up a position which would enable him to intercept the German squadron, irrespective of which passage it might attempt.

The weather on 23 May was again unfavourable for reconnaissance, but clearer towards the edge of the ice than further south. At 7.22 p.m. the *Bismarck* was sighted from the cruiser *Suffolk*, heading south-west with the *Prinz Eugen* astern of her. The *Suffolk* took cover in the bank of mist to port, but maintained radar contact. About an hour later she broke cover to make a further visual contact. At the same time her sister-ship, the *Norfolk*, also sighted the enemy. The two cruisers continued to shadow the German squadron until shortly after midnight, when they lost contact in a snowstorm.

Meanwhile Admiral Holland was closing with the enemy at high speed and on a course which, had he maintained it, would have put him in a position to bring the superior firepower of his two capital ships to bear on the *Bismarck* in the early hours of 24 May. As it was, on learning that the cruisers had lost contact he seems to have assumed that the reason must be that the German squadron had either doubled back or shifted to a southerly or south-easterly course. At 12.17 a.m. he changed his heading from north-west to north and reduced his speed. About a quarter of an hour later he told his squadron that, if the enemy had not been sighted by 2 a.m., he would turn south, but that his destroyers were then to continue to search to the north.[90] A visual reconnaissance in the twilight of the northern night by the aircraft carried by the *Prince of Wales* would have been feasible in normal circumstances, but none was made because visibility for some hours after midnight was poor.

At 1.47 a.m. Holland announced that he proposed to concentrate the fire of his two heavy ships on the *Bismarck* and leave the *Prinz Eugen* to be dealt with by Wake-Walker's cruisers. He did not know that, although the German ships had maintained their south-westerly course, they had changed places, so that the *Bismarck* was now between the *Prinz Eugen* and the cruisers.

Exactly an hour later, the *Suffolk* regained contact with the enemy. From that time until action was joined, she and the *Norfolk* transmitted frequent reports of the enemy's course, speed and position.[91]

Meanwhile Holland had carried out his intention of turning to the south soon after 2 a.m., and at 3.40 a.m. he turned towards the enemy. But by holding to the north between 12.17 and 2.10 a.m. he had allowed the German squadron to draw ahead, with the result that his final approach was made at an angle which prevented the after-turrets of his ships from opening fire. Moreover, although the German ships were sighted at 5.35 a.m. and the *Bismarck* was almost immediately seen from the control position of the *Prince of Wales* to be the right-hand ship, Holland still thought she was the left-hand one. At 5.49 a.m. he ordered that the fire of both capital ships should be concentrated on the left-hand ship. This obviously mistaken order was disregarded aboard the *Prince of Wales*, but so far as the *Hood* was concerned it was not countermanded until a few seconds before fire was opened at approximately 5.53 a.m. It is therefore probable, and indeed there is a good deal of evidence to suggest, that only the *Prince of Wales* fired at the *Bismarck*.

However that may be, it is certain that the *Hood*'s fire was ineffective. The *Bismarck*'s was accurate. About 6 a.m. the *Hood* blew up with a tremendous explosion and was lost with all but three of her company of 95 officers and 1,324 ratings. The destroyers, far away to the north, took no part in the action. The *Prince of Wales* scored two hits on the *Bismarck* and was hit by shells from both German ships before turning away. She then joined Wake-Walker's cruisers in an attempt to shadow the German squadron until Tovey arrived with the main body of the fleet.

That Tovey would arrive in time to intercept it seemed to him and the Admiralty far from certain. By doubling back at high speed, the enemy might yet shake off his pursuers.

We now know that the German commander, Vice-Admiral Günther Lütjens, took a rather different view. The *Bismarck* was losing oil as a result of one of the hits scored by the *Prince of Wales*. Lütjens decided to send the *Prinz Eugen* away and make for a French port, steaming at a reduced speed in order to conserve fuel. He signalled his intentions to the naval authorities ashore, and at noon on 24 May his control was transferred from Wilhelmshaven to Paris. Eventually the *Prinz Eugen* reached Brest without him.

As the naval Enigma was not yet being read currently at Bletchley, the *Bismarck*'s signals were not decrypted until 28 May, when all was over.[92] The naval section of the GC & CS did, however, learn from its study of the traffic of the transfer of her control to Paris.[93] But either this evidence failed to reach Tovey, or he did not regard it as conclusive. Although he learned from Wake-Walker's cruisers at 1.20 p.m. that the *Bismarck* had altered course to the south and reduced her speed to about 24 knots, he still thought she might make for a German or a Norwegian port. At 2.40 p.m. he sent the 2nd Cruiser Squadron and the *Victorious* ahead of his main body with orders to proceed to a position from which an attack by torpedo-bombers could be launched. One Swordfish from the *Victorious* scored a hit on the *Bismarck* shortly after midnight, but Tovey's hope of damaging her so severely that she would be forced to reduce her speed still further was not fulfilled.

In the early hours of 25 May the *Suffolk* again lost touch with the *Bismarck*. However, a little before 9 a.m. Lütjens transmitted a signal from a position which, according to the Admiralty's calculations, suggested that he was making for Saint Nazaire or Brest. On that assumption, Force H was brought up from Gibraltar and the *Rodney* was ordered to cover the northern approaches to the Bay of Biscay. The bearings were signalled to Tovey's flagship, but her navigating officer's estimate of the *Bismarck*'s position differed from the Admiralty's. On the strength of it, Tovey set course for the gap between Iceland and the Faeröes. The discrepancy was noticed at the Admiralty, but it was not brought to Tovey's attention because the Operational Intelligence Centre could not be sure that his ships had not obtained more accurate bearings on the *Bismarck* than were obtainable ashore.[94]

The *Bismarck* transmitted two more signals during the forenoon of 25 May. Again the Admiralty's fixes suggested that she was making for a French port. Nevertheless, for reasons which remain obscure, the Admiralty hedged its bet at 2.28 p.m. by redirecting the *Rodney* towards the Iceland–Faeröes gap. But at 6.5 p.m. it countermanded this instruction and once more ordered the *Rodney* to a position covering the approaches to the Bay of Biscay. Five minutes later, Tovey came independently to the conclusion that after all the *Bismarck* must be making for the French Atlantic coast, and at last set course in the right direction.[95]

Almost at that very moment, Luftwaffe Enigma traffic clinched the matter. By 6.12 p.m. the Operational Intelligence Centre knew that the Chief of Staff of the Luftwaffe, who was in Athens in connection with the invasion of Crete, had asked for personal reasons to be informed of the *Bismarck*'s destination, and had been told that it was Brest.[96]

Impressive confirmation was received on the following day. At 10.30 a.m. on 26 May the crew of a long-range maritime reconnaissance aircraft of Coastal Command sighted the *Bismarck* about 700 miles west of Brest. The aircraft passed so close to her that she opened fire on it.

This meant that, if the *Bismarck* could still make 24 knots, she would soon be close enough to the coast to receive continuous air cover. Tovey's flagship, joined at 6 p.m. by the *Rodney*, was 130 miles away. Force H, consisting of the battlecruiser *Renown*, the carrier *Ark Royal* and the cruiser *Sheffield*, was much closer, and between the *Bismarck* and her destination. Her fate was sealed when, shortly before nightfall, one of two hits scored by Swordfish from the *Ark Royal* damaged her propellers and jammed her rudders, so that her progress became slow and erratic. Attacked during the night and early on 27 May by a destroyer flotilla ordered to join Tovey, and later by the *King George V*, the *Rodney* and the cruiser *Dorsetshire*, she sank at 10.36 a.m. with her flag still flying. The *Dorsetshire* and a destroyer rescued 110 survivors.

Viewed from the intelligence aspect, the *Bismarck* affair invites the comment that the British commanders and staff officers concerned received some good information from a variety of sources, that the use they made of it was sometimes erratic, but that the information was far from complete and that they made some good as well as some bad guesses.

Chiefly as a result of the breaking of the naval Enigma, the Royal Navy was able within a few weeks of the sinking of the *Bismarck* to intercept all nine of the supply ships stationed by the Germans in the Atlantic and elsewhere to refuel and reprovision U-boats and surface raiders.[97] Five were sunk or captured, the rest scuttled by their crews. From the beginning of June, when the traffic was first read currently, the Admiralty was reluctant to use it to intercept ships whose whereabouts would not otherwise have been known, for fear that the Germans might suspect that their signals were being read. We now know that they did have their suspicions, but came to the conclusion that Enigma was impregnable. They were somewhat reassured by a report from the Abwehr to the effect that the British were known to have learnt of the *Bismarck*'s move from Gdynia to Bergen from a source other than signal intelligence.[98]

These events were followed by a marked falling-off in the activities of surface-raiders. Between the outbreak of war and June 1941, 161 British, Allied or neutral merchant vessels had been sunk by surface warships or merchant raiders, mostly German. In the second half of 1941 only nine were sunk. The figure for all theatres rose in 1942 to 61. Thereafter until the end of the war surface raiders sank only six British, Allied or neutral merchant vessels, the last in March 1944.

But none of this meant that the U-boat was permanently defeated. Germany and Italy responded to Pearl Harbor by declaring war on the United States. Early in 1942 the U-boat force opened a new phase of the Battle of the Atlantic by extending its operations to North American waters. Almost simultaneously, boats working in the Atlantic stopped using the normal naval Enigma key and were alloted a cypher of their

own called Triton.[99] The American authorities, although all the
experience accumulated by the British since 1939 was at their disposal,
were extraordinarily slow to adopt such obvious precautions as the
convoying of coastal traffic, the blacking-out of coast towns and the
effective dimming of illuminated buoys and beacons. Many ships which
had crossed the Atlantic safely, or were about to join ocean convoys,
were sunk off the East Coast of the United States or in the Caribbean or
the Gulf of Mexico. Moreover, as escort vessels were still scarce and the
GC & CS did not succeed in breaking Triton until December, losses
elsewhere were heavy. We now know that the Germans calculated that
Britain would be brought to her knees if submarines could sink an
average of 700,000 tons of merchant shipping a month. That was more
than they could manage, but the monthly average for all theatres in 1942
was well over 500,000 tons, and this figure does not include the 61 ships
sunk by surface raiders, 220 sunk by mines, aircraft or patrol vessels, or
223 lost from unknown causes.[100] The average for the first five months of
1943 was about 356,000 tons. Thereafter sinkings fell off sharply. But the
ability of the British to read most of the German Navy's wireless traffic
did not prevent the U-boat menace from continuing to cause them great
anxiety until the war was almost over.

Nor did it prevent the Germans from defying Britain's control of the
narrow waters in February 1942 by passing the *Scharnhorst*, the
Gneisenau and the *Prinz Eugen* through the English Channel. As a *Times*
leader-writer pointed out, nothing like it had happened in home waters
since a Dutch admiral sailed up the Thames in the seventeenth century.

The accomplishment of this feat was all the more mortifying for the
British because the Germans had long been expected to attempt it.
From the time in the spring of 1941 when the battlecruisers were known
to have arrived at Brest after a foray in the Atlantic, the Admiralty had
thought it probable that, unless they were irretrievably damaged by air
attacks in the meantime, sooner or later they would be ordered back to
Germany. They were closely watched by air reconnaissance throughout
their stay, and frequent reports of the progress of repairs to the
Gneisenau were received from well-wishers who included a French
naval officer employed at the dockyard.[101]

We now know that the immediate cause of the move was Hitler's
conviction in the early part of 1942 that a British invasion of Norway was
imminent. At a conference on 12 January he declared that every German
warship not in Norwegian waters was in the wrong place. The new
battleship *Tirpitz* duly moved from the Baltic to Trondheim a few days

later by way of the Kiel Canal and Wilhelmshaven. The *Scharnhorst*, the *Gneisenau* and the *Prinz Eugen*, under the command of Vice-Admiral Otto Ciliax, were to follow during the period before the new moon in the second week of February. They were not to leave Brest before nightfall, and – if they got so far – would therefore reach the Dover Strait in daylight.

The British knew nothing of this conference. During the next two to three weeks, however, they learned from their principal informant at Brest, Lieutenant Philippon, and from two other informants there, that the *Scharnhorst*, the *Gneisenau* and the *Prinz Eugen* were ready to put to sea, and that Philippon expected them to leave under cover of darkness. At the same time, signal intelligence showed that the destroyers which had accompanied the *Tirpitz* to Trondheim had been ordered to Brest. There were also indications that German minesweepers were paying special attention to waters through which the ships would pass if they went up-Channel, and that aircraft and patrol vessels were receiving orders consistent with preparations for a sortie.[102]

In the light of this evidence Commander N. E. Denning, head of the Operational Intelligence Centre and a future Director of Naval Intelligence, reported at the end of January that all three of the German heavy ships at Brest were now seaworthy and that a major operation seemed probable. He added that conditions for an up-Channel dash would be particularly suitable on 12 February.[103]

The Naval Staff accepted the substance of Denning's conclusions, but were not convinced that the German commander would choose to leave Brest after dark at the cost of having to negotiate the Dover Strait in daylight. An Admiralty appreciation of 2 February concluded that in any case the Brest squadron was more likely to make for German waters than to attempt a sortie against ocean trade or take refuge in an Italian port, and in all probability would prefer the Channel route to a long northabout passage west of Ireland. 'We might well', the compilers of the appreciation wrote, 'find the two battlecruisers and the eight-inch cruiser ... proceeding up-Channel.'[104]

On the following day the Admiralty's views were signalled to naval commands at home and conveyed by liaison officers to the appropriate RAF commands. Counter-measures were put in hand, but these were of a very modest character. No heavy ships were ordered to Portsmouth or Plymouth. Admiral Tovey had at Scapa Flow the *King George V*, the *Renown*, the *Rodney*, the carrier *Victorious*, four cruisers and thirteen destroyers. The *Rodney*, with most of Force H from Gibraltar, was already earmarked to escort a large troop-carrying convoy about to leave the Clyde for the Middle East. The rest of the Home Fleet, it was thought, might be needed at any moment to take care of the *Tirpitz*. The Commander-in-Chief, Plymouth, and the Flag Officer, Dover, each received a fast minelayer. The Commander-in-Chief, The Nore, was told to be ready to reinforce the Flag Officer, Dover, with six torpedo-carrying destroyers and six motor torpedo-boats. The only modern submarine available was authorized to enter the Brest roads at her commander's discretion, and two old boats normally used for training were stationed further to seaward. Six Swordfish torpedo-bombers of the Fleet Air Arm were moved from Lee-on-Solent to Manston, near Ramsgate.

The only other torpedo-bombers available in February were fourteen Beauforts of Coastal Command at Leuchars, in Scotland; twelve at St Eval, in Cornwall; and seven at Thorney Island, near Portsmouth. About a dozen bomber-reconnaissance aircraft, also under Coastal Command, were stationed on the East Coast. Bomber Command had about 240 aircraft considered suitable for day-bombing, but their crews were not adequately trained to identify and attack warships at sea. Fighter Command had plenty of aircraft in the south, and was in the habit of searching daily for hostile shipping between the mouth of the Somme and Ostend. Its aircraft would also be available to escort and cover bombers and torpedo-bombers if the necessary arrangements could be made in time. Finally, Hudson aircraft of Coastal Command, equipped with radar capable in theory of detecting large ships at ranges up to thirty miles, were to reconnoitre nightly off Brest, between Ushant and the Ile de Bréhat, and between Le Havre and Boulogne.

The shortcomings of this plan were considerable, to say the least. No single officer was responsible for its execution. The steps taken by the Admiralty showed that they regarded the Flag Officer, Dover, as likely to play a crucial role, but he had no power to issue orders to units not under his command or expressly put at his disposal. None of the naval commands from Plymouth to The Nore had any ships which could be relied upon to sink battlecruisers. Destroyers and motor torpedo-boats could not be expected to prove a match for heavy ships protected by a destroyer screen whose strength the Admiralty estimated at five large and five small flotilla vessels. As the Admiralty also estimated that the German squadron would have 'twenty fighters constantly overhead', the torpedo-bombers would be in no better case. Co-ordinated attacks by Swordfish and Beauforts with fighter support would be hard to arrange, not only because their bases were far apart but also because the Swordfish were much slower than the Beauforts and both were considerably slower than the fighters which would be called upon to cover and escort them. Bomber Command would have to rely on crews with little experience of attacking moving targets, and the bombs normally carried by its aircraft could damage but not sink armoured warships. Armour-piercing bombs which *could* sink warships were available, but these were effective only if dropped from heights at which accurate bombing was possible only in clear weather.

The radar-equipped Hudsons began their special patrols on 3 February, and the mining of channels known to be of special interest to the enemy was stepped up. The fourteen Beauforts from Leuchars were ordered to Norfolk on 11 February, but they did not move until the following day because East Anglian airfields were snowbound. Five of them left without torpedoes, and there were none at the fighter base to which they were diverted.

We now know that Admiral Ciliax intended to start at 7.30 p.m. on 11 February, but was delayed by a raid on Brest by Bomber Command. He left at 10.45 p.m. and rounded Ushant soon after midnight. The night was very dark. By 5.15 a.m. on 12 February he was abreast of the Channel Islands. From that point he kept as near as he could to his own side of the water, passing close to Cap Gris Nez and not far outside the Frisians.

Coastal Command's night patrols were wholly ineffective. The first Hudson sent to patrol off Brest returned to base about 7.30 p.m. because its radar equipment had broken down. The same crew left about two hours later in another aircraft and patrolled until they were relieved soon after midnight. The departing German ships were not detected, and we now know that they were within range of the second aircraft for only a few minutes.[105] The one and only Hudson sent to patrol between Ushant and the Ile de Bréhat also suffered a radar failure. It returned to base about 9.50 p.m. No relief aircraft was sent, and the Flag Officer, Dover, was not told that the patrol had failed.[106] The third patrol, between Le Havre and Boulogne, was carried out more or less as planned, but the German squadron did not arrive off Le Havre until about 8 a.m. and was therefore never within range of it.

Fighter Command's contribution began with a report of considerable activity by patrol craft from two Spitfire pilots sent to make the usual early-morning reconnaissance between Ostend and Boulogne. From 8.25 a.m. hostile aircraft were detected by radar north of Le Havre. This was not unusual, but fighters were sent to search between Boulogne and

Fécamp. Heavy jamming was reported by radar stations on the South Coast from 9.20 a.m. This ought to have aroused suspicion. It failed to do so because jamming had been experienced on a number of occasions in recent weeks. The pilot of one of the fighters sent to search between Boulogne and Fécamp reported what he described as a convoy of twenty to thirty ships off Le Touquet, but it was only when he was interrogated after landing that he identified one of the ships he had seen as a capital ship.[107] The battlecruisers were first positively identified when Group Captain Victor Beamish, commanding the Kenley Sector, flew right over them at 10.42 a.m. while carrying out a freelance offensive patrol with the leader of the Kenley Wing as his companion.[108] As he was flying too low to be in radio contact with Kenley, his news did not become known until he landed at 11.10 a.m. It reached the Flag Officer, Dover, from Fighter Command at 11.25 a.m.

By that time Lieutenant-Commander E. Esmonde, commanding the Swordfish at Manston, was aware that something unusual was happening and had brought his aircraft to immediate readiness. After co-ordinated attacks by Swordfish and Beauforts had been discussed and rejected as impractical, it was agreed that he should attack about 12.45 p.m. with cover and escort form five fighter squadrons due over Manston at 12.25 p.m. Only one squadron had arrived when, at 12.28 p.m., he decided that he could wait no longer. The others followed, and two of them reached the target area while he was in contact with the enemy. All the Swordfish were lost, and no hits were scored.[109]

The Beauforts were no more successful, although their losses were less calamitous. The twelve from St Eval arrived too late to find the enemy in gathering darkness, and two failed to return. Six from Thorney Island and seven from Leuchars launched torpedoes but scored no hits, and one Beaufort from Thorney Island was shot down. No hits were scored by Coastal Command's bomber-reconnaissance aircraft or Bomber Command's bombers. Torpedoes were fired, without result, from four motor torpedo-boats and five destroyers.[110]

So once more good intelligence failed to yield good results. Except that the evidence that Ciliax would leave Brest after dark was not conclusive, the naval and air authorities could hardly have wished for a better forecast of the enemy's course of action than they received. It is unlikely that the Admiralty and Admiral Tovey would in any circumstances have agreed to strengthen the naval commands in the south at the expense of the Home Fleet and ocean convoys, but possible that such forces as were available might have been more effectively disposed if they had been convinced that the battlecruisers were likely to appear in mid-Channel in full daylight.

The fact remains that the up-Channel dash of the Brest squadron, although brilliantly successful, brought Germany no strategic benefit. The removal of the battlecruisers from Brest relieved the British of the threat of an Atlantic foray from that quarter. Both battlecruisers struck mines during the voyage, and the *Scharnhorst* was seriously damaged. Early in 1943 she made two attempts to reach Norwegian waters, but on each occasion naval Enigma gave warning of her intention, and she turned back after being sighted.[111] She afterwards succeeded in joining the *Tirpitz* in the extreme north of Norway, where her presence was revealed by air reconnaissance in March.[112] Enigma messages decrypted in the third and fourth weeks of the following December revealed that she was ready to put to sea, and finally that she had done so.[113] On 26 December she was intercepted and sunk off the North Cape by the battleship *Duke of York* and cruiser and destroyer forces of the Home Fleet, commanded since May by Admiral Sir Bruce Fraser. Her last message, duly intercepted and decyphered by the British, was to the effect that she would fight to the last shell.[114] Fraser's cruisers and destroyers made a long search for survivors in the icy darkness, but succeeded in finding only thirty-six.[115]

The *Gneisenau* was outwardly in good shape when she reached Germany on 12 February 1942, but in fact she had made her last voyage. She was twice hit by heavy bombs during a raid by Bomber Command on Kiel on the night of 26/27 February. The German naval authorities estimated that the cumulative effects of these hits, the damage done to her at Brest and her contact with a mine on 12 February would take a year to repair. The attempt was abandoned early in 1943, and she became a useless hulk.

EIGHT

The Eastern Front

In the summer of 1940 the British government began an attempt to improve relations with the Soviet Union by sending a new ambassador to Moscow. This was Sir Stafford Cripps, an austere left-wing intellectual who so far differed from the traditional image of John Bull as to be a strict vegetarian.

On his way to Moscow, Cripps told *The Times* correspondent in Sofia that, in his opinion, war between Germany and Russia was inevitable. At an interview with the Soviet Commissar for Foreign Affairs on 14 June, he went far beyond a mere expression of opinion. He told Molotov that, 'according to our information', Germany would 'turn east' if France collapsed. At the beginning of July he said much the same to the Greek Minister in Moscow, adding that Hitler would like to launch an attack in the autumn but would have to defer it until the spring of 1941.[1]

These were remarkable statements. 'According to our information' implied that the British government had positive evidence either that the Germans were making active preparations to 'turn east', or that they had expressed in the context of recent events a firm intention to do so. But the government had no such evidence. Hitler had said or written on a number of occasions that he regarded it as his destiny to rid the world of bolshevism and to win living-space for the German people in Eastern Europe. There were rumours in diplomatic circles to the effect that the Russians were alarmed by German successes in Western Europe and that an eventual clash between Germany and the Soviet Union was almost certain. But what Hitler would do at the end of his campaign in France and the Low Countries could not have been known to the British government, because it was not yet known to Hitler himself.[2] The swiftness of his victory had taken him and his military advisers by surprise.

We now know that it was not until 21 July, when Hitler had already called for plans to invade Britain but was far from sure that their execution would be necessary or even possible, that he ordered OKH to begin preliminary studies for an attack on the Soviet Union.[3] By that time he had become suspicious of Soviet intentions in the Baltic States and the Balkans, and had been shown signals intercepted by the Italians which suggested that the Russians were playing a double game with Germany and Britain.[4] At further conferences on 29 and 31 July he told the service chiefs that destruction of the Soviet Union would become the key to the problem of ending the war if he decided not to invade Britain.[5]

But Cripps was not alone in believing as early as June and the first part of July that Hitler had designs on Russia. On 26 June Churchill sent Stalin, through Cripps, a warning similar to that already given by Cripps to Molotov.[6] On the following day he expressed to General Smuts, and on 8 July to Lord Beaverbrook, the opinion that Germany would 'recoil eastwards' if she failed to conquer Britain, or perhaps would move in that direction in any case.[7]

As contributions to an attempt to improve relations with the Soviet Union, the warnings given by Cripps and Churchill in June were perhaps unwise. If Stalin knew or guessed that they were premature, that would go some way to explain his subsequent attitude to such communications. On 1 August the Soviet government publicly accused Britain of trying to drive a wedge between Russia and Germany. From that time until German troops crossed the demarcation line in Poland on 22 June 1941, Stalin repeatedly dismissed as 'British provocation' reports that Germany was about to invade Russia, even when they came from agents whose loyalty to the Soviet cause was not in doubt.

He did not have to wait long for such reports. The Soviet Military Attaché in Berlin warned Moscow before the end of July that the Germans were preparing to make war on the Soviet Union. Moreover, MI 6 knew that he had done so.[8] The source of his information remains obscure. He was in touch with at least two agents in Berlin who had access to the secret files of the Air Ministry and the Foreign Ministry but not, so far as is known, to those of OKH or OKW. As knowledge of the instructions given by Hitler on 21 July is said to have been still confined at the end of July to Hitler himself and a few very senior officers, it seems possible that the attaché had no specific information and was merely repeating gossip current in diplomatic circles.

But more specific though less sweeping reports were soon forthcoming. The substance of those received by the British from a variety of sources up to the end of 1940 can be broadly summarized as follows:

1 The Germans were expanding their army and forming new armoured and mechanized divisions.

2 They had moved possibly as many as 60 divisions (an exaggeration) from Western Europe to Occupied Poland, ostensibly for training in an area beyond the reach of British air reconnaissance.

3 They were moving troops to Finland and demanding transit rights through Finland to Northern Norway.

4 The Russians were putting pressure on the Finns to demilitarize certain areas.

5 They were falling behind in the delivery to Germany of raw materials to which the Germans were entitled by the terms of the economic pact.

6 They were reluctant to part with materials needed for their own defence. At the same time, they accused the Germans of not fulfilling their side of the bargain, and in particular of sending to Finland goods which apparently they were unable to send to Russia.

7 The Germans were developing west-to-east road and rail communications in Slovakia.

8 They were stepping up their espionage and counter-espionage activities against the Soviet Union.

9 The Abwehr was recruiting specialists on the Ukraine, the Crimea and the Caucasus.

10 Abwehr officers had told the representative of MI 6 in Helsinki that Germany would attack the Soviet Union in the spring of 1941.

11 The Swedish government was convinced that Germany would soon attack the Soviet Union, but that nevertheless the Germans were taking care not to antagonize the Russians.

12 Dispossessed owners of property in the Baltic States had said openly that they would soon regain their estates in the wake of the German Army.

There is no reason to suppose that the Russians were not equally well informed. According to statements made after the war by organizers of Soviet espionage networks, Moscow was kept well posted by its agents with information about Germany's intentions and the build-up of German forces in Eastern Europe. Moreover, it is probable that a good deal of the information received by the British was intentionally leaked, through the enigmatic Rudolf Rössler, to the Swiss-based Soviet espionage network organized by the Hungarian-born veteran Communist Alexander Rado. Whether Rössler really was in touch with the high-level informants in Berlin of whose identity Moravec claimed to be aware seems rather doubtful. There is no doubt that by 1940 he was in touch with British and Allied intelligence agencies, or that his association with them and with Rado's network had the tacit approval of the Swiss military authorities.

But none of this evidence convinced either the Russians or British Military Intelligence that a German invasion of the Soviet Union was inevitable. The Russians hoped that, if the worst came to the worst, they could buy the Germans off. British Military Intelligence could not bring itself to believe that the Germans would commit themselves to so hazardous an undertaking while Britain was undefeated.[9] That Hitler would try to seize by conquest what he could surely obtain more cheaply by negotiation seemed to the War Office both too good to be true, and inconsistent with all that he had said about not exposing Germany to a two-front war. From the British point of view, an added complication was that a good deal of the evidence which pointed to preparations to attack the Soviet Union seemed equally consistent with preparations to invade Greece as the prelude to an advance through Turkey to the Middle East. On that basis, the transfer of divisions to Poland could be construed as a defensive measure, intended merely to discourage Soviet intervention.

That, as we now know, was just what the Germans wanted the British to think. The essence of their deception plan for Operation Barbarossa was that logistic preparations in Eastern Europe should be represented as preparations for a postponed Operation Sea Lion but that, lest this pretence should fail to convince, they should also be represented as preparations to hold off the Russians while German troops moved into the Balkans. But we also know that the authorities in Whitehall reached this conclusion not because they were taken in by Hitler's deception plan, but because they had already got hold of the wrong end of the stick without any prompting from the Germans. On the very day in January 1941 when Hitler reaffirmed his intention of invading Russia in the middle or at the end of May, the Future Operations (Enemy) Section of the Joint Intelligence Committee endorsed the view held by the War Office that the German troops in Poland had been sent there to guard against a Russian attack while Germany marched into the Balkans.[10]

During the next three months the British received many more reports of German intentions, moves and preparations. Some seemed to point unmistakably to an impending attack on the Soviet Union. Others could be interpreted in the opposite sense, or were ambiguous. A report received from an agent at the end of January said that German preparations for war with Russia were almost unconcealed, that besides moving troops from Western Europe to Poland the Germans were building airfields along the line of the railway from Poznan to Lodz and recruiting Russian-speaking Germans and Russian émigrés.[11] Another, received early in February, said that German military formations, mostly armoured, were arriving in East Prussia and that the railway between Berlin and Warsaw was congested with traffic.[12] In the middle of February the Abwehr's principal hand-cypher, first read in December, confirmed earlier reports that German intelligence and counter-intelligence agencies were paying special attention to the Soviet Union, although the same source showed that they were also keenly interested in Near Eastern and Middle Eastern countries.[13] Reports received in London by the first week of March indicated that Germany was strengthening her ties with Finland, that German officers were organizing military and air bases close to the Russo-Finnish frontier and that German agents were fostering subversive movements in the Ukraine and the Caucasus. They also showed that Germany had asked the Rumanian government for plans of bridges across the Pruth and the Dniester and that the Hungarian General Staff expected her to attack the Soviet Union in the summer.[14] Later in March an agent expressed the opinion that Germany would turn against Russia after occupying Greece, Yugoslavia and European Turkey in the spring. Almost simultaneously, the GC & CS decrypted a message in which the Japanese Ambassador in Berlin reported that Admiral Räder doubted whether Germany would be wise to attack Britain or British interests in the Middle East, had hinted at offensives in some other direction, and had suggested that Japan should attack Singapore.[15]

However, the British also learned between January and March that Germany and the Soviet Union had renewed their economic pact and signed a Pact of Friendship, and that the Greek and Turkish diplomatic representatives in Moscow believed that reports of an impending invasion of Russia were being spread by the Germans to conceal preparations to invade Greece and Turkey. Reports to the effect that the Germans were building fortifications along the demarcation line in Poland seemed, too, to support the belief that their attitude to the Soviet Union was more defensive than offensive. Furthermore, they were known in March to be moving divisions westwards to Belgium and Occupied France. Some British specialists on the German Order of Battle suggested that these were training divisions which were being got out of the way as the prelude to an attack on Russia. The Military Intelligence Branch was not entirely convinced by this argument, but agreed that the moves pointed to a redistribution of the Wehrmacht's resources rather than the strengthening of any particular area.[16]

Some further information, so striking that according to Churchill's subsequent account it 'illuminated the whole Eastern scene in a lightning flash', was received in the last week of March. Luftwaffe Enigma revealed on 26 March that three armoured divisions, an SS division, a corps headquarters and the headquarters of an armoured group, with other details, had been ordered from the Balkans to the neighbourhood of Cracow. On the following day the same source revealed that within twelve hours of the *coup d'état* in Yugoslavia the move had been halted, the first formations to entrain had been ordered to remain in sidings, and the Chief of Staff of the Luftwaffe and the commander of Luftflotte 4 had been summoned to Berlin for a conference with Göring.[17]

Churchill's interpretation of these events was that Hitler had assembled powerful forces in the Balkans to overawe Yugoslavia and Greece, had thought it safe to reduce them when Yugoslavia agreed to join the Rome–Berlin axis, but had changed his mind on learning of the *coup d'état*. It seemed to follow that an attack on the Soviet Union was coming, but would not be delivered until the situation in the Balkans was cleared up.

On 30 March Churchill asked the Foreign Secretary and the Chief of the Imperial General Staff, then in Athens, to comment on these conclusions.[18] On 3 April he addressed to Stalin, through Cripps, a message incorporating the gist of the Enigma information, attributing it in the interests of security to 'a trusted agent'. Fearing that the Russians would regard the message as provocative, Cripps withheld it until 19 April, when he submitted it with a message of his own to Andrei Vyshinsky, the Deputy Commissar for Foreign Affairs. In the meantime he urged upon Vyshinsky the seriousness of the German threat to the Soviet Union and the importance of supporting the Balkan states.[19]

The Russians received many other reminders that their situation was precarious. From 20 March the United States government plied the Soviet Ambassador in Washington with warnings based on the Japanese diplomatic traffic which the Signal Corps had begun to read in the previous September.[20] These appear to have been of a general character and not to have included detailed information about the German plan or the date when effect might be given to it. The Swedish authorities acquired from their intelligence service, and communicated to the United States Ambassador in Moscow on 24 March, some valuable information about German intentions.[21] The Yugoslav Military Attaché in Berlin, also apparently well-informed about these matters, passed his material to Moscow by way of London.[22] Information about German troop movements acquired by agents of the Vichy government reached the Russians through diplomatic channels and probably also through their Swiss network.

They also had sources of their own. In October 1940 Cripps told the Foreign Office, in effect, that the Russians were terrified of simultaneous attacks by Germany and Japan.[23] It was largely to assess the reality of this danger that one of the Soviet Union's ablest agents, Richard Sorge, had been sent to Tokyo in 1933.[24]

Sorge was the son of a prosperous German mining engineer who worked for some years in Russia but returned to Germany when Richard was three. Richard's mother was Russian. He served during the first half of World War I in a volunteer battalion of the German Army, and sustained wounds which left him with a slight limp. Although not formally discharged from the army until 1918, he spent the last two years of the war reading economics at the University of Berlin and afterwards at Kiel, where he came under strong left-wing influences. He went to Hamburg early in 1919 with the intention of writing a thesis, but afterwards followed his economics tutor, a Communist, to a technological college at Hamburg. He joined the German Communist Party soon after the armistice, but left it in 1925 to become a member of the Communist Party of the Soviet Union. From 1924 to 1929 he spent most of his time in Moscow, where he was employed at the headquarters of the Comintern. After attending the Sixth World Congress of the Comintern in Moscow in 1928 he visited Sweden and the United Kingdom, and in 1929 he was recruited by Soviet Military Intelligence and assigned to its Far Eastern section. He was then ordered to return to Berlin and establish a respectable front as a journalist specializing in sociological, economic, agricultural and Far Eastern questions. His former association with the German Communist Party was known to the authorities, but was not held against him in view of his excellent war record, academic qualifications and obvious ability. He signed contracts with two publishing firms and in due course left Berlin armed with an introduction from the Foreign Ministry to the German Consul-General at Shanghai. He was suspected by the Shanghai police almost immediately after his arrival in China of being a Soviet agent, but he was not molested and was able to travel widely and make a number of contacts with Communists and crypto-Communists of various nationalities.

In view of the widely-held belief that the Soviet intelligence effort was almost fatally handicapped by conflicts between rival agencies, it is of some interest that no objection was made to his being briefed for his mission to China by a variety of mentors. These included Jan Berzin himself, members of his staff, representatives of the Comintern, the Soviet Communist Party and its Central Committee in Moscow, and at least two officials of the People's Commissariat for Foreign Affairs.

Sorge left Shanghai at the end of 1932 and reached Moscow early in 1933. He claimed afterwards that, on being told that he would soon be sent abroad again, he himself suggested that his next mission should be to Japan. He was briefed by representatives of Military Intelligence, the GPU, the Comintern and the Commissariat for Foreign Affairs. No objection was made to his seeking advice from holders of key positions in the secretariat of the Central Committee of the Communist Party as well as his own department's experts on Far Eastern affairs. He left Moscow early in May for Berlin, where he reported to the police and applied for a new passport. Three German newspapers or periodicals, one of them an organ of the National Socialist Party, agreed that he should send them occasional articles from Japan, and so did a Dutch financial newspaper, the *Algemeen Handelsblad* of Amsterdam. Travelling by way of Cherbourg, New York, Washington (where he called on the Japanese Ambassador), Vancouver and Yokohama, he reached Tokyo in the autumn of 1933 and presented letters of introduction to the German Ambassador, members of his staff, and the head of the Information Department of the Japanese Foreign Ministry.

Apart from himself, Sorge's Japanese network consisted initially of Branko Vukelic, a left-wing intellectual of Serb extraction with a Danish wife, a small son, little experience of espionage and no money; Yotoku Myagi, an Okinawa-born Communist who had lived mostly in the Philippines and California, knew very little about Japan and did not even know he was to be a spy until Sorge told him so; and a wireless-operator too timid to do much transmitting. To this rather unpromising team Sorge soon added Hotsumi Ozaki, a crypto-Communist newspaper correspondent with friends in high places whom he had met in Shanghai. Ozaki's knowledge of political tendencies enabled Sorge to assure Moscow that, although many Japanese officers thought otherwise, the party which favoured war with the Soviet Union was unlikely to prevail. During the undeclared war with China he furnished both excellent information about the strength and Order of Battle of the Japanese Army, and background material which encouraged the Soviet military authorities to take a tough line when Japanese forces clashed with Soviet and Mongolian troops in 1938 and 1939. He established cordial relations with the German Ambassador and the service attachés, was formally admitted to membership of the Tokyo branch of the National Socialist Party, but did himself no harm in the eyes of his friends at the embassy by openly criticizing aspects of the régime which could not be expected to appeal to the patriotic but sturdily-independent freelance journalist he professed to be.

In the summer of 1935 Sorge interrupted his stay in Tokyo to visit Moscow and report to Berzin's successor, General Uritsky. Travelling by way of the United States, he completed the journey from New York with a forged passport, so that his true passport would not show that he had been to Russia. While in Moscow he arranged that Ozaki should be recognized as a member of his circuit.

Sorge's usefulness to Soviet Military Intelligence became greater than ever after his return to Japan and the outbreak of war with China. In the spring of 1938 Dr Herbert von Dirksen, German Ambassador in Tokyo since 1934, was posted to London and succeeded by Major-General Eugen Ott, the former Military Attaché. Sorge had always been on good terms with Dirksen; Ott was a close friend. A few months later, Ozaki received a part-time government appointment as an adviser on Chinese affairs to the Chief Secretary of the Japanese Cabinet. Finally, after the outbreak of World War II Sorge began to work on a part-time basis for the German Embassy as compiler of news-bulletins. As he was already well known to the staff as a friend and confidant of the Ambassador, this meant that he could take almost any document he chose to the room allotted to him, and study or copy it at leisure. From that time until his circuit was blown and he was arrested by the Japanese in the early winter of 1941, he was very well placed to furnish information about German as well as Japanese intentions. It has been claimed that he warned Moscow of the precise date of the German attack. If he did have prior knowledge of the date, he was better informed than Yosuke Matsuoka, the Japanese Foreign Minister. The event came as a surprise to Matsuoka, although he had been given hints and warnings by Ribbentrop and the Japanese Ambassador in Berlin.[25]

The Swiss network, too, is said to have informed Moscow of the date first chosen for the attack, and of its postponement as a result of developments in the Balkans. Thümmel may perhaps have been the ultimate source of its knowledge. He is known to have warned the British as early as August 1940 of the Abwehr's growing interest in Russia, and to have given them some account in the following March of preparations for Barbarossa.[26] By 23 May the British received from him an account of proposals that were being made for the administration of areas of the Soviet Union to be occupied by German troops.[27] It has been claimed that only a few days later he gave Moravec the date when Barbarossa would be launched. But there appears to be no surviving documentary evidence that this further report reached MI 6 or Rössler.

Apart from those attributed to the Swiss network, the Russians had in Germany and German-occupied territories a considerable number of informants who reported through various channels. For a number of reasons, their attempt to weld these into a coherent system of interlocking espionage networks was not very successful.

In the first place, it must be borne in mind that the primary target of the Soviet intelligence agencies during the greater part of the period between the wars was not Germany but France. At the end of World War I France was by far the world's strongest military power. As financial backer, political mentor and armourer of a string of anti-Communist buffer states in Eastern Europe, she was the natural enemy of bolshevism. There was a strong Communist Party in France, but it did not always take kindly to dictation from Moscow. Although in its post-war form it dated only from 1920, it inherited traditions which went back to the 1870s. By various expedients the Soviet intelligence agencies succeeded in extracting a great many reports, ostensibly intended only for the eyes of the party leaders, from French Communists employed at dockyards, arsenals, military establishments, arms factories and elsewhere; but much of the information they contained was of doubtful value. Some of it was spurious information, concocted by the French counter-intelligence service and passed on by intermediaries who had warned the authorities of attempts to suborn them and agreed to co-operate with the police. As political propagandists the Soviet manipulators of the Comintern made considerable headway in France, but the ultimate effect of Soviet-inspired industrial unrest and class-hatred was to undermine the capacity of the French to resist National Socialist aggression.

As long as France remained the potential enemy, the Soviet leaders saw in Germany their most promising ally in a hypothetical war against her and her client-states in Eastern Europe. Diplomatic relations with the Weimar Republic were initiated on an informal basis soon after the end of World War I and formalized by the Treaty of Rapallo in 1922. Co-operation was both economic and military. The foundations of German air power in World War II were laid at a training establishment in Russia, attended by nearly all the officers who afterwards attained high rank in Göring's Luftwaffe.[28]

But friendly relations with the Weimar government did not prevent the Soviet leaders of that era from aiming at its eventual overthrow and replacement by a Communist régime subservient to Moscow. When the French sought in 1923 to solve the reparations problem by invading the Ruhr, the time seemed ripe for such a transformation; but attempts by emissaries of the Red Army and the Comintern to precipitate a *coup d'état* were unsuccessful. The Soviet authorities then remodelled their clandestine apparatus in Germany with a view to using it largely as an instrument of industrial and scientific espionage. Communists or Communist-sympathizers succeeded in infiltrating many research establishments maintained by large industrial firms or sponsored by the state. Other tasks undertaken by the German Communist Party on Moscow's behalf included training in sabotage and subversion, and the selection of candidates for indoctrination in Russia as agents of military intelligence, the security service or the Comintern.[29]

Soviet intelligence foresaw Hitler's rise to power, but the scope and staying-power of the National Socialist movement were at first seriously underestimated. In 1932 the Comintern advised its henchmen in Germany to make preparations to go underground.[30] In due course, privileged members of the party were able to leave the country with forged documents made ready before the agency responsible for their fabrication moved to safer quarters. Records too valuable to be destroyed were sent to Moscow or stored in safe-deposits rented in the names of persons not known to the police.

Once in power, the National Socialists aimed at destroying the German Communist Party and, as far as possible, eliminating the influence of the Comintern as a factor in German politics, but stopped short of severing diplomatic and economic relations with the Soviet Union. Party headquarters and the premises of Moscow-oriented organizations not protected by diplomatic immunity were searched, but the sanctity of the Soviet Embassy and the headquarters of the Soviet trade delegation in Berlin was respected. Large numbers of Communists or suspected Communists were interrogated. They furnished a good deal of information about the party, but few of them knew more about its links with Soviet intelligence agencies than the cover-names of persons who had provided their sole means of communication with mysterious organizations which some of them had heard referred to as Grete (Military Intelligence) or Klara (the Foreign Department of the security service).

Even so, it had to be assumed that virtually the whole of the Soviet under-cover apparatus in Germany had been compromised by these investigations. Once convinced that National Socialism was not a passing phenomenon but had come to stay, the Russians proceeded to disband it, retaining only the nucleus of a new military espionage network to be organized from a base or bases outside Germany. Although progress was delayed by Berzin's dismissal, the Stalinist purges, oscillations of foreign policy and internal squabbles, the ultimate outcome was the formation of the Swiss network and of a Western European network operating at first from Brussels and later from German-occupied Paris.

In the meantime the German Communist Party became a wholly illicit organization, much reduced in numbers by arrests, defections and emigration. There remained in Germany a large number of opponents of National Socialism, of whom some were crypto-Communists but many were not. Dislike of the upstart Hitler was particularly strong in the higher ranks of the army and the civil service. Not many serving officers and civil servants were willing to carry their distaste for the régime to the length of imparting secrets of state to foreign governments, or were in a position to do so. Of those who were, some approached the British or the French, and a few the Czechs; others established contact with the Russians, usually through the Soviet Embassy in Berlin. By 1936 Harro Schulze-Boysen, a young air force officer employed in the intelligence branch of the German Air Ministry, was in touch with the embassy and furnishing information about the Luftwaffe's role in the Spanish Civil War. He seems to have been motivated in the first instance by dislike of the National Socialist Party and its methods rather than Marxist leanings. Later, he and his wife Libertas, with the crypto-Communist civil servant and economist Arvid Harnack, helped to organize a resistance movement thought to have had about a hundred members, of whom only a small proportion were aware that espionage on behalf of the Soviet Union was among its functions. Rudolf von Scheliha, who began to supplement his income by selling secrets to the Russians when he was serving in 1937 at the German Embassy in Warsaw but was posted in 1939 to the Foreign Ministry, was an agent of a different stamp. One of the few Soviet agents who seems to have been actuated purely by mercenary motives, he was also one of the best paid.

In addition to these and other agents or sub-agents whose names are known, according to Moravec there were in Germany about ten serving officers who regularly supplied Rössler with information about naval, military and air force matters, and whose identity he did not reveal to Moscow or to members of the Swiss network.[31] Moravec's account does not give their names, although it hints that Moravec knew who they were. Nor does it explain how the expatriate Rössler was able to recruit such well-placed informants, or how they managed to communicate with him without detection. An explanation suggested by David Kahn in his monumental book on codes and code-breaking is that one of the informants was Fritz Thiele, second-in-command of OKW's signal organization.[32] If that is so, Thiele must have had quite a lot of encyphering to do, as presumably he would not have risked showing the plain-text originals of his and the other informants' messages to his cypher-clerks. An alternative explanation is that Rössler really had no informants in Germany, but merely acted as a channel of communication for information supplied to him by Allied and neutral intelligence agencies.

However that may be, the Russians are known to have made strenuous attempts towards the end of 1939 and later to improve their intelligence cover in Germany. The partition of Poland between German and Soviet occupation forces was followed by the repatriation of thousands of men and women of German origin hitherto domiciled there or in the Baltic States. Many of them reported on their arrival in Germany that the Comintern or the NKVD had tried to enlist them as spies.[33] The publicity given in Germany to these attempts to suborn German nationals did not make for good relations between Berlin and Moscow, and it seems unlikely that the Russians gained much from this haphazard method of recruitment.

Germany's occupation in 1940 of Denmark, Norway, the Netherlands, Belgium and northern and western France led to the penetration of some Soviet circuits by agents of the Gestapo or the counter-intelligence branch of the Abwehr. It also gave Soviet agents opportunities of infiltrating German organizations in the occupied countries in the guise of interpreters, clerks, typists, and contractors for goods or services. The outcome was a progressive tightening-up by the Germans of security precautions. But that, as SOE was to discover, did not prevent the French Communist Party from building up a strong resistance movement.

*

In the spring of 1941 a steady flow of information pointing to German preparations for war with the Soviet Union reached Whitehall from a variety of sources. Between the beginning of April and the third week of May the War Office received numerous reports of troop-movements in Finland, Northern Norway, Poland, Czechoslovakia, Austria, Hungary and Rumania. There was also evidence from signal intelligence that the headquarters of Luftwaffe formations, with ancillary units, were being ordered from Western Europe or the Balkans to areas within striking-distance of Russia or the Russian zone of Poland, and that provision was being made for the reception and interrogation of Russian-speaking prisoners-of-war.[34] While some of this evidence was compatible with the belief that the Germans intended merely to frighten the Russians into making large economic concessions, it seemed scarcely probable that they would go to the length of ordering up a prisoner-of-war cage and printing Russian money unless they really meant to fight.

Even so, the War Office still could not bring itself to believe that Germany would risk war with the Soviet Union while Britain remained undefeated.[35] Its attitude was based largely on the commonsense argument that Hitler would be very unwise to commit himself to a two-front war for the sake of exchanging the solid benefits of the economic pact with Russia for the uncertain spoils of conquest and the prospect of an expensive military occupation of as much of European Russia as he might hope to seize. That view was not, however, entirely unsupported by evidence. Early in April the British Embassy in Washington reported that, according to Japanese diplomatic traffic read by the Americans, Göring had told the Japanese Foreign Minister that Germany would not attack the Russians without first making a further attempt to beat the British.[36] Although he was not expressly reported as saying so, the implication was that Göring believed, or at any rate hoped, that Britain might yet be knocked out of the war by blockade and bombing. In April and the first half of May the Luftwaffe was still making heavy night attacks on London, Belfast, Birmingham, Bristol, Coventry, Glasgow, Hull, Liverpool, Plymouth and Portsmouth. As the Air Ministry now conceded, it did not have enough first-line aircraft and crews to go on doing that and at the same time support a major assault on the Soviet Union by land forces. On the other hand, preparations already made in Poland, Finland, Northern Norway and Rumania would enable it to switch units to the Eastern Front at short notice if the need arose. For that reason, Air Intelligence was readier than Military Intelligence to accept the view advanced by the GC & CS that a German attack on the Soviet Union in the early summer was not merely possible but probable.

On 23 May the Joint Intelligence Committee summed up the outlook in a paper expressly devoted to Germany's intentions towards Russia.[37] The committee – now a much more authoritative and self-confident body than it had been in 1939 and 1940 – agreed that the Germans could not, at one and the same time, attack the Soviet Union and invade the United Kingdom, but thought that Sea Lion was unlikely to be launched in the immediate future. Domination of the Soviet Union, on the other hand, was – or at any rate had become – 'a fundamental German objective'. Germany could not fight a long war without a bigger economic contribution from the Soviet Union than she was receiving under the economic pact; the question was whether she would seek to obtain it by diplomatic pressure or by fighting. After reviewing the arguments on both sides, the committee concluded that Hitler's best course would be to formulate demands backed by the threat of force, but that he might have to fight if he saw that otherwise his demands were not going to be met.

However, the committee was not content to leave the matter there. By stating in its appreciation that Germany, 'with her usual thoroughness', was 'making all preparations for an attack so as to make the threat convincing', it implied that it knew for a fact that the Russians were negotiating with the Germans and were being pressed to make concessions. Although rumours to that effect were circulating in diplomatic quarters, such was not the case. Apart from these rumours, there was no evidence that negotiations were in progress.

On the very day when the Joint Intelligence Committee's paper was circulated, Thümmel warned London not to be deceived by reports of Russo-German negotiations, which he likened to a time-fuse.[38] Luftwaffe Enigma revealed a few days later that Fliegerkorps II was asking for maps of Latvia, Lithuania, part of Rumania and most of Poland. It also showed that the commanders of five Fliegerkorps and two anti-aircraft formations whose headquarters were known to be moving to Eastern Europe were included in a list of officers invited to a conference on 4 June which would also be attended by Luftflotte commanders. By the end of May there was ample evidence from

Luftwaffe and railway Enigma of preparations for the massing of land and air forces behind the demarcation line in Poland and the frontier between Rumania and the Ukraine. The Commander-in-Chief of the German troops in Rumania was known to be planning a personal reconnaissance of the frontier-area, and an assault-boat company formerly associated with Sea Lion to be among units due to move by rail to Eastern Europe. Enigma messages showed, too, that further reinforcements had arrived in Northern Norway.[39]

In face of this evidence, the theory that Hitler intended merely to frighten the Russians into making concessions became hard to maintain. Not much was known in London about the Red Army's dispositions, but it was believed to be making fairly extensive defensive preparations. We now know that the Soviet military authorities had in fact begun to move not merely small bodies of troops but whole divisions from the Far East to European Russia and the Baltic States. According to the Soviet official history, these were not disposed in accordance with any systematic plan of defence.[40] They would seem merely to have been held ready to move to their final positions on receipt of a warning-order. No such order was, however, received by commanders in the field. Soviet troops and air squadrons were forbidden to reconnoitre German-held territory or to open fire on German aircraft which violated Soviet air-space. Stalin and Molotov continued to assert until well past the eleventh hour that Germany was not going to attack the Soviet Union, and that reports that she intended to do so were malicious fabrications. Stalin is even said to have ordered that agents who submitted such reports should be punished, although it is not suggested that the order was obeyed.

In England the broad situation at the end of May was that rather different views of the outlook were held in Whitehall and at Bletchley. The Joint Intelligence Committee still belived that Germany was negotiating with the Russians and might pose a new threat to British interests in the Mediterranean and the Middle East if they gave way. The GC & CS, while conceding that doubtless Hitler would be unwise to commit himself to a long two-front war with the Soviet Union and the British Empire, pointed out that he might not think that a war with the Soviet Union need be a long one.[41] Its opinion that Germany was not seeking merely to overawe the Russians but was poised for a lightning-stroke against them was soon reinforced by further evidence. In the first week of June signal intelligence revealed that the move of Luftflotte 2 to Eastern Europe was virtually complete and that the Germans were transmitting spurious messages in an attempt to conceal the departure of units from Northern France and the Low Countries.[42] At the same time there was a marked increase in Luftwaffe wireless traffic in Northern Norway, where a dearth of landlines compelled newly-arrived units to put their signals on the air. On 3 June the GC & CS decrypted a signal in which the Italian Ambassador in Moscow reported that his German colleague had assured him that Germany was not negotiating with the Russians.[43] On 7 June the Swedish government, which had sometimes provided valuable information in the past, gave the Foreign Office a warning to the effect that Hitler would attack the Soviet Union in the middle of the month.[44] On 8 June a signal was decrypted in which Luftflotte 2 told Fliegerkorps VIII, whose long-expected transfer from Greece to Poland was known to have begun, that its units were not to move to their forward bases before 16 June. Two days later, the commanders of all Luftwaffe formations mentioned in recent Enigma traffic were summoned by Göring to a conference to be held at his headquarters on 15 June.[45]

Even the Foreign Office and the Joint Intelligence Committee found this evidence impressive. On 10 June the Foreign Secretary gave the substance of it to the Soviet Ambassador, receiving in exchange an assurance that the Soviet Union was not negotiating with Hitler and would make no deal with him.[46] The Joint Intelligence Committee still thought the Russians might yield to German demands, but conceded that it was at least possible that they would find themselves at war in the second half of the month. Cripps, on a visit to London, confessed that he did not know whether Russo-German negotiations were in progress, but added that he expected Germany to issue an ultimatum when she was ready for war.[47] In the light of this admission the War Cabinet felt unable to decide on 12 June whether Hitler would attack the Russians without further ado, or give them a chance of yielding by demanding control of the Ukraine and the Caucasus.

Immediately after this inconclusive meeting, there arrived in Whitehall the decrypt of a message sent by the Japanese Ambassador in Berlin on 4 June. This was part of a long account of an interview with Hitler. The Ambassador reported Hitler as saying that the Russians, although outwardly friendly, were habitually obstructive, and that he had decided that Communist Russia must be eliminated. After explaining why he thought the issue must be faced now rather than five or ten years later, the Führer said that he would have Rumania and Finland as allies, and that the campaign would not be a long one. The

Ambassador added that, although neither Hitler nor Ribbentrop had mentioned a date, his impression was that the attack would be made soon.[48]

This message does not seem to have been taken very seriously by Matsuoka, but it made a great impression on the British. Within a few hours of the arrival of the decrypt, the Joint Intelligence Committee announced that Hitler had made up his mind to attack the Soviet Union and that matters seemed likely to come to a head in the second half of June.[49] On the following day the Foreign Secretary told the Soviet Ambassador that the evidence for a German offensive was increasing, and offered to send a military mission to Moscow.[50] The Chiefs of Staff thereupon instructed the Joint Planners and the Joint Intelligence Committee to make arrangements for a mission to be sent when the Germans opened their attack. On 17 June, after further decrypts had yielded convincing evidence that the attack was imminent, the Air Ministry directed Bomber, Fighter and Coastal Command to consider ways and means of reversing the eastward flow of German aircraft from France and the Low Countries, 'particularly in the event of operations developing against Russia'.[51] Meanwhile the Soviet government lived up to its reputation for unpredictable behaviour by publicly announcing that rumours of an impending German offensive were groundless.

*

From the intelligence aspect, one of the most interesting features of Operation Barbarossa is that, despite the numerous warnings received by the authorities in Moscow, its launching on 22 June 1941 found the Russians largely unprepared.[52] Many units close to the frontier or the demarcation line were overrun in the first few hours, with the result that troops sent to reinforce them became committed to encounter-battles and suffered heavy losses. As an ambitious programme of airfield construction had yet to be completed, fighter aircraft in the West were concentrated at a limited number of bases where they could not be adequately dispersed or protected against blast-damage. Apart from the unsatisfactory disposition of their forces the Russians were hampered, too, by shortages of up-to-date weapons and equipment. Their armies in the West had fewer than 1,500 modern tanks, and only about a quarter of their older tanks were serviceable. They were also short of mechanized transport. Most Russian aircraft in service on all fronts in the early summer of 1941 were obsolete or obsolescent by Western European standards. Some very good tanks, aircraft and anti-tank weapons were in production, but they were still coming forward only in small numbers.

British estimates of the fighting value of the Soviet Army were based not so much on factual knowledge of these deficiences as on its poor showing against Finland in the winter of 1939–40, the not unfounded belief that many of its ablest officers had been executed or dismissed between 1936 and 1938, and a general impression that Soviet industry was backward, poorly organized and inefficient. Cripps told the War Cabinet on 16 June that he and other heads of mission in Moscow did not expect the Red Army to withstand a German onslaught for more than three or four weeks.[53] The Joint Intelligence Committee estimated on 9 June that the Germans could occupy the Ukraine and reach Moscow in four to six weeks; on 14 June it changed its estimate to a minimum of three or four and a maximum of about six weeks.[54] In the light of these predictions and of agents' reports to the effect that large numbers of German troops were about to move to France, the Chiefs of Staff ruled on 25 June that anti-invasion forces in the United Kingdom should be kept on the alert and brought to their highest state of efficiency by the beginning of September. This ruling was based on the assumption that the Germans could be ready to invade the United Kingdom some four to eight weeks after defeating the Russians.

We now know that the Germans themselves did not expect to be finished with the Soviet Union in less than about five months. Their plan was founded on the belief that the Russians would do everything they could to hold their chief centres of production, and that therefore it was on the approaches to Leningrad and Moscow and in the neighbourhood of Kiev and Kharkov that their strongest forces would be deployed and could be brought to battle. Three German army groups, the southernmost reinforced by Hungarian, Italian and Rumanian contingents, were to advance respectively through the Baltic States to Leningrad, towards Smolensk and Moscow, and in the general direction of the Ukraine and the Donetz basin. The ultimate aim was to occupy virtually the whole of European Russia west of a line from Archangel on the White Sea to Astrakhan on the Caspian.

This plan involved a wide dispersal of German forces and posed some awkward problems. In 1940 some 3,500 aircraft had sufficed to support parallel thrusts by two army groups into the Low Countries and across the Meuse between Sedan and Dinant. With fewer aircraft immediately available, the Luftwaffe was expected in 1941 to support divergent thrusts by three army groups on a thousand-mile front. After making provision for the Mediterranean theatre, home defence and anti-shipping operations in United Kingdom waters, it had only about 2,700 bombers, fighters and reconnaissance aircraft left for Barbarossa. To Göring, and still more to his operational and administrative staffs, the launching of the operation was bound to seem foolhardy. But Hitler brushed aside objections by asserting that the Soviet régime would collapse at the first blow 'like a pricked soap-bubble'.

As things turned out, the Germans made a good start except on the right, where Army Group South's advance was delayed by heavy rain and the difficulty of co-ordinating operations by troops of four different nationalities. For more than a week the Soviet authorities did little or nothing to controvert Hitler's judgement that they were men of straw. Stalin then took heart of grace, announced a scorched-earth policy, and appealed to the patriotism of the Russian people. By the middle of July Army Group North was checked between Lake Peipus and Lake Ilmen, Army Group Centre outside Smolensk. In Britain, the Joint Intelligence Committee expressed on 23 July the opinion that Germany was so deeply committed in Russia that she could be reckoned incapable of disengaging before September the large forces needed to invade the United Kingdom. The Chiefs of Staff agreed that invasion before the spring of 1942 had become improbable, and early in August the directive which called for the highest state of readiness by the beginning of September was rescinded.[55]

The transition from peace to war went some way to raise the status of Soviet military intelligence in relation to that of other intelligence organizations. At staff conversations with the British and later the Americans, Soviet intelligence was represented by the military intelligence branch, while other clandestine organizations remained in the background. Early in 1941 the state security service had achieved ministerial status as the People's Commissariat for State Security (the NKGB), but soon after the German invasion it was again placed under the Commissariat for Internal Affairs (the NKVD). This arrangement held good until 1943, when it became once more the NKGB. It was not until after the war, when the term commissariat was dropped, that the NKVD was transformed into the MGB. In 1953 the former NKVD, now the MVD, was once again made ultimately responsible for security, but after Beria's execution control was vested in a committee, the KGB of a new generation of spy-stories.[56]

None of this made much difference to the security service's powers or functions. At all times its primary task was to ensure the supremacy of the central government by stamping out and ruthlessly punishing dissent or deviationism. For that purpose it posted agents or informers in every government department or agency, regional or central, every Soviet embassy or legation, every officers' mess or club, every unit or formation of the armed forces down to battalion level or its equivalent, every important factory or workshop. Workers, managers, officials, soldiers, sailors, airmen, masters and crews of merchant vessels, even spies were spied upon.

Nor did the outbreak of war curtail the activities of the foreign department of the security service and other clandestine organizations in countries with which the Soviet Union found herself allied. On the contrary, these organizations took full advantage of the additional facilities for espionage provided by the despatch of purchasing commissions or specialist missions to such countries. The efforts of large numbers of Soviet citizens who arrived in the guise of members or minor employees of bodies with diplomatic or quasi-diplomatic status supplemented those of agents already present. In Britain, attempts begun soon after the October Revolution of 1917 to enlist support for anti-capitalist doctrines and foment industrial strife had led to setbacks which included the failure of a projected Triple Strike of miners, dockers and transport workers in 1921 and the swift collapse of a General Strike in 1926. More subtle attempts made later to suborn promising members of the intelligentzia had yielded far better results. Well-placed informants recruited in academic circles in the 1930s included the physicist Alan Nunn May, who was to furnish data bearing on the Anglo-American nuclear research and development programme between 1943 and 1945; Donald Maclean and Guy Burgess, both afterwards employed by the Foreign Office; Kim Philby, who was to hold in World War II an important post in MI 6; and the art historian Anthony Blunt, who confessed to the British security authorities in 1964 that he had acted as a talent-spotter for the Soviet intelligence apparatus while holding a fellowship at Cambridge a quarter of a century earlier and had passed information to the Russians while serving in World War II in MI 5. Similar attempts to debauch promising candidates for employment in the higher echelons of the public service were made about the same time in the United States. According to an estimate volunteered many years later by the self-confessed former Soviet agent Whittaker Chambers, the Soviet Union had on the eve of World War II about seventy-five well-placed informants in the Department of State, the Department of Justice, the Treasury and other government departments or agencies.

However, these infiltrations were made primarily with long-term ends in view. What the Soviet authorities needed, as a matter of urgency, to know in the summer of 1941 was what the Germans and the Japanese were doing or were about to do. The outbreak of war made communication with Moscow hazardous for agents who had hitherto communicated through the Soviet Embassy in Berlin. Rudolf von Scheliha became unable or unwilling to provide much information in such circumstances, and an attempt to contact him by courier in the autumn of 1941 led to his arrest and execution. Schulze-Boysen and leading members of his organization were arrested about twelve months later. The Russians afterwards made attempts to introduce new agents into Germany by dropping them from their own or Allied aircraft, but these were not very successful. Few of the hastily-trained refugees or prisoners-of-war chosen for the work had much aptitude for evasion or stood much chance of gaining access to secret material even if they did succeed in eluding the police and the counter-intelligence authorities. Many were caught, or gave themselves up, within a few hours of their arrival.

Sorge was fortunate enough to be outside the jurisdiction of the Gestapo, and his clandestine activities were totally unknown to his friends at the German Embassy. The Japanese counter-intelligence authorities kept an eye on him as a matter of routine, but he had excellent cover as a respected journalist whose mildly bohemian bachelor existence was punctuated by regular visits from a quiet, well-behaved Japanese mistress against whom nothing was known. Within a few weeks of the German invasion of Russia, he was able to tell Moscow, on the highest authority, that the Japanese government had no immediate intention of attacking the Soviet Union and that its eyes were fixed on Indo-China and the Netherlands East Indies.[57] This information may also have reached the Russians from the Western Allies, whose knowledge was derived from the reading of Japanese diplomatic traffic; but Sorge's contribution was doubly valuable because it came from a source which no one could suspect of being influenced by the British. On the strength of it, the Soviet High Command further reduced its forces in the Far East by moving to European Russia substantial formations which arrived in time to take part in the defence of Moscow and the Soviet counter-offensive in the winter of 1941–42.

Unfortunately for Sorge, the security authorities arrested in the meantime a Japanese suspected of being an agent of the Comintern. He was not a member of Sorge's network, but the authorities traced a link between Ozaki and a woman whose name the suspect mentioned in a statement by which he hoped to exculpate himself. They arrested Ozaki in the middle of October 1941, Sorge and his wireless-operator a few days later. Although Sorge argued in his defence that he was no enemy of the Japanese and that one of the main objects of his mission had been to avert war between Japan and the Soviet Union, he and Ozaki were hanged some three years later.

The Swiss network, too, had the advantage of operating outside the reach of the Gestapo and the Abwehr. Moreover the Swiss government, although officially neutral, was well disposed towards the Allied cause. These advantages were offset to some extent by isolation. The Soviet Union was not diplomatically represented in Switzerland. Switzerland had no common frontier with any neutral country, except in so far as Vichy France could be considered a neutral country. This meant that the Swiss network could receive funds only through devious channels which the Russians seem not to have been good at exploiting. It also meant that the network's reports to Moscow had to be transmitted by wireless from buildings not immune from search. The Swiss military authorities might be willing to turn a deaf ear to its illicit transmissions as long as they could be assumed not to threaten the national interest; they could not guarantee that the civil authorities would always do so. Rado suggested more than once that the network should take refuge with the British rather than risk capture, but Moscow would not hear of it.[58] In the autumn of 1943 two or its three wireless operators were arrested. The Englishman Alexander Foote, who was the third wireless operator and Rado's deputy, was arrested about a month later. He was released in the following September, but by that time Rado was in hiding and the network had disintegrated.

After the liberation of France, Rado and Foote reported independently to the Soviet Military Mission in Paris. Their estimates of the chances of reviving the Swiss network on French soil differed so widely that both were summoned to Moscow for interrogation. Rado slipped away when their flight to Russia by way of Egypt and Iran was interrupted at Cairo, but was afterwards arrested by the British as an alleged deserter and sent against his will to the Soviet Union, where he survived a long term of imprisonment. Foote satisfied his interrogators, took advantage of a visit to Berlin on Soviet business to take refuge in the British zone, and eventually returned to England to write a book about his experiences and enter the service of the British government in a capacity less exciting than that of a secret agent.[59] Rössler was convicted by a Swiss military court of having taken part in illicit activities, but no penalty was imposed in view of his services to Switzerland.

In the meantime the Swiss network, and Rössler in particular, furnished Moscow with a stream of information about the dispositions and intentions of German Army and Luftwaffe formations on the Eastern Front. Rössler never revealed his sources, but it is hard to see how he managed to provide almost daily information about these matters unless he had access to information derived from the reading of Enigma messages either before or after their encypherment. According to Foote, the Soviet High Command based its decisions largely on Rössler's reports. But this does not mean that the Russians always made good use of what the Swiss network and their field intelligence and air reconnaissance systems had to tell them. Allegedly because Stalin refused to countenance a withdrawal they failed, for example, to pull out of the Kiev pocket in September 1941 in time to avoid enormous losses, although both the commander and the political commissar on the spot had a good idea of what was coming. Stalin is said to have intervened with almost equally dire consequences at Kharkov in the following summer, although it has also been alleged that on that occasion Rössler failed, for once, to give Moscow adequate warning.

Not only public and private acknowledgements by the Russians themselves of the help they received from Rössler, but also the impartial testimony of results, show that in general the intelligence they received was good. The planning of their counter-offensive at Stalingrad in November 1942 bears witness to accurate knowledge of the weak points in the enemy's line. They did not succeed, except to a limited extent, in hiding their build-up for the offensive, but fortunately for them Hitler paid little heed to warnings from the Sixth Army's intelligence officers.[60]

Manstein's counter-thrusts west of the Donetz in the following February and March caught the Russians unprepared, but that was the last important occasion on which their intelligence system was found wanting. At Kursk in the summer of 1943 they were forewarned of the enemy's intentions, they were not misled by his deception-plan, and they made good use of patrols and air reconnaissance to keep themselves informed of the state of his preparations. In the ensuing battle they were in the fortunate position of having more combatant troops, more major formations, more tanks and more guns within reach of the battlefield than the enemy could muster. Moreover, they were not inferior in the air. But they would not have enjoyed these advantages if they had allowed themselves to be taken by surprise.

This state of affairs reflected the remarkable all-round improvement in the Soviet armoury which had occurred since 1941. That improvement was due largely to the foresight which led the Russians to move enormous quantities of plant and machinery in the summer and autumn of 1941 from Leningrad, Moscow, the Ukraine and the Donetz basin to safer quarters, and to their policy of concentrating production on a limited range of weapons. But the Russians also owed something to large contributions made by the Western Allies. According to figures published on the authority of the Commissariat for Foreign Trade, they received between 1941 and the early summer of 1944 alone no less than 5,480 British and 3,734 American tanks and 5,800 British and 6,430 American aircraft, in addition to huge quantities of raw materials and a wide range of other products.* During the currency of their lend-lease agreement with the United States, they received from the Americans alone aircraft, tanks, motor vehicles, naval and other vessels, weapons and ammunition, with spares, to the value of $4,651,582,000, and other products and materials to the value of $4,826,084,000. The second category, incidentally, includes such unwarlike items as cosmetics, cigarette-cases, fishing-tackle, gramophone records and false teeth.

The carriage of these goods to the Soviet Union imposed a tremendous burden on the Western Allies. At the end of 1942 a system was introduced by which American-built aircraft consigned to the Soviet Union were flown across the Bering Strait from Alaska to Siberia. These aircraft could, and did, carry small amounts of freight. Almost everything else had to be taken by sea to Vladivostok, Archangel or Murmansk, or to the Persian Gulf for transit to the Soviet Union through Iranian territory. Vladivostok was, in principle, reserved for bulk cargoes, mainly of food for consumption in the Soviet Union's eastern provinces. Conditions imposed for political reasons by the Russians ensured that comparatively little use was made of the route through Iran. So the majority of all goods consigned to the Soviet Union from the United Kingdom or the eastern seaboard of North America travelled from Iceland to Archangel or Murmansk in convoys escorted and covered by the British Home Fleet.

A more perilous route would be hard to imagine. Apart from the ever-present risk from U-boats, the Arctic convoys were exposed

* 'British', in this context, includes equipment built in Canada.

throughout the daylight hours to the threat of attack by German aircraft based in Norway – and in summer the daylight hours were twenty-four out of twenty-four. In winter, darkness gave some protection, but ships moving in convoy had then to do their best to keep station in conditions which sometimes included winds of gale or hurricane force and waves up to seventy feet high. Water shipped over the bows became solid ice almost as soon as it touched the deck. Even in summer, polar ice prevented the convoys from standing far enough to the north to be entirely out of range of air attack from Norwegian bases. Furthermore, as a result of Hitler's conviction that the British intended to land in Norway, from the early part of 1942 the Germans had a substantial surface fleet in Norwegian waters. An attack on an Arctic convoy by the *Tirpitz* could be disastrous.

The first contribution made by either of the Western Powers to the Soviet armoury was a cargo of mines delivered by the British minelayer *Adventurer* to Archangel at the end of July 1941 in the course of an expedition against enemy shipping.[61] A convoy consisting of the old carrier *Argus* and a single merchant vessel, carrying 48 Hurricanes, left Iceland some three weeks later and was escorted and covered by six flotilla vessels and three cruisers. The merchantman duly disembarked her aircraft at Archangel and the carrier flew hers to Murmansk.

In the meantime Stalin confessed that the situation was tense, but added that the Soviet Union could hold out for three or four years if she were assured of an adequate supply of aluminium. Later he asked for 30,000 tons of aluminium by the beginning of October, 400 aircraft and 500 tanks a month for an indefinite period, and a second front in France or the Balkans. He said that, without such assistance, the Soviet Union would be either defeated, or crippled for a long time to come.[62]

The British and United States governments then agreed to meet Stalin's demands for tanks and aircraft at the cost of reducing allocations to the British forces in the Middle East. The British promised him 2,000 tons of aluminium a month, and undertook to meet his requirements for an array of raw materials which included such diverse commodities as cobalt, cocoa beans, diamonds, wool and zinc. The Russians announced their intention of buying in the open market large quantities of food, including North American wheat and sugar from the Netherlands East Indies.[63] Soon afterwards the United States government entered into the first of a series of lend-lease agreements by which it pledged itself to meet Soviet requirements on a gigantic scale.

Such was the price demanded by the Soviet Union for staying in the war and making a major contribution to the defeat of the German Army. Neither the British nor the American intelligence organizations could produce in 1941 much factual evidence about the state of the Soviet economy or the staying-power of the Soviet Union's armed forces. They were not in a position to make any authoritative comment on Stalin's prognostications, or to challenge the opinion currently held in diplomatic circles that, without outside assistance, the Russians would collapse in a few weeks, or at best in a few months.

The first of a series of numbered Arctic convoys, PQ 1, left Iceland on 29 September 1941, escorted by a cruiser, two destroyers and an anti-submarine group. It was accompanied by an oiler which was to refuel the escort in the far north and then return with the ship which had carried the Hurricanes to Archangel and had left that port with her escort on 28 September. PQ 2 left on 18 October, PQ 3 on 9 November and PQ 4 on 17 November. By the middle of November the port of Archangel had begun to freeze. It soon became clear that the Russians would not be able to keep it open throughout the winter with ice-breakers, as they had hoped to do.[64] The decision was therefore made to divert some ships to Murmansk, which the Germans had been expected but had failed to capture in the first stage of their advance. Later it was decided that Murmansk should be the destination of all ships for the rest of the winter.

Chiefly because the U-boat force and the small German bomber force in Northern Norway had other preoccupations, but also because the Luftwaffe's anti-shipping units were in the midst of a switch from the bomb to the torpedo, the early Arctic convoys did not meet much opposition. Until the end of 1941 the convoys ran steadily and without loss. PQ 7, which left in two parts at the end of 1941 and the beginning of 1942, lost one ship out of eleven. All eight ships of PQ 8 reached Murmansk on 17 January, although one was damaged by a torpedo and one of its two escorting destroyers was sunk. PQ 9 and PQ 10, with ten ships between them, and PQ 11 with thirteen ships, were not located by the enemy and arrived unscathed.

Nevertheless the outlook in the early part of 1942 seemed to the British far from reassuring. Even when no losses were suffered, the use of warships to escort merchant vessels on the round trip to Murmansk or Archangel and back meant that the Home Fleet was deprived of their services for three weeks or more. Apart from the *Scharnhorst*, the *Gneisenau* and the *Prinz Eugen* at Brest, the Germans were believed to have ready for sea a substantial surface fleet consisting of the *Tirpitz*, the pocket-battleship *Admiral Scheer*, the *Hipper* and perhaps four light cruisers and twenty destroyers.[65] On learning on 17 January of indications that the *Tirpitz* might be at sea, Admiral Tovey postponed the next Arctic convoy and took the main body of his fleet to Iceland to cover the northern passages to the Atlantic.[66]

On 23 January the *Tirpitz* was photographed in a narrow fiord east of Trondheim, camouflaged and heavily protected by nets. We now know that she had gone there in response to Hitler's insistence that all available surface warships should be concentrated in Norwegian waters to counter the supposed threat of a British invasion.*

It was then agreed that the Arctic convoys should be continued, even though this meant that the passages from the North Sea to the Atlantic might sometimes have to be left inadequately guarded. Accordingly, PQ 9 and PQ 10 left together on 1 February, PQ 11 on 6 February. Churchill suggested to the Chiefs of Staff on 25 January that 'the entire naval situation throughout the world' would be altered if the *Tirpitz* were destroyed.[67] Bomber Command sent sixteen aircraft to attack her on the night of 29/30 January, but no hits were scored.

In the third week of February, after the Brest squadron had completed its up-Channel dash, signal intelligence revealed exceptional air activity in Norway. On 19 February the *Tirpitz* was seen to be under way, although still in the fiord in which she had been anchored since January. Tovey took the main body of the fleet to sea and steamed towards Tromsö, but nothing happened. On the following day there were indications, again from signal intelligence, that a further move of German warships to Norway was in prospect. On 21 February two large ships and three destroyers were seen in the southern part of the North Sea, heading north at high speed. The large ships were the *Admiral Scheer* and the *Prinz Eugen*. They were seen again on 22 February. A British submarine torpedoed and damaged the *Prinz Eugen* on 23 February, but she and the *Scheer* succeeded in joining the *Tirpitz* at Trondheim.

Surveying the situation in the light of these developments, Tovey felt that the luck which had hitherto attended the Arctic convoys could not last. The presence of a powerful German surface fleet in Norwegian waters meant that future convoys would have to be covered by heavy ships during part of the voyage. Although we now know that the first of the long-range bomber crews who were retraining with torpedoes would not be ready for active operations before April, the Luftwaffe already

* See page 179.

had in Northern Norway about sixty long-range bombers, some thirty dive-bombers and fifteen torpedo-carrying seaplanes, in addition to small numbers of FW 200s and BV 138 flying-boats for long-range maritime reconnaissance. U-boats had already begun to lie in wait for merchant shipping off the Kola Inlet. Attempts had been made to persuade the Russians to do something about the U-boats and provide air cover over the approaches to Murmansk, but without much success.

Tovey asked on 26 February that in future the sailings of outward-bound and homeward-bound convoys should be synchronized, so that two convoys could be covered simultaneously as they moved in opposite directions through the area of greatest danger between Jan Mayen Island (north-west of Trondheim) and Bear Island. Accordingly, on 1 March PQ 12 left Iceland and PQ 8 the Kola Inlet. Both were fairly large convoys, of sixteen and fifteen ships respectively, and they were the first of their kind to be covered by the main body of the Home Fleet.

PQ 12 was sighted near Jan Mayen Island at noon on 5 March by the crew of an FW 200. Their report prompted the commander of the German squadron, Admiral Ciliax, to put to sea with the *Tirpitz* and three destroyers. Her departure was missed by crews of Coastal Command who were keeping a special watch, but was accompanied by exceptional wireless activity. She was sighted on the following day (and reported as either a battleship or a heavy cruiser) by the submarine *Seawolf*.

Tovey, with two battleships, a battlecruiser, the carrier *Victorious*, a heavy cruiser and twelve destroyers, was patrolling south of the convoy route when the *Seawolf*'s report reached him from the Admiralty soon after midnight on 6/7 March. A long search for the *Tirpitz* culminated in an unsuccessful attack by twelve Albacore torpedo-bombers from the *Victorious* on 9 March. Led by an officer who had only just taken over command of the squadron and had never flown with it before, they attacked from astern when the *Tirpitz* was steaming into the wind, thus forfeiting speed and giving the target more time to dodge.

Ciliax's search for the convoys was no more successful, although one of his destroyers sank a straggler from PQ 8. He anchored off Narvik late on 9 March and returned safely to Trondheim on 13 March.

The two convoys passed each other some 200 miles south-west of Bear Island about noon on 7 March. The Admiralty ordered PQ 12 to pass north of Bear Island. The commodore of the convoy and the senior officer of the escort agreed to disregard the order, observing that there was pack-ice even to the south of the island.

Two lessons could be drawn by the British from these events. One, which the Admiralty did draw, was that very high standards of individual and collective training were needed for success in torpedo-bomber operations. The other, which it failed to draw, was that, although the Operational Intelligence Centre in consultation with the GC & CS was undoubtedly better placed than any officer afloat could be to evaluate and interpret intelligence of the kind it was now receiving, the Naval Staff in London might be very badly placed to say what officers a thousand miles away should do. The order given to PQ 12 to go north of Bear Island was ill judged, to say the least. Not surprisingly, Admiral Tovey made some scathing remarks about 'the detailed instructions' signalled from the Admiralty.[68] But Admiral of the Fleet Sir Dudley Pound, the First Sea Lord, was unrepentant.

The conclusion drawn by the German Naval Staff was that the *Tirpitz* had been lucky to emerge unscathed, and henceforth should be put at risk only in a dire emergency. Hitler, although no less determined that Germany's last battleship should be used with extreme caution, nevertheless insisted that Arctic convoys must be attacked not only by U-boats and aircraft but also by surface warships.

In the third week of March the Germans carried their policy of concentrating their surface warships in Norwegian waters a stage further. The *Hipper* left Brunsbüttel on 19 March and joined the *Tirpitz* at Trondheim two days later. Signal intelligence revealed her departure, but attempts by reconnaissance aircraft and shore-based torpedo-bombers of Coastal Command to find and sink her during the voyage were unsuccessful. Later the pocket-battleships *Scheer* and *Lützow*, with six destroyers, moved to Narvik, leaving the *Tirpitz*, the *Hipper* and four destroyers at Trondheim.

Four more Arctic convoys, with their homeward-bound counterparts, were run between 20 March and the end of May. Their fortunes were various. PQ 13 was scattered by a gale, and five of its nineteen ships were sunk by aircraft and destroyers. QP 9, also of nineteen ships, had a safe passage. PQ 14 ran into ice. Sixteen ships out of twenty-four turned back, and one of the eight which went on was sunk by a U-boat. QP 10 lost four ships out of sixteen. PQ 15 and QP 11, with thirty-eight ships between them, lost three sunk by torpedo-bombers and one by a destroyer; in addition two cruisers of the covering force were lost. PQ 16, a big convoy of thirty-five ships, was attacked repeatedly by aircraft and lost seven ships. QP 12 started with fifteen ships. One had to turn back, but the rest arrived without loss at Reykjavik on 29 May.

By that time the Luftwaffe had, and was known to have, a very substantial anti-shipping force in the neighbourhood of the North Cape. It included about a hundred Ju 88s which could be used for dive-bombing as well as level bombing; some thirty Ju 87 dive-bombers; about sixty torpedo-bombers and torpedo-carrying seaplanes; and enough long-range or very-long-range reconnaissance aircraft to cover virtually the whole of the area from Norway to the polar ice and from Jan Mayen Island to the Barents Sea. PQ 16 had been continuously shadowed and repeatedly attacked by aircraft for five days on end, with the result that 77 of the 201 aircraft, 147 of the 468 tanks, and 770 of the 3,277 other vehicles it carried had gone to the bottom of the sea.[69] Thus there was a strong case for suspending Arctic convoys until the autumn brought shorter days.

However, the British government was under strong pressure from Moscow not to cut off supplies, and from Washington not to allow a big backlog of undelivered cargo to build up in Iceland or in British and American ports. In these circumstances the Admiralty decreed that PQ 17, a large convoy of thirty-six ships carrying about 300 aircraft, some 600 tanks, more than 4,000 other vehicles and well over 15,000 tons of miscellaneous cargo, should leave for Archangel on 27 June and pass north of Bear Island in order to stay as far as possible from the German air bases in the neighbourhood of the North Cape. It was to be protected during the first part of the voyage by three minesweepers and four trawlers, and from 30 June by a long-range escort force of six destroyers, four corvettes and two submarines under Commander J. E. Broome. Additional protection would be provided by two anti-aircraft ships, and there would also be three rescue ships. Close cover during part of the voyage was to be provided by two British and two American cruisers and three destroyers under Rear-Admiral L. H. K. Hamilton. The main body of the Home Fleet, consisting of the *Duke of York*, the American battleship *Washington*, the *Victorious*, two cruisers and fourteen destroyers, was to provide distant cover by taking up a position north-east of Jan Mayen Island.

This plan was based on the Admiralty's belief that the convoy was likely to be attacked not only by aircraft but also by surface forces, and that these might include the *Tirpitz*. In principle Hamilton's cruiser force was not to go beyond Bear Island, but provision was made for him to go as far east as the meridian of the North Cape if the convoy was threatened by a force he could fight, or in other words by one which did not include the *Tirpitz*.[70]

Admiral Tovey made it clear to the Admiralty that, apart form thinking the time of year unsuitable for an Arctic convoy, he disliked many features of this plan. The convoy was, in his opinion, too large, and the close escort was too weak. If there had to be a midsummer convoy, then it ought, in his judgement, to sail in two parts.[71] He did not believe that the Germans would risk sending the *Tirpitz* to attack the convoy in view of her narrow escape in March, but thought that in any case Hamilton's cruisers ought not to go further east than Bear Island. Beyond that point they could not be adequately protected against aircraft or U-boats, and their extrication would be difficult if they were damaged. But Admiral Pound, the First Sea Lord, insisted that the operation must be carried out as planned. What was worse, in the course of a telephone conversation with Tovey he revealed that he might order the convoy to scatter if it appeared to be in imminent danger.[72] Tovey was convinced that this was the biggest mistake that could be made. Experience had shown that, as long as a convoy stayed together and the ships kept station, they could protect each other and be protected by their escort. Ships which scattered could receive no protection. They could be picked off one after another.

The convoy left Iceland in good order on the scheduled date. Except that two ships turned back at an early stage, everything began extremely well. U-boats and shadowing aircraft were sighted on 1 July, but the U-boats were driven off, and an attack by torpedo-bombers was unsuccessful.

By arrangement with the Russians, a number of Catalinas of Coastal Command flew to the neighbourhood of Murmansk between 1 and 4 July, reconnoitring Norwegian waters on the way. Continuous cover of the danger-area by these and home-based aircraft throughout the critical period was planned, but a gap occurred between 11 a.m. and 5 p.m. on 4 July as the result of an accident to an aircraft. There was, however, no interruption of the watch kept by signal intelligence. The *Tirpitz* and the *Hipper* were known by 2 p.m. on 3 July to have left Trondheim, but whether this meant that they would be used against PQ 17 was not clear.

We now know that the German commander, Admiral Schniewind, had been ready since the middle of June with a plan to move the Trondheim squadron to Vestfiord (south-west of Narvik) and the Narvik squadron to Altenfiord (near the North Cape) as soon as PQ 17 was known to be approaching. His intention was that the two squadrons should put to sea when the convoy was well past Jan Mayen Island, make rendezvous a hundred miles north of the North Cape, and attack it more or less in that area. We also know that what actually happened was that the *Tirpitz*, the *Hipper* and the *Scheer*, with six destroyers, assembled at Altenfiord on 3 July. The *Lützow* and three destroyers ran aground near Narvik. Permission to use the *Tirpitz* against the convoy, which only Hitler could give, was not granted until the forenoon of 5 July. By that time the situation had changed so much that Schniewind's intervention was not required. He sailed during the afternoon of 5 July and set an eastward course, but abandoned the operation after a few hours.

Late on 3 July PQ 17 passed about thirty miles north of Bear Island. Hamilton decided to stay close to the convoy for the time being, as he had been authorized to do at his discretion. About noon on the following day the Admiralty gave him permission to go even beyond the meridian of the North Cape if the need arose.[73] Tovey added that he was to turn back once the convoy reached that line, or earlier if he thought fit, unless the Admiralty assured him that there was no risk of his meeting the *Tirpitz*. In the meantime the convoy lost one ship, torpedoed by a solitary aircraft which emerged from a blanket of fog. At 6 p.m. on 4 July Hamilton announced his intention of turning back at 10 o'clock. About 8.30 p.m. some twenty-four torpedo-bombers attacked the convoy. Three ships were damaged, two of them so badly that they had to be abandoned and sunk by their own side. Even so, the outcome of this encounter with a fairly large torpedo-bomber force was regarded by competent eye-witnesses as encouraging. They were struck by the excellent discipline with which the convoy and the escort defended themselves and each other. They felt, in the words of the official history, that 'provided the ammunition lasted PQ 17 could get anywhere'.[74]

But meanwhile the authorities ashore had embarked on a course which was to lead PQ 17 to disaster. At 7.30 p.m. the Admiralty responded to Hamilton's announcement that he proposed to turn back at 10 p.m. by signalling to him that 'further information' might be available shortly, and that he was to remain with the convoy 'pending further instructions'. This message was sent in the knowledge that, although nothing had been heard of the *Tirpitz* since the afternoon of the previous day, when she was known to have left Trondheim with the *Hipper*, the Operational Intelligence Centre was awaiting a batch of decrypts which might show what she was doing. But the decrypts, when they arrived, showed only that she had reached Altenfiord late on 3 July and that her accompanying destroyers had been ordered to refuel. They did not show whether she had put to sea again. Nevertheless the very experienced Commander Denning was confident that she had not. He felt sure that, if she had left Altenfiord, her departure would have been accompanied by exceptional wireless activity, as had happened when she put to sea in March to search for PQ 12.

The First Sea Lord refused, however, to regard this negative evidence as conclusive. About the time when the convoy was being attacked by the torpedo-bombers, he summoned a staff meeting. No record appears to have been made of the proceedings. What we do know is that the conclusions reached by the Naval Staff were that the enemy's surface forces might deliver an attack at any time after 2 a.m. on 5 July, and that such an attack might overwhelm not only the convoy but also Hamilton's cruisers and Broome's destroyers if all stayed together.[75] To break up the convoy would mean exposing some or all of the merchant vessels to almost certain air and underwater attacks which individual ships would have virtually no chance of repelling, but the effects of a surface attack on the convoy and its escort and close cover were deemed likely to be even more calamitous.

Accordingly, the dire decision was made to break up a convoy which was in excellent shape and still had eight hundred miles to go. Soon after 9 p.m. the Admiralty despatched the following signal, addressed to Hamilton:[76]

Most Immediate. Cruiser force to withdraw to westward at high speed.

This was followed at 9.23 p.m. by:

Immediate. Owing to threat of surface ships convoy is to disperse and proceed to Russian ports.

According to standing instructions, an order to a convoy to disperse meant that its ships were to break formation and proceed to their destinations. As Archangel was the destination of all the ships in PQ 17, the effect of compliance with the order signalled at 9.23 p.m. would have been to keep the ships fairly close to each other until some of them lagged behind the rest or were picked off by the enemy. Since that was not what the Admiralty intended, the following signal was sent at 9.36 p.m.:

Most Immediate. My 9.23 of the 4th. Convoy is to scatter.

All these signals were sent on the authority of the First Sea Lord, but not before he had discussed the situation with other officers and had been assured that there was no evidence that the *Tirpitz* had left Altenfiord. The puzzling switch from 'Most Immediate' to 'Immediate' in the second signal and back to 'Most Immediate' in the third had no operational significance and appears to have been merely a slip. Hamilton was ordered in the first signal to proceed at high speed not because his presence was urgently required to westward of his position but because U-boats were reported to be concentrating on the route by which he would withdraw. However, he was not told that. Nor was either he or Broome told of the reasoning which led the Admiralty to conclude that the convoy should scatter. The Naval Staff would have incurred no reproaches if they had made it clear that, although there was no evidence that the *Tirpitz* had left Altenfiord and some reason to think that she had not, they feared that she might have done so while Coastal Command's watch was interrupted. They could then have summed up the arguments for and against scattering the convoy, and have left it to the officers afloat to decide what should be done in the light of the intelligence available and their knowledge of the situation at sea. We now know that, if they had done that, the convoy would not have scattered.

As it was, they not only made an indefensible decision but conveyed it in misleading terms to the officers required to act upon it. The three signals sent after 9 p.m. were bound to give the impression that positive evidence received by the Admiralty since 7.30 p.m. indicated that an attack by surface forces was imminent. The order to Hamilton to withdraw 'at high speed', the coupling of orders to break up the convoy with a reference to surface ships, inevitably led Hamilton and Broome to conclude that a situation calling for prompt and drastic action had arisen. Both expected the enemy to come over the horizon at any moment. Hamilton obeyed the order to steam westwards at high speed in the belief that his role was to lead the *Tirpitz* away from the merchant ships and towards the main fleet. Broome, intensely reluctant to leave his charges but recognizing that he could not escort a convoy which would cease to be a convoy when it scattered, took his six destroyers to reinforce Hamilton's cruisers and ordered the rest of the escort to proceed independently to Archangel. When the enemy failed to appear, he expected to be ordered back to help the scattered merchant ships, and gave Hamilton a hint to that effect. But Hamilton, although he too was puzzled, thought a major surface action might still be imminent. He concluded that the best service the cruisers and destroyers could render was to join the main fleet as soon as possible. Tovey afterwards endorsed Broome's decision to join Hamilton, but thought Broome's flotilla should have been sent back when no enemy surface force appeared. In the absence of positive information about the whereabouts of the *Tirpitz* it would, however, have been difficult for Hamilton to know just when that should be done.

To the commodore of the convoy, the order to scatter came as such a surprise that he asked for it to be repeated.[77] In the outcome, the ships did not scatter to the extent contemplated by the Admiralty. Some proceeded singly, others in small groups escorted and screened by the anti-aircraft ships, minesweepers, trawlers and corvettes. Most made not for the White Sea but for Novaya Zemlya. Seventeen, and also a rescue ship, were sunk between 4 and 7 July by U-boats and aircraft. Small convoys were improvised to take the surviving ships to Archangel, but not without further losses. Altogether, of the thirty-six merchant vessels which left Iceland on 27 June two turned back at an early stage, thirteen were sunk as a result of air attacks and ten by U-boats. Eleven, in addition to two of the three rescue-ships, survived. About two-thirds of the tanks, aircraft and miscellaneous stores consigned to the Russians, with roughly three-quarters of the other vehicles, were lost.[78] While it is manifestly impossible to say precisely what would have happened if the order to scatter had not been given, there can be little doubt that losses would have been much lighter if Pound had paid more heed to his intelligence officers, or had accepted Tovey's opinion that the Germans were unlikely to risk their only battleship in close proximity to a convoy escorted by ships heavily armed with torpedoes.

The fact remains that Denning was unable to give a categorical assurance that the *Tirpitz* was not at sea at 9 p.m. on 4 July. He could only say that he was satisfied that she was not, and expected to be told by signal intelligence when she did put to sea. He would have had a stronger case if he had been able to produce recent evidence from photographic or visual reconnaissance that she was still in the fiord with the *Hipper* and the *Scheer*. About two hours after the order to scatter was given, the GC & CS furnished another item of information in the shape of a decrypted message to U-boats off the North Cape that there were no German surface forces in that area. But even that was not regarded as conclusive. What the Naval Staff wanted was positive evidence.

In preparation for the next Arctic convoy, the authorities did what they could to ensure that in future positive evidence would be forthcoming. A long-range maritime reconnaissance squadron and four PR Spitfires were sent to the neighbourhood of Murmansk. In addition two squadrons of Hampden bombers were sent to provide a striking-force, and an Area Combined Headquarters was set up on Russian soil to co-ordinate naval and air operations. At the same time, the Admiralty accepted Tovey's argument that there was not much point in stationing the main body of the Home Fleet north-west of Bear Island to provide distant cover for a convoy in the Barents Sea. It would have to be protected by destroyers which could be better used to escort the convoy. The aim should be to give the convoy not only adequate protection against aircraft and U-boats, but also an escort powerful enough to deter the enemy's surface force or, if the need arose, to fight it.

PQ 18 consisted of thirty-nine merchant ships, one rescue ship, one oiler and three minesweepers which would accompany it throughout the voyage, and two fleet oilers. In accordance with Tovey's recommendations, it was given not only a close escort of two destroyers, two anti-aircraft ships, two submarines, four corvettes, three minesweepers and four trawlers, but also a 'fighting destroyer escort' of one light cruiser and sixteen destroyers. There was also a carrier force of one escort carrier and two destroyers. A single officer, Rear-Admiral R. L. Burnett, was put in command of the entire escort force. The distant covering force was reduced to two battleships, a cruiser and five short-range destroyers under the second-in-command of the Home Fleet. Tovey, afloat in his flagship but in direct touch with the Admiralty and the GC & CS, controlled the operation from Scapa Flow. He said afterwards that he found this arrangement 'advantageous'.

On the whole, the plan worked well, although it would have worked still better if a second escort carrier had been available. The main body of the convoy left Loch Ewe on 2 September. Warned by their reconnaissance aircraft on 8 September that it was north of Iceland, the Germans disposed twelve U-boats in three groups along the course they expected it to take. On 10 September they moved the *Scheer*, the *Hipper*, the light cruiser *Köln* and some destroyers to Altenfiord, leaving the *Tirpitz* at Narvik. These moves were duly noted by the British. Some anxiety was felt in London and at Scapa Flow when the *Tirpitz* was found on 14 September not to be at her usual berth. A reconnaissance from the Murmansk area showed that she had not joined the ships at Altenfiord, and there was no exceptional wireless activity to indicate that she had put to sea. She was in fact exercising in Vestfiord, and was back in the usual place by 18 September. Attacks by aircraft and U-boats cost PQ 18 thirteen ships and the homeward-bound QP 14 three out of fifteen, but the Germans lost forty-one aircraft and four U-boats. They attributed their failure to repeat the success achieved against PQ 17 to the fact that

PQ 18 'maintained ... close formation in the face of heavy and persistent attacks'. The PQ and QP series of Arctic convoys ended when QP 15 reached United Kingdom waters after losing two ships out of twenty-eight.

In November the Luftwaffe responded to Allied landings in North-West Africa by transferring to the Mediterranean theatre all the Ju 88 and He 111 bombers and torpedo-bombers hitherto in Northern Norway. Its anti-shipping force in the far north was thus reduced to a few dive-bombers and torpedo-carrying seaplanes, and a number of maritime reconnaissance aircraft which continued to operate for the benefit of U-boats and surface ships. Air Intelligence was aware of this transformation, but Churchill and the War Cabinet ruled that, after PQ 18, there should be no more outward-bound Arctic convoys until the end of the year. In the meantime thirteen British or American merchant ships sailed independently to and twenty-three from Russia. No escort was given, but trawlers were provided for life-saving. Of these thirty-six ships, three turned back, five were sunk by enemy action, one succumbed to natural hazards and twenty-two arrived safely.

When regular convoys were resumed in December 1942, the designation JW replaced PQ, QP was replaced by RA, and the numbering of the new series began at 51. These changes were made in the interests of security. Security was also much aided by the fact that henceforth outward-bound convoys assembled not in Icelandic but in Scottish waters. The first of them, JW 51A, reached its destination without being spotted by the enemy, as did the first incoming convoy, RA 51. JW 51B was partially scattered by a gale. The *Hipper*, the *Lützow* and six destroyers put to sea when the main body of the convoy was south of Bear Island, but the German commander had orders not to engage a superior or even an equal force and not to risk the torpedoing of his heavy ships in a night action. Five destroyers of the escort held him off for four hours. He was then driven away by two light cruisers. Hitler's comments on this action were so scathing that Admiral Räder resigned his post and was succeeded by the U-boat expert Admiral Dönitz. The Naval Intelligence Division expected the change to be followed by a stepping-up of U-boat attacks on Arctic convoys, but JW 52 lost no ships and JW 53 was not molested by the enemy, although a gale forced some of its ships to turn back. RA 53 was scattered by winds approaching hurricane force and lost three ships sunk by U-boats as well as one which foundered.

Arctic convoys had then to be suspended for more than six months because every available escort vessel was needed to win the second round of the Battle of the Atlantic. They were resumed at the beginning of November 1943 and continued, with an intermission in the summer of 1944, until the end of the war with Germany. Very few merchant ships were lost, despite the presence of a substantial U-boat force in Norwegian waters and the return of some sixty or more Ju 88 torpedo-bombers to Northern Norway during the last winter of the war. The intelligence contribution to the sinking of the *Scharnhorst* when she put to sea for the purpose of attacking JW 55B in December 1943 has already been described.* A long watch on the *Tirpitz* by air reconnaissance culminated in her destruction in November 1944 by aircraft of Bomber Command.

From first to last, 811 merchant vessels left Iceland or Scotland for the White Sea or the Kola Inlet in convoys protected by the Home Fleet. Thirty-three turned back and fifty-eight were sunk. Seven hundred and twenty completed the voyage, delivering about four million tons of cargo which included approximately five thousand tanks and more than seven thousand aircraft. Convoys in both directions cost the lives of 2,783 sailors and merchant seamen and the loss of eighty-nine merchant vessels and eighteen warships.[79] Losses might well have become prohibitive if the authorities had not been well served by intelligence or had failed to profit by the lessons of PQ 17 and PQ 18.

*

With the failure of the German offensive at Kursk in the late summer of 1943 the war entered a new phase. At Teheran in the following October the Western Allies committed themselves to a landing in France by the early summer of 1944; the Russians, although they had signed a five-year neutrality pact with the Japanese in 1941, volunteered to join the war against Japan when Germany was defeated. Thereafter things might still go wrong for the Americans and the British, but the Russians could scarcely fail to defeat the German armies on the Eastern Front. In the meantime they received from their allies such excellent information about German dispositions and intentions that the collapse of their Swiss network hardly mattered.

* See page 184.

A remarkable feature of the Soviet intelligence effort was the high proportion devoted to espionage in allied countries. It is no exaggeration to say that in the latter part of the war the various intelligence agencies paid more attention to the discovery of Allied than of German secrets. Political and military espionage in the United States was organized on a massive scale by senior members of the staff of the Soviet Embassy in Washington. The American security authorities, preoccupied with the activities of Axis agents at home and in Latin America, paid little heed to those of Soviet agents masquerading as diplomatic or consular officials, press correspondents or members of quasi-permanent or *ad hoc* missions. Some use was made of American informants recruited earlier from Communist cells or study groups, but from the end of 1943 or the early part of 1944 only the services of those willing to observe the rules of conspiracy as laid down in Moscow were retained.[80]

Industrial espionage on a still larger scale was organized by the Soviet Purchasing Commission. All employees who were members of the Soviet Communist Party were required in the latter part of the war to obtain as much information as possible about manufacturing methods and processes and technical developments for the benefit of Russian industry and its post-war reconstruction and expansion.[81] The Russians became avid collectors of trade publications, patent specifications and technical handouts which they were allowed to acquire openly. There is reason to suspect that these were valued not only for their own sake, but also as a cloak for material obtained by clandestine methods.

The ferrying of American-built aircraft to the Soviet Union by way of the Bering Strait provided the Russians with a very simple means both of smuggling illicit material out of the country and of smuggling in persons whose credentials might not bear examination.[82] The aircraft were flown by American crews to Great Falls, Montana. There they embarked cargoes of lend-lease material packed by American civilians under Russian supervision. They were then flown, again by American crews, to Fairbanks, Alaska. From Fairbanks Soviet crews flew them to Siberia and on to Kuibyshev, Moscow or elsewhere. Smaller numbers of aircraft flew in the opposite direction to bring back crews needed to fly out more aircraft. In 1943 there were no facilities at Great Falls for the censorship of outgoing mail, and the customs and immigration authorities were represented only by one elderly official who had to be summoned from his office in the town, four miles away, when his services were needed at the airport. Passengers arriving from Fairbanks could easily escape interrogation by jumping over the railings and driving away in taxis. As a rule, no examination was made of outgoing personal luggage or, once they had been packed, of crates containing lend-lease material. No aircraft could, however, leave Great Falls without clearance from Major Jordan, the American officer responsible for expediting the despatch of material, or in Jordan's absence from an American duty officer.

Jordan's suspicions were aroused when the Soviet Purchasing Commission took to including in its consignments large numbers of cheap suitcases, all of the same pattern, which the Russians at first described as personal luggage and later as receptacles for material 'of the highest diplomatic character'.[83] He took it upon himself to examine some of them. According to his subsequent account, based on hasty jottings made at the time, they contained among other things technical publications; commercial catalogues; maps of the Panama Canal Zone; a large map or plan of what he afterwards knew to be the site of the nuclear installation then under construction at Oak Ridge, Tennessee; and photostatic copies of American official documents from which the margins had been trimmed, perhaps to save weight or possibly to remove security classifications. He reported his findings to the security authorities, but for a long time nothing happened. Eventually the State Department warned the Soviet Embassy that henceforward censorship, customs and immigration regulations would be enforced, and officials were posted to Great Falls for the purpose. But these reforms had no practical effect. The Russians continued to defy the regulations, knowing that the authorities could have enforced them only if they had been willing to incur the odium of holding up entire plane-loads of lend-lease material.

As the attitude of the Roosevelt administration to the Soviet Union was founded on Roosevelt's personal conviction that it could best secure Stalin's co-operation both during and after the war by treating him with the utmost liberality, the reluctance of government officials to do anything to annoy the Russians is understandable. Cases of alleged espionage on behalf of the Soviet Union were investigated from time to time, but little was done about them until the war was over, or almost over. The definition of lend-lease was extended to cover not only a wide range of consumer goods, but also plant, equipment and raw materials clearly intended by the Russians for use after the war. Large numbers of Soviet officers and civilian officials were allowed to visit factories and military establishments and make notes of what they saw.

Establishments to which Soviet officers and officials were admitted did not, however, include those concerned with nuclear research or the preparation of fissionable material. For information about the progress of Anglo-American nuclear research and development programme, code-named the Manhattan Project, the Russians relied on agents.[84] These differed a good deal in knowledge and status. At one end of the scale was the machinist Corporal David Greenglass, who did not know he was making parts for an atomic bomb until his wife Ruth told him so; at the other were physicists of the calibre of Alan Nunn May, Bruno Pontecorvo and Klaus Fuchs. Somewhere between came Julius Rosenberg, who furnished his sister Ruth Greenglass with the knowledge which enabled her to enlighten her husband, and the go-between Harry Gold. Gold was neither a scientist nor a skilled craftsman, but he had a long experience of industrial espionage and the advantage of being, so to speak, conspicuously inconspicuous. His appearance was so nondescript that even people who had met him several times could not remember what he looked like.

May's recruitment by Soviet intelligence in the 1930s has already been mentioned.* Pontecorvo, a former colleague of the distinguished physicist Enrico Fermi, arrived in Canada in 1943, worked for a time at McGill University in Montreal, and was afterwards transferred to the nuclear research establishment at Chalk River. He met May in Montreal, but probably neither man knew the other was a Soviet agent. Fuchs, a German refugee and a convinced Communist, was sent by the British to a camp in Canada in 1940, but afterwards allowed to return to the United Kingdom. In the early summer of 1942, when he was working on a nuclear research project at the University of Birmingham, he got in touch with Semion Kremer, a civilian employed by the Soviet Military Attaché in London. He continued to meet Kremer from time to time until, in December 1943, he was sent to the United States. There he worked first at Columbia and afterwards at Los Alamos. Soon after his arrival he was approached by Harry Gold on behalf of Anatoli Yakovlev, Soviet Vice-Consul in New York and the principal organizer of nuclear espionage in the Eastern and Southern states.

How Yakovlev's network functioned is well shown by the example of a visit made by Gold to New Mexico in the early summer of 1945. One evening in May Gold met Yakovlev by appointment at a café near 42nd

* See page 205.

Street and Third Avenue, New York. Yakovlev told him that, travelling as 'Dave of Pittsburgh', he was to go to Santa Fé and meet Fuchs. He was then to go on to Albuquerque and pick up some drawings which were being prepared by a Mr X, to whom he was to introduce himself by saying that he came from Julius. For the same go-between to meet, in rapid succession, two agents both working at Los Alamos was contrary to the strict rules of conspiracy which the Russians were usually careful to observe, but Yakovlev decided to risk it because the courier who was to have fetched the drawings was unable to make the journey. Moreover, as Gold had never met Mr X and would have to get in touch with him when he arrived at Albuquerque, he had to be told that Mr X's real name was Greenglass. This, too, was irregular. It was also very unfortunate for Greenglass because, when Fuchs and Gold were arrested some five years later, Gold was able to name him as a source. However, to make sure that Gold got hold of the right man Yakovlev gave him one half of the top of a packet of raspberry jelly (US Jello). The other half had already been given to Greenglass by his brother-in-law, Julius Rosenberg.

Gold duly travelled by train to New Mexico a few days later, met Fuchs and was given a report which he afterwards put in an envelope marked 'Doctor'. He then took another train to Albuquerque, where he registered at the Hotel Hilton not as Dave of Pittsburgh (which would certainly have looked odd), but in his own name. In the forenoon of Sunday, 3 June, he called on the Greenglasses at their flat at 209 North High Street, went through the prescribed recognition procedure, and was asked to come back in the afternoon, when a report which was to accompany the drawings would be ready. He spent most of the next few hours reading a thriller in his hotel bedroom. In due course he collected the drawings and the report. These went into a second envelope which he marked 'Other'.

The rules of conspiracy were breached yet again when, much to Gold's embarrassment, the Greenglasses insisted on walking part of the way to the station with him. He arrived in New York fairly late on 5 June and met Yakovlev in Brooklyn at ten o'clock that evening. Both men carried newspapers. Inside Gold's were the two envelopes. He and Yakovlev walked together for a few minutes before exchanging newspapers. They then chatted for a few minutes before parting. The mission was over.

In addition to the material brought by Gold from New Mexico and transmitted by Yakovlev to Moscow, the Russians received a brief account of the testing of the experimental bomb at Los Alamos on 16 July. So the lack of surprise with which Stalin greeted Truman's announcement at Potsdam on 24 July that the Western Allies had a new weapon of extraordinary power is understandable.

NINE

The Far East and the Pacific

The broad situation in the Far East on the eve of World War II was that the Japanese, without ever formally declaring war on China, had occupied large tracts of Chinese territory and forced the Chinese Nationalist government of Chiang Kai-shek to take refuge at Chungking, deep in the Yangtze gorges. In the summer of 1939 they persuaded the British government to assent to the proposition that Japanese forces in China were entitled to take measures to safeguard their security and maintain order in areas under their control; but they were unable to prevent the United States government from denouncing, with effect from the early part of 1940, the commercial treaty negotiated between Japan and the United States in 1911. They had begun some months earlier to put strong pressure on the British and the French to cut off supplies to Chiang Kai-shek and surrender Chinese assets in their custody, but were nevertheless anxious to avoid an open conflict with France and Britain.

The Japanese government of the day was also anxious to avoid, or at any rate postpone until the 'China incident' was over, the confrontation with the Soviet Union which some Japanese strategists regarded as inevitable. Fear of the Russians had led Japan to conclude with Germany in 1936 an Anti-Comintern pact which her statesmen now had some cause to regret. The link with Hitler's Germany made even the best-intentioned Japanese suspect in Western eyes. At the same time the pact was bound to be an obstacle to good relations with Russia, yet it did not bind Germany to come to the aid of Japan if the Russians attacked her.

In the spring of 1939 the Germans pressed the Japanese to replace the Anti-Comintern pact by a military alliance. When the Japanese declined on the ground that such an alliance might involve them in hostilities with the Western Powers, Ribbentrop warned them that their refusal might drive Germany to conclude a non-aggression pact with the Soviet

Union.[1] Despite this broad hint, the Moscow Pact caused such consternation in Tokyo that the government fell from office. It was replaced by one whose leader, General Noboyuki Abe, considered his predecessor's attitude to the China question woefully mistaken. Abe aimed at making peace with Nationalist China, conciliating the Russians, and convincing the Western Powers that Japan had no intention of riding roughshod over their interests in East Asia. But he failed to persuade the Americans to negotiate a new commercial treaty, was accused of truckling to them without gaining anything in return, and early in 1940 had to make way for another stop-gap administration. His successor, Admiral M. Yonai, was equally unsuccessful. Pressure from advocates of a more aggressive policy then brought to office a government which represented an uneasy coalition between moderate and extremist elements. It was headed by a respected moderate, Prince Konoye. Its War Minister was General Kideki Tojo, a former Chief of Staff of the Kwantung Army in Manchuria; its Foreign Minister a relatively inexperienced diplomat, Yosuke Matsuoka, who had studied law in the United States and had little use for traditional methods of diplomacy.

Matsuoka was an unabashed admirer of totalitarian methods. He believed that Italy was bound to become subservient to Germany but that Japan, because of her physical remoteness from Europe, could join Hitler in carving up the British Empire without forfeiting her independence. He envisaged a division of the spoils which would give her the dominant position in Greater East Asia as far west as Burma and as far south as New Caledonia. Ultimately her sphere of influence might include India, Australia and New Zealand, although possibly India might have to be offered to the Russians as the price of their acquiescence in these designs.[2]

Against the background of Hitler's triumphs in Western Europe in the summer of 1940, Matsuoka persuaded his colleagues and the Privy Council to give their reluctant assent to a Tripartite Pact which bound Germany, Italy and Japan to give each other full political, economic and military support in the event of an attack on any of them by a power not already involved in the European war or the Sino–Japanese dispute. Secret understandings which accompanied the pact pledged Germany to give Japan 'all possible assistance' should she go to war with Britain, and in the meantime to help her prepare for such a contingency by giving her 'all possible technical and material aid'. Japan did not undertake to go to war with Britain, but she did promise to take all measures, short of war, that might be needed to complete the overthrow of the British Empire and prevent the United States from intervening.

In the teeth of adverse comments from the Emperor and the naval Commander-in-Chief, Admiral Yamamoto, the pact was signed at the very moment when the Germans were forced to recognize that their attempt to establish favourable conditions for a landing in Britain had failed. The Russians, when formally notified that signature of the pact was imminent, made the disconcerting remark that they were entitled by the terms of the Moscow Pact to scrutinize any such document before the formalities were completed.

Matsuoka's further aims included transformation of the Moscow Pact into a ten-year non-aggression pact between Germany, Italy, Japan and the Soviet Union. Although Hitler and Ribbentrop gave him a strong hint in the spring of 1941 that Germany might soon be at war with Russia, he persisted in wooing the Russians but had to be content with the five-year neutrality pact already mentioned.*

Early in June the Japanese Ambassador in Berlin reported after an interview with Hitler that the Führer had made up his mind to attack the Soviet Union. Nevertheless, Matsuoka was flabbergasted when the Ambassador telephoned on 22 June to say that the attack had begun. He then proposed that Japan should herself go to war with Russia, but omitted to consult his colleagues before broaching the matter with the Emperor. A few weeks later the entire Cabinet resigned as a first step towards the formation of a new government from which Matsuoka was excluded. In the meantime the decision was made to send troops to southern Indo-China for the purpose of occupying bases for a possible invasion of the Netherlands East Indies. The authorities agreed at an Imperial Conference on 2 July that this should be done even at the risk of war, but an earlier decision to go to war with the Western Powers only if the national existence was at stake was not rescinded.

The Western Powers had some difficulty in interpreting the shifts of Japanese policy. During the lifetime of the Abe government the United States Ambassador in Tokyo, J. C. Grew, urged the State Department without success to make concessions to Japan in order to keep Abe in office and extremists out. The Secretary of State, Cordell Hull, was profoundly shocked by outrages committed by the Japanese in China, and he had no faith in promises of better behaviour in the future. The Western Powers were also handicapped by lack of unanimity about the best means of resisting Japanese encroachments. The essence of

* See page 223.

Britain's long-term plan for the defence of Western interests in South-East Asia and the South-West Pacific was the presence at Singapore of a fleet strong enough to dominate the South China Sea and thus prevent the Japanese from disembarking and supplying expeditionary forces which might otherwise threaten Malaya, Borneo, the Indonesian archipelago or the Philippines. The British were unable after the fall of France to provide such a fleet, and they saw little prospect of doing so before the spring of 1942. They proposed in the summer of 1940 that the Americans should help them to keep the Japanese in check, either by sending warships to Singapore or by banning exports to Japan. If neither course was acceptable then the Americans would, they thought, be well advised to join them in an attempt to settle the Sino–Japanese dispute by mediation. But Roosevelt and Hull were unwilling, with a presidential election in the offing, to do anything that might be represented by their political opponents as a subordination of American to British interests. They refused to send American warships to Singapore or mediate between Japan and China, and they declined until the election was over to impose more than a partial embargo on trade with Japan.

At the same time, Roosevelt was aware of the value of contact with British sources of information and of the shortcomings of his own intelligence organization. On the outbreak of World War II at least half a dozen different bodies in the United States were concerned with various aspects of foreign intelligence and internal security, but no single authority was in a position to furnish the President or the Chiefs of Staff with comprehensive intelligence appreciations.[3] A Joint Committee on Intelligence Services existed for the purpose of co-ordinating the activities of the various agencies, but its functions did not include collation, interpretation or analysis. Adolf A. Berle, appointed Assistant Secretary of State on Roosevelt's recommendation in 1938, was the nearest equivalent to a Chief of Intelligence, but he did not possess – and his predecessors since 1927 had not possessed – a staff trained to interpret and analyse information from all sources. The signal intelligence services maintained by the army and the navy were potentially valuable sources of information, but they did not have much to offer until, in the autumn of 1940, they began to read the Japanese diplomatic cypher. For espionage in foreign countries the Department of State and the service departments depended on a system by which, in effect, the service attachés were empowered to recruit agents and sub-agents on the understanding that they must not be caught doing so. The Federal

Bureau of Investigation – formed in 1908 as the Bureau of Investigation, with a great-nephew of Napoleon as its first chief – was responsible for internal security, and from 1940 for counter-espionage not only at home but also in Latin America and the Caribbean. Distinct from the FBI was the Secret Service, formed soon after the Civil War for purposes which included the detection of fraud, and which still include the provision of a presidential bodyguard. Other agencies whose reports contributed in some measure to the intelligence picture were the customs and immigration services and the federal communications organization.

With the President's approval, C made contact early in 1940 with the FBI.[4] In May Colonel (afterwards Sir) William Stephenson was appointed British liaison officer with the American intelligence services. Almost simultaneously, Roosevelt took the first step towards a unified intelligence organization by appointing Colonel 'Wild Bill' Donovan Co-Ordinator of Information and asking him to assess the ability and determination of the British to carry on the war.[5] Stephenson proposed that Donovan should visit London and see for himself how events were shaping. At a time when the United States Ambassador, Joseph Kennedy, was predicting Britain's imminent collapse in face of German air power, Donovan reported that in his opinion the RAF would defeat the Luftwaffe. In the light of his report and a visit to London by an American delegation at the end of August 1940, the President authorized full disclosure to the British of relevant information from American diplomatic and consular sources.[6] In the event, the Americans did not have a great deal to communicate until they became active belligerents in 1941, but personal contacts were useful to both sides. Representatives of the FBI were attached to MI 6 as pupils, and they had something to contribute as well as something to learn.

Donovan's appointment as Co-Ordinator of Information proved not to be the answer to Roosevelt's problems. The American Chiefs of Staff feared that, having direct access to the President, he might tender advice which differed from theirs; Berle complained of the difficulty of knowing what conception Roosevelt had of his co-ordinator's responsibilities.[7] Donovan himself recognized by the summer of 1941 that his terms of reference were too wide. On 13 June he was given a new post as Director of an Office of Strategic Services responsible not to the President but to the Joint Chiefs of Staff. His brief was to collect and analyse such strategic information as the Chiefs of Staff might require, to plan and carry out such special operations as they might order him to undertake. The FBI retained its existing responsibilities for domestic security and counter-espionage, while Berle was relegated, in effect, to the role of watchdog on behalf of the Department of State.[8]

In the meantime the American signal intelligence services had begun to read Japanese diplomatic traffic. Within a few weeks of the formation of the OSS, they decrypted a summary sent by the Japanese Foreign Ministry to embassies and legations of the conclusions reached at the Imperial Conference on 2 July.[9] A signal transmitted a few days later by the South China Army gave details of impending moves in Indo-China and made their purpose clear. On the initiative of the President and his advisers, the Western Powers responded to these disclosures by imposing stringent economic sanctions on Japan. Japanese assets throughout the British Empire and the United States were frozen, three-quarters of Japan's foreign trade was brought to a standstill, and nearly nine-tenths of her imports of crude oil and refinery products were cut off at the source. The effect was to create precisely those conditions in which even the most pacifically inclined members of the Japanese ruling class were prepared to countenance war with the Western Powers if all else failed.

There was nothing in the signals decrypted up to that time to suggest that the Japanese were contemplating a surprise attack on the United States Fleet at Pearl Harbor if war did come. Evidence that the Abwehr was keenly interested in the naval base and its defences was, however, available to the FBI by the third week in August 1941. It was contained in a list of questions put to a double agent employed by the British double-cross organization, who was being sent to the United States by way of Lisbon.[10] But the significance of these questions in the context of current relations between Germany and Japan does not seem to have been apparent to the Americans at the time, obvious though it may seem in retrospect.

In any case, the Japanese were still not convinced that war was inevitable. On the contrary, they made strenuous attempts to settle their differences with the Western Powers by means of diplomatic negotiations in Washington. On 6 August Konoye offered to enter into an undertaking not to advance beyond Indo-China, and to withdraw from Indo-China on the termination of the 'China incident', if the Americans would lift their economic embargo and suspend military preparations in the Philippines. When these proposals were rejected, he suggested that he and Roosevelt should meet. Roosevelt was not unwilling, but Hull insisted that there should be no summit meeting unless the Japanese first put their cards on the table. Konoye then yielded to the Japanese

Army's insistence that a time-limit should be set to the negotiations, but told Grew that he still saw no reason why war should not be averted if only he and Roosevelt could meet. No progress having been made by the middle of October, he resigned and advised the Emperor to 'put the responsibility squarely on the army' by appointing a government headed by General Tojo.[11]

We now know that Tojo agreed at an Imperial Conference on 5 November that further attempts should be made to come to terms with the Americans, and that Japan should go to war only if these were seen by 25 November to have failed. An experienced professional diplomat, Saburo Kurusu, was sent to Washington to help the Ambassador, Admiral Kichisaburo Nomura.

By the end of the first week in November Roosevelt and Hull knew from decrypted messages that Nomura had been warned that 25 November was the deadline.[12] On 7 November Nomura submitted proposals for a comprehensive settlement of outstanding issues. These provided for the withdrawal of Japanese forces from most but not all parts of China within two years of a satisfactory agreement with Chiang Kai-shek or his successor. On 18 November Hull rejected these proposals on the ground that public opinion in the United States would not tolerate a comprehensive settlement as long as Japan remained friendly with Hitler's Germany. Nomura and Kurusu then proposed an interim agreement which envisaged the prompt withdrawal of Japanese forces from southern Indo-China and their withdrawal from the whole of Indo-China on the conclusion of an equitable settlement of the China problem. The Americans were asked in return to call a halt to military moves in South-East Asia and the South-West Pacific, lift the economic embargo, help the Japanese to bargain for supplies of raw materials from the Netherlands East Indies and, in effect, put pressure on Chiang Kai-shek to come to terms with Tojo's government. Hull showed these proposals and American counter-proposals on 22 November to the Australian, British, Chinese and Dutch envoys in Washington, summoned the envoys to a further meeting on 24 November, but on 26 November suddenly gave up the whole idea of an interim agreement and offered to come to terms with the Japanese only if they withdrew their forces from the whole of China and relinquished even the extraterritorial rights to which they were entitled under treaties of long standing.[13]

The Japanese were staggered by this announcement. Nevertheless, Tojo and his colleagues agreed to make a further attempt at a peaceful settlement and to extend the deadline to 29 November. We now know that their final decision to go to war was not made until 1 December. In the meantime the American authorities, aware that the earlier deadline had been reached, warned appropriate commanders that an aggressive move by Japan might be expected within the next few days.[14] No specific mention was made of Pearl Harbor in this warning, issued on 27 November. The possibility of a surprise attack by carrier-borne aircraft on American possessions in the Central Pacific had been considered on a number of occasions in the past, but the kind of aggressive move the authorities now had in mind was an attempt to put troops ashore in Siam, Malaya, the Philippines or possibly Borneo.

Chiefly because all eyes were therefore focused on South-East Asia and the South-West Pacific, the significance of a conspicuous gap in Japanese naval traffic in the latter part of November and the first week in December was missed. As a rule, the Japanese Navy changed its call-signs at invervals of approximately six months. It changed them, not unexpectedly, on 1 November, but then changed them again on 1 December. Many of the new call-signs introduced at the beginning of November were identified in the meantime, but contact with the 1st and 2nd Carrier Squadrons was lost. In the light of traffic analysis, American intelligence officers concluded, correctly, that a new task force was being formed to support a southward drive.[15] They also concluded, incorrectly, that in all probability the missing carrier squadrons were somewhere in Japanese home waters, preparing to support such a movement.[16] In fact the 1st and 2nd Carrier Squadrons, with the 5th Carrier Squadron and other warships, were already steaming towards the Central Pacific with orders to turn back if and when they received a coded message to be sent if the negotiations in Washington were successful.

In the meantime the Americans received many indications that a crisis was impending. They intercepted as early as 19 November, and decrypted nine days later, a signal to the effect that if international communications were severed, an imminent breakdown of diplomatic relations would be announced by the inclusion of a special weather forecast in the daily Japanese-language short-wave news broadcast. 'East wind rain' would mean that relations with the United States were in jeopardy, 'north wind cloudy' would indicate an imminent breach with the Soviet Union, 'west wind clear' would herald trouble with Britain.[17] As international communications were not in fact severed before the outbreak of war, these signals were never sent, and the special listening-watch kept by the Americans was unrewarding. Signal intelligence did, however, intercept and decrypt in the first few days of December instructions to a number of diplomatic and consular officials to destroy cypher material or prepare to do so. The Americans also bugged and recorded, on 6 December, what seemed a sinister but was in fact a perfectly above-board telephone conversation between the editor of a Japanese newspaper and its correspondent in Honolulu.[18]

While intelligence officers in Hawaii were chasing this hare, the local office of the Radio Corporation of America transmitted to Tokyo a coded message which purported to be signed by the Japanese Consul-General. Its originator was Takeo Yoshikawa, a Japanese secret agent ostensibly employed by the consulate as a secretary. The gist of Yoshikawa's report was that virtually the whole of the Pacific Fleet was at Pearl Harbor, except that no carriers were present. The message was intercepted, and a teletyped version reached Washington soon after midnight.[19] It was of cardinal importance to the Japanese Navy, but its value was not apparent to the American officer who received the teletype, because the code used was one not generally employed for important messages. The teletype was therefore put aside to be dealt with later. Even if it had been decrypted on the spot, it would probably not have convinced American intelligence officers that Pearl Harbor was about to be attacked, because reports from consular officials about shipping movements were not uncommon.

In any case the Signal Intelligence Service and its naval counterpart, OP-20-G, had other preoccupations. During the afternoon of 6 December and the following night the Japanese transmitted, in fourteen parts, a long message in English which rehearsed Japanese grievances against the Western Powers and concluded with an expression of regret that diplomatic negotiations must be broken off. It was preceded by a pilot message which instructed the Japanese Embassy in Washington to put the text 'in nicely drafted form' before presenting it to the Department of State at a time to be communicated later.[20] The first thirteen parts were transmitted and decrypted in time for the President and a number of other authorized recipients to see them before midnight, but were not seen that night by the Chief of Staff of the Army, General George C. Marshall, or the Chief of Naval Operations, Admiral Harold S. Stark. The fourteenth part was circulated before 10 a.m. on Sunday, 7 December, and a copy of the complete text was delivered to the Department of State in time for a conference at 10 a.m. between Hull and the heads of the service departments.[21] The message showed clearly that the Japanese Foreign Ministry regarded the diplomatic negotiations as over, but it did not mention war.

On the other hand, a decrypted signal instructing the Japanese Embassy to destroy all cypher material, including the one cypher machine not already destroyed, did suggest that hostilities were imminent.[22] More revealing still was the promised time-of-delivery message. This instructed Nomura to present the fourteen-part message to the Department of State (and preferably to the Secretary of State in person) at 1 p.m. The choice of 1 p.m. on a Sunday for the delivery of an important diplomatic communication struck both naval and army intelligence officers as more than odd. At 1 p.m. by Washington time the sun would not have risen in South-East Asia or the South-West Pacific, but dawn would be breaking in Hawaii. Colonel Rufus S. Bratton, the Military Intelligence Division's Far Eastern expert, thought this so significant that he tried to get in touch with General Marshall and, on learning that Marshall had left for his usual Sunday-morning ride, sent an orderly to look for him.[23] Lieutenant-Commander Alwyn D. Kramer, a Japanese-language expert working in OP-20-G, interrupted a meeting of senior officers to break the news to his immediate superior and Admiral Stark.

However, as the navy was concerned only with the naval base at Pearl Harbor while the army was responsible for the defence of the Territory of Hawaii as a whole, nothing could be done until Marshall, having received Bratton's message, reached his office about 11 a.m. Marshall then drafted the following signal:[24]

> Japanese are presenting at one p.m. Eastern Standard Time what amounts to an ultimatum also they are under orders to destroy their code machine immediately Stop Just what significance the hour set may have we do not know but be on alert accordingly Stop

At Stark's request, he added: 'Inform naval authorities of this communication.' Stark offered to have the signal sent with all speed, but Marshall told Bratton to take it to the War Department's communications centre for transmission to the commanding generals in the Philippines, Hawaii and the Caribbean and on the West Coast. Bratton, by that time somewhat agitated, asked the communications centre how long transmission would take and was told that the signal could be mechanically encyphered in three minutes, on the air in eight and in the hands of addressees in twenty. He reported this to Marshall, who seems not to have understood and twice sent him back to the communications centre for further information before its chief, Colonel Edward French, received authority to go ahead. The time was then one minute past noon, and French had discovered in the meantime that, because of jamming, his ten-kilowatt transmitter could not be heard in Honolulu. He therefore passed the encyphered signal by teleprinter to Western Union for transmission by RCA's forty-kilowatt equipment. It reached Honolulu at 7.33 a.m. by local time, but the Japanese telegraph-boy to whom its delivery was entrusted was delayed by traffic jams and stopped by the National Guard and the police, with the result that he did not reach the commanding general's administrative headquarters at Fort Shafter until some four hours later.[25]

Thus the excellent information furnished to the authorities in Washington by the Signal Intelligence Service and OP-20-G did not prevent the Japanese from achieving tactical surprise at Pearl Harbor. The broad situation in Hawaii on 7 December was that the naval commander believed the army commander to be maintaining a continuous radar watch for hostile aircraft, while the army commander assumed that his naval colleague was mainttaining an effective search by long-range maritime aircraft for approaching warships.[26] Both were mistaken. The Japanese carrier force reached its flying-off position at first light without detection by any of the thirty-three flying-boats at the navy's disposal. Only three of these were on patrol, and they were not searching in the right direction. The army's radar watch was not continuous and was organized on a training basis. In view of the 'war warning' of 27 November the army commander had, however, arranged that operators should man their sets daily from 4 a.m. to 7 a.m. instead of doing all their training in normal working hours. On weekdays they would then train for another four hours before going off duty. As 7 December was a Sunday no provision was made for stations to be on the air after 7 a.m., but an inexperienced duty officer, himself under training, would remain at the report centre until 8 a.m. Two enlisted men manning a station in the extreme north of Oahu detected at 6.45 a.m. what we now know to have been a seaplane reconnoitring on behalf of the Japanese carrier force, but the duty officer did not regard the approach of a single aircraft as a reason for prolonging the watch after the scheduled time.[27] A request by the two men to be allowed to go on manning their set until a truck arrived to take them to breakfast was, however, granted. About two minutes after the watch ended they detected what they estimated to be a force of not less than fifty aircraft approaching from the north, but their attempt to convince the duty officer that something exceptional was happening was unsuccessful. The officer thought they must have detected American aircraft on a training or a delivery flight.

Except in so far as suspicion was aroused by an encounter with a submarine about a mile off Pearl Harbor between 6.30 and 7 a.m., the defenders were caught completely unprepared when a first wave of 183 Japanese carrier-borne aircraft arrived shortly before eight o'clock. Very few anti-aircraft guns ashore or afloat were fully manned. Live ammunition for the guns had to be extracted from locked boxes or fetched from depots.[28] Aircraft on the ground were not dispersed, but parked close together so that they could be more easily guarded against saboteurs. Of the eight battleships at Pearl Harbor, one was in dry dock and the others were berthed in two lines, unprotected by anti-torpedo nets or baffles. All seven of these were sunk or crippled. The battleship in dry dock escaped lightly, although she was hit by a bomb which exploded in the casemate of a 5-inch gun. In just over two hours 353 Japanese aircraft, of which 29 were lost, sank or damaged 18 American warships and auxiliaries, destroyed or damaged 349 American aircraft and killed or wounded 3,581 American sailors, marines and soldiers. The Pacific Fleet was saved from irremediable disaster by the absence of its carriers and the failure of the Japanese to destroy naval installations ashore.

At the time the Americans regarded the attack as an infamous breach of Article I of the Hague Convention, which forbids the opening of hostilities without prior delivery of a declaration of war or ultimatum. We now know that the Japanese Foreign Minister, Shigenori Togo, was not quite as unscrupulous as he seemed, although he was certainly not blameless. He regarded the fourteen-part message as a formal rejection of what he conceived to be Hull's virtual ultimatum of 26 November, and therefore tantamount to a declaration of war. He meant it to be delivered before hostilities began. The naval authorities did not tell him when Pearl Harbor was to be attacked, but only that delivery of the message at 1 p.m. would suffice. They afterwards admitted that they had miscalculated, that the message would have come too late even if it had been delivered punctually. In the event it was not delivered until 2.30 p.m. because, as a result of Togo's insistence that junior members of the staff of the embassy should not be used for its transcription, it had to be laboriously typed out by the First Secretary.

The American authorities in the Philippines received official notification from Washington of the attack on Pearl Harbor about four hours before the first bombs fell on northern Luzon. Nevertheless, attacks on their bases in the neighbourhood of Manila some two and a half hours later found them still largely unprepared. Japanese airmen whose mission had been delayed by fog over their airfields in Formosa were astonished to find large numbers of aircraft parked in the open with little or no attempt at dispersal or concealment. They destroyed nearly a hundred American aircraft on the ground and in the air for the loss of seven of their own.[29] Two days later, bombing started uncontrollable fires in the Navy Yard at Cavite and destroyed the entire reserve stock of torpedoes for American submarines operating from Manila Bay. By the end of the fifth day of hostilities the Japanese had virtually undisputed control of the sea and air approaches to the Philippines, and their troops were already ashore on the north, east and west coasts of Luzon.

The situation in South-East Asia in November 1941 was that the British did not expect to be able to hold Hong Kong for more than a brief period in the event of war, but hoped to have at Singapore by the spring of 1942 a fleet strong enough to prevent the Japanese from invading Malaya, Borneo or the Indonesian archipelago, or from pushing past the Indonesian archipelago to threaten Australia, Burma, India or Ceylon. If the diplomatic negotiations entrusted to Hull failed to avert war in the meantime, the Japanese could be expected to disembark troops at Singora and Patani, in Southern Siam, in order to gain access to roads linking Siam with Malaya and running down the west coast of the Malay peninsula. Alternatively, or in addition, Japanese troops might land at Kota Bharu, on the east coast of Malaya. There were few roads in eastern Malaya, but a railway linked Kota Bharu with Johore and Singapore.

The arrival at Singapore at the end of November of the new battleship *Prince of Wales* and the old battlecruiser *Repulse*, sent in the hope that they might have some deterrent effect, gave the British naval commander, Admiral Sir Tom Phillips, a weak and unbalanced fleet of two capital ships, three light cruisers and six destroyers. There were also two Australian destroyers in the area. No help could be expected from the United States Pacific Fleet, nearly six thousand miles away, but the commander of the small United States Asiatic Fleet in the Philippines, Admiral Thomas C. Hart, intended to send four of his thirteen destroyers to Singapore on the outbreak of war. The Dutch authorities in the Netherlands East Indies had three light cruisers, six destroyers and thirteen submarines based on Java.

In these circumstances the British had virtually no chance of gaining control of the South China Sea by the exercise of surface power. The commander of their land and air forces, Air Chief Marshal Sir Robert Brooke-Popham, had been told at the time of his appointment in 1940 that he would have to rely on air power until a balanced fleet became available. But the only aircraft he had in Malaya in December 1941 were 24 obsolescent torpedo-bombers, 35 light bombers, 72 fighters and 27 reconnaissance aircraft. The land forces would provide one corps of two infantry divisions for the defence of northern Malaya, in addition to garrisons for Singapore and Penang and a small reserve. About half this force would be needed to hold airfields built when the RAF expected to have many more aircraft in Malaya than had arrived, so only one division would be available to bar the routes to the south. This was the 11th Indian Division, consisting of the 6th and 15th Indian Infantry Brigades and a detached force called Krohcol.

The situation was complicated by the existence of alternative plans for the 11th Indian Division. If Brooke-Popham ordered Operation Matador, the two infantry brigades would move well into Siamese territory to meet the enemy at or near Singora; Krohcol a short distance into Siam to block the road from Patani at a position called The Ledge. If he decided against Matador, the two brigades would occupy a prepared position at Jitra, on the Malayan side of the frontier, but Krohcol would still have to advance to The Ledge to prevent the Jitra position from being turned. Matador would be feasible only if the troops began their advance at least twenty-four hours before the enemy reached Singora, and in any case might be ruled out on political grounds.

On 21 November Brooke-Popham asked the Chiefs of Staff in London to define the circumstances in which Matador would be permitted. They replied on 25 November that the government could not commit itself in advance but that he could expect a decision within thirty-six hours of the receipt of a firm report that Japanese forces were bound for Singora. As the Japanese were known already to have substantial forces in southern Indo-China and could reach Singora within thirty-three hours of leaving Saigon, Brooke-Popham then proposed that he should be allowed to order Matador as soon as reconnaissance aircraft reported that a Japanese convoy was approaching the Siamese coast. The Chiefs of Staff at first rejected this proposal, but on 5 December, after the United States government had been consulted, they told Brooke-Popham that he could order Matador without further reference to higher authority if he had good reason to believe that the Japanese had entered Siam or were about to disembark troops in the Singora–Patani area.[30]

In the meantime pro-Japanese members of the Siamese government were reported by a secret source to have asked the authorities in Tokyo to furnish them with a pretext for inviting Japanese forces to enter Siam by staging a feint towards the Singora–Patani area and thus luring Brooke-Popham to send troops across the frontier without good cause.[31] Opinion in Siam was believed to be generally favourable to the British, but likely to swing in the opposite direction if they jumped the gun.

On December 6 Japanese convoys were reported to have left Saigon and Camranh Bay. There were also reports that transports and warships were approaching the Gulf of Siam, and that Siamese frontier guards were obstructing roads south of Singora and Patani.[32] After consulting the naval authorities, Brooke-Popham brought the land and air forces to instant readiness, but decided not to order Matador until he was sure that Japanese forces were bound for Siam.

This excess of caution cost him his only chance of giving effect to Matador. A flying-boat sent early on the following day to the eastern part of the Gulf of Siam failed to return. Nothing more was known until, in the afternoon, a few transports and warships were seen in positions which suggested that landings in Siam might be imminent. We now know that the transports arrived off Singora and Patani about 2.20 a.m. on 8 December by local time. This was about ten minutes before Nomura handed the fourteen-part message to Hull in Washington.

In the meantime three transports were seen anchoring off the east coast of Malaya near Kota Bharu. Covered by fire from a light cruiser and a destroyer flotilla, Japanese troops began to come ashore in landing-craft soon after midnight. Arrangements were promptly made for troops, landing-craft and transports to be attacked by aircraft which, as things turned out, might with advantage have been held back to deal with the transports soon to arrive off Singora and Patani.

About 4 a.m. bombs aimed by fewer than twenty Japanese crews in bright moonlight at airfields on Singapore Island fell in built-up areas, causing about 200 civilian casualties. The defences received good warning from the radar chain, but no public warning was issued because, in the absence of any ultimatum or declaration of war, the ARP centre intended to go into action on the outbreak of hostilities was not manned.

Heavy air attacks on airfields in northern Malaya began about 7.30

a.m. About half an hour later Brooke-Popham received a signal from London authorising him to send troops across the Siamese frontier at his discretion if the Japanese came ashore at Kota Bharu. Although aware that they had already begun to do so he judged, correctly, that the main effort would be made elsewhere. Believing that he might yet have an opportunity of ordering Matador if the Japanese postponed landings in Siam on political grounds, or to keep him guessing, he decided to take no further action for the time being.

About 9.15 a.m. a badly-damaged reconnaissance aircraft landed in northern Malaya with the news that Japanese troops were streaming ashore from a large concentration of ships off Singora and Patani. When a signal to that effect reached Booke Popham half an hour later, he had no choice but to abandon Matador and order the Jitra alternative. However, the executive order could not be given until the commander of the land forces returned about 11 a.m. from a routine meeting of the Legislative Assembly. Two hours then elapsed before it reached the corps commander. The 11th Indian Division, after standing by for Matador since the afternoon of 6 December, received orders at 1.30 p.m. to move its main body to Jitra, send a delaying column along the trunk road towards Singora, and despatch Krohcol to The Ledge. Most of its arrangements for supply and transport had therefore to be changed at the last moment.

Krohcol reached the Siamese frontier at 3 p.m. There it was delayed for twenty-four hours by roadblocks manned by Siamese constabulary who had no orders to admit British troops. On 10 December it was met five miles short of its objective by Japanese troops. The 6th and 15th Infantry Brigades, joined by the 28th Indian Infantry Brigade from corps reserve, reached the Jitra position punctually, but found it incompletely prepared and partly waterlogged. To buy time for eleventh-hour improvements, the divisional commander fought a number of delaying actions. Consequent losses led him to break up the 28th Brigade instead of holding it in reserve. Thus he had no divisional reserve when the enemy made contact with his main position.

Between the evening of 11 December and the following morning, an advanced guard of the Japanese 5th Division launched probing attacks along the axis of the trunk road at Jitra, but made only a shallow penetration. The Japanese also sent patrols east of the road to feel for the British flank. Inaccurate reports of their progress in that direction gave the British divisional commander the impression that his right was threatened with envelopment. He was also troubled by his lack of reserves, the knowledge that his was the only division that could be used to bar the main routes to the south, and the possibility that a column advancing from The Ledge might turn his whole position. He asked on 12 December for permission to withdraw to an alternative position, but was told that his orders to fight at Jitra still held good.

We now know that the Japanese commander on the spot decided about midday on 12 December to relieve the advanced guard and attack during the coming night with the six battalions of his main body, but intervened too late to prevent the advanced guard from launching a fresh assault. It was halted by a counter-attack after advancing about three-quarters of a mile, but a gap about half a mile wide opened in the British front.

The divisional commander found on visiting the forward area in the afternoon that the brigadier responsible for the threatened sector was confident that he could restore the situation, but that alarmist rumours were circulating in the rear.[33] On his return to headquarters he was given inaccurate reports to the effect that disaster had overtaken one of the forward battalions. He also received a somewhat highly-coloured account of Krohcol's misadventures. At 7.30 p.m. he renewed his request for permission to withdraw. He was told that there was believed to be only one Japanese division on his front, that his best course might be to dispose his forces in depth, and that he could withdraw at his discretion. At 10 p.m. he ordered his troops to disengage and start withdrawing at midnight to the south bank of a river about ten miles to the rear. This move was intended as the first step towards withdrawal to the partly-prepared alternative position at Gurun to which he had proposed on the previous day to fall back.

Thus the British abandoned the Jitra position without waiting for the enemy's main body to attack it. The projected assault by six battalions of the Japanese 5th Division was not delivered, and an attack made by a smaller force soon after midnight was not successful.

The 11th Indian Division's attempt to retreat by a single route, in darkness and extremely unfavourable weather, proved disastrous. Some units never received the order to withdraw. Some tried to circumvent traffic-jams on the trunk road by taking to the country, with the result that they became irretrievably separated from the main body, or had to abandon guns and vehicles stuck in the mud. On the morning of 13 December the 15th Indian Infantry Brigade was down to a quarter of its strength and had to be withdrawn into reserve.

Nevertheless the Japanese were successfully held on that day by the

6th Brigade and elements of the 28th. During the following night the division continued its retreat to Gurun, in pouring rain. After a series of inconclusive engagements there the corps commander received permission to pull it back by stages to what was believed to be a naturally strong position some ninety miles to the south.

Thereafter the Japanese 5th Division, reinforced by elements of the Imperial Guards Division and later by the 18th Division, romped through the mainland of Malaya without ever having to fight a major battle. The British, with only about a tenth of the air support available to the Japanese, fought a series of expensive delaying actions in the hope of denying the enemy access to airfields which might be used for attacks on convoys bringing reinforcements and supplies.

Singapore, although described as a fortress in some British official documents, was unfitted to withstand a siege. Its formidable coast defences covered only the seaward approaches. Mangrove swamps hampered observation of the narrow channel separating it from Johore. Three of its four airfields could be swept by observed artillery fire from the mainland. It had a large civilian population, much swollen by refugees. Air and artillery bombardments which cut telephone-lines in the north-west corner of the island preceded landings after nightfall on 8 February by assault troops of the 5th and 18th Divisions. Elements of the Imperial Guards Division landed about twenty-four hours later. The defenders were soon forced back to a line covering the town of Singapore. Streets became blocked with rubble. Essential services were threatened with breakdown by a shortage of water caused by fractured mains. Armed deserters began forcing their way aboard ships bound for Sumatra and Java. On 15 February the garrison surrendered on the understanding that the Japanese commander would protect civilian life and property.

*

Could better intelligence have helped the Western Powers to avoid some or all of these disasters?

Obviously, more precise information about the enemy's plans and methods and the extent and quality of his resources would have been valuable. As it was, the performance of his aircraft was, in general, seriously underestimated, even though most of the types used in 1941 and 1942 had already been seen in China. The *Prince of Wales* and the *Repulse*, sunk off the east coast of Malaya on 10 December by dual-purpose aircraft which doubled as long-range bombers and torpedo-bombers, were sighted four hundred miles from the nearest Japanese airfield in Indo-China by C5M2 land-based reconnaissance aircraft whose radius of action Allied intelligence officers estimated at not more than three hundred.

The fact remains that most of the calamities suffered by the Western Powers were due not so much to a lack of knowledge as to errors of judgement, inadequate resources, or a combination of the two. Everything the Japanese did at the outset of hostilities was foreseeable, and indeed at one stage or another had been foreseen. 'The most likely and dangerous form of attack on Oahu', the commanders of the American naval and army air forces in the Central Pacific wrote in the spring of 1941, 'would be an air attack launched from carriers'.[34] In spite of this warning, the attack delivered in December caught the Americans unprepared because evidence from traffic analysis was misinterpreted, and because the Japanese were judged incapable of mounting more than one major operation at a time. Once they were known to be preparing for a southward drive from Indo-China, the risk of a surprise attack on Oahu was not taken seriously. The commanders in the Central Pacific busied themselves with preparations to reinforce the Philippines and to recapture or relieve them if they were captured or beleaguered.

The Philippines were not defensible with the means available in 1941. Until the summer of that year the Americans did not even hope to do more than hold a small part of Luzon until a relieving force arrived from the Central Pacific. Glowing reports of the B-17 bomber then engendered the belief that a resolute commander might be able to hold the whole of Luzon. Lieutenant-General Douglas MacArthur, a former Chief of Staff of the United States Army, was called out of semi-retirement as Field Marshal of the Armed Forces of the Philippines and promised substantial reinforcements. These were to include a hundred B-17s by the spring of 1942. MacArthur planned to use them both to supplement attacks on an invasion force by submarines and naval aircraft, and to make spoiling attacks on airfields in Formosa. But only thirty-five B-17s arrived before the outbreak of hostilities, and about half of them were destroyed on the ground in the first few hours. No spoiling attacks were delivered in the meantime, because a preliminary reconnaissance was felt to be essential.[35]

Hong Kong, defended by six regular battalions and six volunteer companies with some artillery but virtually no air support, could not be expected to hold out for more than a few weeks against an augmented Japanese division supported by some eighty aircraft. On the other hand, the British did hope to hold Malaya. Their belief that the enemy would aim at disembarking most of his expeditionary force in Siam and making a diversionary landing at Kota Bharu was correct. They recognized that they could prevent him from doing so only by gaining control of the South China Sea, and that this would also help to safeguard the Philippines, Borneo and the Netherlands East Indies. Their hope of using aircraft as a substitute for a strong fleet was unrealistic, because no suitable air striking force was available. Six well-trained, well-equipped torpedo-bomber squadrons in Malaya, supported by half the Hurricanes squandered in futile offensives over Northern France, would have been worth far more to the British in 1941 than their home-based long-range bomber force.

As it was, they had to fall back on land forces with meagre air support. Their intelligence sources told them on 6 December that a Japanese force was moving towards the Gulf of Siam, but did not provide the firm evidence of its destination which was needed before effect could be given to Matador. Whether Matador could have succeeded if it had been ordered in a good time is debatable. Japanese air superiority might have been decisive in any case. On the other hand, the British would have had the advantage of arriving in Siam before the Japanese could establish air bases there.

Air Chief Marshal Brooke-Popham's reluctance to commit himself to the Jitra alternative until he learned on 8 December that the Japanese were already landing in Siam is understandable, but lack of information was not responsible for the long delay that then occurred before the 11th Indian Division received its orders. The quality of much of the information that reached British commanders thereafter was poor. Airfields in northern Malaya were abandoned partly on the strength of premature reports that their capture was imminent, although the fear that they might be heavily attacked from the air was also a contributory factor. A false report of landings on the east coast of Malaya far south of Kota Bharu led to the loss of the *Prince of Wales* and the *Repulse*. The estimate received by the commander of the 11th Indian Division of the strength of the Japanese force on his front was accurate, but the reports on which he based his decision to withdraw from the Jitra position were not. Allied intelligence officers who had previously underestimated the fighting value of Japanese troops tended from the moment when the enemy came ashore in South-East Asia and the South-West Pacific to err in the opposite direction. Japanese units and formations were thought to have been specially trained and equipped for jungle warfare in tropical conditions. In fact, the Japanese High Command had based its long-term training and re-equipment programmes chiefly on the assumption that sooner or later the army would have to fight the Russians in Manchuria.

*

Early in 1942 the Western Allies set up a short-lived ABDA command to co-ordinate the operations of American, British and Dutch forces in an area extending from Burma in the west to Darwin in the east. By the time its commander, Field-Marshal Wavell, reached his headquarters in Java in the middle of January, the Japanese were already preparing to advance on the Indonesian archipelago from captured bases in the Philippines, Borneo and Celebes. He came to the conclusion that the best he could do with the forces likely to be at his disposal before the spring was to try to hold a line from Singapore through Sumatra and Java to Darwin. The campaign in Malaya was going badly, but reinforcements, equipment and supplies, including crated Hurricanes, were still reaching Singapore by sea. Large numbers of American aircraft would, it was hoped, arrive in March or April if communications with the United States could be kept open.

ABDA received useful intelligence about Japanese shipping movements from air reconnaissance and coast-watchers, but its naval resources consisted only of nine American, British and Dutch cruisers, twenty-five American, British and Dutch destroyers, two sloops and forty American and Dutch submarines. There were also three American seaplane-tenders with a complement of twenty-five Catalinas. As most of the surface ships were needed for convoy escort, only small striking-forces could be improvised. Some Japanese transports were sunk in the second half of January, but the enemy could not be prevented from establishing forward bases within striking distance of the Indonesian archipelago.

On 1 February Allied reconnaissance aircraft sighted about twenty transports, accompanied by warships, in the Makassar Strait, between Borneo and Celebes.[36] A hastily-assembled striking-force of two American and two Dutch cruisers and four American and three Dutch destroyers, under Rear-Admiral K. W. F. M. Doorman of the Royal Netherlands Navy, left Sourabaya late on 3 February to engage them, but turned back after attacks by land-based aircraft from Kendari, in

Celebes, had damaged both American cruisers. Aircraft from Kendari, supported by long-range fighters from Borneo, also attacked ABDA bases in Java. On 9 February the Japanese disembarked troops at Makassar, near the southernmost extremity of Celebes, without interference from Doorman's force, which had withdrawn to the south coast of Java and could not put to sea in time to intervene.

On the same day the first of two convoys carrying a Japanese infantry regiment left Indo-China for Sumatra. A naval force which included the light carrier *Ryujo* sailed on 10 February to cover both convoys. Again, no fault can be found with the warning given by intelligence. Wavell was satisfied by 11 February that Sumatra was threatened with invasion. All available Allied bombers attacked the leading convoy during the night of 13/14 February and on the following day. Five cruisers and ten destroyers under Doorman's command left the western extremity of Java late on 14 February, but once more Japanese air superiority proved decisive. Attacked by aircraft from the *Ryujo* and also by land-based bombers, Doorman turned back on the following day for lack of fighter cover. Transport aircraft which carried paratroops to Sumatra did not arrive without warning, but they were met only by anti-aircraft fire because all availabe Allied fighters were already committed to attempts to repel landings from the sea.

Allied forces in Sumatra then withdrew in haste to Java, leaving the invaders to occupy strategic points throughout the island while other Japanese forces landed in Bali and Amboina. On 19 February Darwin was attacked by aircraft from carriers which reached the Banda Sea without detection, and also by land-based bombers from Kendari.

ABDA was disbanded on 25 February. The commanders of the naval, land and air forces in Java then became responsible to the Governor-General of the Netherlands East Indies. A strong Japanese force was known to be approaching from the Makassar Strait, another believed to be assembling off the north coast of Sumatra. To meet the double threat, the naval commander formed a Western Striking Force of three cruisers and two destroyers based on Batavia, and a Combined Striking Force of five cruisers and nine destroyers based on Sourabaya.

The Western Striking Force, after repeatedly searching in vain for the convoy said to be off Sumatra, obeyed orders to make for Ceylon if it was not found by the afternoon of 28 February. Admiral Doorman, commanding the Combined Striking Force, left Sourabaya at 6.30 p.m. on 26 February with orders to engage an invasion force whose last reported position was 190 miles north-east of his base. He failed to find it, but was told as he was entering harbour to refuel his destroyers on the following day that two convoys had been sighted and that one of them was only eighty miles away.

Doorman promptly put to sea again. With his two 8-inch and three 6-inch cruisers and nine destroyers, he was outwardly well-equipped to deal with the two 8-inch and 5.5-inch cruisers and fourteen destroyers of the Japanese covering and escort force, but he could not afford to exchange ship for ship with it at the cost of allowing the transports to reach their destination without opposition. He was also handicapped by the difficulty of controlling a mixed fleet with no common tactical doctrine, and still more by a lack of precise information about the whereabouts of the enemy's warships and transports from either shipborne or shore-based aircraft. We now know that the Japanese commander, warned by his own aircraft of Doorman's approach, sent the transports to the rear with a close escort of two destroyers and prepared to engage Doorman with the rest of his force. Doorman, after losing some ships sunk or crippled by gunfire, torpedoes or mines, and sending others away to refuel, protect damaged ships or pick up survivors, was left at nightfall on 27 February with a force much reduced in firepower, but still amply strong enough to sink the Japanese transports if only he could find and reach them. While attempting to do so in bright moonlight, he was engaged by the enemy's heavy cruisers and went down with his flagship. That settled the fate of Java.

*

In the meantime Japanese forces from Siam began to invade Burma. They started by seizing airfields in the extreme south as bases for attacks on Rangoon. Rangoon had a good early-warning system, and was well defended by one RAF squadron and one of three 'volunteer' squadrons sent by the Americans before the war to guard the American-financed road linking Lashio in Burma with Kunming in China. The attacks did no great damage, but created a social problem by driving many Burmese and Indian workers to leave their jobs and take refuge in the jungle, or set out on foot for India.

The British military authorities in the Far East calculated that the Japanese would not be able to maintain more than about two divisions in Burma unless they held Rangoon.[37] They might try to reach Rangoon from the Bangkok railway either by advancing from its northern terminus at Chiengmai towards the Shan States and then turning south, or by marching westwards through Raheng to the neighbourhood of

Moulmein and skirting the Gulf of Martaban. The former seemed their more likely course until they were found to be assembling a large force at Raheng. This was the Fifteenth Army, consisting of the 33rd and 55th Divisions less one regiment.

Major-General J. G. Smyth, V.C., commanding the 17th Indian Division, arrived at Rangoon early in 1942 and was given the task of opposing the Fifteenth Army. He proposed to stand on the line of the River Sittang, but was ordered to fight further forward. On 30 January his most forward and least experienced brigade, which he had asked in vain to be allowed to pull back, was attacked at Moulmein by the 55th Division. Its commander made a brilliantly-improvised withdrawal on the following day with the help of a more experienced brigadier sent forward for the purpose. After fighting delaying actions on the Salween and the Bilin, Smyth succeeded in uniting his force on 20 February at a point about fifteen miles from the bridge across the Sittang by which it was to withdraw. This was a railway bridge, decked so that military vehicles could use it.

What followed rubbed home the lesson that even the most carefully considered military plan can go wrong without good intelligence and security in the field, good staff work in the rear, and a little bit of luck. Smyth recognized that the Japanese might try to outflank him by marching through the jungle. He did not know that, enlightened by intercepted orders repeated by at least one of his subordinate commanders in clear, they were laying an ambush for him. Had he known it, he could have moved his whole force across the Sittang before the trap was sprung. As it was, he decided to move his divisional troops and one brigade part of the way to the river on 21 February, leaving his other two brigades to follow when the head of the column started to cross the bridge on 22 February. That would give him time to satisfy himself that arrangements for guarding the bridge and for traffic control were adequate. It would also enable him to fight a strong rearguard action if the enemy followed him along the road.

The leading brigade and divisional details duly set out for the bridge on 21 February, a day of sweltering heat. Their vehicles raised a dust-cloud visible for miles. They were bombed and machine-gunned not only by the Japanese 5th Air Division, but also by Allied airmen who had been ordered to attack a non-existent Japanese column on another road. Thereafter everything went wrong. Soon after the column began to cross the bridge on the following morning, it was held up for more than an hour by a vehicle which ran off the decking. Only divisional headquarters and about a third of the leading brigade had reached the west bank when the Japanese burst out of the jungle. Troops of the leading brigade who were waiting to cross had to turn and fight. Both brigades coming up behind them were attacked. Finally, as the result of a misunderstanding the bridge was blown early on 23 February when two-thirds of the division was still on the wrong side of it.[38]

Fortunately for the British, the Japanese were slow to follow up. During his final approach to Rangoon at the end of the first week in March, the commander of the 33rd Division adopted a proposal from one of his regimental commanders that he should clear the Prome–Rangoon road of troops. This was intended to conceal the direction of his advance. In fact, it allowed the British to escape and begin a long retreat to the Indian frontier.

The British also emerged without disaster from an attempt by the Japanese to repeat on a smaller scale their exploit at Pearl Harbor. Signal intelligence revealed towards the end of March that a powerful striking force of carriers and battleships was about to enter the Indian Ocean, primarily for the purpose of attacking British naval bases at Colombo and Trincomalee.[39] Admiral Sir James Somerville had recently arrived to take command of a revived Eastern Fleet which, although it included five old battleships, two fleet carriers and the small carrier *Hermes*, would be no match for the striking force, commanded by Vice-Admiral Chuichi Nagumo, which had already attacked Pearl Harbor and Darwin.

Expecting the enemy to arrive on the following day, Somerville put to sea on 31 March with the intention of keeping out of his way by day and attacking him at night. No hostile warships having appeared by the evening of 2 April, he concluded that the operation had been postponed. He took the main body of his fleet to Addu Atoll, in the Maldive Islands; ordered the cruiser *Dorsetshire* to resume an interrupted refit at Colombo; and sent the *Hermes* and one destroyer to Trincomalee to prepare for a forthcoming expedition to Madagascar. He was therefore 600 miles away when, in the afternoon of 4 April, the crew of a reconnaissance aircraft sighted Nagumo's force 360 miles south-east of Ceylon.

Admiral Sir Geoffrey Layton, who was responsible for the defence of the island, promptly cleared Colombo of all ships which could be got to sea. At dawn on 5 April Nagumo's force was seen to be only 120 miles away. Attacks by carrier-borne aircraft began about 8 a.m. No warships were caught in harbour, but the *Dorsetshire* and a sister-ship, the

Cornwall, were sunk at sea while trying to join the fleet. Damage to installations ashore was relatively light.

Nagumo then spent some days searching in the wrong direction for Somerville's fleet. His whereabouts remained unknown until the afternoon of 8 April. His force was then sighted 400 miles east of Ceylon. Layton, who had been given dictatorial powers over the civil as well as the naval and military authorities ashore, ordered warships, auxiliaries and merchantmen to leave Trincomalee and steer south, hugging the coast. They were well out of the way when attacks by carrier-borne aircraft began early on 9 April; but the *Hermes*, her accompanying destroyer, a corvette and two tankers were sunk during the return voyage. Only twenty-two fighters, as compared with forty-two used at Colombo, were available for the defence of Trincomalee. Heavy damage was done to installations ashore, and for the time being the port became unusable.

Nagumo's force consisted of five carriers, four battleships, three cruisers and eight destroyers, with about three hundred aircraft of which he lost only seventeen. A separate force under Vice-Admiral J. Ozawa, consisting of a light carrier and some cruisers and destroyers, attacked unescorted groups of merchant vessels in the Bay of Bengal. Between 4 and 9 April Ozawa sank more than 100,000 tons of merchant shipping and dropped bombs at two points in Madras. Japanese submarines sank another 32,000 tons.

The threat to Ceylon cost the British anxieties which persisted for some time after Nagumo withdrew his carriers to Japan to prepare for operations elsewhere. On 8 April, after the attack on Colombo but before the attack on Trincomalee, Somerville and the Admiralty agreed in principle that he should send his slower ships to Kilindini, in Kenya, and use for his faster ships the base at Addu Atoll which, although unprotected against air attacks, had the advantage over Colombo and Trincomalee that its existence was rightly thought to be unknown to the Japanese. A week later Churchill, fearing that the Japanese might try to invade Ceylon or southern India before the Eastern Fleet could be strengthened in the summer, sent a request to Roosevelt that the United States Navy should consider whether it could either reinforce Somerville, or help the Admiralty to do so by reinforcing the Home Fleet. Roosevelt declined on 17 April to send American warships to the Indian Ocean, but offered as a temporary measure to replace battleships of the Home Fleet that might be sent there.

We now know that the Japanese had no plans for the invasion of

Ceylon or southern India, and no intention of repeating Nagumo's incursion. We also know that the American authorities were aware, when Roosevelt replied to Churchill, of indications from signal intelligence that the Japanese intended within the next few weeks to send a carrier force to the Coral Sea.[40] The President made no direct reference to this evidence in his reply. He may perhaps have had it in mind when he added that measures were in hand in the Pacific which he hoped Churchill would 'find effective' when they were disclosed to him.

TEN

The Defeat of Germany and her Allies

The Axis Powers planned to drive the British from the Mediterranean and the Middle East in 1942 by a series of co-ordinated blows. Intensified air attacks were to pave the way for an invasion of Malta by German and Italian airborne forces. The Axis forces in North Africa, assured by the elimination of Malta of uninterrupted supplies, were to advance to the Suez Canal. If all went well, their arrival at the western gates of the Middle East would coincide with that of an army group from the southern sector of the Eastern Front in the Caucasus. With the oilfields of the Middle East, the Caucasus and Rumania under their control or within their grasp, Germany and her European allies would have the British at their mercy. Meanwhile Japan would take care of the Americans.

Hitler and Mussolini had yet to sanction this programme when Rommel went some way to demonstrate its feasibility by driving the Eighth Army from western Cyrenaica. Encouraged by the safe arrival at Tripoli of a convoy carrying 54 tanks and other equipment and supplies, he attacked on 21 January and soon had the British guessing. The GC & CS had read some army Enigma traffic in the previous September, but it was not read regularly before April.[1] As a rule, Luftwaffe traffic yielded valuable information about the German Army's moves and dispositions; but the weather in North Africa was so bad in the early part of 1942 that Rommel received little air support after the first few days. For the same reason, less information than usual was forthcoming from air reconnaissance. By the end of the first week in February Benghazi had been lost, the Eighth Army driven back to a defensive position with its right on the sea at Gazala and its left at Bir Hacheim.

General Ritchie had been given command of the Eighth Army in

November to tide over an emergency. He was still in command when Rommel attacked in January. His handling of the retreat was not altogether reassuring. Nevertheless Auchinleck decided not to replace him, feeling that two changes of command within three months might unsettle the troops and be misinterpreted by press and public.

To the accompaniment of devastating air attacks on Malta, both sides in the Desert War then prepared to take the offensive as soon as they felt strong enough. On the Axis side, the general intention was that Rommel should aim at capturing Tobruk by the beginning of the last week in June, but should not continue his advance to Cairo and Alexandria until Malta's fate was settled. On the British side, Churchill was determined that Auchinleck should engage the enemy in strength before Malta was starved out. Keith Park, who as commander of the fighter group responsible for the defence of south-east England had played a leading part in defeating the Luftwaffe in 1940, succeeded in preserving the air defences from disintegration with the help of aircraft flown from British and American carriers. A fast minesweeper brought ammunition. Otherwise little could be done to reprovision the island. The situation in May was that stocks of flour and unmilled grain would provide bread until July if the mills were not destroyed by bombing in the meantime. Almost everything else was so scarce that survival seemed improbable unless a fairly large convoy could be brought from Alexandria or Gibraltar before the end of June.

In these circumstances, and under pressure from London, Auchinleck agreed on 19 May to fight a major battle in time to divert the enemy's attention from a convoy due about the middle of June. By that time he had known for more than a week that Rommel was preparing to attack the Eighth Army and would almost certainly do so before Ritchie was ready to pass to the offensive.[2]

What the sources could not tell Auchinleck and Ritchie was where Rommel's attack would fall. The Gazala–Bir Hacheim position was not a continuous line. It consisted of a number of wired 'boxes', some close together and some separated by gaps up to thirteen miles wide. Each box was prepared for all-round defence and garrisoned by an infantry brigade group or its equivalent. The whole front was covered by minefields and screened by patrols, but the system was not intended to present an impregnable obstacle to the enemy. Its purpose was to canalize his advance and set the stage for a decisive counter-stroke by the two armoured divisions of the 30th Corps. The counter-stroke would have to be delivered before the enemy reached a crucial supply-dump at Belhamed, about forty-five miles east of the centre of the forward position.

The question was whether Rommel would turn the southern flank of the position, or come through one of the gaps after clearing a passage through the minefields. But it was not of paramount importance, because in either case he would have to wheel to the north to reach Tobruk and the coast road. What Auchinleck did think of paramount importance was that the Eighth Army's armour should not be committed piecemeal, as had happened in the past. Ritchie's armoured divisions, the 1st and 7th, must fight as divisions and be handled by the corps commander as a corps. The aim should be to draw the enemy towards a junction of roads and tracks near El Adem, about fifteen miles west of Belhamed. There the armoured divisions would be able to launch concerted attacks with support from artillery favourably sited on high ground to the north. Auchinleck strongly advised Ritchie to put both divisions in the neighbourhood of El Adem while he awaited Rommel's attack, but did not insist on his doing so.

The outcome was that Ritchie and his subordinate commanders dispersed their counter-attack forces over an area of hundreds of square miles in an attempt to cover both lines of approach. The two armoured brigades of the 1st Armoured Division took up positions close to the route the enemy was likely to follow if he came from the west. This placed them more or less where Auchinleck wanted them to be. The one armoured brigade of the 7th Armoured Division they put about twenty miles south-west of El Adem, its two motor brigades still further to the south and south-west. In theory these widely scattered formations could still be brought together for a concerted effort once the enemy's intentions were clear. Whether in practice the corps commander would be able to unite them after action was joined was another matter.

Late on 26 May two Italian corps on Rommel's left, with some German lorried infantry, approached the northern sector of the Gazala–Bir Hacheim position and began to dig in to the accompaniment of an intense artillery bombardment. At dusk, and later in bright moonlight, large numbers of tracked and wheeled vehicles were seen approaching the southern flank. They belonged to Rommel's two Panzer divisions, his light division, and an Italian armoured division. No steps were taken to withdraw the 7th Armoured Division's motor brigades from their exposed positions. Both were attacked early on 27 May by superior forces and driven back. The division's armoured brigade was engaged by the 15th Panzer Division while assembling for a counter-attack, suffered but also inflicted fairly heavy losses, and eventually withdrew towards Belhamed. The divisional commander was captured with three of his staff when his advanced headquarters was overrun, although he escaped a few days later. Thus the corps commander had no chance of handling his two divisions as a corps. Indeed, some considerable time elapsed before he even knew what had happened to one of them.

After rounding the southern extremity of the mined area, the two Panzer divisions and the light division pushed to the north and north-east, leaving the Italian division to engage the 1st Free French Brigade Group in its box at Bir Hacheim. Ritchie still had large undefeated forces with which he hoped to cut them off and annihilate them. The fact remains that he failed to do so. A counter-attack by the 1st Armoured Division on the two Panzer divisions, planned for 28 May, was not carried out because one of the Panzer divisions was short of fuel and ammunition and therefore did not come forward to be attacked. On the following day Rommel in person led his supply columns to the forward area. Unable to reach the coast as he had planned to do, he then concentrated his mobile formations in a defensive position east of the minefields, protecting them with a thick anti-tank screen. Poorly co-ordinated counter-attacks failed either to dislodge them, or to prevent Rommel from opening a new supply route after overwhelming the 150th Infantry Brigade Group in its box near the centre of the Gazala–Bir Hacheim position. On 11 June, after driving the Free French with great difficulty from Bir Hacheim, he launched a fresh attempt to reach the coast road. By 14 June he was so close to it, and had destroyed or disabled so many of the Eighth Army's tanks, that Ritchie ordered the withdrawal to the Egyptian frontier of two divisions of the 13th Corps, leaving the third at Tobruk. Pounded by dive-bombers, the garrison of Tobruk surrendered a week later.

The battle of Gazala–Bir Hacheim proved, if proof were needed, that good intelligence and a preponderance in armour were not enough to ensure success. Ritchie received more than a fortnight's warning of Rommel's attack. On 26 May Rommel had about 330 German and 230 Italian tanks. The Eighth Army had about 850, with more to come from reserves in Egypt or held by units available as reinforcements. Qualitatively there was not a great deal to choose between the equipment of the British and the Axis forces. Each side had some weapons or items of equipment envied by the other, but the differences were not so great that they could be expected to prove decisive. Whether precise knowledge of Rommel's intentions would have helped the British is doubtful, to say the least. Indeed, if Ritchie had known for certain before the battle began that Rommel would come round his southern flank, he would probably have been even less inclined than he already was to accept Auchinleck's proposals for the disposition of his armour. His reluctance to wait until the enemy reached the neighbour-hood of El Adem before counter-attacking in strength is understandable in view of his responsibility for the valuable stores dumped at Belhamed in readiness for an offensive; but the consequences were precisely those feared by Auchinleck.

Rommel's political masters responded to the fall of Tobruk by cancelling the airborne expedition to Malta and authorizing him to follow the enemy into Egypt. Ritchie had already ordered a further retreat, to Mersa Matruh, when Auchinleck relieved him and took over direct command of the Eighth Army. As the Matruh position could easily be turned, Auchinleck decided to fight only a delaying action there and make his main stand in the thirty-eight-mile-wide gap between El Alamein and the virtually impassable Qattara depression. This had long been recognized as a suitable place for a defensive battle, and some work had been done upon it in consequence of orders given by Auchinleck soon after his arrival in the theatre in 1941. There he fought, in the first few days of July, what proved to be the decisive battle for Egypt.

Intelligence made, as it were, a negative contribution to this battle. Rommel's knowledge of the Alamein position was not up to date. He attacked without waiting to make a thorough reconnaissance, and met opposition where he did not expect it. Later, his signal intelligence service made a positive contribution by warning him of an impending counter-attack, with the result that he was able to extricate his depleted mobile formations under cover of an improvised anti-tank screen. Attempts made later in the month to break through his front were unsuccessful, although we now know that they failed only by a narrow margin.

Rommel could therefore be expected to make a fresh attempt to reach Alexandria and Cairo when he received a further supply of tanks. Auchinleck and his staff drew up a defensive plan designed to ensure that the mistakes made at Gazala were not repeated. The essence of their strategy was to hold the northern sector of the Alamein position in such strength that Rommel would be able to attempt an enveloping movement only by passing his mobile formations south of a feature called the Bab el Qattara and wheeling to the north. Half-way to the coast road he would be met by armoured brigades supported by artillery on the high ground of the Alam el Halfa ridge, some fifteen miles south-east of El Alamein. In other words, the Alam el Halfa ridge would play the part which Auchinleck had intended the high ground near El Adem to play in the battle of the Gazala–Bir Hacheim position.

However, the battle of Alam el Halfa was not destined to be fought by Auchinleck. After the fall of Tobruk a new Commander-in-Chief of the Mediterranean Fleet, Admiral Sir Henry Harwood, sent all unessential warships and merchant vessels south of the Suez Canal and divided the rest of his fleet between Port Said, Haifa and Beirut. A start was made with the transfer of staffs ashore from Alexandria to the Canal Zone, and preparations were made to demolish installations and stores and block the harbour. When the Eighth Army fell back to the Alamein position, Auchinleck gave orders that plans should be made to fight the enemy in the Valley of the Nile if the need arose. These were sensible precautions, because Alexandria was now within reach of the enemy's escorted bombers, and no one could be absolutely certain before the battle began that the Alamein position would be held. But they gave rise in Cairo and Alexandria to rumours that the British were preparing to clear out of Egypt. The evil effects of this crisis of confidence persisted long after any real danger of a break-through at El Alamein had disappeared.

The impression received in London towards the end of July was that, although undoubtedly the Eighth Army had stemmed the tide of Axis success by winning the battle afterwards called First Alamein, all was not well with the Middle East Command. During a visit to Egypt early in August Churchill was angered by the discovery that no responsible commander or staff officer expected the army to be ready to renew the offensive before September. The outcome was the Cairo purge. Auchinleck was replaced as Commander-in-Chief in the Middle East by General Alexander, who had led the retreat from Burma to India; command of the Eighth Army was offered to Lieutenant-General W. H. E. Gott, hitherto commanding the 13th Corps; new commanders were chosen for both the 13th and the 30th Corps; and some of the ablest members of the staff were sacked.

Gott accepted the appointment with misgivings, but was killed when an aircraft in which he was travelling to Cairo was forced down by the enemy. Command of the Eighth Army then went to Lieutenant-General B. L. Montgomery. As Montgomery was no more willing than Auchinleck had been to commit himself to a premature offensive, and was backed by Alexander, the ultimate effect of these chops and changes was that the start of the offensive which Auchinleck might have launched in September was fixed for the night of 23 October.

In the meantime ample evidence was received that Rommel hoped to launch in late August the turning movement south of the Bab el Qattara predicted in July.[3] Adopting the substance of the plan inherited from Auchinleck, Montgomery strongly reinforced the Alam el Halfa ridge and prepared to fight a tank battle with ample support from massed artillery and anti-tank guns. The approach of Rommel's mobile formations to the southern part of the Eighth Army's minefield was reported by air reconnaissance late on 30 August. Finding it broader than they expected, they took so long to get through it that the two Panzer divisions fell about six hours behind schedule and, in order to save fuel, had to wheel prematurely to the north instead of first making a wide sweep to the east. On approaching the Alam el Halfa ridge in the afternoon of 31 August, the 21st Panzer Division came under heavy fire from the 22nd Armoured Brigade and its supporting artillery in dug-in positions. The 15th Panzer Division was still working its way towards the ridge when both divisions were ordered to halt until they could be replenished and refuelled.

On the following day, after a night of almost continuous bombing and an attempt by the 15th Panzer Division to seize the ridge, Rommel abandoned his attempt to reach the coast road for fear of exhausting his small reserve of fuel. Profiting by Montgomery's reluctance to commit the whole of his armour without knowing whether it would be led into a trap, he succeeded on 3 and 4 September in withdrawing his mobile formations behind the Axis minefield. In the whole battle the British lost more aircraft and more tanks destroyed or put out of action than the Germans and Italians, but their losses in killed, wounded and missing were much lighter.[4]

Rommel, already ill before the battle, then went home for treatment. He was temporarily replaced as commander of the Panzerarmee Afrika by General Georg Stumme. General R. von Thoma assumed command of the Afrika Korps in place of General Walter Nehring, who had been wounded at an early stage of the advance to Alam el Halfa. Neither of these newcomers had any experience of desert warfare.

On the eve of the October offensive, the Eighth Army had a numerical superiority over the Germans and Italians of more than two to one in men and something like five or six to one in modern gun-armed tanks. As the British were also greatly superior in the air, they were able to check their information from signal intelligence by frequent air reconnaissance, and at the same time prevent the enemy from seeing much of their own preparations. The Eighth Army was, in addition, better provided than ever before with field, medium and anti-tank guns.

Even so, to break through a defensive position progressively strengthened since the beginning of July was not likely to be easy. Montgomery's first attempt was unsuccessful. Four infantry divisions were given the task of opening corridors through which two armoured divisions were to pass. The time needed to clear mines was underestimated, with the result that tanks piled up behind the infantry and came under strong artillery fire from first light on 24 October.

Stumme having died of heart failure on the first day of the battle, Rommel interrupted his convalescence to resume command of the Panzerarmee. He found when he arrived late on 25 October that, although the army's front had not been breached, a fairly deep wedge had been driven into it.

Montgomery made three attempts at a break-through. The second, launched on 28 October, failed for much the same reasons as his first on 23 October. The third began in the early hours of 2 November. It started badly, but attrition on both sides led by the evening of that day to a situation in which the Afrika Korps had only about thirty fit tanks left, while the Eighth Army still had about six hundred. Rommel then decided to fall back to Fuka, about fifty miles to the west. Although hampered by an untimely standfast order from the Führer, he succeeded in extricating the greater part of his surviving troops at the cost of abandoning much of their equipment. His retreat did not stop at Fuka. But it did not give the Allies control of the Sicilian Narrows, and it left them still a long way from defeating Germany and her allies.

*

When the British left the mainland of Europe in 1940, they hoped to return in two years' time after crippling Germany's war economy by air bombardment and organizing powerful partisan forces throughout occupied Europe. By the summer of 1942 it was obvious that these hopes were premature. Bombing had not done much to reduce Germany's output of war material, the Special Operations Executive could not claim that it had yet fulfilled its mandate to 'set Europe ablaze', and the British Army was not ready for a large-scale opposed landing in occupied territory. In the meantime the strategic outlook had changed in consequence of Germany's intervention in Libya, her invasion of Russia, and developments in the Far East and the Pacific. The Russians and their left-wing supporters in Allied countries were demanding a Second Front in Europe, the Americans active employment for the troops they had begun to assemble in the United Kingdom to fight Germany. Despite Roosevelt's incautious remark to Molotov in the early summer of 1942 that he hoped and expected to organize a second front in Europe by the end of the year, the United States Army was, however, in no better position than its British counterpart to undertake so ambitious an enterprise.

But there were other places besides Europe where a new front might be opened. Eventual participation by American land and air forces in a hypothetical campaign against Axis troops in Africa had been contemplated by the United States Chiefs of Staff as at least a remote possibility as early as 1939. The situation when the United States became an active and overt belligerent in 1941 was that the British were already fighting the Germans and Italians in Cyrenaica and that a plan existed for British troops to land in Algeria (Operation Gymnast) if and when the Eighth Army was ready to push westwards into Tunisia. At the Arcadia Conference a few weeks later, Churchill suggested that American troops might, at the same time, land 'by invitation' in French Morocco. Neither the American nor the British Chiefs of Staff at first took kindly to this proposal, but ultimately they were induced by pressure from Roosevelt and Churchill to concede that a landing somewhere in North Africa was the only practical means by which American troops could take part in the war against the European Axis in 1942. Reinforcement of the Eighth Army by American troops was not regarded by the United States Chiefs of Staff as an acceptable alternative.

Roosevelt and Churchill believed that, because the United States had maintained diplomatic relations with Vichy during the German occupation of northern and western France, the French might not mind having their North-West African possessions invaded by American troops. Super-Gymnast – renamed Torch in July 1942 – was therefore represented, with some economy of truth, as essentially an American enterprise. Major-General Dwight D. Eisenhower, already commander-designate of United States land forces in Europe, was appointed Supreme Commander. Frenchmen whose active support or passive acquiescence the Americans hoped to secure were told that the expedition would be supported by British naval and air forces, but not that the British Army was to contribute thousands of troops, or that all the troops in Algeria, once they were ashore, were to go under command of the newly formed British First Army.

The project having been accepted in principle, an Anglo-American planning staff did their best to reconcile conflicting opinions about the best means of giving effect to it. One school of thought held that, as the purpose of the operation was to gain control of the Sicilian Narrows by the prompt capture of Tunis and Bizerta, the landings should be made as far east as possible, not a thousand miles away in French Morocco. Against this it was argued that dependence on a single line of communication through the Straits of Gibraltar would be hazardous, and that landings east of Oran – itself six hundred miles from Bizerta – would expose the troops to air attacks from Luftwaffe bases in Sicily and Sardinia. Eventually the planners compromised on landings by 24,500 American troops in Morocco, 18,500 American and a few British troops at Oran, and about 10,000 British and roughly the same number of American troops at Algiers. Attempts to seize crucial objectives in eastern Algeria and Tunisia within the first few days would be mounted from Algiers. The troops bound for Morocco would be brought from the United States by an American naval task force. Those bound for Algeria would start from United Kingdom ports and be escorted and covered by British naval forces.

In the meantime the Americans undertook the delicate task of sounding influential Frenchmen about their attitude to the project. As Roosevelt and Churchill agreed that General de Gaulle should not be consulted, his London-based intelligence organization was by-passed.[5] Discreet enquiries elicited a good deal of information about the situation in Algeria and Morocco, but some obscurities remained. The Americans did not, for example, gain a clear insight into the complexities of the chain of command of the French armed forces, and in consequence the powers of local commanders were overestimated. Also, inaccurate reports encouraged their belief that General Henri-Honoré Giraud was the most suitable candidate for leadership of the French in North Africa.

Giraud had commanded the Seventh and later the Ninth Army in 1940. He had been captured by the Germans, but had escaped in the spring of 1942 and been allowed to live under surveillance near Lyons. On the eve of Torch he was smuggled by submarine and flying-boat from the south of France to Gibraltar. When he arrived on 7 November he learned to his astonishment that landings in Algeria and Morocco were due not in December, as he had supposed, but early on the following day. Eisenhower was equally astonished to learn that Giraud (who was very much senior to him in substantive rank and a far more experienced commander) had been promised the supreme command. After a stormy interview, Giraud agreed to serve under Eisenhower on the understanding that he was to be head of the French forces and administration in North Africa.

Notwithstanding the soundings made by the Americans both in North Africa and at Vichy, the landings achieved complete surprise so far as the Germans were concerned. In the interests of deception the British had plied the Abwehr, through their double agents, with reports that preparations were being made for landings in Norway and Northern France, that a large convoy was to be passed to Malta, and that rumours of an impending expedition to Dakar were current in Britain.[6] We now know that, although some of these reports were not without effect, the true cause of the surprise achieved by Torch was that the Germans did not reckon with the possibility that Algeria and Morocco might be invaded by troops carried directly from Britain and the United States. They accepted an air reconnaissance report to the effect that shipping assembled at Gibraltar on 4 November included few landing craft and only two passenger ships as evidence that no invasion of North-West Africa was imminent.[7]

Unfortunately for the Western Allies, local commanders on whose help they relied were almost as much in the dark. Major-General* E. Béthouart, commanding a French division at Casablanca, had been consulted at an early stage, but he did not learn until late on 7 November that American troops were due in Morocco in a matter of hours.[8] Even then he was not told where they would disembark. Assuming that they would land at Rabat because it was the seat of government and not defended by coast defence batteries, he sent officers there to welcome them. He then arrested members of the German Armistice Commission, put the Army Commander under escort, and informed the Commander-in-Chief and the Resident-General that Giraud was coming to liberate North-West Africa and had appointed him commander of the land forces in Morocco. The result was that Béthouart was himself arrested on a charge of treason, although he was afterwards released. American forces approaching Casablanca were met by fire from coast defence guns and warships, including the incomplete and immobile battleship *Jean Bart*, and resistance did not cease until 10 November.

* i.e., *Général de Division*.

Much the same happened elsewhere. At Oran coast defence batteries did not open fire until after landings had begun, and then not very effectively, but an attempt to seize the harbour by direct assault was strongly resisted. At Algiers the conspirators occupied police headquarters and arrested unsympathetic officials, but they soon lost control of the situation and were themselves arrested or had their orders countermanded. An appeal broadcast on Giraud's behalf evoked no enthusiasm. His image was not enhanced by his failure to appear until 9 November, when he arrived in a British submarine masquerading as an American one and was coolly received by local dignitaries and brother-officers.

The situation was complicated, although in a sense it was simplified, by the presence in Algiers of the redoubtable Admiral Darlan, who had come to visit a son ill in hospital but may also have had other reasons for being where the action was. A realist with a strong anti-British bias, Darlan was generally regarded in Britain and the United States as an arch-collaborationist. From Eisenhower's point of view he had, however, the threefold advantage of representing the legally constituted government, enjoying the respect of most Frenchmen of all parties, and being more or less in Eisenhower's power. When Giraud was found to have virtually no following in North Africa, a deal with Darlan became inevitable. The outcome of negotiations, threats and table-thumpings was that Darlan agreed to order a cease-fire throughout Algeria and Morocco, ensure that the French fleet at Toulon did not fall into Axis hands, and urge the Governor of Tunisia to resist Axis attempts to seize ports and airfields.

However, even with 15,000 French troops in Tunisia on their side – to say nothing of more than 100,000 in Algeria and Morocco – the Western Allies proved incapable of reaching Tunis and Bizerta before mud and rain stopped their advance in the last week of December. In the meantime the Germans, besides joining the Italians in invading what had hitherto been Unoccupied France, rushed troops by sea and air to Tunisia. The French admiral at Toulon, declining Darlan's invitation to bring his fleet to North Africa, scuttled it just as the Germans were about to seize it. A young French royalist and pro-Gaullist relieved the Western Allies of embarrassment by assassinating Darlan, and, on Giraud's orders, was executed for his pains.

Eisenhower defended his deal with Darlan by pointing out that the situation confronting him in Algeria was utterly different from that which he had been led to expect. If his expectations were belied, the fault lay not so much with the Allied intelligence agencies as with the American diplomats who had largely usurped their functions. But the forces at his disposal by the second half of November were numerically so much superior to the enemy's that his failure cannot be attributed merely to inadequate information. The Germans had about 3,000 combatant troops in Tunisia by the middle of November, about 10,000 by the end of the month, about 25,000 by the middle of December. By a combination of bluff and bold tactics, they successfully resisted all attempts by some 40,000 British, American and French troops of the First Army to dislodge them.

Thereafter the Germans built up their strength in Tunisia to a point at which withdrawal became impossible and supply increasingly difficult. To the troops brought by sea and air were added those brought by Rommel from Tripolitania. Thus the ultimate consequence of the failure of the Western Allies to attain their aims before the winter was that a huge bag of prisoners fell into their hands when the First Army, joined by Montgomery's Eighth Army, at last captured Tunis and Bizerta in the following May. But by that time there was no longer any prospect of their being able to launch before the summer of 1944 the invasion of northern France to which they were committed.

*

Both Torch and the expensive raid made on Dieppe in August 1942 drew attention to the importance of not attempting landings in hostile or doubtful territory without careful preparation based on detailed knowledge of the opposition likely to be met not only from troops and naval and air defences but also from natural or artificial hazards. If the French had offered serious and sustained resistance to Torch, it could have turned out as badly as Dakar. At Dieppe the troops met obstacles of whose existence they had not been warned.[9]

By 1943 the Western Allies were well placed to apply the lesson. Their photographic and visual air reconnaissance organizations were extremely strong, and from May had access to bases throughout North Africa as well as in the United Kingdom, in Iceland and Malta and at Gibraltar. Their signal intelligence services provided them with a steady stream of information about the enemy's plans, dispositions and logistic problems. Their espionage networks and those of London-based exiled governments or quasi-governmental institutions covered most European countries, although not all the material they furnished was reliable, especially where developments in Germany and Austria were concerned. They were in touch with a variety of resistance movements whose ultimate aims did not necessarily coincide with theirs, but which had in common a desire to harass and discomfit the Axis powers. Moreover, as the British double-cross organization virtually controlled the Abwehr espionage network in the United Kingdom, they possessed a ready means of priming the enemy with false information, although they could only do this at the cost of lulling his suspicions by also furnishing him with some genuine material.

The Western Allies had three major strategic aims in 1943. The first in order of importance, though not of time, was to disembark an Anglo-American expeditionary force in Northern France for the purpose of defeating the German forces there and afterwards advancing into Germany (Operation Overlord). The second was to tighten their grip on the central Mediterranean and inflict further losses on the enemy by invading Sicily (Operation Husky). The third was to prepare for Overlord by opening 'visible cracks' in Germany's 'armed structure' by means of air attacks. From the summer they aimed in particular at wearing down the German fighter force. This they hoped to do by attacking airfields, airframe, aero-engine and ball-bearing factories for the twofold purpose of destroying aircraft and components on the ground and forcing the Germans to use up their fighters in defensive battles (Operation Pointblank).

Whether, in view of the progress already made by the Western Allies in the Mediterranean theatre by the summer of 1943, the landing in Northern France which they had once hoped to make in 1942 was still desirable now that it could not be made before 1944 was debatable. However, although the point was made by a number of critics (notably General Smuts), no alternative strategy was seriously considered. Churchill was attracted by the idea of an advance on Vienna through the Balkans, but had come to regard Overlord as 'the keystone of the arch of Anglo-American co-operation'. He insisted that the American case for it should not be challenged, and was allowed by his military advisers to have his way.

The decision to invade Sicily was made in January, but the plan was not finally approved until May. Eisenhower was again Supreme Commander. The British General Alexander, although senior to Eisenhower and a far more experienced commander, served as his deputy. The most interesting feature of the plan was that elaborate steps were taken to give the impression that the Allies meant to land in

Sardinia and Greece and that preparations for landings in Sicily were merely part of a cover-plan. These culminated in a gruesome *ruse de guerre*.[10] The corpse of a man who had died a violent death was dressed in the uniform of a British army officer. Bogus documents in the pockets included a suitably misleading letter addressed by the Vice-Chief of the Imperial General Staff, Lieutenant-General A. E. Nye, to Alexander. The body was placed in the sea where it was likely to be washed ashore and come to the attention of the Germans. Hitler seems to have swallowed the bait, but the Axis commanders in the field did not conclude that the defences of Sicily could safely be neglected.

The rest of the plan was unimpressive. The Allies hoped not only to occupy Sicily, but also to take prisoners. Nevertheless they did not try to bar the enemy's retreat by disembarking troops on the Italian mainland. Large British and American forces were put ashore in the southern part of Sicily. Thence they fought their way against the grain of the country to the northern part of the island while nearly 40,000 German and more than 60,000 Italian troops, with nearly 10,000 vehicles, escaped across the Straits of Messina with little interference from Allied naval and air forces. The most important consequence of the invasion was that on 25 July Mussolini fell from power and was replaced by Marshal Pietro Badoglio.

While the campaign in Sicily was still in progress, Badoglio's government asked the British and American diplomatic emissaries to the Vatican to convey tentative proposals for a negotiated peace to their respective governments.[11] The British Minister replied that his cypher was too old to be safely used for so delicate a communication; the American Chargé d'Affaires that he had no cypher. The Italians had to wait until the middle of August before they were able to make contact with British and American representatives in Portugal. In the meantime the Germans, unaware of these approaches but guessing that Italy might change sides, prepared to meet a situation in which they might, at one and the same time, have to resist Allied landings on the Italian mainland and disarm their former ally.

The Western Allies decided before Mussolini was deposed that their next step after the capture of Sicily should be an invasion of the Italian mainland. By the time their plan was ready they had signed an armistice agreement with Badoglio's government. They expected, therefore, that their troops would be opposed on the mainland only by German formations whose communications seemed likely to be precarious. Even so, they were unwilling to risk major landings beyond the reach of fighter cover. Two divisions of the Eighth Army landed near Reggio, in the toe of Italy, on 3 September, but the main landings were made by one American and two British divisions of the United States Fifth Army (with part of a second American division in reserve) in the Gulf of Salerno early on 9 September. As a last-minute addition to the plan, the British 1st Airborne Division landed from the sea at Taranto on the same day.

Intelligence reports indicated that the Germans had only about two infantry battalions in the neighbourhood of Reggio, and that these were well back from the coast.[12] Nevertheless the landings were preceded by heavy naval and artillery bombardments. No opposition was met on the beaches, and very little during the next few days; but demolitions made the Eighth Army's advance in the general direction of Naples very slow.

Taranto was just beyond the reach of single-seater fighters from Sicily, but the 1st Airborne Division's expedition to Taranto was approved in the light of reports, which proved correct, that the Germans had very few troops in that part of Italy. Taranto, Brindisi, Bari and an important group of airfields near Foggia were occupied without much difficulty. But these acquisitions proved of limited value because the planners had made no provision to exploit such gains by a lightning advance up the east coast.

The situation that developed on the west coast was very different. Large convoys carrying Allied troops bound for the Gulf of Salerno left Oran and Tripoli on 5 and 6 September, and were joined by smaller convoys from Algiers, Bizerta, Palermo and Termini. Their destination was supposed to be a profound secret, but for two reasons it was not hard to guess. In the first place, the past performance of the Western Allies suggested that they would play for safety by making their main landing within but fairly close to the limit of fighter cover, and within striking distance of a large port. Secondly, Allied security was poor.[13] Places near Salerno were mentioned by name in an administrative order which was widely circulated. Rumours of an impending expedition to the neighbourhood of Naples were current well before the event. When outlining on 18 August the steps to be taken if and when the Italians succumbed to pressure from the Allies, Hitler described the stretch of coast between Naples and Salerno as the area most immediately threatened, adding that it must be held. Field-Marshal Kesselring, the senior German Commander in Italy, put six of the eight divisions at his disposal in the southern part of the country, holding only two in reserve near Rome. On 22 August he told General S. von Vietinghoff, commanding the newly formed Tenth Army, to regard Salerno as 'the centre of gravity'.

Vietinghoff learned in the early afternoon of 8 September that the Allied convoys had been sighted off the north-west corner of Sicily.[14] As he had already posted his best-armed formation to resist landings in the Gulf of Salerno and arranged for it to be reinforced in case of need, he had nothing left to do but call his troops to readiness.

The signing of an armistice agreement between Italy and the Western Allies on 3 September, hitherto kept secret, was announced by Eisenhower in a broadcast from Algiers at 6.30 p.m. on 8 September, about nine hours before the landings began. The announcement came as a surprise to Kesselring and his staff, but it did not find them without a prearranged plan to prevent the Italian Army from going over to the other side. An attempt to occupy the Italian GHQ and capture the whole of the General Staff was only partially successful, but Kesselring went on to negotiate an agreement by which Italian soldiers who laid down their arms were allowed to go home without interference and Rome was declared an open city. We now know that the Germans regarded themselves as very lucky to have avoided a situation which would have put their communications at the mercy of a hostile army and made it impossible for them to keep Vietinghoff supplied.

As things were, his army fought so well that Naples, which the Allied planners had expected their troops to enter on the third day, did not fall until the beginning of October. The Germans then withdrew by stages to a 'winter line' some eighty miles from Rome. The Allied advance in prematurely wintry weather was so slow that Hitler relinquished, at any rate for the time being, his earlier intention of ordering a progressive retreat to northern Italy and agreed that the winter line should be held as long as possible.

The Salerno landings and the advance to the winter line cost the Fifth Army about 12,000 American and 10,000 British casualties by the middle of November. Attempts to break through the winter line close to its western extremity cost the best part of another 18,000 by the end of the year. We now know that, according to Kesselring's Chief of Staff, the Western Allies could almost certainly have occupied Rome without much difficulty, and at a far lower cost, if they had adopted a bolder strategy in September. Even the information they then had might well have led them to conclude that landings near Rome were more likely to succeed than landings south of Naples if they had been willing to discard the axiom that troops should not be disembarked in large numbers without fighter cover. Apart from their losses, the penalty they paid for their excess of caution was that, when Eisenhower and Montgomery left the Mediterranean theatre at the end of 1943 to prepare for Overlord, the Fifth and Eighth Armies were still a long way from Rome and condemned to fight on a front where lack of room for manoeuvre largely nullified the advantages they gained from their excellent signal intelligence services and the air superiority which enabled them to reconnoitre freely. Even the ability to land troops behind the enemy's lines which they derived from command of the sea was threatened by demands for the transfer of assault vessels to the Overlord theatre.

*

At the Teheran Conference in November 1943, the Grand Alliance agreed that in 1944 the Americans and the British should give priority in the war against Germany to Overlord and a subsidiary landing in the south of France. (This was Operation Anvil, afterwards Dragoon). In Italy General Alexander (responsible after Eisenhower's departure to a British Supreme Commander, General Maitland Wilson) was to confine himself to attempts to capture Rome and advance to a line from Pisa to Rimini.

The outcome of a close debate between the British and American service chiefs was that Alexander managed to retain enough assault craft to put about 50,000 troops ashore in January at Anzio, some thirty-five miles south of Rome. At the same time the Fifth Army tried, without success, to break through the enemy's line between its western extremity and Cassino, where it intersected one of two main highways to Rome. Further attempts to take Cassino were made in February and March. The February assault was accompanied by a heavy air attack on the monastery which dominated Mount Cassino, delivered in the belief that the Germans were using it as a stronghold. There was no evidence that they were so using it, and we now know that they were not. The attack reduced the monastery to a heap of ruins which provided legitimate cover for German troops. The March assault was preceded by artillery and air bombardments of Cassino itself. These blocked the streets with fallen masonry which helped the defenders by serving as an anti-tank barrier.

If Cassino recalled the Western Front of World War I, Anzio was reminiscent of Gallipoli. Intelligence reports indicated before the landing that the Germans had scarcely any troops in the vicinity. The reports were accurate, but the Allied commander on the spot hesitated so long before pushing inland that the enemy was able to bring up elements of eight divisions to oppose him. Yet another attack on Cassino, begun by the Eighth Army on 11 May, was needed before the Germans withdrew from the winter line and the troops at Anzio were able to break out of their bridgehead. The Fifth Army entered Rome on 4 June, two days before the launching of Overlord.

*

Overlord can be said, in a sense, to have begun with the directive given to the British and American heavy bomber forces in the European theatre after the Casablanca Conference in January 1943 to attack German submarine construction yards, the German aircraft industry, and a variety of other objectives with a view to the progressive destruction and dislocation of Germany's military, industrial and economic system and the undermining of her will to fight. By that definition, Overlord started badly. Attacks made on industrial targets before and after the issue in June of the Pointblank directive, which gave priority to attempts to wear down the German fighter force, did not prevent the Germans from greatly expanding their output of fighter aircraft in 1943 and increasing their fighter strength in the West by some six hundred aircraft. The intelligence authorities furnished commanders with good target data, but underestimated the recuperative powers of German industry and the amount of slack in Germany's economy.

Moreover, the attacks were expensive. The British Bomber Command, restricted to night attacks on whole towns, made about 18,000 sorties between 3 March and 13 July. Nearly nine hundred aircraft failed to return and another two thousand were damaged, some of them beyond repair. A remedy advocated by the resourceful Dr Jones was the dropping of large numbers of strips of foil (code-named Window) to confuse the enemy's radar; but there was strong opposition to it on the ground that its use might prompt the Germans to adopt it. This argument was weakened by a report from a Danish agent which indicated that the idea had already occurred to them.[15] Nevertheless it was not until 23 June 1943, some eighteen months after the launching of the project, that Jones won his case by persuading Churchill to back it. Window was first used a month later during a raid on Hamburg. It was instantly successful, although the Germans soon made a come-back by recasting their control-system. We now know that the Luftwaffe had considered a device similar to Window in 1942 and that a report on experiments made early in 1943 had convinced Göring that it should not be used because such a weapon would be far more valuable to the expanding British Bomber Command than to the diminishing German bomber force.

American bombers, attacking precise objectives in daylight, were still more vulnerable. In the first half of 1943 the United States Eighth Air Force made about 4,500 bomber sorties to places within reach of its escort fighters. About 250 aircraft were lost and some 1,300 damaged. Raids on more distant objectives, undertaken after the issue of the Pointblank directive, were still more expensive because the bombers could not be escorted much beyond the German coast. On 17 August 146 bombers were sent to attack the Messerschmitt factory at Regensburg on the Danube, 230 to tackle a ball-bearings factory at Schweinfurt, near Würzburg. Sixty bombers were lost and more than a hundred damaged. Another sixty were lost, seventeen damaged beyond repair and well over a hundred less seriously damaged when 291 bombers were sent to make a further attack on Schweinfurt on 14 October. It was only when, in 1944, the Americans achieved the seemingly impossible by providing them-selves with escort fighters which combined a long endurance with a high performance that their losses ceased to approach the prohibitive. Ultimately the Allied bomber forces attained their aim not by attacking objectives directly associated with the manufacture of aircraft and components, but by concentrating on synthetic oil plants as Bomber Command had tried with inadequate resources to do in 1940. Declining output forced the Luftwaffe to restrict at first training and transport flights, then test flights and finally even operational flights by first-line aircraft.

*

Operational planning for Overlord was begun in the summer of 1943 by an Anglo-American staff under a British chief, Lieutenant-General Sir Frederick Morgan. The planners could not tell at all precisely how the enemy's troops in Northern France would be disposed in the following summer, but one thing seemed certain: the assault would fail if there was a large armoured force close to the area in Normandy west of the Seine where the Allies proposed to establish their bridgehead. As they could not hope to conceal the build-up of their forces in the United Kingdom, they would have to convince the enemy that the invasion was coming elsewhere or, if he did guess that landings were to be made in Western Normandy, that these were not to be the main landings. They would also have to impede the movement of his reserves by attacking his communications.

If these conditions were met, and if the security of the base could be assured, the operation should stand a good chance of success. Much of the German Army was heavily engaged on the Eastern Front and likely to remain so for some time. The Fifth and Eighth Armies were holding down substantial forces in Italy. The Special Operations Executive, at the cost of shifting its allegiance in Yugoslavia from the royalist Mihailovitch to the Communist Tito, was helping partisan forces in the Balkans to keep the Germans busy and their High Command anxious about the possibility of an Allied follow-up. In France and the Low Countries, resistance workers hitherto restricted to occasional acts of sabotage could be expected to make valuable contributions to the harassing of the enemy's communications.

The security of the base could, however, by no means be taken for granted. The Luftwaffe's effort against the United Kingdom in 1943 and the early part of 1944 was not impressive, but there were growing indications that the enemy had something else in prospect.

The Oslo report of 1939 had referred to the development by the ordnance department of the German Army of gyroscopically-stabilized missiles propelled by rockets. It had also mentioned Peenemünde, although not in the same context. Germany's Baltic coast was visited for the first time by a photographic reconnaissance aircraft on 29 October 1940, but no special attention was paid to Peenemünde because the chief purpose of the sortie was to discover whether invasion forces were assembling in Baltic ports. The first significant cover of Peenemünde was obtained on 15 May 1942 when a PRU pilot, after photographing Kiel, flew on to Swinemünde, noticed an airfield close by at Peenemünde, and decided that the place was worth photographing. His photographs showed large circular earthworks which were taken as evidence that 'heavy constructional work' was in progress.[16]

No evidence which linked these earthworks with the missiles mentioned in the Oslo report was received until, in the following December, a new agent of unknown reliability sent the first of a number of reports to the effect that trials of a long-range rocket had been made recently near Swinemünde.[17] Later reports referred specifically to Peenemünde. None of this evidence indicated that the United Kingdom was imminently threatened with attacks by long-range missiles, but a considerable stir was made by the circulation to military and air intelligence officers in the last week of March 1943 of the transcript of a bugged conversation between two well-informed prisoners-of-war.[18] These were General H. von Thoma and Lieutenant-General Ludwig Crüwell, both captured in North Africa. Discussing 'this rocket business', Thoma had referred on 22 March to 'huge things' which would go fifteen kilometres into the stratosphere and had only to be aimed at an area to produce frightful effects. He had also said that, as he knew he and Crüwell were being held somewhere near London and they had heard no big bangs, the rocket programme must have been held up.

Dr Jones and his staff concluded from the transcript that evidently they would have to take 'this rocket business' seriously and learn more about it. The photographs of Peenemünde taken in the previous May were re-examined, and fresh cover was ordered. With four sets of photographs before them, the interpreters drew attention in April not only to the circular earthworks but also to a large elliptical one which looked something like a football stadium.

Military Intelligence went rather further. The matter was brought to the attention of the Vice-Chief of the Imperial General Staff, Lieutenant-General A. E. Nye. Nye consulted the Scientific Adviser to the Army Council (Professor C. D. Ellis) and the Director and Controller of Projectile Development at the Ministry of Supply (Dr A. D. Crow). He then authorized the circulation to the Chiefs of Staff and others of a paper about possible counter-measures, to which was annexed a speculative account of the kind of rocket Crow and Ellis believed the Germans might think worth developing.[19]

The result was that the alarm was sounded in high places before the nature of the real or supposed threat was known. The Prime Minister and the Minister of Home Security, Herbert Morrison, were warned that the Germans appeared to be developing a new weapon of which no reliable account could be given. On the recommendation of the Chiefs of Staff, a junior member of the government was put in charge of what were called 'the scientific investigations to be put in hand'. This was Duncan Sandys, Joint Parliamentary Secretary at the Ministry of Supply.

Sandys said after the war that, although he might appear to have been duplicating the work of the intelligence staffs, he did not view his appointment in that light. His job, as he saw it, was not so much to discover the precise characteristics of the still-hypothetical rocket as to make sure that counter-measures were taken in good time.[20] However, he soon became aware of the difficulty of persuading people to countenance counter-measures to a threat that could not be defined, and even of convincing them of its existence. In practice he was compelled to act to some extent as a kind of supernumerary scientific intelligence officer without academic qualifications. Inevitably his first report, circulated in the middle of May, incorporated a tentative account of the possible dimensions and performance of the large rocket, and inevitably it was based more on the speculations of his scientific and technical advisers than on factual evidence of what the enemy was doing. The gist of it was that the missile might be a multi-stage rocket about twenty feet long and ten feet in diameter, weighing up to seventy tons and using an unknown propellant to deliver a warhead weighing up to ten tons at a range of a hundred to a hundred and fifty miles.[21] The Ministry of Home Security calculated that one such warhead might kill six hundred people and that one an hour for thirty days might kill more than a hundred thousand.[22] But would the Germans really be able to develop, and to use in face of Allied air superiority, a missile so massive that presumably it would be transportable only by rail?

The first authentic information about dimensions was received in June, when objects rightly thought to be rockets were photographed at Peenemünde. They seemed to be about forty feet long and six or seven feet in diameter.[23] Useful reports were received in the same month from informants who included impressed foreign workers and a disaffected German officer employed in the weapons department of the German Army. Some of them were confusing because the British did not yet know – although they soon began to suspect – that two distinct weapons were under development at Peenemünde. One was the A 4 liquid-fuelled rocket (V 2) on which the German Army had been working for years. The other was the FZG 76 pilotless aircraft, or flying bomb (V 1) adopted by the Luftwaffe in 1942. The German officer described 'the secret weapon to be used against London' as 'an air-mine with wings and a rocket-drive', to be launched by catapult.[24] That did not sound much like a rocket; it did sound like a pilotless aircraft with some form of jet-propulsion.

At a meeting of the Defence Committee (Operations) on 29 June, Sandys asked Churchill to agree that Bomber Command should attack Peenemünde as soon as the nights were long enough. Lindemann, raised to the peerage as Lord Cherwell, said he would play the part of devil's advocate. He argued that the story of the rocket was a hoax: the objects photographed at Peenemünde were dummies, put there to divert attention from preparations to use some other weapon, possibly a pilotless aircraft. Jones supported Sandys by pointing out that Peenemünde was one of the two most important experimental establishments possessed by the Germans: they would hardly stage a hoax whose probable effect would be to call down an attack upon it. The committee then agreed that Peenemünde should be bombed. It was also agreed that Sandys, in close association with Jones, should look into the whole question of jet-propulsion as applied by the Germans to aircraft, whether piloted or pilotless.

Nearly six hundred aircraft of Bomber Command attacked Peenemünde on the night of 17 August. Thereafter most trial launchings of the rocket were made at Blizna, in Poland. Partly but not solely in consequence of the raid, a plan to assemble production models of the rocket at Peenemünde, Friedrichshafen and Wiener Neustadt was abandoned in favour of assembly in an underground factory at Niedersachswerfen, near Nordhausen in the Harz Mountains. The chance destruction in a raid on Hamburg of a factory which made some of the special vehicles used for transporting, fuelling and servicing the rocket helped to delay its introduction, but the chief cause of delay was a series of technical imperfections which led to premature bursts and other troubles.

As a result of the move to Blizna, after a long delay a stream of reports about activities there reached London from local agents of the Polish intelligence service. They suggested that the rocket was still not ready for operational use. In the meantime evidence from other sources confirmed that there were two distinct weapons. The disaffected German officer reported about the middle of August that the 'air-mine' he had mentioned earlier was a pilotless aircraft, adding that there was also a rocket called A 4 and that rocket attacks on London were scheduled to begin on 20 October.[25] Finally, the existence of V 1 was established beyond dispute by the arrival in a turnip-field on the Danish island of Bornholm of a pilotless aircraft which miscarried. Photographs and drawings of the remains, made by a Danish naval officer, were given to the British by the Danish Chief of Naval Intelligence.[26]

A remarkable report was received about the same time from a multi-lingual French agent described at the time as *une jeune fille la plus remarquable de sa génération* and now known to have been Jeannie Rousseau, afterwards Vicomtesse de Clarens. It was an account of experiments made at Peenemünde and elsewhere on the island of Usedom with a variety of weapons, including an 'atmospheric bomb' which took off vertically with a deafening roar. The source, as we now know, confused V 1 with V 2, but stated correctly that a Colonel Wachtel was forming an organization to be called Flakregiment 155 W, which would be stationed in France and man a large number of 'catapults'.[27]

Some indirect clarification of Wachtel's role was provided early in September by a Luftwaffe Enigma message which called, as a matter of urgency, for anti-aircraft protection for the ground organization of Flakzielgerät 76. Jones guessed, correctly, that this was a cover-name for the German pilotless aircraft, because the word means 'anti-aircraft target apparatus', and towing a target for anti-aircraft gunners was the purpose for which pilotless aircraft had hitherto been used.[28] He reported in the middle of September that the Germans were developing an important ground organization which was probably connected with preparations for attacks on the United Kingdom by pilotless aircraft, adding that good reports had been received of the development of such a weapon and also of the development of long-range rockets. Almost simultaneously, Sandys retired at his own request from the search for the pilotless aircraft, leaving the Air Ministry to deal with that part of the enquiry while he continued his search for the long-range rocket.

During the next few weeks a flood of reports about unusual constructions in Northern France arrived from agents and resistance workers who had been briefed to look for them.[29] The most numerous were those called by the British ski sites. Their characteristic features included a rectangular concrete slab with a small hut or shelter at one end of it and parallel rows of concrete studs at the other; a square building with a twenty-two-foot opening across almost the whole width of one side; and a small number of buildings about ten feet wide and up to 260 feet long, curved at one end. There were usually three of these ski-shaped buildings. In each case the longer axis of the rectangular slab was aligned on London, and the square building was precisely in line with it and had its open side facing in the same direction. By the last week in November Air Intelligence identified ninety-five of these sites, out of ninety-six now known to have been built.

On 13 November Constance Babington Smith of the Central Interpretation Unit spotted, on exceptionally clear photographs of Peenemünde taken nearly five months earlier, a very small aircraft with a wing-span of roughly twenty feet.[30] As a sub-agent with engineering experience and first-hand knowledge of an almost-completed ski site had reported that the square building was constructed entirely of non-magnetic materials, this find was consistent with the belief that it was intended to house a pilotless aircraft of that size while the compass was being set, and that the ski-shaped buildings were for the storage of others to which the wings had not yet been fixed. Signal intelligence revealed about the same time that a German unit on which a special watch was being kept was tracking objects which moved seawards from the Baltic coast at speeds up to 400 miles an hour, and had mentioned FZG 76. Finally, photographs taken on 28 November showed that at Zempin, near Peenemünde, there were buildings similar to those seen at ski sites and that an aircraft similar to the one spotted by Constance Babington Smith was in position on what was evidently a launching-ramp.

The ski sites were attacked from 5 December by British fighter-bombers and American tactical bombers, and later by American heavy bombers. We now know that soon after the attacks began General Erich Heinemann, the officer responsible for directing the V 1 and V 2 offensives, pronounced the ski sites needlessly elaborate and far too conspicuous and vulnerable. He ordered that work should be continued on them only as a blind, and that simpler sites should be constructed. Agents began to report the existence of 'modified' sites in February 1944, but it was only towards the end of April that the first of them was spotted on a reconnaissance photograph.[31] Sixty-six were identified up to 12 June. Apart from one experimental attack, no attempt was made during that time to bomb them. This was partly because they made awkward targets, partly because the Allied air commander and his staff attached little importance to them and were preoccupied with other matters. Their attitude was not unreasonable in view of a ruling from Churchill that, in the event of a conflict between defensive and offensive aims, the offensive should have priority. Intelligence officers at Fighter Command – reduced for the time being to a subordinate status as ADGB – thought, however, that Air Chief Marshal Leigh-Mallory and his intelligence staff were taking the threat to the base from secret weapons a bit too lightly.[32]

Sandys continued his efforts to plumb the mysteries of the rocket until November 1943, when the Chiefs of Staff ruled that the Air Ministry should co-ordinate intelligence on rockets as well as pilotless aircraft, and should also co-ordinate counter-measures to both weapons. In the meantime a British engineer, Isaac Lubbock, drew attention to experiments made in the United States with liquid fuels pumped into the combustion chamber of a rocket, and showed that a liquid-fuelled rocket with dimensions similar to those of the rockets photographed at Peenemünde was technically feasible. Little further progress was made until reports began to arrive from the Poles in the following March. Even then, not much was learnt before the summer except that the Germans appeared to be experimenting with a weapon of longer range than the FZG 76 which made a large crater, and that rail-tanks thought to contain liquid air were reaching Blizna.

*

The Allies based their deception-plan for Overlord on the assumption that they would not be able to prevent the Germans from knowing that they intended to land troops somewhere in France within reach of their single-seater fighters, or in other words somewhere between Cherbourg and Dunkirk. Something could be done to exploit Hitler's notorious nervousness about landings in more distant places, such as Norway or South-West France; but the chief aim must be to convince the enemy that the main effort was coming later than it was, and would be made not west but east of the Seine. The enemy must also be made to think after D-day that landings already made were only the prelude to a bigger effort further east.

While Overlord forces were assembling in the Midlands and West and South-West England steps were taken, therefore, to give the impression that the main assembly areas were in the East and South-East and in Scotland. The assault and follow-up forces were drawn from the British Second Army and the United States First Army, forming the Twenty-First Army Group. To this genuine formation was added, in the bogus order of battle concocted for the misinformation of the Germans, a spurious First United States Army Group (Fusag), notionally consisting of the United States Third Army (which existed and would cross the Channel in due course) and a mythical British Fourth Army.[33] Double agents sent reports to the effect that detailed plans had been made (and leaked by a railway clerk) to move Fusag's forces by rail to ports suitable for an expedition to the Pas de Calais. They also reported that few or no troop movements were visible in the West of England but that an officer had told a woman friend in an unguarded moment that a landing was to be made in the Bay of Biscay about the middle of June.[34]

However, the authorities could not rely on planted reports alone to persuade the enemy to accept a false order of battle. Because the double-cross organization was confident that there were no German agents in the United Kingdom who had not been safely rounded up or turned, they were willing to take the risk that the Germans might receive through diplomatic channels, or from agents in neutral countries, reports which, even though inaccurate or invented, might be believed and might contradict the picture the Allies were trying to build up. But double agents, to preserve their credibility, had to transmit a proportion of genuine information and, above all, to refrain from sending inherently improbable reports whose falsity might be exposed by, for example, air reconnaissance. In any case their reports were more likely to be believed if apparent corroboration was forthcoming. Means of providing such corroboration included actual movements of troops towards areas where troops were notionally assembling, offensive sweeps by the Home Fleet towards Norway, the artful placing of dummy assault craft and simulated supply-dumps, the issue of orders and regulations governing access to prohibited or restricted areas. On the borderline between deception and security, special care was taken not to betray an overriding interest in the area where the troops were to land. Beaches east as well as west of the Seine were examined at close quarters by small inter-service recon-naissance teams which did not always escape the enemy's notice. In the course of softening-up attacks by Allied aircraft, two objectives east of the Seine were bombed for every one west of it.

These measures were highly effective. Notwithstanding the popular belief that documents abstracted by the agent Cicero from the safe of the British Ambassador in Ankara betrayed the secrets of Overlord to the enemy, until the Allies landed the Germans were almost completely in the dark as to where the invasion was coming. Until a few hours before that, they had no idea that landings were imminent.

In the meantime, different authorities held different views, and sometimes changed them in the light of genuine or false reports. The branch of OKH responsible for studying the armies of the Western Allies reported in April that Allied dispositions pointed to landings 'in the area of the Eastern Channel ports'.[35] On 13 May it mentioned growing evidence that the focal point of Allied troop movements was in Southern or South-Eastern England.[36] Rommel (Inspector of Coast Defences and commanding Army Group B in Northern France and the Low Countries) thought on 5 June that the pattern of Allied bombing pointed to landings in the Pas de Calais.[37] Luftflotte 3 predicted landings in the neighbourhood of the Baie de la Seine and Dieppe,[38] but stationed about a quarter of its aircraft in South and South-West France. Reconnaissance aircraft paid some attention in May to ports and harbours between Portland and Portsmouth as well as Dover and

Folkestone; towards the end of March, and again between the latter part
of April and the end of May, unsuccessful air attacks were made on
objectives in the triangle Bristol–Falmouth–Portsmouth. The Commander-in-Chief West (Rundstedt) reported on 22 May that the focus
of the Allied assembly seemed to have shifted to the Portsmouth–
Southampton area, but the last situation report circulated by his
headquarters before D-day said only that probably the invasion would
come somewhere between Normandy and the Scheldt, that landings
further west were possible, and that there was no immediate prospect of
invasion.[39] Admiral Theodore Krancke, commanding Naval Group
West, reported on 4 June that, although air reconnaissance in May had
not sufficed to give a clear picture of measures taken by the Allies, they
seemed consistent with preparations to invade at some future date
rather than immediately.[40] Rommel spent the night before the landings
at home in Germany. Naval patrols ordered for that night were
countermanded because the weather was unfavourable though not
prohibitive, and army officers ordered to report for an exercise at
Rennes on 6 June received no contrary instructions.

The Germans did, however, receive a last-minute warning, although
it was not very effective. On 1 June (as on 1 May) the BBC broadcast a
great many coded messages to resistance circuits in France. These
included a slightly misquoted version of the first three lines of Verlaine's
Chanson d'automne. The rest of the first stanza, again slightly misquoted,
followed on 5 June. Probably as a result of the penetration of a particular
circuit some months earlier, the Paris branch of the German security
service, the Sicherheitsdienst, was aware that these lines were a call to
action, although not of their precise significance.[41] When the second half
of the stanza was picked up shortly before 9.30 p.m. by the wireless
section of the SD in the Avenue Foch, a warning was passed by
telephone to the headquarters of Commander-in-Chief West.[42] The
Fifteenth Army, whose area of responsibility included the Pas de Calais
and part of Normandy, warned its corps about an hour later that
intercepted messages pointed to invasion within forty-eight hours.[43]
The Seventh Army, on whose front the main weight of the assault was
about to fall, took no action.

Allied intelligence was generally good. Besides throwing a good deal
of light on Rundstedt's and Luftflotte 3's views and expectations,
decrypted Enigma messages identified by the end of May between a half
and two-thirds of the divisions the Germans would have in Northern
France and the Low Countries on D-day. All armoured divisions were

correctly located and all army and corps commands identified.[44] The Allies also had the benefit of a detailed report sent to Tokyo by the Japanese Military Attaché in Berlin after a conducted tour of the defences in Normandy.[45] The Luftwaffe's effort on D-day was greatly overestimated, not because of any lack of information about Luftflotte 3's resources but because the intelligence officers who made the estimate felt bound to assume that fighters normally reserved for the defence of the Reich would be used.[46]

In response to the messages broadcast by the BBC, resistance workers in North-West Europe began during the night of 5/6 June a tremendous effort against German communications, using explosives furnished by Special Force Headquarters (formed by the fusion of SOE and its American counterpart, SO). About 950 rail-cuts were made in France alone. As a result of these efforts, Allied bombing of communications and Allied command of the air throughout the daylight hours, the Germans had great difficulty in reinforcing, and even supplying, their formations in Normandy.

However, despite the advantages the Allies derived from naval and air superiority and their ability to put down an immense weight of fire on the coast defences, they only just managed to establish and consolidate their beach-heads. It seems very unlikely, therefore, that the landings could have succeeded if the deception plan had failed. The plan for the assault phase of Overlord (Operation Neptune) involved the movement to the central part of the English Channel from widely-separated assembly ports of more than four thousand vessels carrying the assault and follow-up forces and more than twelve hundred warships of the escort and covering forces, as well as the prompt arrival off the French coast of bombardment vessels from anchorages as far away as Belfast and the Clyde. The Allies would have faced an awkward situation if, after the plan was adopted, the Germans had moved strong armoured forces to Western Normandy. As it was, they had one armoured division in the Seventh Army's area, five in the Fifteenth Army's, and three (of which two were refitting) under Army Group G in South and South-West France. But none of these divisions was at the immediate disposal of the army commander in whose area it was stationed. Three of the nine were in Army Group B's reserve, three in Army Group G's and three in the reserve directly controlled by OKW.

Fortunately for the Allies, the Germans not only allowed themselves to be surprised, but believed even more strongly after than before D-day that the main assault would come in the Pas de Calais. On 9 June a double agent in whom they had boundless confidence sent them a report . in which he exaggerated the number of divisions at Eisenhower's disposal by about fifty per cent, pointed out that no Fusag formations had landed in Normandy, and drew the inference that the D-day landings were only a diversion and would be followed by landings further east.[47] They promptly ordered two armoured divisions in the general direction of the Pas de Calais and countermanded orders to an infantry division to move away from its position north of the Somme. Mil. Amt (which had taken over from the Abwehr in the previous February) was so far from suspecting the author of the report of being a double agent that it described his work as particularly valuable.[48]

However, the landings in Normandy did not end the threat to the base from secret weapons. On 10 June an agent reported that a train of thirty-three wagons, each carrying three objects described as rockets but more likely to be pilotless aircraft, had passed through Ghent, heading towards France.[49] A recently-appointed Director of Operations (Special Operations) at the Air Ministry thought surviving ski sites might be capable of a modest effort against London, but discounted any serious threat from the modified sites until, on the following day, air reconnaissance disclosed considerable activity at six of nine modified sites photographed. At four of them launching-ramps had been equipped with rails, and at all six a characteristic building had been completed since the sites were last photographed.[50] On 12 June Air Intelligence warned all concerned of indications that pilotless aircraft might be used 'at an early date'. Only a few hours later, General Heinemann left his headquarters near Paris to supervise, from Wachtel's command post near Amiens, the early stages of an offensive due to begin that night.

We now know that the intention was to start with a salvo on London from 64 modified sites and continue with harassing fire until about 5 a.m. on 13 June. By that time about 500 missiles should have been launched. As only a few sites had received the prescribed equipment, in fact the best Wachtel could do on the first night was to launch ten missiles, half of which crashed almost immediately. By 15 June he was ready for a fresh start. He succeeded between 10 p.m. and noon on the following day in launching 244 missiles from 55 sites. Although many never came within sight of shore and only about half of those that did reached the Greater London area, ADGB gave effect to a plan to use guns, fighters and a balloon barrage to explode the missiles in the air or bring them down in open country. A public announcement that the Germans were using 'flying bombs' was made, and a 'staff conference' summoned by Churchill agreed that Eisenhower should be asked to sanction attacks on launching and supply sites by the bomber forces under his control.

On Sunday, 18 June, a flying bomb hit the chapel at Wellington Barracks, killing or seriously injuring 180 people. Eisenhower thereupon ruled that, for the time being, attacks on targets associated with the flying bomb and the long-range rocket should take precedence over everything except the urgent requirements of Overlord.

By that date four of eight supply sites associated with the ski-site programme had been heavily bombed since 13 June, but no modified sites had been attacked. There was no evidence that the ski sites or the supply sites were in use. On the other hand, there were indications during the latter part of the month that the Germans had three 'depots' and were interested in worked-out gypsum mines at Nucourt and Saint Leu d'Esserent, in the valley of the Oise, and a disused railway tunnel at Rilly-la-Montagne, near Rheims.[51] So it is not surprising that intelligence officers and operational commanders were dissatisfied with a target-list compiled by the Directorate of Operations (Special Operations), which allotted first place to 'large sites' which had no known connection with the flying-bomb offensive, and second place to the supply sites. Under pressure, the Air Ministry agreed in the second week of July that in future evidence bearing on what were called 'Crossbow' targets should be collated by Air Intelligence and that target-lists should be compiled by a Joint Crossbow Target Priorities Committee on which both the Air Ministry and the United States Strategic Air Forces in Europe were represented. At its first meeting on 21 July, the committee recommended that priority should be given to attacks on storage depots and industrial and production centres, and that harassing attacks should be made on 57 modified sites. Responsibility for the detailed planning of attacks was transferred on the following day to an existing Combined Operational Planning Committee of British and American officers. These reforms went some way to stifle criticism, but the system did not make for swift decisions followed by prompt action.

In the meantime a definite link was established between Wachtel's organization and the sites in the valley of the Oise. The United States Eighth Air Force attacked Nucourt and Saint Leu d'Esserent in the last week of June; the British Bomber Command attacked Saint Leu on the night of 4 July and again three nights later. These attacks were followed by a marked but temporary decline in Wachtel's scale of effort, and their success was confirmed by Enigma traffic. But so many targets competed for the attention of the bomber forces that, although three more attacks were made on Nucourt in the first half of July, no co-ordinated attempt was made to knock out all three depots. Harassing attacks on the modified sites were not very effective. In the outcome Wachtel was defeated, almost on the eve of the capture of his sites by the advancing Overlord forces, by a redeployment of the defences which gave gunners a clear field of fire over the sea and enabled them to use proximity fuses. On 28 August guns, fighters and the balloon-barrage accounted respectively for sixty-five, twenty-three and two of ninety-seven missiles observed by the defences. Three fell short or wide, and only four reached Greater London. Thereafter about twelve hundred missiles aimed at the United Kingdom were launched from aircraft and 275 from sites in the Netherlands, but very few reached their targets.

In June the long-range rocket came into the picture again. Within a few hours of the first abortive V 1 attack on London, an experimental, remotely-controlled version of the A 4 launched from Peenemünde was misdirected by the controller and landed in Sweden instead of splashing into the Baltic.[52] Examination of the remains revealed traces of hydrogen peroxide, which had also been found in wreckage examined by the Poles, and the design of one of the pumps used to feed the combustion chamber suggested that liquid air or liquid oxygen might be one of the liquids used. A prisoner taken in Normandy said he had been on the staff of a colonel whose task was to choose and develop sites for the launching and storage of rockets. This disclosure was followed by the capture of a launching-site near Bayeux, and soon afterwards of documents which revealed the whereabouts of others.

Inspection of this site near Bayeux demolished the belief, long held by British ballistic experts, that a massive installation was needed to launch the rocket. The site consisted merely of slabs of concrete let into the surface of a tree-lined road flanked by newly-constructed loop-roads. A fresh scrutiny of reconnaissance photographs then revealed a rocket standing on a similar slab at Blizna.

Almost simultaneously, an analysis of references in Enigma traffic to numbered items of equipment suggested that the Germans must have made about a thousand rockets. Duncan Sandys, now Chairman of a Crossbow Committee appointed by the War Cabinet, concluded that an offensive with rockets might be imminent; but Jones and others pointed out at a meeting of the committee on 25 July that there was no evidence that the special troops needed to service and launch the missile had been brought from Germany.[53]

Churchill announced at the same meeting that he had received 'a very civil reply' from Stalin to a request that British experts should be allowed to visit the German establishment at Blizna when the Russians captured it. A mission assembled in the Middle East at the end of July. It was held up by the Soviet authorities in Teheran and again in Moscow, and did not reach Blizna until September. Its members were then allowed by their Soviet escort to talk to sympathetic Poles and take away selected items of equipment. The most important of these were packed in crates. The Russians afterwards announced that the crates had been temporarily lost in transit between Blizna and Moscow, but promised to find them and send them on without undue delay. When they arrived in London, they were found to contain not the items chosen, but parts of old aero-engines.[54]

Happily the British did not depend on Stalin for their technical data. On 28 July the leader of a Polish network (an NCO whose deputy was a colonel) arrived in London with a sackful of exhibits retrieved under the noses of the Germans. He had cycled 200 miles with them to a secret rendezvous, still in German-occupied territory, where he was picked up by an Allied aircraft. He said that a high proportion of the rockets launched from Blizna had exploded prematurely and that this had caused the Germans a great deal of anxiety.[55]

In the light of the Polish evidence and further information from Normandy, there emerged by the first week of August a new conception of the A 4 as a liquid-fuelled, gyroscopically-stabilized rocket which could be transported by road and did not need to be launched from a mortar, as had hitherto been supposed, but rose under its own power from a simple launching-pad. All this was correct; but the experts consulted by Sandys continued to overestimate the weight of the rocket and its warhead, chiefly because they could not bring themselves to believe that the Germans would bother to develop an expensive rocket unless it delivered a bigger explosive charge than the cheap and easily-constructed flying bomb. This argument, although the experts buttressed it by reference to the dimensions of a crater photographed in Poland, was fallacious, because the flying bomb was the newer weapon. It occurred to Jones that an analysis of reports which mentioned liquid air or liquid oxygen as one of the fuels might be illuminating, because their authors could be assumed to have better access to technical data than others. He found that there were five such reports. Four estimated the total weight of the rocket at respectively seven, eight, eleven and eleven to twelve tons; the fifth gave no figure. Three put the weight of the warhead at one ton, one at one to one-and-a-half tons, and one at two tons. At a meeting of the Crossbow Committee on 10 August he announced, amidst general incredulity, that in his opinion the all-up weight of the rocket was about twelve tons and that of the warhead about one ton.[56] His figure for the warhead was confirmed a few days later by a reconstruction of the rocket which had crashed in Sweden. We now know that in fact the rocket weighed approximately 12.7 tons with a full load of fuel and that its warhead weighed approximately one ton.

On 26 August Jones completed a detailed report which was circulated on the following day. It included accurate estimates of the dimensions of the rocket and a description of the procedure for servicing and launching it. The maximum range was given as 200 to 210 miles. As a result of objections from Sandys, the report was withdrawn a few days later; but Jones's reputation in intelligence circles was such that the confidence of intelligence officers at the operational commands in the essential accuracy of the report remained unshaken. The report was of particular interest to the author of this book, because he was the member of the intelligence staff of ADGB responsible for keeping the Chief Intelligence Officer, Vorley Harris, and the Air Officer Commanding, Sir Roderic Hill, informed about the threat from the rocket.

When Jones wrote his report, the Air Staff expected rocket attacks on the United Kingdom to begin in the first half of September. But on 2 September the Director of Intelligence (Research) declared that the threat would disappear when parts of Northern France and Belgium within 200 miles of London were 'neutralized by the proximity of our land forces and the operations of our Tactical Air Forces'.[57] Four days later, the Vice-Chiefs of Staff committed themselves to the opinion that rocket attacks on London need no longer be expected.[58]

A map and a ruler were enough to show that this was wrong. Even though driven from Northern France and Belgium, the Germans could still fire rockets at London from Western Holland. Hill was therefore relieved to learn that the Chiefs of Staff had decided that he should continue his existing radar watch for ascending rockets, if only as a precaution against attacks on targets other than London.

We now know that the Germans hoped at the end of August to start on or about 7 September a two-pronged offensive from Belgium, using two batteries under Gruppe Nord to fire at London and two under Gruppe

Sud to fire at Paris. In consequence of the Allied advance, Gruppe Nord was diverted on 5 September to The Hague. Gruppe Sud, after moving from the Rhineland to Venlo and afterwards to Euskirchen, was ordered to prepare for attacks on targets in Northern France and Belgium. An experimental battery was brought in to open the attack on Paris. After two abortive attempts on 6 September, it succeeded early on 8 September in launching a round which fell within the built-up area. It then moved to Walcheren to augment Gruppe Nord's effort against London.

At 6.40 p.m. on 8 September a rocket launched by Gruppe Nord landed at Chiswick, killing three people and seriously injuring ten. Another, which landed sixteen seconds later near Epping, caused no casualties. A further twenty-five rockets fell on or near the United Kingdom during the next ten days. Of the total of twenty-seven, sixteen reached Greater London. Eight landed in Sussex or Essex, two in the sea but within sight of shore, and one on a mud-flat in the Thames Estuary. Altogether about thirty-five rockets were launched between 8 and 18 September, most of them by the two regular batteries of Gruppe Nord from the outskirts of The Hague and the rest by the experimental battery from Walcheren.

As ADGB was responsible for the armed reconnaissance of launching-sites, a method had to be found of pinpointing the sites without delay. It was expedient that this should be done at the headquarters of ADGB, so that as little time as possible elapsed before the information reached the squadrons which would act upon it. An unorthodox but effective arrangement was made, by which information from radar, sound-ranging, flash-spotting, agents and signal intelligence was passed as soon as it arrived to a special section of the intelligence staff consisting initially of one officer. Radar, sound-ranging and flash-spotting at ranges of the order of 200 miles proved too inaccurate for the precise location of sites, but the sight and sound of an ascending rocket could not be concealed from observers close at hand. The best information came from agents or resistance workers who risked death or torture to transmit reports to an aircraft off the coast which relayed them to the United Kingdom. Their contributions made it possible to establish the point of origin of almost every rocket fired from Western Holland within a short time (sometimes only a few minutes) of its arrival. Missiles which failed to arrive were also detected and reported. Although fighter or fighter-bomber pilots could seldom hope to reach the site from which the last rocket had been launched before the launching-team packed up and moved on, study of the enemy's habits soon provided data on which forecasts of the group of sites likely to be used on a given occasion could be based. It also enabled the rocket section at ADGB to establish the location of stores, barracks and rail sidings associated with the rocket, concert arrangements with Bomber Command to attack them when opportunities arose of doing so without undue risk to civilians, and order the necessary target-material. Two storage sites were attacked on 14 and 17 September.

Early in October two intelligence officers from ADGB visited Belgium to discuss the intelligence aspect of counter-measures with the Second Tactical Air Force, a mobile radar unit and a sound-ranging and flash-spotting regiment. They reported on their return that in recent weeks at least fifty rockets and an unknown number of flying bombs had been aimed at Continental targets. The Chiefs of Staff then sent a mission to advise General Eisenhower on counter-measures to both weapons. By that time Hitler had decreed that Antwerp should be the sole continental target for the long-range rocket, but flying bombs continued to be aimed at both Antwerp and Brussels. On the mission's recommendation, a Crossbow section was established within the Air Defence Division of SHAEF. As there was no equivalent on the Continent of the bomb-census which functioned in Britain, one of its tasks was to organize teams of observers in jeeps to report the fall of shot.

*

On 4 September the Allies captured Antwerp, but omitted to seize the crossings of the Albert Canal and left the Germans in possession of both banks of the West Scheldt, connecting Antwerp with the sea. For the time being their prize, the greatest port in North-West Europe, was useless to them as a port of supply.

Eisenhower's intelligence staff estimated a few days later that, although nominally the Germans had forty-eight divisions in the West, the effective strength of the forces available for the defence of the 'West Wall' would not exceed the equivalent of about fifteen, to which another five or six might be added by the end of the month.[59]

This estimate was not far wrong. Rundstedt reported to OKW on 15 September that Army Group B was fighting on a front of 250 miles 'with the strength of about twelve divisions'.[60] Although in some respects the enemy was even weaker than the Allies thought, it was not because of any serious defect in their assessment of his capabilities that they failed early in September to follow their leap forward from the Seine with a further rapid advance which, according to Rundstedt's Chief of Staff, would have enabled them to break through the German front with ease at any point they chose. They lost their chance of ending the war with Germany by Christmas because they were unable to agree in time on a strategy that could be adopted with supplies insufficient for the advance on a broad front envisaged in SHAEF's 'overall stategic plan'. This plan (generally regarded as characteristically American but drawn up by three British members of Eisenhower's staff)[61] dated from early May and was not intended to meet such a situation as arose at the end of August and early in September.

On 17 September the Allies at last began the attempt to break through the German front north of Eindhoven on which they had agreed after weeks of sometimes acrimonious debate. Again, their information about the enemy was fairly good. The sector from Eindhoven to Maastricht, almost undefended on 4 September, was known to be held by an improvised force which had fought well when the British began to push across the Albert Canal on 7 September. Eisenhower's intelligence staff were aware by the time the operation was launched (although apparently the commander of the British 1st Airborne Division was not) of evidence that two SS Panzer divisions had arrived in the neighbourhood of Arnhem to refit.[62] Although they had been sent there for rest and rehabilitation, their intervention in an emergency was predictable, and therefore not unexpected so far as SHAEF was concerned.

Operation Market Garden involved the capture by airborne forces of nine bridges over three major rivers and five minor waterways to pave the way for an advance by a single corps on a very narrow front. A Dutch resistance worker, Christiaan Lindemans, is alleged to have betrayed the plan to the Germans.[63] Although it has been stated on the authority of a British investigator that he failed to make contact with the enemy, the truth would seem to be that he did succeed in conveying his warning to the local office of the German counter-intelligence service, but was not believed.[64] Army Group B stated after the event that the operation came as a surprise.[65] Preliminary air attacks on gun positions were taken for attempts to destroy the bridges.

Five bridges across minor waterways and two across the Maas were captured by American airborne troops on the first day, but the advance of the British 30th Corps along a single road through Eindhoven was slower than had been expected. The next bridge to the north, across the Waal at Nijmegen, fell to simultaneous assaults from north and south by American paratroops and British armour. The great steel bridge across the Lower Rhine at Arnhem, which was to have been taken by the British 1st Airborne Division, eluded capture. As the division landed about seven miles north-west of the bridge and Army Group B's headquarters were in the western outskirts of the town, it does not seem a matter for wonder that the Germans recovered from their surprise in time to seize the southern end of the bridge and organize an effective counter-stroke on the north bank. The division was also handicapped by cloudy weather which delayed the arrival of reinforcements and reduced the amount of air support it could be given.

On the first day of the Arnhem operation, informants on the spot reported that rocket-launching troops were leaving The Hague. We now know that the main body of Gruppe Nord withdrew to Burgstein-furt, near Münster, and the experimental battery to Zwolle. SS General Kammler, who had assumed command of the organization when the SS gained control in August, moved his headquarters from Nijmegen to Darfeld, also near Münster. The arrival of a rocket at Lambeth late on 18 September showed that the withdrawal was not yet complete.

As London was now out of range, Kammler ordered the experimental battery to keep the offensive against the United Kingdom alive by moving a few days later to Staveren, in Friesland, and opening fire on Norwich and Ipswich. Between 25 September and 12 October it aimed 43 rockets at Norwich and one at Ipswich. The nearest approach to a hit on either target was one round which fell harmlessly in the outskirts of Norwich on 3 October. Locations indicated by some early reports included Apeldoorn, Vlieland and Terschelling as well as Staveren, but after a few days a group of launching-sites was identified about five miles east of Staveren, and there were indications that supplies were reaching a railhead about twelve miles away at Sneek.[66]

On 30 September Kammler ordered one battery of Gruppe Nord to return to The Hague. News of the move reached London and the headquarters of ADGB at Stanmore on 3 October, well before the first rocket aimed at London since 18 September fell at Leytonstone late that evening.[67] Soon after the middle of the month (when ADGB became Fighter Command again), the troops at The Hague were joined by the experimental battery.

From that time until the spring of 1945 both London and Antwerp were under attack. Between 3 October 1944 and 27 March 1945 about 1,300 rockets were aimed at London (as compared with 55 between 8 and 18 September); 501 fell within the London Civil Defence Region and 496 elsewhere on land. As each rocket on land killed or seriously injured an average of eight or nine people (and three which fell in crowded places killed or injured 684), much thought was given to methods of reducing the scale of attack. Intelligence provided good information about storage-sites, communications and buildings used by the launching-troops, but the use that could be made of it was limited by the extent to which the authorities were willing to divert aircraft from other tasks, and in the case of Gruppe Nord by the extent to which the lives of Dutch civilians could legitimately be put at risk in order to save lives in the United Kingdom.

The second point was discussed, at Air Marshal Hill's suggestion, with the Dutch authorities in London. The conclusion reached was that attacks on targets adjacent to built-up areas were permissible as long as they could be considered 'reasonably discriminating'. In substance, the attitude of the authorities to the first point was that Hill must do what he could with his own resources and occasional contributions by other commands, and that no major diversion of bomber forces from Overlord and the bombing of Germany would be justified unless the enemy substantially increased his scale of attack. They pointed out that repeated attacks made by the Allied tactical air forces on the enemy's communications, even though not specifically directed against Cross-bow targets, should do something to keep the scale of effort within bounds.

In general, Hill's policy was to use his fighter-bombers only against sites at least 250 yards from the nearest building still occupied by Dutch civilians, or against buildings known to have been taken over by the Germans. On 21 and 22 February he tried, on the recommendation of his intelligence staff, the experiment of concentrating his entire effort on a single target. The target chosen was the Haagsche Bosch, a wooded, park-like area where up to twenty or thirty rockets at a time had been seen on air photographs taken since December. The outcome of thirty-eight attacks was that only one rocket was launched during the next two-and-a-half days, the Germans were reported to be moving to new positions, and no rockets were seen on photographs of the Haagsche Bosch taken on 24 February. Unfortunately the Second Tactical Air Force, disregarding a new target-list issued by Fighter Command, chose the Haagsche Bosch as the target for a rare intervention by medium bombers on 3 March. Still more unfortunately, an incorrect allowance was made for wind. No bombs fell within 500 yards of the intended aiming-points, and heavy damage was done to a built-up area about a mile away.[68]

In the meantime General Sir Frederick Pile of Anti-Aircraft Command suggested that barrage-fire might be used to explode rockets before they reached the target. If 150 proximity-fused shells were fired at a given rocket there might, he thought, be a fifty-to-one chance of success.[69] One scientist consulted by the Crossbow Committee, however, put the odds against success at a hundred to one, another at a thousand to one.[70] Later, a panel of scientists reported that the odds might shorten to thirty to one if the number of rounds fired at a given rocket could be increased from 150 to 400.[71] The Chiefs of Staff decided on 30 March that, even so, the prospects of success were too slender to justify an unexplained volume of fire which might frighten the public, and in any case by that time Gruppe Nord had launched its last rocket.

The use of the double-cross organization to deceive the enemy about fall of shot was discussed from the time when the first flying bombs arrived in the summer of 1944. There was so much coming and going between England and the Continent after D-day that MI 5 could no longer be sure that the Germans had no agents in Britain who had not been put away or turned. Moreover, photographic reconnaissance could reveal points of impact although not the times at which flying bombs had fallen. Even more care than usual had therefore to be taken that double agents did not blow the whole system by transmitting reports that were demonstrably false. As the enemy tended to aim short, the framers of the deception plan proposed to induce him to shorten his aim still further by dwelling on incidents north and west of the target and saying as little as was consistent with credibility about incidents south and east of it.[72] Although objections were made on the ground that this would be an interference with Providence and would favour Westminster, Belgravia and Mayfair at the expense of less prosperous quarters south of the Thames, eventually their recommendations were accepted. When, later, Wachtel's former headquarters in France were overrun, captured documents showed that sample bombs had carried radio transmitters which revealed their points of impact, but that he and his staff had preferred the evidence planted on them.[73]

V 2 posed similar problems, with the added complication that, as the rockets were launched singly and usually at well-spaced intervals, the enemy could calculate the time of arrival of each missile. On the other hand he could not know, except from agents, where any particular missile fell. It was therefore decided that double agents should report the genuine points of impact of missiles which fell in Central London, but that in each case the time given should be the time of arrival of a missile which fell from five to eight miles short.[74] If he believed the reports, the enemy would be led to conclude that missiles which fell short were bang on target and those that did hit the target overshoots. The inherent inaccuracy of the A 4 makes it hard to say how far the deception plan succeeded. But it is a fact that nearly forty-seven per cent of all rockets aimed at London, apart from abortive or grossly inaccurate rounds whose fate remains unknown, fell short of the target in Essex or Kent or in the sea.[75]

*

On 1 September 1944 Eisenhower assumed direct responsibility for co-ordinating the operations of the Overlord land forces, a function hitherto delegated to Montgomery. After the failure of Market Garden he reverted to the strategy of simultaneous advances on more fronts than one, although he conceded that priority should go to an attempt to seize the Ruhr. But before that could be done the enemy had to be pushed from positions covering the estuary of the Scheldt so that Antwerp could be used as a port of supply. This proved an uphill task, to which the intelligence agencies and resistance movements could make no major contribution.

Clearance of the seaward approaches to Antwerp was completed early in November, but much minesweeping and other preliminary work had to be done before the port became usable. In the meantime Eisenhower sanctioned an ambitious attempt by General Omar H. Bradley's Twelfth Army Group, supported by Montgomery's Twenty-First Army Group on its left, to close up to the Rhine, establish bridgeheads on the right bank, and occupy the Ruhr and the Saar.

The weather in the middle of November was appalling, and the landing in the South of France on which the American Chiefs of Staff insisted had done little or nothing to ease Eisenhower's problems. The failure of the November offensive left the Allies standing on a 600-mile front. The United States First Army, now part of the Twelfth Army Group, held a front of nearly 150 miles, with its left north of Aachen and its right on the Moselle. The better part of its troops were in the left-hand sector, preparing to resume the offensive in due course. Its right-hand sector in the Ardennes was held by a single corps of four divisions and a cavalry group on a front of nearly eighty miles. The sector was regarded by the Americans as a quiet one, although there was a fair amount of patrol activity by both sides.[76]

The Allies knew as early as October that the Germans were forming a new Sixth Panzer Army partly from divisions taken out of the line to refit.[77] Its role was obscure, and the enemy took care that it remained so. To conceal OKW's intention of using the new army, with the Fifth Panzer Army on its left, to sweep through the Ardennes, across the Meuse and on to Antwerp and Brussels, reports were circulated to the effect that it was to be used for a counter-attack when the Allies resumed their attempt to reach and cross the Rhine. Its arrival west of Cologne early in November therefore caused no particular alarm.

Thereafter the Allies received a great deal of information which might have been, but was not, interpreted as evidence of an impending offensive in the Ardennes. Air reconnaissance (intermittent because the weather was often bad) detected a considerable flow of reinforcements to the Western Front (but not exclusively to the sectors opposite the First Army).[78] Signal intelligence revealed the establishment of two new wireless networks and exceptional security precautions.[79] The Germans were known to be forming a special unit, manned by English-speaking officers and other ranks, with first call on captured American equipment and uniforms (and this led the Allies to suspect that attempts might be made to kidnap Eisenhower and other senior officers).[80] From early December prisoners-of-war repeatedly referred to preparations for an offensive which most of them thought would start soon after the middle of the month.[81] At the same time, air reconnaissance reported a substantial build-up of German forces in the Bitburg–Wittlich area, immediately opposite the First Army's weakly-held right-hand sector.[82] A German woman who came through the Allied lines on 13 December said there were many Panzer troops and guns at Bitburg and that during the past three days she had seen troops and vehicles moving from that direction with pontoons, small boats and other equipment suitable for crossing rivers.[83] The First Army's intelligence staff, noting that flying-bomb attacks on Antwerp and Liège had ceased on 1 December, suggested that the reason might be either that the railways were too congested with troops and military equipment to carry the missiles, or that the launching-units might be moving to new positions in readiness to support an offensive. Nevertheless they did not conclude that the all-out offensive predicted by a prisoner whom they described as 'extremely intelligent' was imminent. The enemy, they thought, might perhaps launch a limited offensive to boost morale, but was more likely to remain on the defensive until the Allies resumed their advance.[84] At Supreme Headquarters at Versailles a limited offensive by the Sixth

Army was considered possible, but improbable except in the context of a defensive battle.[85]

In the event, the assault launched before dawn on 16 December by the two Panzer armies, supported on the extreme left by the Seventh Army, not only caught Eisenhower and his subordinates unprepared but astonished them by its weight and scope. Reports that the enemy had opened an attack in the Ardennes reached Versailles fairly early in the day, but the news that a weak part of the Allied line was being attacked in strength was not broken to Eisenhower until the afternoon.[86] At the time he was conferring with Bradley and others about the next stage of the Twelfth Army Group's offensive and a lack of reinforcements for it. He claimed after the war to have recognized immediately that something more than a local attack was in progress; Bradley, on the other hand, confessed in his memoirs that he thought the Germans were delivering merely a spoiling attack.[87] By the evening of 17 December forward troops of the 1st SS Panzer Division were at Stavelot, twenty miles behind the First Army's front and barely eight miles from its headquarters at Spa. On 23 December elements of the 15th Panzergrenadier Division reached Celles, only four miles from the Meuse at Dinant.

Nevertheless the offensive failed, not only because the Allies soon recovered from their surprise and responded to the threat with a combination of counter-attacks and measures to safeguard the crossings of the Meuse, but also for other reasons. Among these were an improvement in the weather which enabled the Allies to make some use of their air superiority; the inability of the German High Command to keep its mobile formations adequately supplied with fuel; and the preference given to the Sixth Panzer Army over the Fifth, which had further to go but a better chance of success because it was attacking the weakest part of the Allied line. The Germans paid heavily for their failure to seize opportunities of capturing huge reserves of fuel which would have given their Panzer units a new lease of life. Accurate knowledge of the location of Allied fuel dumps, punctually disseminated, might have made all the difference. So neither the Allied nor the German intelligence authorities earn top marks for their performance on the eve of the battle.

Apart from costing the Allies (and also the enemy) heavy losses, the Battle of the Ardennes delayed the start of the Twenty-First Army Group's advance to the Rhine by four to five weeks. It also shook SHAEF's reputation as an authority on what would happen next. An allegation often made during the last few months of the war was that the situation-maps at Versailles did not accurately show the disposition of Eisenhower's own forces, let alone the enemy's.

In fact the Germans were able, after their withdrawal from the occupied countries, to improve their security by making more use of landlines which could not be tapped or cut by resistance workers. This did not apply to Italy, where partisans were particularly active in the last few months of the war, and in any case messages had still to be put on the air when communications were interrupted by bombing. In the spring of 1945 the enemy caused some perturbation at Bletchley by introducing a modified version of the Enigma machine.[88] However, as there were not enough of the new machines to go round and some units used their old machines to encypher signals encyphered by others with the new, the setback was not very serious. Enigma continued until the end to reveal the growing disintegration of the Wehrmacht under the impact of simultaneous assaults from east, west and south. On the other hand, the work of SHAEF's intelligence officers was not made easier by the spate of wild rumours which reached the Allies towards the end of the war from the other side of the lines.[89]

In Italy the Germans made a step-by-step withdrawal, after the fall of Rome, to a new line north of Florence, picturesquely called the Gothic Line. Alexander lost seven divisions withdrawn for the landing in the South of France on which the Americans insisted, but was nevertheless ordered to keep up pressure on the enemy in order to prevent the transfer of German divisions to the Western Front. Operation Anvil (renamed Dragoon) gave the Allies access to Marseilles as an additional port of supply, but it did not draw off any German divisions from the West. Its ultimate effect was to add to Eisenhower's forces the ten Allied divisions which landed on the Côte d'Azur, while the forces opposing him were increased by eleven weak divisions which retreated from the South of France and two divisions brought from Italy.[90] All these moves were revealed by intelligence, and were understandably regarded by the British as justification of their argument that Anvil would weaken Alexander but not the German armies in the West.

Between the last week of August and the end of 1944 the Allies broke through the Gothic Line and went on to capture Ravenna, but failed to take Bologna. Alexander then went over to the defensive.

With his force further reduced by the transfer of the two divisions of the 1st Canadian Corps to the Western Front, but still with seventeen British and American divisions, six independent armoured brigades, four independent infantry brigades and six Italian combat groups under command, Alexander prepared early in 1945 to resume the offensive against twenty-three weak German divisions and four scratch divisions raised in Northern Italy by the German-liberated and still defiant Mussolini. The Allies were also supported by some 60,000 Italian partisans working behind the German lines. They had almost undisputed command of the air and were well provided with good modern weapons, ammunition and equipment. Unlike the enemy, they had ample reserves of fuel.

By that time the German commanders in Italy knew that they could expect little from Berlin except orders to hold on at all costs. Their communications were so precarious, their movements so circumscribed by lack of fuel, air attacks and partisan activities that they could scarcely hope to stage an orderly retreat across the Alps, even if withdrawal were permitted. As they were bound to be defeated when their supplies ran out, it does not seem surprising that they opened negotiations for a cease-fire without waiting for the Allies to launch their spring offensive. Cautious approaches by SS General Karl Wolff, at first through Italian and Swiss intermediaries, led to highly-secret meetings between Wolff and the head of the OSS network in Switzerland, Allen Dulles.[91] Although the first steps were taken as early as February, complications arising from changes in command, mutual distrust and objections made by the Russians to conversations from which they were excluded delayed agreement until after the Allies opened their offensive in the second week of April. But on 23 April Wolff and Vietinghoff – who had succeeded to the chief command when Kesselring was injured in a car-crash – decided to disregard stand-fast orders and negotiate a cease-fire. In accordance with an instrument of surrender signed on 29 April, all Axis forces in Italy laid down their arms on 2 May. The German forces in North-West Europe surrendered two days later at Montgomery's headquarters on Lüneburg Heath. A formal surrender of all German forces was made at Eisenhower's headquarters at Rheims on 7 May in the presence of representatives of Britain, France, the Soviet Union and the United States. Eleventh-hour messages intercepted and decrypted by the British included a signal to one of their double agents instructing him to keep in touch and replying to a question about a lost suitcase.[92]

ELEVEN

The Defeat of Japan

When the ABDA command was wound up early in 1942, the Western Allies agreed that henceforth the British should direct operations in the area westwards from Singapore to the Mediterranean, the Americans in the whole of the Pacific. Chiang Kai-shek, with the rank and style of Generalissimo but guided by American military and air advisers, would take care of China. The British and the Americans were to be jointly responsible for the North and South Atlantic and the European theatre. Commanders in all theatres would, in theory, be required to conform to a grand strategy framed by the Combined Chiefs of Staff under the direction of the British and United States governments. Australia, China, the Netherlands and New Zealand would be represented on advisory councils in London and Washington.

In practice, considerable departures were made from this programme. The appointment of an American Supreme Commander for Torch extended the principle of joint responsibility to the Mediterranean theatre as far east as Tunisia. Burma ceased to be an exclusively British area of responsibility when, late in 1943, a British Supreme Commander with an Anglo-American staff was appointed to direct operations in South-East Asia. Chiang Kai-shek did not take kindly to foreign guidance, and had to be threatened with the withdrawal of American supplies before he agreed in 1944 to send an expeditionary force across the Sino-Burmese frontier. The Combined Chiefs of Staff never had more than a loose control of operations in the Pacific theatre or the allocation of equipment as between that theatre and other theatres. 'The war' meant to most Americans the war in the Pacific, but even the American Chiefs of Staff, in their joint capacity, had some difficulty in imposing their will on commanders in that area and adjusting inter-service rivalries.

The Americans divided the Pacific theatre into a South-East Pacific Area covering the approaches to the Panama Canal and the West Coast of South America; a South-West Pacific Area which included in the first instance Australia, the Indonesian archipelago as far west as Java, Borneo, the Philippines, Celebes, New Guinea, the Bismarck archipelago and the Northern Solomons; and a Pacific Ocean Area extending from the Aleutians in the north to New Zealand in the south. The Pacific Ocean Area was in turn sub-divided into areas covering respectively the North, Central and South Pacific.

When these arrangements were made, the Allies had already agreed to stand on the defensive against Japan until Germany was defeated, with the proviso that this should not preclude them from establishing bases for a future offensive. In any case it was obvious that the Japanese must be prevented from cutting communications between Australasia and the United States by seizing outposts in the Pacific south of the equator. Forces had been sent as early as January from the Common-wealth countries and the United States to set up new bases, or strengthen existing garrisons, in Fiji, Samoa, New Caledonia and the southern part of New Guinea. In the course of the next few months work had begun on an Allied naval and air base at Espiritu Santo in the New Hebrides. American troops had joined the Australian garrison of Port Darwin, and MacArthur was promised two American divisions to supplement the substantial Australian forces already under his com-mand.

Signal intelligence and reconnaissance were generally the best sources of information about Japanese resources, dispositions and intentions. The Americans had not provided themselves in peacetime with a Far Eastern espionage network comparable with Sorge's, partly because national policy precluded the employment of unassimilated descendants of Japanese settlers in the United States as secret agents. Little information could be expected from prisoners-of-war, because the Japanese considered surrender in the field dishonourable and therefore preferred death in battle or suicide to capture. On the other hand, a good deal was learnt from captured equipment, and occasionally from captured documents. In the South-West Pacific valuable warnings and reports were received from a coast-watching service organized by the Royal Australian Navy, and in South-East Asia the British made considerable use of irregular forces and of agents dropped behind the Japanese lines by SOE.

American signal intelligence made its first important contribution to operations in the Pacific theatre about four months after Pearl Harbor. By 17 April 1942 the Americans knew from intercepted and decrypted naval traffic that a large Japanese convoy could be expected to enter the Coral Sea early in May.[1] The Japanese plan, as we now know it, was to disembark a small landing-party, carried in one transport escorted by two destroyers, at Tulagi in the Central Solomons for the purpose of establishing a seaplane base for immediate use, and a much larger force carried in eleven transports escorted by six destroyers at Port Moresby, on the south coast of Papua–New Guinea. Close support was to be provided by two light cruisers, a seaplane-carrier and three gunboats; close cover by the light carrier *Shoho*, four heavy cruisers and a destroyer. The fleet carriers *Zuikaku* and *Shokaku*, accompanied by two heavy cruisers and six destroyers, were to provide distant cover by rounding the south-eastern extremity of the Solomons, engaging any Allied warships found in the Coral Sea, and flying off aircraft to attack Allied fighter bases in Queensland.

To counter the threat, the Americans assembled a task force under Rear-Admiral F. J. Fletcher. It consisted of a carrier group comprising the *Yorktown* and the *Lexington*, with four destroyers; an attack group of five cruisers and five destroyers; a support group of three cruisers and two destroyers; and a so-called search group consisting of one seaplane tender. The Americans, like the Japanese, would have about 140 carrier-borne aircraft at their disposal, but they would also receive such support from shore-based aircraft in Australia and New Guinea as could be provided after other commitments were met.

Fletcher, flying his flag in the *Yorktown*, assembled the carrier group west of the New Hebrides on 1 May. Soon afterwards he ordered the carriers to refuel. The *Lexington* was still refuelling when, late on 3 May, he learned that Japanese troops had been seen earlier in the day disembarking at Tulagi. He took the *Yorktown* to Tulagi during the night, attacked shipping there without much effect on the following day, and did not again make rendezvous with the *Lexington* until 5 May. By that time the Japanese carrier striking force had rounded the Solomon Islands; the Port Moresby invasion force, accompanied by the support force and followed by the covering force, was heading for the south-eastern extremity of New Guinea. Fletcher spent most of 6 May refuelling from an accompanying oiler and searching with his aircraft for the enemy.

On the following day the commander of the Japanese carrier force located Fletcher's fleet, but the striking force he despatched succeeded in finding and sinking only the oiler and a destroyer. Almost simultaneously, an airman from the *Yorktown* sighted the two cruisers and two of the three gunboats of the Japanese support force, but the combination of a mistake in identification and a cyphering error led to their being reported as two carriers and four heavy cruisers. A striking force then despatched by Fletcher failed to find either the support force or the carrier force for which it was mistaken, but did find and sink the *Shoho*, which went down with all but three of her aircraft. Two days later the American and Japanese carrier forces located each other more or less simultaneously and launched simultaneous attacks. The *Shokaku* was seriously and the *Zuikaku* slightly damaged by dive-bombers from the *Yorktown*; but both American carriers were hit, and the *Lexington* had afterwards to be abandoned and sunk. The Japanese commander, believing that both American carriers had been sunk, abandoned the attempt to invade Port Moresby and ordered a general withdrawal.

The Battle of the Coral Sea was the first in naval history in which all the damage suffered on both sides was inflicted by aircraft from warships which never came within sight of each other or used their main armament. It was a typical encounter in more ways than one. The Americans had the benefit of excellent strategic intelligence, but their tactical intelligence left a good deal to be desired. They suffered a tactical defeat by exchanging the *Lexington* for the less valuable *Shoho*, but gained a strategic victory by preventing the enemy from reaching Port Moresby.

The issue in the Coral Sea had yet to be decided when the Americans decrypted the first of a series of messages which convinced them that a bigger operation was impending. As before, their information came from the reading of a naval cypher on which both American and British cryptanalysts had worked.[2] We now know that the Japanese intended to change the cypher on 1 May, but were unable to do so because the printing of new tables was not completed in time. Had they carried out their intention, in all probability the new cypher would not have been broken in time to prepare the Americans for what proved to be a decisive battle.

As it was, the evidence pointed to a feint towards the Aleutian Islands as cover for an expedition to an objective which could be either Midway Island or Oahu in the Hawaiian Islands. The United States Pacific Fleet's Combat Intelligence Unit at Pearl Harbor was fairly sure that the co-ordinates AF, mentioned in the traffic, indicated Midway, but decided to put the question to the test by asking the garrison to transmit in clear a message, sure to be monitored by the Japanese, to the effect that the island's distillation plant had broken down. When the traffic referred two days later to a shortage of water at AF, there could no longer be any doubt about the matter.[3]

The Japanese were expected to use at least four and perhaps as many as six carriers in the coming battle. The Americans had only the *Yorktown*, the *Enterprise* and the *Hornet*. The naval authorities in Washington therefore asked the British to help either by sending a carrier to the South-West Pacific, or by attacking Rangoon and the Andaman Islands or Japanese communications between Rangoon and Singapore. But their request, with the intelligence on which it was based, was not signalled to London until 19 May, and the matter was not fully explained even to the head of the British Admiralty Delegation in Washington until three days later.[4] Two British carriers were under repair at Kilindini, but neither could have reached the Pacific in time to be of use. The British contribution had to be limited to a diversionary movement by the Eastern Fleet towards Ceylon.

In the event, the *Zuikaku* and the *Shokaku* did not complete their repairs in time to take part in the Battle of Midway Island. Admiral Yamamoto had the fleet carriers *Akagi*, *Kaga*, *Hiryu* and *Soryu*, with a complement of 272 aircraft, and the light carriers *Ryujo*, *Junyo*, *Hosho* and *Zuiho*, with 121 aircraft. He also had five seaplane carriers, but two of these were used to transport motor torpedo-boats and midget submarines, and the rest carried only 34 aircraft between them. Surprise was of the essence to his plan. On 3 June four lightly-escorted transports were to disembark about 2,000 men in the Western Aleutians under cover of attacks by aircraft from two of his light carriers on Dutch Harbor, in the Eastern Aleutians. Four battleships would then engage the force the Americans could be expected to send towards the Aleutians. On the following day aircraft from the four large fleet carriers were to attack Midway Island as the prelude to landings by some 5,000 men from twelve transports and supply-ships. All American heavy ships not already sunk or crippled would then be brought to action and destroyed either by carrier-borne aircraft or by the battlefleet.

The warning given by his Combat Intelligence Unit went a long way to compensate the American commander, Admiral Nimitz, for his numerical inferiority in carrier-borne aircraft. Moreover, he was in a position to supplement the 233 aircraft carried by the *Yorktown*, the *Enterprise* and the *Hornet* with about 300 naval and army aircraft based ashore in Midway and the Aleutians or Alaska. He formed a small North Pacific Force of cruisers, destroyers, submarines and light naval craft to take care of the Aleutians with support from shore-based aircraft. To fight the enemy in the Central Pacific and defend Midway Island he formed a Carrier Striking Force consisting of two task forces built round his three carriers. The rest of the Carrier Striking Force consisted of eight cruisers and fifteen destroyers included in the two task forces, and an oiler group of two oilers and two destroyers.

The North Pacific Force was commanded by Rear-Admiral Robert A. Theobald. In the interests of security, Theobald was not given a full account of the evidence which pointed to landings in the Western Aleutians under cover of diversionary attacks on Dutch Harbor.[5] Nimitz's caution is understandable, but it put Theobald at a disadvantage. Suspecting that Nimitz had been hoaxed and that the enemy's real intention was to gain a foothold at Dutch Harbor itself or in Alaska, he kept the main body of his small force too far to the east to intercept the transports bound for the Western Aleutians.[6] The Japanese commander, helped by thick weather which enabled him to put his light carriers within striking distance of Dutch Harbor without detection by reconnaissance aircraft or naval patrol craft, succeeded in disembarking troops on the remote and inhospitable islands of Attu and Kiska and withdrawing with the loss of only a few aircraft shot down by anti-aircraft guns or shore-based fighters. A projected landing at Adak, about midway between Kiska and Dutch Harbor, was abandoned.

In the Central Pacific, almost everything went wrong for the Japanese. Knowledge of Yamamotos's intentions not only enabled the Americans to guard against surprise; it also helped them to avoid committing their precious carrier force too soon.

This they might easily have done in less favourable circumstances, because the organization of Yamamoto's Combined Fleet was extremely complex. In addition to the battleships assigned to support of the expeditions to the Aleutians, the fleet comprised a First Mobile Force consisting of the four large carriers, two battleships, two heavy cruisers and twelve destroyers; a Main Body of three battleships, a light carrier, thirteen destroyers, and two seaplane carriers bringing motor torpedo-boats and midget submarines; and a Midway Occupation Force. The last was made up of an invasion force of transports and supply ships, with a close escort of destroyers and a light cruiser; a close support force of four heavy cruisers, and two destroyers; a covering force of two battleships, a light carrier, four heavy cruisers and eight destroyers; and miscellaneous forces for reconnaissance and minesweeping.

The invasion force was sighted from a reconnaissance aircraft 700 miles west of Midway about 9 a.m. on 3 June. It was at first thought to be part of the Main Body, but was afterwards correctly identified.[7] To await the arrival of the enemy's carrier force, the American Carrier Striking Force took up a position about 300 miles east-north-east of Midway. Admiral Fletcher, commanding the task force built around the *Yorktown* and also the Carrier Striking Force as a whole, learned in the late afternoon that bombers from Midway had attacked the invasion force during the day, but had scored no hits.

We now know that Admiral Nagumo, commanding the First Mobile Force, reached his flying-off position 240 miles north-west of Midway about twenty minutes before sunrise on 4 June. He sent seventy-two bombers, with an escort of thirty-six fighters, to attack the island. Although he knew nothing of Fletcher's whereabouts, he kept back ninety-three bombers, armed with torpedoes and armour-piercing bombs, to deal with any American warships that might appear. About an hour after his arrival, his presence was reported by the crew of a reconnaissance aircraft, who also saw some of his aircraft in the air. Fighters took off from Midway to intercept them, and bombers were sent to attack his ships. These efforts were unsuccessful, but they led Nagumo to conclude that his attempt to knock out the defences of the island had failed. At 7.15 a.m. he decided to launch a second attack. Accordingly, he gave orders that bombers not committed to the first attack should exchange their torpedoes and armour-piercing bombs for bombs suitable for dropping on targets ashore. Less than a quarter of an hour later, the crew of a reconnoitring seaplane reported that 'ten enemy ships' were approaching from a point north of Midway. Although he was not to learn until another half-hour had elapsed that they included at least one carrier, he decided after anxious thought to countermand the further attack on Midway. He then arranged that torpedo-bombers which had not yet exchanged their torpedoes for bombs should retain them.

Fletcher knew nothing of what was passing through Nagumo's mind, but received shortly after 6 a.m. a report of his whereabouts.[8] He ordered Rear-Admiral R. A. Spruance, commanding the task force which included the *Enterprise* and the *Hornet*, to close with the enemy, locate his carriers and attack them. Spruance did not at first intend to launch his aircraft until about 9 a.m., when he could expect to be a hundred miles or so from his objective. He was persuaded by his Chief of Staff, Captain Miles Browning, that he would stand a better chance of catching Nagumo at a disadvantage if he launched them a good deal earlier. Between 7 and 8 a.m. he despatched twenty-nine torpedo-bombers, sixty-seven dive-bombers and twenty fighters, retaining only eight dive-bombers and thirty-six fighters to protect his force. Fletcher, following in the *Yorktown*, contributed about half his aircraft and kept the rest to deal with any Japanese warships that might turn up unexpectedly.

The result was that aircraft from all three American carriers approached Nagumo's force just when he had finished recovering the aircraft sent to Midway at dawn, was making a desperate attempt to refuel and rearm them before action was joined, and had turned to port with the intention of engaging the one American carrier of whose approach he was aware. Most of the American torpedo-bombers were shot down by Nagumo's fighters or anti-aircraft guns, and they scored no hits. The *Hornet*'s dive-bombers went astray. But dive-bombers from the *Enterprise* and the *Yorktown*, meeting little opposition because the torpedo-bombers had drawn most of the enemy's fire, disabled and sank the *Akagi*, the *Kaga* and the *Soryu*. Aircraft from the *Hiryu* then disabled the *Yorktown*, but the *Hiryu* was herself put out of action by dive-bombers from the *Enterprise*, which included a few transferred from the *Yorktown*. She sank next morning. Thus the First Mobile Force lost all four of its carriers, with their entire complement of aircraft.

This was a blow from which the Japanese were never fully to recover. They still had the *Zuikaku*, the *Shokaku* and the newly-completed *Junyo*. To these they added later in the year the *Junyo*'s sister-ship, the *Hiyo*. These two ships carried up to 53 aircraft apiece, as compared with up to 73 carried by the *Soryu* and the *Hiryu*, up to 84 by the *Zuikaku* and the *Shokaku*, and up to about 90 by the *Akagi* and the *Kaga*. In 1944 they completed the 29,000-ton *Taiho* and the 64,000-ton *Shinano*, which carried respectively 53 and 47 aircraft, but both were sunk soon after completion. Two battleships, the *Hyuga* and the *Ise*, were modified in 1943 as battleship-carriers, but each carried only 22 dual-purpose seaplanes designed to double the roles of reconnaissance aircraft and dive-bomber. A more promising venture was the development of light carriers, displacing about 17,000 tons, with carrying-capacities comparable with those of large fleet carriers. The fact remains that, partly because they squandered carrier aircraft and crews on operations from shore bases, after Midway the Japanese never had a carrier force as good as that of 1941 and early 1942.

*

The first offensive operation of any consequence undertaken by the

Americans, apart from the propagandist Tokyo raid and some attacks by carrier-borne aircraft on Japanese outposts in the Central and South-West Pacific, was an expedition to the Solomon Islands in August 1942. The Joint Chiefs of Staff decided at the beginning of July that preparations should be made for step-by-step advances towards New Ireland and New Britain, immediately east of New Guinea, and that these should start with the expulsion of the Japanese from Tulagi and the establishment of American bases there and elsewhere in the British Solomon Islands Protectorate. The Santa Cruz Islands, at the south-eastern extremity of the Solomons, at one time seemed a convenient point of departure, but were afterwards found unsuitable.

A few days after this decision was made, the Joint Chiefs learned that Japanese troops and engineers had crossed the Iron Bottom Sound from Tulagi and were building an airfield on the much larger island of Guadalcanal.[9] Clearly the enemy would have to be expelled from Guadalcanal as well as Tulagi before the Southern Solomons became a secure base for a northward advance.

Inasmuch as preparations for Torch would be making heavy demands on Allied resources by the time the expedition to the Solomons could be mounted, the operation was not well timed. It was also badly planned. The planners estimated that there were 5,000 Japanese on Guadalcanal.[10] In fact there were only about half as many, and not more than 600 of these were combatant troops; but Tulagi and the adjacent islets of Gavutu and Tanambogo were garrisoned by about 1,500 men. The American expeditionary force – the first despatched to enemy-held territory since 1898 – consisted of some 19,000 officers and enlisted men of the United States Marine Corps, carried with their equipment and supplies in twenty-three transports and supply-ships escorted and supported by eight cruisers (three of them Australian) and fifteen destroyers. This was not only an unnecessarily large force, it was also a much larger one than the Americans would be able to maintain without great difficulty once the supplies it carried with it were exhausted. All the marines were to be carried in one lift, so there would be no follow-up formations to exploit a success or redeem a failure. Unloading was expected to take four days, and the transports and supply-ships and their escort would be vulnerable to air attacks until it was completed. The planners arranged, therefore, that air support should be given by aircraft based in New Caledonia, the New Hebrides, Fiji, Samoa, New Guinea and Australia. But aircraft from bases as far away as New Caledonia, the New Hebrides, Fiji and Samoa would not be able to spend much time over the Solomons, and the amount of support that could be given by aircraft from New Guinea and Australia would depend on the circumstances prevailing in the South-West Pacific Area at the time. It was therefore arranged that additional support should be given by aircraft from the carriers *Saratoga*, *Enterprise* and *Wasp*, which would be accompanied by the battleship *North Carolina*, six cruisers and sixteen destroyers. But the carriers were too valuable to be risked within reach of shore-based aircraft from New Britain and New Ireland once their presence became known to the enemy, so the planners had to agree that the Air Support Force should withdraw after forty-eight hours, when the unloading of equipment and supplies would be only half completed.[11]

The execution of the plan, too, left a lot to be desired. The landings were to have been made on 1 August, but they had to be postponed until 7 August because preparations could not be completed in time for the earlier date to be met. On 21 July Japanese troops began to land on the north coast of Papua. The result was that some of the aircraft with which the South-West Pacific Area Command was to have covered the Solomons for the benefit of the expeditionary force from the South Pacific Sub-Area had to be diverted to other tasks. Nevertheless preparations continued on the assumption that somehow or other enough aircraft to support the landings and the unloading of stores would be found. The arrival of the expeditionary force came as a complete surprise to the Japanese, but was reported to the authorities at Rabaul in New Britain by the troops at Tulagi,[12] who resisted stoutly until they were overcome by sheer weight of numbers on 8 August. The landings on Guadalcanal met no opposition, the Japanese having withdrawn to another part of the island. The sturdy Melanesian inhabitants were loyal to the British and willing to furnish the Americans with information, but the marines did not seize their opportunity of securing a large bridgehead while the enemy was absent. They occupied only a small area which they extended on 8 August to include the partially-completed airfield but not the neighbouring Mount Austen, which according to the plan was to have been captured on the first day. In the meantime equipment and supplies were dumped ashore more or less at random.[13]

The Japanese response was prompt and energetic. Aircraft arrived from New Britain within the first few hours, but were intercepted by fighters from the *Saratoga* and the *Enterprise*. They withdrew with fairly heavy losses after scoring one hit on a destroyer. On the following day a coast-watcher gave eighty minutes' warning of the arrival of forty-three aircraft. Nineteen were shot down by fighters from the *Enterprise*, but a second destroyer was hit and a transport was set on fire.

In the meantime the Japanese commander in New Britain hastily assembled a naval striking force of seven cruisers and one destroyer. It was sighted off Bougainville in the forenoon of 8 August by the Australian crew of a reconnaissance aircraft, but anti-aircraft fire prevented them from closing the range and they mistook it for three cruisers, three destroyers and two seaplane-carriers or gunboats.[14] As they completed a long reconnaissance flight before returning to their base in New Guinea, their report did not reach Guadalcanal until the late afternoon. The reference to seaplane-carriers or gunboats led the commander of the invasion force, Rear-Admiral Richmond K. Turner, to conclude that the Japanese intended to establish a temporary base somewhere in the Northern or Central Solomons and that he could expect an air attack on the following day rather than a night attack by surface craft, for which three cruisers would not suffice.[15] He was not told that a special reconnaissance of the approaches to Guadalcanal which was to have been made for his benefit had been cancelled because of unfavourable weather. Nevertheless eight cruisers and eight destroyers were ordered to patrol to seaward of the transport anchorages during the hours of darkness as a precaution against the unexpected.

Soon after 6 p.m. Admiral Fletcher, commanding the Air Support Force and nominal commander of the entire expeditionary force, proposed in a signal to Admiral Nimitz that, as he had lost twenty-one of his ninety-nine fighters, might be attacked by large numbers of Japanese aircraft and was in danger of running out of fuel, he should withdraw immediately instead of waiting until the stipulated forty-eight hours had expired.[16] He then set off towards the New Hebrides without waiting for a reply. He did not consult Turner, but his signal to Nimitz was intercepted and read aboard Turner's flagship. Turner was appalled by it. After conferring with the commander of the marines and the British commander of the escort force, he decided that the transports, supply-ships and escort and close-support forces should withdraw early on the following day, but that every effort should be made in the meantime to unload essential stores.

Fletcher's decision would seem not to have been justified by anything that had happened, or any intelligence that had been received, up to the time when it was made, though allowance must be made for his knowledge that the loss of his carriers would be a major calamity for the

Allies. Turner's response to it is understandable. As head of the War Plans Division during the planning stage, he had argued that the Air Support Force should stay until unloading was completed, but had failed to persuade his superiors not to sanction its withdrawal after forty-eight hours. Fletcher's unilateral decision to withdraw it after only thirty-six hours confronted him with the hard choice between risking a disaster to the transports and supply-ships and their accompanying warships, and sending them away prematurely.

Turner's conference ended a few minutes before midnight. Meanwhile the Japanese cruiser force, under Vice-Admiral G. Mikawa, was hastening towards its objective. Mikawa expected to reach it about 1 a.m. on 9 August. At 11 p.m. he sent two seaplanes to make a final reconnaissance of the Iron Bottom Sound, where many transports and warships had been reported at noon. Although the night was very dark, one of them was sighted by the lookout of an American destroyer and recognized as an aircraft of a type commonly used as spotters by Japanese cruisers; but atmospherics prevented the destroyer's report from being read aboard Turner's flagship.[7] It was read aboard other Allied warships, but little attention was paid to it, or to less precise reports from other ships of the proximity of unidentified aircraft, in the absence of a warning from Turner. The result was that Mikawa, narrowly escaping detection by a radar-equipped American destroyer as he entered the sound, achieved surprise. With the help of searchlights and of flares dropped by his seaplanes, he sank or disabled four Allied cruisers within an hour, while a fifth departed on a wild-goose chase in pursuit of his only destroyer, which doubled back to the north-east. The transports and supply-ships, thereafter more or less at his mercy, escaped destruction because he then withdrew in the belief that he might be attacked by carrier-borne aircraft if he failed to reassemble his scattered force and retreat to a safe distance before daybreak.

Fletcher, having as yet received no reply from Nimitz, turned back towards Guadalcanal at 1 a.m. About 3 a.m. he received a vague and belated report to the effect that there had been some kind of surface action there. This was followed half-an-hour later by permission to withdraw. He then resumed a south-easterly course without waiting to hear more.

In the light of the night's events, Turner decided early on 9 August to accept the risk of air attack by continuing to disembark stores until the afternoon. The transports, supply-ships and surviving warships then withdrew, leaving the marines with rations for about a month, but with only about half their quota of ammunition, no radar or coast-defence guns, and none of the heavy equipment they were to have used to complete the airfield and build offices and living-quarters. On 15 August four converted destroyers brought bombs, fuel and ammunition. Two days later the airfield was pronounced fit for use in dry weather – not often experienced in the Solomons – and on 20 August a merchant vessel transformed into an escort carrier delivered a first instalment of nineteen fighters and twelve dive-bombers.

The Japanese underestimated the strength of the American expeditionary force even more grossly than the Americans had overestimated that of the Japanese garrison before the landings. At first putting it at no more than 2,000 of all ranks, they concluded that fairly modest reinforcements would suffice to restore the situation. The outcome was a series of hard-fought naval battles precipitated by the attempts of both sides to reinforce or supply their troops. Once the airfield was completed and fully equipped, the Americans generally had the advantage in daylight; at nightfall control of the seaward approaches passed to the Japanese, whose naval forces were better trained than the United States Navy in night fighting and had better torpedoes. Between August 1942 and February 1943 the struggle for Guadalcanal cost the Allies two large fleet carriers, eight cruisers and fourteen destroyers. The Japanese lost two battleships, one light carrier, four cruisers, eleven destroyers and six submarines. On land, intelligence furnished by native troops of the small British Solomon Islands Defence Force raised in peacetime by the British was of some help to the marines in organizing their perimeter and resisting counter-attacks, but they remained pinned to a bridgehead about seven miles wide and less than three miles deep. Early in December their commander was relieved by an army officer of equivalent rank. The 1st Marine Division was then withdrawn to Australia and replaced by part of an infantry division. Further arrivals, including hitherto uncommitted regiments of the 2nd Marine Division, brought the strength of the American garrison in early January to roughly 50,000.

By that time the Japanese had raised the strength of their own garrison to some 25,000, but had come to the conclusion that they could not continue to maintain it except at a price the navy was not prepared to pay. They had therefore decided to withdraw it to New Georgia, in the Central Solomons. The Allies had already noticed on reconnaissance photographs an airfield built there by the Japanese, but they interpreted its construction as evidence that the enemy was preparing not to leave

Guadalcanal but to mount a new series of air attacks on their positions.[18] They also observed the arrival of destroyers sent by the Japanese to take away their remaining troops, but supposed them to be bringing reinforcements. An encircling movement intended by the new American commander to annihilate the enemy was completed thirty-six hours after the last of his troops embarked for New Georgia.

*

The Allies continued throughout the war in the Far East and the Pacific to make a somewhat wayward use of the information furnished by their intelligence agencies, but became increasingly adept at turning the unexpected to good account. They were handicapped to some extent by their lack of a common purpose and the inability of the Combined Chiefs of Staff to enforce the equitable distribution of resources which it was their business to bring about. The British and United States governments had agreed that some items of equipment should be produced mainly in the United States and others mainly in the United Kingdom. An elaborate system of boards and committees was intended to ensure that output was pooled and distributed according to needs, but practice fell short of theory. Not only British but also American commanders outside the Pacific theatre sometimes had great difficulty in obtaining their fair share of American-made equipment (notably assault shipping and transport aircraft) which the American authorities in Washington wished to assign to the Pacific Ocean Area or the South-West Pacific. For much of the war the British front in South-East Asia seemed to most of those who served there a 'forgotten front'. It was not forgotten by the War Cabinet or the British Chiefs of Staff, but their attempts to secure what might have seemed a reasonable degree of priority for its needs were often unsuccessful.

Inevitably, the British and the Americans had different aims. Apart from the fact that command of the sea had long been a bone of contention between them, the British wished to end the threat to India, recapture Burma and Malaya and see the Netherlands East Indies returned to their Dutch allies. The Americans were less than enthusiastic about the restoration of British and Dutch colonial rule in South-East Asia and Indonesia, but determined to recapture the Philippines, prop up the Nationalist régime in China, and fight their way to a suitable point of vantage for the invasion of Japan. These aims they hoped to attain by making convergent thrusts towards Formosa or the mainland of China by way of New Guinea and the Philippines on the left and the Gilbert, Marshall, Caroline and Mariana Islands on the right. The strategy of simultaneous advances along two axes was open to serious objections on grounds of extravagance, but a powerful argument in favour of a thrust to the Marianas was that their capture would bring Japanese industry within reach of American bombers.

Some strategists believed that all this was unnecessary, that the Allies did not need to mount expensive offensives in South-East Asia, the South-West Pacific and the Pacific Ocean Area. Japan had begun the war with barely enough merchant shipping for her peacetime needs. We now know that between the outbreak of hostilities and the end of 1943 she acquired not far short of an additional two million tons from new production and captured or requisitioned vessels, but lost very nearly three million. Thus she suffered a nett loss of more than a million tons. Allied intelligence officers did not have the precise figures before them at the time, but knew that her losses were substantial. They concluded that a situation could arise in which she would have great difficulty in supplying her forces overseas and importing from her newly-acquired territories the raw materials for which she had gone to war. On that basis it could be argued that nothing more was needed to compel her to ask for terms than a redoubled effort by Allied submarines and aircraft against her merchant fleet.

This argument was sound as far as it went, but it did not allow for the possibility that Japan might either substantially increase her output of ocean-going merchant vessels or manage to make do with fewer ships. The former she failed to do. The latter she succeeded in doing by cutting civilian consumption, relying more and more on local produce to feed her troops, carrying essential military equipment in warships or auxiliaries, linking Burma with Siam by a narrow-gauge railway built with forced labour, and in extreme cases even leaving beleaguered garrisons to fend for themselves. In the latter part of the war she was driven to station her major warships where they could be most easily fuelled rather than where they were most needed. We now know that the carrying-capacity of her merchant fleet fell by the summer of 1945 to little more than a quarter of the peacetime figure, yet her troops continued to fight bravely until the end. So doubtless the Allies were right not to rely on maritime blockade alone to bring her to her knees.

Whether the means on which they did rely enabled them to make the best use of their strength and their knowledge of her weaknesses is another matter. The American authorities claimed, with some justice, that their two-pronged offensive put them in a position to keep the enemy guessing and shuttle their major warships between the Pacific Ocean Area and the South-West Pacific. On the other hand, it absorbed what some critics thought was an inordinately high proportion of Allied resources. There was fierce competition for the rest between British forces in South-East Asia, an American-trained and American-led Chinese force on their left, American air forces in China and the organizers of an air-lift to China, to say nothing of Allied forces in the Atlantic and the European and Mediterranean theatres. On the manifold problems of procurement, production and distribution thus engendered was superimposed the problem of keeping Stalin and Chiang Kai-shek supplied. The Western Allies had no effective control over the use made by Chiang Kai-shek of what was sent to him, but were aware that a high proportion of the equipment and supplies he received from them and from the Soviet Union failed to reach his troops. Nor, for that matter, had they any control over the ultimate destination of the enormous tribute levied by Stalin.

The first offensive attempted by the British in South-East Asia was conspicuously unsuccessful. Wavell, viewing the situation in Burma from the standpoint of Delhi, proposed in the summer of 1942 to advance about the end of October to the Chindwin between Homalin in the north and Kalewa in the south, and if all went well to swing his left and centre by the end of the 1942–43 dry season to the Irawaddy, where he hoped to be joined by Chinese troops from Yunnan for an eventual advance to Mandalay, Rangoon and Lower Burma. Under pressure from Churchill, he agreed to undertake only a limited offensive on the Chindwin front and put his main effort into an advance from Chittagong along the coast of Arakan towards the island of Akyab. This was to have been the prelude to a seaborne expedition across the Bay of Bengal, with Rangoon and Bangkok as its ultimate objectives; but eventually the whittling away of Wavell's resources to meet demands from other theatres reduced the operation to an attempt to take Akyab, without the aid of assault craft, from the neighbouring Mayu peninsula. The troops made a creditable advance of about a hundred miles from Chittagong, but were unable to capture the Mayu peninsula in face of opposition from a garrison ordered to hold it at all costs. Wavell's estimate of the enemy's resources was not seriously at fault, but he underestimated the inherent difficulty of the enterprise with the means at his disposal.

In the meantime a reconnaissance party parachuted behind the Japanese lines found that the enemy was very thin on the ground in Northern Burma.[19] An outpost was established in Burmese territory at

Fort Hertz, a disused landing-ground close by was made serviceable, and an infantry company was flown in and afterwards supplied by air from Dinjan, near Ledo in Assam. A project which envisaged the construction of a road through wild country between Ledo and Myitkyina, on the Irawaddy, was then revived, and a plan was made for Chiang Kai-shek's American military adviser, General Stilwell, who had escaped to India when Burma fell, to advance along it in due course with two Chinese divisions which had also reached India from Burma, and to be reinforced by additional Chinese divisions from Yunnan. By the end of 1942 it was, however, clear not only that a long time was likely to elapse before Chiang Kai-shek could be prodded into action, but also that the American engineers who were to build the road would not be able to start until the 1942–43 dry season was almost over.

Wavell had then to consider what should be done with the special long-range penetration force under Orde Wingate (then a lieutenant-colonel but soon to become a brigadier and afterwards a major-general) whose formation he had sanctioned in the summer. Formally designated the 77th Indian Infantry Brigade but generally known as the Chindits, the force consisted essentially of a number of self-contained columns about 300 to 400 strong, each with its own fighting troops, medical, signals and air liaison sections, sabotage group, and platoon of scouts, guides and interpreters. The authorized establishment of each column included fifteen horses, a hundred mules, and small numbers of anti-tank rifles, mortars, heavy and light machine-guns and light anti-aircraft weapons. The purpose for which the brigade was formed was to help Stilwell's advance, and an advance towards the Irawaddy between Katha and Myitkyina by British troops on Stilwell's right, by operating behind the enemy's lines and disrupting his communications. It was also to supply target data for air attacks and exploit 'any opportunities created by its presence within enemy territory'.[20] By the time the Chindits completed their training early in 1943, there was no longer any reasonable prospect of a successful advance to the Irawaddy before the monsoon broke in May. Nevertheless Wavell decided that, in order that their enthusiasm should not be blunted, the Chindits should be allowed to carry out their part of the operation. At the same time he sanctioned the formation of a second long-range penetration brigade, to be called the 111th Indian Infantry Brigade. Both he and Wingate recognized that irregular forces could attain no strategic aim unless they were followed up by regular troops, but felt that a sortie behind the enemy's lines was worth attempting if only for the first-hand knowledge and experience it could be expected to provide.

The Chindits, divided into a Northern and a Southern Group, crossed the Chindwin at two widely-separated points in February. Supplied by air, they spent some weeks behind the Japanese lines and did some damage to communications. Both groups, less elements which turned back early, crossed the Irawaddy, but the Northern Group, led by Wingate in person, did not reach the area where Wingate had told the commander of the Southern Group he would meet him. At the beginning of the last week in March both groups were ordered to disperse, and the troops to make their own way back to base, using methods of survival in which they had been trained. About two-thirds of the three thousand men who had crossed the Chindwin in February returned to India by the first week in June, but many sick or wounded had to be left behind in the hope – not always well founded – that sympathetic villagers would look after them.

Wingate's exploit made a tremendous impression on Churchill and the American Chiefs of Staff. The British military authorities in India were not so enthusiastic. They recognized that Wingate had proved that irregular forces could operate behind the enemy's lines as long as they did not venture beyond the range at which they could be supplied from the air. His experience had also shown that, in any future operation of the kind, provision would have to be made not only for supplies to be flown in, but also for sick, wounded or exhausted men to be flown out. Auchinleck, who succeeded Wavell as Commander-in-Chief when Wavell became Viceroy, was nevertheless obliged to form six long-range penetration groups instead of two, and to meet Wingate's demand for predominantly British troops by breaking up a British division. The Americans formed a long-range penetration force which became known (from the name of its commander) as Merrill's Marauders.

Strategically the most important consequence of the first Chindit operation was that it convinced a newly-appointed commander of the Japanese Fifteenth Army, Lieutenant-General R. Mutaguchi, that his hold on Upper Burma was precarious, and would remain so unless and until he could push his forward positions well beyond the Chindwin. He persuaded his superiors to sanction an updated version of a plan made in 1942 for the capture of Imphal and Kohima, on the Indian side of the frontier with Burma.

The substance of the Japanese plan was that early in 1944 Mutaguchi, with the equivalent of about three-and-a-half divisions, was to advance on Imphal and Kohima from the line of the Chindwin while one division of the Burma Army, on his right, prepared to resist an Allied thrust from Ledo and another guarded his flank and rear against a possible attack by Chinese forces from Yunnan. Three weeks before he launched his offensive, one division of the Twenty-Eighth Army, on his left, was to stage a diversion by attacking and encircling British positions in Arakan. This was the 55th Division, commanded by Lieutenant-General T. Hanaya.

As things turned out, Mutaguchi derived no benefit from the diversion, because he had to await the arrival of reinforcements from Siam and was therefore unable to start before the second week in March. Hanaya was ready by the beginning of February, and dared not delay his attack for more than a few days for fear that, if he did, the British would forestall him.

His offensive, begun under cover of darkness and mist in the early hours of 4 February, achieved tactical but not strategic surprise. Lieutenant-General W. J. Slim, commanding the Fourteenth Army, expected his troops in Arakan to be attacked and their positions to be infiltrated.[21] A study of Japanese tactics had convinced him that in jungle warfare nothing was to be gained from attempts to hold continuous fronts. He impressed upon subordinate commanders that they must be prepared to stand fast even though surrounded, adding that if necessary they would be supplied by air. On 2 February he told his administrative staff to 'start packing day and night' so that they would have supplies ready to be dropped to encircled troops. The result was that, although Hanaya succeeded in getting across the enemy's lines of communication, he was soon in difficulties. From 9 February the invested British received daily deliveries not only of rations and ammunition but also of cigarettes, rum, razor-blades, mail and newspapers. The investing Japanese ran short of supplies, were driven back by a counter-attack, and on 24 February called off their offensive.

By early March the Allies were aware that Mutaguchi was making active preparations for the main attack. Lieutenant-General G. A. P. Scoones, commanding the 4th Corps, proposed to withdraw troops of the 17th Indian Division which were preparing for a limited advance across the Chindwin, and concentrate on holding Imphal and Kohima and assembling the largest possible force for a counter-attack. Slim agreed, but stipulated that the order for withdrawal should not be given until Scoones was satisfied that a major offensive had begun.[22] In the meantime the long warning given by intelligence enabled Scoones to prepare for the withdrawal by dumping supplies along the 17th Indian Division's route, and to stock Imphal and its neighbourhood for a siege.

Japanese patrols appeared on 12 March in rear of the 17th Indian Division's forward positions. On the following day Scoones sanctioned the withdrawal and told the 20th Indian Division, on the 17th Division's left, to hasten the removal of engineer and labour units from vulnerable positions in the frontier area.

The decision to withdraw came as a great surprise to most of the 17th Indian Division. The divisional commander did not issue the order until 1 p.m., and the troops were given until 5 p.m. to start moving. As a result of the slow start and misunderstandings among subordinate commanders, the division had to be reinforced by two brigades from the corps reserve before it could be extricated. To provide a new reserve, Slim arranged for the whole of the 5th Indian Division, with its guns, mules and jeeps, to be flown from Arakan by twenty-five RAF and about twenty American transport aircraft. The American Chiefs of Staff made difficulties about the diversion of resources from the air-lift to China, but Mountbatten (a substantive Captain but an Acting Vice-Admiral and a temporary Admiral) used his authority as Supreme Commander to ensure that Slim did not lose his chance of a decisive success for want of a few aircraft.

The Japanese were handicapped from the start by having to march through rough country where there were few roads suitable for wheeled traffic. Mutaguchi hoped to supply part of his force from Kalewa, on the Chindwin, by using roads which he wrongly believed the British to have made usable in all weathers; the rest would have to depend for at least three weeks on what they carried with them or were fortunate enough to capture. To make matters worse, Mutaguchi had not yet received the whole of his reinforcements from Siam; but he could not afford to postpone the launching of his offensive at the cost of reducing his chances of capturing his objectives before the monsoon broke. As there were no bridges across the Brahmaputra and no broad-gauge railways in the part of India south and east of it, the Allies too faced problems of supply; but they had developed since 1942 an advanced depot at Dimapur capable of handling a thousand tons of stores a day and of accommodating a month's supply for three divisions. It was linked by a good all-weather road with Kohima and Imphal, and by a narrow-gauge railway with Ledo and the terminus of the air-lift to China at Dinjan. Roads and narrow-gauge railways also provided links with river-ports on the south bank of the Brahmaputra. By the time the Japanese reached the Dimapur–Kohima–Imphal road at the end of March and early in April, the Allies had in the Imphal area about 155,000 British and Indian troops with large stocks of ammunition and rations for five weeks. From the middle of April until the end of June these were supplemented by supplies brought by transport aircraft which also flew in about 12,500 troops as reinforcements for the 4th Corps and flew out roughly the same number of sick or wounded and about 43,000 non-combatants. As Mountbatten had predicted when arguing with the Americans about the diversion of transport aircraft, Slim was thus able to employ on a larger scale in Assam and Manipur the tactics he had used so successfully in Arakan. The Allied forces invested at Kohima and threatened with investment in the Imphal area were well supplied, while their Japanese assailants were soon in desperate straits.

Of the three divisions which provided most of the Japanese Fifteenth Army's fighting troops, the most favourably placed was the 33rd, on the Japanese left, since it was able to receive some supplies from Kalewa along fair-weather roads. Even so, its commander recognized by the last week in March that his attempt to encircle the 17th Indian Division had failed. He urged, in vain, that the offensive should be called off. The 31st Division, on the extreme right, received no supplies at all. It managed to reach the Dimapur–Kohima–Imphal road on both sides of Kohima, but failed to subdue the garrison and was strongly counter-attacked. On 25 April its commander flatly refused to part with an infantry regiment for the benefit of the 15th Division on his left. Thereafter his situation became so precarious that he was obliged to retreat under cover of a rearguard action and tell Mutaguchi that the Fifteenth Army's failure to supply him made it impossible for him to carry out his orders. The 15th Division did receive some supplies. It reached the road from Dimapur at a point about twelve miles north-west of Imphal, and also further north, but was unable to do more without the help which the 31st Division refused to give. In the second half of April it went over to the defensive. Although an emissary from Imperial General Headquarters reported in the middle of May that the Fifteenth Army's offensive stood little chance of success, Mutaguchi continued until late in June to hope that the 33rd Division might be able to fight its way to Imphal from the south. He then proposed a general withdrawal, to which Imperial General Headquarters assented early in July. At the end of that month there remained of his army of more than 84,000 of all ranks fewer than 31,000 still fit to march, let alone fight.

The launching of Mutaguchi's offensive coincided with the early stages of a long-delayed attempt by Stilwell's Northern Combat Area Command to advance from Ledo to the northern terminus of the railway from Rangoon at Myitkyina. This was notable for the contributions made to it by irregular forces.

Originally, Stilwell's advance was to have been synchronized with an advance by Chinese forces from Yunnan, limited offensives by the British on the Chindwin front and in Arakan, and an airborne expedition to Indaw – a valuable objective because it was not only linked by surface communications with Rangoon and Myitkyina but also served by two airfields. The Chindits, renamed Special Force, were to have contributed to this programme by helping Stilwell and the troops from Yunnan to get forward, and assisting in the capture of Indaw. The British offensives on the Chindwin front and in Arakan were dropped when intelligence gave warning of the impending Japanese offensives in both areas, and the expedition to Indaw had also to be dropped because the large number of transport aircraft needed to lift an orthodox airborne force of the required strength could not be found. The capture of Indaw by Special Force alone was an attractive possibility, but regular forces would still be needed to hold the place if indeed it could be captured by such means.

The tasks assigned to Special Force when the programme was recast in February 1944 were to help Stilwell, create favourable conditions for an advance by the Chinese from Yunnan, and inflict as much damage, confusion and loss as possible on the enemy's forces in North Burma. Of the six long-range penetration brigades formed up to that time, one (the 16th) was to march by a roundabout route from Assam to the neighbourhood of Indaw; two (the 77th and the 111th) were to be flown to landing-zones east of the Irawaddy. The others (the 14th, 23rd and 3rd West African) were held in reserve 'for relief or exploitation', and would not be at Wingate's disposal unless Slim released them. Advanced parties of the 77th and 111th Brigades were to be carried in towed gliders to the landing-zones and prepare them for the reception of transport aircraft which would bring the rest of the troops, with their equipment and supplies. They would then be held as 'strongholds' with the help of field and anti-aircraft guns additional to the normal establishment of long-range penetration brigades.

The 16th Brigade, commanded by Brigadier B. E. Fergusson, left early in February, but was still a long way from its destination when, on 5 March, an assemblage of notables, which included Wingate and Slim, gathered to watch leading elements of the 77th and 111th Brigades depart. About thirty minutes before zero hour, Wingate was handed reconnaissance photographs which showed that one of the two landing-zones he had chosen was obstructed by felled trees.[23] These were afterwards found to have been put there to dry by foresters who knew nothing of Allied or Japanese intentions. The outcome of a hurried conference was a decision to go ahead with the operation, but at first use only the unobstructed landing-zone. Later a reserve landing-zone was brought into use. About 9,000 men of the two brigades, with 1,300 animals and 250 tons of stores, were flown in by 13 March. Two strongholds were established, and a blocking-position on either side of the railway north of Indaw was occupied. Most of the 111th Brigade joined the 77th at the blocking-position, but part of it moved north to harass the enemy in the Sino-Burmese frontier area between the west bank of the Salween and Myitkyina. Considerable damage was done to the enemy's communications, and counter-attacks were successfully repelled.

The 16th Brigade was not so fortunate. On 20 March Wingate met Fergusson in the field and told him to attack Indaw without delay.[24] Fergusson received the impression that he was to be supported by leading elements of the 14th Brigade, but it is hard to believe that this was what Wingate intended to convey. As early as 8 March, Slim had transferred the 14th and 23rd Brigades to the Fourteenth Army's reserve for possible use in the Imphal operations. It was not until 21 March – the day after his interview with Fergusson – that Wingate persuaded Slim to release the 14th Brigade and allow him to fly it to a landing-zone west of the Irawaddy, where he proposed to establish a new stronghold. Wingate's intention (which apparently he failed to make clear to Slim) was to use the 14th Brigade not to support Fergusson or help Stilwell, but to harass what he believed to be the Japanese 15th Division's line of communication along a track linking Wuntho on the Rangoon–Myitkyina railway with Sittaung on the Chindwin. Notwithstanding allegations of deviousness made by Wingate's critics, it seems unlikely that he intentionally misled either Fergusson or Slim about the role of the 14th Brigade. On the other hand, he was wrong in thinking that the 15th Division was receiving supplies by the Wuntho–Sittaung route.

Fergusson's attempt to capture Indaw and its airfields was unsuccessful. In view of the arrival of the 77th and 111th Brigades in the neighbourhood, it does not seem surprising that the Japanese garrison had been reinforced. The 16th Brigade suffered serious losses.

Wingate was killed on 24 March, when an aircraft in which he was returning from a second visit to Burma crashed in Assam. His successor, Brigadier W. D. A. Lentaigne, at first proposed to use part of Special Force to help Stilwell, part against the Japanese Fifteenth Army's communications. When it became clear that the Fifteenth Army was not receiving supplies by any route within his reach, he decided in consultation with Slim that helping Stilwell must be his main task.[25] The battered 16th Brigade was flown back to India, and arrangements were made for the 77th, 111th and 14th Brigades, joined by the 3rd West African but not the 23rd, to move towards the area Stilwell was approaching.

Stilwell disliked this plan, fearing that the effect would be to draw the enemy to his front.[26] Eventually he agreed that Special Force should go under his command when it reached a point about twenty-five miles from Myitkyina.

Stilwell misemployed the Chindits, as he misemployed Merrill's Marauders, by giving them tasks which could have been tackled with confidence only by orthodox formations with artillery support and secure communications. They held up supplies to the troops opposing Stilwell and pinned down the equivalent of a Japanese division,[27] but these gains were offset by an alarmingly high rate of wastage from combat casualties, sickness and exhaustion. The second Chindit operation – like the first, although for different reasons – was therefore not a fair test of the long-range penetration concept. At the end of a long siege, Stilwell's Chinese formations, British long-range penetration brigades and American composite units succeeded early in August in entering Myitkyina. But they did so only after the Japanese garrison had withdrawn, and at the cost of heavier losses than were inflicted on the British in the whole of the fighting at Imphal and Kohima.

*

In the South-West Pacific Allied aircraft, malnutrition and tropical diseases took a heavy toll of the Japanese force which set out in July 1942 to march from the north coast of Papua to Port Moresby. In September the survivors were halted by the Australians some thirty miles short of their objective. They were then driven back to their starting-point at Buna, and early in 1943 Buna and its immediate neighbourhood were occupied by Allied troops.

The focus of strategic interest in New Guinea then shifted to the Huon peninsula and Nassau Bay, some two hundred miles north-west of Buna. To forestall an Allied move in that direction, the Japanese took steps to strengthen their hold on bases they had established early in the war at Lae, Salamaua and Finchshafen. These were not at first successful. A convoy bound with reinforcements for Lae was spotted by air reconnaissance within twenty-four hours of its departure from Rabaul, with the result that early in March Allied bombers sank all eight of the transports and four of the eight destroyers of which it was composed.[28] Documents carried in sealed tins by survivors captured by the Australians gave a complete order of battle of the Japanese Army.[29] Thereafter supplies and reinforcements had to be sent by submarine, or in powered barges which hugged the coast.

Spoiling attacks on Allied bases by aircraft disembarked from carriers were also unsuccessful. Moreover, the losses they entailed made recovery from the damage done to the Japanese carrier force at Midway doubly difficult.

Finally, signal intelligence revealed to the Allies that two bombers were to carry Admiral Yamamoto and members of his staff to a conference in the Solomons on 18 April. Both aircraft were intercepted and shot down, with the loss of all aboard.

These reverses did not shake the determination of the Japanese that the Seventeenth Army in the Solomons and the Eighteenth Army in New Guinea, supported respectively by the 7th and 6th Air Divisions, should do everything in their power to prevent the Allies from breaking through to the Bismarck archipelago. Naval support would be limited in the first instance to aircraft, cruisers and destroyers, but these could be supplemented, if the need arose, by heavy ships from Truk, in the Caroline Islands.

MacArthur prepared for an offensive due to start at the end of June by forming, without prior consultation with the Australian government or military authorities, an all-American force of approximately corps strength which he called the Alamo Force. His intention was that the Australian New Guinea Force, joined by a small part of the Alamo Force, should drive the enemy from the Huon peninsula and afterwards move in a westerly direction towards the frontier between Australian-administered and Dutch-administered New Guinea. The main body of the Alamo Force was to occupy Kirina and Woodlark Islands, in the Trobriand group between New Guinea and the Solomons, as the prelude to landings in the western part of New Britain. In the Solomons forces controlled ultimately by MacArthur, but under the tactical command of Vice-Admiral W. F. Halsey, were to capture the islands of the New Georgia group and continue to the Northern Solomons, administratively part of the mandated Territory of New Guinea.

Originally MacArthur had hoped to take Rabaul. Intelligence reports indicated that Rabaul was strongly held but that the Admiralty Islands were not, although the natural harbour adjoining the main island of Manus was one of the finest in the world. The Joint Chiefs of Staff therefore directed MacArthur to go straight to the Admiralty Islands once both shores of the Vitiaz Strait (between New Guinea and New Britain) were in his hands. Rabaul was to be 'neutralized' by encirclement.

While preparations for this three-pronged offensive, and for a separate offensive in the Central Pacific, were going forward, substantial forces were diverted on political rather than strategic grounds to the recapture of Attu and Kiska, in the Aleutians. About 2,500 Japanese held out for a fortnight against an American division which landed on Attu on 11 May under cover of a bombardment by three battleships. Kiska was rightly believed to be more strongly held, but fog helped the 5,000 Japanese there to withdraw without detection on the night of 15 July. Heavy bombardments were wasted on positions no longer occupied by the enemy before some 30,000 American and 5,000 Canadian troops went ashore in dismal weather, to be greeted by three yellow dogs which barked defiance at them. They spent five days searching the island before they were satisfied that the enemy had gone.

In the South-West Pacific the jungle, rather than the weather, was the chief obstacle to observation of the enemy's positions. Sites cleared by the Japanese, even though camouflaged, could usually be seen on air photographs, but these did not always show whether they were active. On the other hand, the Allies gained a good deal from operating largely in territory only sparsely occupied by the enemy. The Alamo Force occupied Kirina and Woodlark Islands at the end of June without opposition. The American infantry regiment which landed at the same time south of Salamaua met little resistance in the early stages, and was guided ashore by Australian forces already present. About ten days before Halsey's assault on the main island of New Georgia was due Major D. G. Kennedy, an officer of the British Solomon Islands Protectorate Defence Force who was acting as coast-watcher in the southern part of the island, reported that the Japanese were active in his area and were closing in on him. Halsey thereupon disembarked four companies of infantry and marines ahead of schedule, thus gaining some degree of tactical surprise. Marines and infantrymen who afterwards landed in the northern part of the island were met by a party of 200 Melanesian porters organized by an Australian coast-watcher, Flight-Lieutenant J. A. Corrigan. Troops raised locally and commanded by Major M. Clemens, also of the British Solomon Islands Protectorate Defence Force, joined the Americans in capturing the adjacent island of Rendova.

In general, the policy of the Japanese Seventeenth Army was to offer little more than token resistance on the beaches and concentrate on preparing for counter-attacks by running reinforcements and stores to the Central Solomons in warships. The outcome was a series of naval actions not unlike those precipitated by the expedition to Guadalcanal in the previous year. These reached something of a climax on the night of 6 August, when six American destroyers surprised a Japanese destroyer flotilla and sank three of its four destroyers at no cost to themselves. A week later the last of the outnumbered garrison of the main island of New Georgia withdraw northwards to Kolombangara. On 15 August the Americans, adopting the leapfrogging strategy which they afterwards used with great success, made an unopposed landing on Vella Lavella, still further to the north. The Japanese held out in the Central Solomons until the end of September and then withdrew their surviving troops to the large island of Bougainville, garrisoned by an infantry division, four independent battalions and some 20,000 marines. Allied landings at the beginning of November were followed by a prolonged stalemate which had no adverse effect on MacArthur's subsequent operations.

In New Guinea the purpose of the Allied advance from Nassau Bay was to push the Japanese back to Salamaua and hold them there while preparations were made for a major assault on Lae. In the early hours of 4 September the main body of the Australian 9th Division, making the first landings by Australian troops in enemy-held territory since Gallipoli, was put ashore on two beaches east of Lae by an American naval task force. On the following day American paratroops, accompanied by an Australian artillery detachment and followed by American and Australian engineers, seized a disused airfield at Nadzab, north-west of Lae. The Australian 7th Division was then flown in. By 16 September both Lae and Salamaua were in Allied hands, and Australian troops were pushing in a north-westerly direction towards the head-waters of the Markham River and the Bismarck Sea.

A further landing had then to be made north of Finchshafen, and a large tract of mountainous country to be cleared of the enemy. The landing was successful, but was soon followed by indications that a newly-arrived infantry regiment, joined by units which had retreated from Lae, Salamaua and Finchshafen, was preparing for a counter-attack. These culminated in the capture on 15 October of an order to the effect that a bonfire on a prominent hilltop would give the signal for its launching. Probing attacks in daylight on 16 October suggested that the offensive was imminent, but such heavy rain began to fall towards nightfall that the Australians doubted whether the bonfire could be kindled. During the night and in the early hours of the following day the Japanese launched two attacks from the west and also succeeded in putting a few specially-picked troops ashore from barges. The attacks were repelled with some difficulty, and a counter-attack restored the situation.

The Japanese then withdrew to the neighbourhood of Madang (140 miles north-west of Lae) under cover of a holding action in mountainous country to the south of it. Although the formal order for the withdrawal was not issued until 4 January 1944, by the end of 1943 they were so obviously in full retreat that on 2 January an American task force landed in an intermediate position at Saidor to cut them off. Thousands escaped along jungle tracks skirting Saidor on the south, but the pursuing Australians killed 734, found 1,793 dead, and took 48 prisoners at a cost to themselves of three killed and five wounded.

In the meantime MacArthur secured the far side of the Vitiaz Strait by disembarking troops in the western part of New Britain. Originally he intended to synchronize landings in the Admiralty Islands with an assault by Halsey's forces on Kavieng, in New Ireland, but the Joint Chiefs of Staff accepted a proposal from Halsey that Kavieng, like Rabaul, should be by-passed. As a contribution to their encirclement, Halsey made an unopposed landing on Emirau Island, north-west of New Ireland.

MacArthur's assault on the Admiralty Islands was scheduled for the beginning of April. The strength of the Japanese garrison was estimated at 4,600 – rather more than the true figure – but the crew of a reconnaissance aircraft which flew low over the islands on 23 February reported no signs of Japanese occupation.[30] MacArthur thereupon ordered a reconnaissance in force of the small island of Los Negros, hoping to seize it by a *coup de main* and use it as a stepping-stone to Manus. A six-man team which made a preliminary reconnaissance after landing without detection on 27 February signalled, however, that the island was 'lousy with Japs'.[31] Nevertheless about a thousand American troops, accompanied by twenty-five Australian officers and other ranks and twelve Papuan policemen, began the reconnaissance in force two days later. By 9 March an Australian fighter squadron was operating from an airstrip captured on the first day. The whole of the Admiralty Islands were soon in Allied hands, although mopping-up continued until May.

These operations effectively cut off about 140,000 Japanese troops in New Britain, New Ireland and Bougainville. Survivors who did not succumb to malnutrition or tropical diseases spent the rest of the war keeping starvation at bay by fishing and growing vegetables.

New instructions given to MacArthur in the meantime directed him to devote 'minimum forces' to the containment of Rabaul and Kavieng, hasten the development of naval and air bases in the Admiralty Islands, and after clearing the Japanese from Madang and its neighbourhood leap forward into Dutch New Guinea. There he was to establish an 'air centre' from which the Japanese-held islands to the west and north-west of New Guinea could be attacked by heavy bombers. In the Central Pacific Admiral Nimitz was to occupy the southern part of the Marianas about the middle of June, by-pass Truk, and come in on the right of MacArthur's advance by reaching the western part of the Caroline Islands in September: The general intention was that Mindanao in the Philippines should be occupied about the middle of November as the prelude to an advance early in 1945 to Formosa, either directly from Mindanao or by way of Luzon. No role was allotted in this programme to the strong fleet which the British wished to send to the Pacific as soon as the war with Germany was over. At the Octagon Conference at Quebec in September 1944 Roosevelt ruled, however, that Churchill's offer of a fleet to serve under Nimitz should be accepted without question.[32]

These plans were made in the light of a good general knowledge of the enemy's intentions, as revealed by signal intelligence. Accurate assessment of Japanese strength in scores of Pacific Islands, many of them occupied by Japanese troops since World War I, was another matter. The Americans, with the advantage of growing naval and air superiority, solved the problem by assaulting only a few islands in each group, leaving the rest to take care of themselves. In this way, and with the help of a vast fleet train which enabled them to keep their heavy ships at sea for long periods, they seized as much as they needed of the Gilbert Islands in November 1943, of the Marshall Islands early in 1944, of the Marianas between June and August of that year. Their capture of Saipan on 9 July was followed by political developments in Tokyo which brought to power a government committeed to an attempt to reconcile the aims of army officers who wanted to continue the war with those of civilians and naval officers who thought Japan should now aim at a negotiated peace.

In New Guinea the Japanese began in the second half of March 1944 what was intended to be a gradual retreat to Dutch New Guinea under cover of a rearguard action at Madang. Much heavy equipment had to be left behind and was captured by the Australians, who entered Madang on 24 April to find that even the rearguard had gone.

MacArthur then relegated the Australian New Guinea Force to minor tasks and prepared, with the United States Sixth Army under command, to establish himself in strength in a remote Dutch colony of which most Europeans and Americans were profoundly ignorant, and whose interior was mostly unknown territory even to the few hundred white residents who had settled on or near the coast.[33] Hollandia, where the Japanese Eighteenth Army hoped to concentrate its forces after their withdrawal across the frontier, was chosen as the site of the great base MacArthur had been ordered to establish, chiefly because the neighbouring Humboldt Bay was the only first-class natural harbour in Dutch New Guinea east of Geelvink Bay, some 400 miles to the west.

The Japanese were known to have established three airfields, and to be building a fourth, near Lake Sentani, about ten miles west of Hollandia. They also had airfields rather more than a hundred miles further west, in the neighbourhood of Sarmi and Wakde Island, and on the Australian side of the frontier at Aitape and Wewak. MacArthur aimed at seizing Aitape by a seaborne assault at the same time as his troops landed in Humboldt Bay and some twenty to thirty miles further west, in Tanahmera Bay.

During the night of 23 March an American submarine put six Australian scouts, four natives of New Guinea and an Indonesian interpreter ashore in Tanahmera Bay for a preliminary reconnaissance. They were cornered by Japanese troops, and only five of them survived. A consequent lack of local knowledge might have proved disastrous if the main landings on 22 April had found the Japanese well prepared. As things were, they were at a serious disadvantage. None of their troops retreating from Australian New Guinea had yet crossed the frontier. At Aitape there were about a thousand Japanese, of whom fewer than a quarter were combatants. The commander at Hollandia, a newcomer, had one division and some indifferent garrison troops with which to give effect to a plan still under discussion. The airfield at Aitape was captured for the loss of two Americans killed and thirteen wounded. At Humboldt Bay the defenders were so shaken by a preliminary bombardment that resistance was slight. At Tanahmera Bay there was no opposition, and this was fortunate because one of the two beaches chosen for the landings was found to be fringed by an impassable swamp, while the other was accessible only at high tide and had no exit except a track too steep and narrow to be used by military vehicles.

By 26 April all the Lake Sentani airfields were in Allied hands, but they proved unsuitable for heavy bombers. Besides seizing Wakde Island and transforming Hollandia into a fully-equipped base with accomodation for 140,000 men, MacArthur therefore sent an expedition to Biak Island, at the mouth of Geelvink Bay, where he hoped to find airfields that would meet the case.

The outcome was a struggle which cost the Americans heavy combat losses and severe wastage from disease. Japanese attempts to reinforce Biak Island from the Philippines were unsuccessful, but a garrison much larger than the Allied estimate put up a tremendous fight.

MacArthur's campaigns in New Guinea culminated at the end of July in the capture of objectives at its western extremity. In the meantime signal intelligence gave warning of an impending attack on the American perimeter east of Aitape by some 20,000 to 30,000 survivors of the Eighteenth Army.[34] An assault launched on 10 July carried them forward about four miles before they were driven back and pinned between the Americans to the west of them and Australian and Papuan forces in their rear.

The Allied programme called next for simultaneous assaults by MacArthur's forces on Morotai (about half-way between the western extremity of New Guinea and Mindanao) and by forces under Nimitz on Pelelieu, at the western edge of the Carolines. Morotai was captured without much difficulty. Pelelieu proved a much harder nut to crack because air reconnaissance did not reveal elaborate defence-works constructed by the garrison with the help of natural caves. Ulithi, also in the Western Carolines, was occupied without opposition.

In the meantime the Joint Chiefs of Staff proposed on the initiative of Nimitz and MacArthur, and the Combined Chiefs of Staff agreed at the Octagon Conference, that after the capture of Morotai and Pelelieu MacArthur should by-pass Mindanao and go straight to Leyte. At the beginning of October they settled a controversial issue by decreeing that Luzon, not Formosa, should be the next objective after Leyte. Nimitz was to push towards Japan by capturing Iwojima and Okinawa, and plans were to be made for an eventual landing on the coast of China north of Formosa, and for an invasion of the Japanese homeland during the winter of 1945–46.

In the following month preparations for the bombing of Japan by aircraft from the Marianas were completed after a long delay. The American authorities hoped to knock out nine aircraft or aero-engine factories believed to be of cardinal importance to the enemy, but these proved very hard to hit from heights of the order of 30,000 feet. Damage-assessment reports indicated that by the end of 1944 only one had suffered major damage. Although we now know that the Japanese considered the threat to their aircraft industry far from negligible, the Americans switched, as the British had done where Germany was concerned, to area attacks. These, and also the erosion of their merchant fleet, caused the Japanese so much anxiety that they no longer hoped to do much more than defend their homeland so resolutely that the Allies might perhaps accept a negotiated settlement rather than risk the losses an invasion of the main Japanese islands must entail.

Early in 1945 Koiso, discredited by his government's inability to defend Japan against area attacks and by Allied progress in the Pacific, laid down his office. He was succeeded by the seventy-nine-year-old Admiral Suzuki, President of the Privy Council. Enquiries had already been made of the Swedish Minister in Tokyo about the chances of a negotiated peace.[35] The new Foreign Minister, Shigenori Togo, preferred an approach to the Russians. He denounced the Anti-Comintern Pact, declared after the German surrender that the Tripartite Pact had ceased to be effective, and urged the Soviet government through diplomatic channels to act as mediator between Japan and the Western Allies. As Togo's messages to the Japanese Ambassador in Moscow were decrypted by Allied signal intelligence and the Ambassador's attempts to enlist the aid of the Soviet government were mentioned by Stalin at the Potsdam Conference, the Allies were well aware before the first atomic bomb was dropped that nothing stood in the way of a negotiated peace except the difficulty of reconciling their declared intention of demanding unconditional surrender with the determination of the Japanese to seek terms which would preserve the monarchy.[36] Their decision to drop the bomb must be judged in the light not only of their genuine wish to escape the heavy losses they expected to incur if they invaded the Japanese homeland, but also of this knowledge and the knowledge that the Russians were making active preparations to join the war against Japan.

Bibliography

Official Histories

Australian

DEXTER, David: *The New Guinea Offensives*. Canberra: Australian War Memorial, 1961

LONG, Gavin: *To Benghazi*. Canberra: Australian War Memorial, 1952

— *Greece, Crete and Syria*. Canberra: Australian War Memorial, 1953

— *The Final Campaigns*. Canberra: Australian War Memorial, 1963

MCCARTHY, Dudley: *South-West Pacific Area, First Year*. Canberra: Australian War Memorial, 1959

MAUGHAM, Barton: *Tobruk and El Alamein*. Canberra: Australian War Memorial, 1966

WIGMORE, Lionel: *The Japanese Thrust*. Canberra: Australian War Memorial, 1951

British (UK)

BUTLER, J. R. M.: *Grand Strategy Volume II*. London: HMSO, 1957

— *Grand Strategy Volume III, Part II*. London: HMSO, 1964

COLLIER, Basil: *The Defence of the United Kingdom*. London: HMSO, 1957.

DERRY, T. K.: *The Campaign in Norway*. London: HMSO, 1952

EHRMAN, John: *Grand Strategy Volume V. Grand Strategy Volume VI*. Both London: HMSO, 1956

ELLIS, Major L. F.: *The War in France and Flanders, 1939–1940*. London: HMSO, 1954

— *Victory in the West: I The Battle of Normandy*. London: HMSO, 1962

— *Victory in the West: II The Defeat of Germany*. London: HMSO, 1968

FOOT, M. R. D.: *SOE in France*. London: HMSO, 1966

FRANKLAND, Noble: See WEBSTER, Sir Charles

GOWING, Margaret: *Britain and Atomic Energy, 1939–1945*. London: HMSO and Longmans, Green, 1964

GWYER, J. M. A.: *Grand Strategy Volume III, Part I*. London: HMSO, 1964

HINSLEY, F. H. (with E. E. Thomas, C. F. G. Ransom and R. C. Knight: *British Intelligence in the Second World War*. vol. i. London: HMSO, 1979

— *British Intelligence in the Second World War*. vol. ii. London: HMSO, 1981

KIRBY, Maj.-Gen. S. W.: *The War Against Japan*. 4 vols. London: HMSO, 1957–1965

KNIGHT, R. C.: See HINSLEY, F. H.

MARSHALL, Howard: *Grand Strategy Volume IV.* London: HMSO, 1972

MEDLICOTT, W. M. *The Economic Blockade.* 2 vols. London: HMSO and Longmans, Green, 1952 and 1959

PLAYFAIR, Maj.-Gen. I. S. O.: *The Mediterranean and Middle East.* vols. i–iv. London: HMSO, 1956–1962

RANSOM, C. F. G.: See HINSLEY, F. H.

ROSKILL, S. W.: *The War at Sea.* 3 vols. in 4 parts. London: HMSO, 1954–1961

THOMAS, E. E.: See HINSLEY, F. H.

WEBSTER, Sir Charles, and FRANKLAND, Noble: *The Strategic Air Offensive Against Germany.* 4 vols. London: HMSO, 1961

WOODWARD, Sir Llewellyn: *British Foreign Policy during the Second World War.* One-volume edition. London: HMSO, 1962

Canadian

NICHOLSON, Lt.-Col. G. W. L.: *The Canadians in Italy, 1943–1945.* Ottawa: Queen's Printer and Controller of Stationery, 1957

STACEY, Col. C. P.: *Six Years of War: The Army in Canada, Britain and the Pacific.* Ottawa: Queen's Printer and Controller of Stationery, 1955

— *The Victory Campaign: The Operations in North-West Europe, 1944–1945.* Ottawa: Queen's Printer and Controller of Stationery, 1960

New Zealand

DAVIN, D. M.: *Crete.* Wellington: War History Branch, Department of Internal Affairs, 1953

United States

CATE, James L.: See CRAVEN, Wesley F.

COAKLEY, R. W.: See LEIGHTON, R. M.

COLE, Hugh M.: *The Ardennes: The Battle of the Bulge.* Washington: Office of the Chief of Military History, 1965

CRAVEN, Wesley F., and CATE, James L. (editors): *The Army Air Forces in World War II.* 6 vols. Chicago: University of Chicago Press, 1948–1955

CROWL, Philip A.: *The Campaign in the Marianas.* Washington: Office of the Chief of Military History, 1960

CROWL, Philip A., and LOVE, Edmund G.: *Seizure of the Gilberts and Marshalls.* Washington: Office of the Chief of Military History, 1955

LEIGHTON, R. M., and COAKLEY, R. W. *Global Logistics and Strategy, 1940–1943.* Washington: Office of the Chief of Military History, 1959

— *Global Logistics and Strategy, 1943–1945.* Washington: Office of the Chief of Military History, 1968

LOVE, Edmund G.: See CROWL, Philip A.

MATLOFF, Maurice: *Strategic Planning for Coalition Warfare, 1943–1944.* Washington: Office of the Chief of Military History, 1959

MATLOFF, Maurice, and SNELL, E. M.: *Strategic Planning for Coalition Warfare, 1941–1942.* Washington: Office of the Chief of Military History, 1953

MILLER, John, Jr.: *Guadalcanal: The First Offensive.* Washington: Historical Division, Department of the Army, 1949

MILNER, Samuel: *Victory in Papua.* Washington: Office of the Chief of Military History, 1957

MORISON, Samuel Eliot: *The History of United States Naval Operations in World War II.* 15 vols. Boston: Little, Brown, 1947–1962. Volumes consulted:

   iii *The Rising Sun in the Pacific, 1931–April 1942*
   iv *Coral Sea, Midway and Submarine Actions, May 1942–August 1942*
   v *The Struggle for Guadalcanal, August 1942–February 1943*
   vi *Breaking the Bismarck Barrier, 22 July 1942–1 May 1944*
   vii *Aleutians, Gilberts and Marshalls, June 1943–April 1944*
   viii *New Guinea and the Marianas, March 1944–April 1944*
   xii *Leyte, June 1944–January 1945*
   xiii *The Liberation of the Philippines: Luzon, Mindanao, the Visayas, 1944–1945*
   xiv *Victory in the Pacific, 1945*

MORTON, Louis: *The Fall of the Philippines.* Washington: Historical Division, Department of the Army, 1948

— *Strategy and Command: The First Two Years.* Washington: Office of the Chief of Military History, 1962

RENTZ, John R. *Bougainville and the Northern Solomons.* Washington: Historical Division, Department of the Army, 1948

— *Marines in the Central Solomons.* Washington: Office of the Chief of Military History, 1952

SMITH, R. R. *The Approach to the Philippines.* Washington: Office of the Chief of Military History, 1955

SNELL, E. M.: See MATLOFF, Maurice

WATSON, Mark: *Chief of Staff: Prewar Plans and Preparations.* Washington: Historical Division, Department of the Army, 1950

Other Published Works

Apart from official histories, so many books and articles have been written since 1945 about a variety of clandestine activities (and in recent years about one aspect of signal intelligence), that a bibliography which aimed at anything like completeness would fill a volume. On the other hand, the list would be quite short if it included only works whose accuracy can be attested.

Again excluding official histories, I think most books on these subjects can be assigned to one or other of the following classes:

1 Reminiscences whose authorship promises important revelations, but which don't really tell us very much except that the author thinks that, on the whole, he and his associates did a good job. Major-General Strong's *Intelligence at the Top* seems to me to fall into this category.

2 Reminiscences which do lift the curtain on matters previously shrouded in secrecy but which, although based on first-hand knowledge, are not always accurate, usually because they were written without access to documentary records. To this class must be assigned Group Captain Winterbotham's highly entertaining but far from reliable *The Ultra Secret.*

3 First-hand accounts of escapes, evasions, or clandestine missions in the

field. These are seldom buttressed with documentary evidence and often inaccurate, but the best of them give a vivid impression of the atmosphere in which clandestine operations were conducted.

4 Accounts of similar experiences written at second hand, but in consultation with the person whose adventures are described. These are sometimes more accurate than first-hand accounts, because the author has not relied solely on the subject's recollections and has gone to some trouble to check his statements. Bruce Marshall's *The White Rabbit* is as exciting as any first-hand account of an agent's experiences could be, and probably more accurate than most.

5 Special studies such as Dallin's *Soviet Espionage* and Kahn's *The Code-breakers*. The value of such books, based as a rule on research rather than direct experience, is largely a function of the extent to which the author has managed to steer clear of unreliable sources.

6 Studies of the influence on Allied operations of intelligence derived from the breaking of high-grade machine-cyphers ('Ultra'). As the authors of these studies do not profess to be concerned with anything but Ultra, it is not their fault that unwary readers may receive a somewhat distorted impression of the role of signal intelligence.

7 Works which reflect both first-hand knowledge of the matters discussed and a fairly extensive acquaintance with documentary sources. Two books which fall into this category are Dr R. V. Jones's *Most Secret War* and Sir John Masterman's *The Double-Cross System*. Others which bear the stamp of authenticity include Patrick Beesley's *Very Special Intelligence*, and *Master of Spies*, by Frantisek Moravec. Moravec is said to have relied largely on an exceptionally good memory, but many of his statements are confirmed by the documentary record.

The list below includes a somewhat arbitrary selection of works drawn from all seven of these classes. It also includes works consulted for background material. All published works referred to in the notes are included.

AMRINE, Michael: *The Great Decision*. London: Heinemann, 1960

ASTIER DE LA VIGERIE, Emmanuel d': *Seven Times Seven Days*. London: MacGibbon and Kee, 1958

AVON, The Earl of: *Full Circle*. London: Cassell, 1960

— *Facing the Dictators*. London: Cassell, 1962

— *The Reckoning*. London: Cassell, 1965

BABINGTON SMITH, Constance: *Evidence in Camera*. London: Chatto, 1957

BARKER, R. *Aviator Extraordinary*. [Sidney Cotton] London: Chatto, 1969

BARNETT, Correlli: *The Desert Generals*. London: Kimber, 1960

BEAMISH, John: *Burma Drop*. London: Elek Books, 1958

BEESLEY, Patrick: *Very Special Intelligence*. London: Hamish Hamilton, 1977

BELOFF, Max: *The Foreign Policy of Soviet Russia, 1929–1941*. 2 vols. London: Oxford University Press, 1947–1949

BENNETT, Ralph: *Ultra in the West: The Normandy Campaign, 1944–45*. London: Hutchinson, 1979

BERTRAND, Gustave: *Enigma, ou la plus grande énigme de la guerre 1939–1945*. Paris: Plon, 1973

BLEICHER, Hugo: *Colonel Henri's Story*. London: Kimber, 1954

BRADLEY, General Omar H.: *A Soldier's Story*. London: Eyre and Spottiswoode, 1951

BUCKMASTER, M. J.: *Specially Employed*. London: Batchworth, 1952

— *They Fought Alone*. London: Odhams, 1958

BULLOCK, Alan: *Hitler: A Study in Tyranny*. London: Odhams, 1952

BUNDY, McG.: See STIMSON, H. L.

BURNS, J. M. *Roosevelt: The Lion and the Fox*. London: Secker and Warburg, 1957

BUTLER, Ewan: *Amateur Agent*. London: Harrap, 1963

CALVOCORESSI, Peter: *Top Secret Ultra*. London: Cassell, 1980

CALVOCORESSI, Peter, and WINT, Guy: *Total War*. London: Allen Lane, 1972

CARRÉ, Mathilde-Lily: *I Was The Cat*. London: Four Square, 1961

CHURCHILL, Winston S.: *The Second World War*. 6 vols. London: Cassell, 1948–1959

CLARK, Ronald W.: *The Birth of the Bomb*. London: Phoenix House, 1961

— *The Man Who Broke Purple*. London: Weidenfeld and Nicolson, 1977

CLAYTON, Eileen: *The Enemy is Listening*. London: Hutchinson, 1980

COLVIN, Ian: *Vansittart in Office*. London: Gollancz, 1965

CONNELL, John: *Auchinleck*. London: Cassell, 1959

COWBURN, Benjamin: *No Cloak, No Dagger*. London: Jarrolds, 1960

CRUICKSHANK, C. *The Fourth Arm: Psychological Warfare, 1938–1945*. London: Davis-Poynter, 1977

DALLIN, David J.: *Soviet Espionage*. New Haven/London: Yale University Press/Oxford University Press, 1955

DEAKIN, F. W., and STORRY, G. R.: *The Case of Richard Sorge*. London: Chatto, 1966

DULLES, Allen W.: *The Secret Surrender*. London: Weidenfeld and Nicolson, 1967

ERICKSON, John: *The Road to Stalingrad*. London: Weidenfeld and Nicolson, 1975

FARRAN, Roy: *Winged Dagger*. London: Collins, 1948

FEIS, H.: *The Road to Pearl Harbor*. Princeton: University Press, 1950

— *The China Tangle*. Princeton: University Press, 1953

— *Churchill, Roosevelt, Stalin*. Princeton: University Press, 1957

FERGUSSON, Bernard: *Beyond the Chindwin*. London: Collins, 1945

— *The Wild Green Earth*. London: Collins, 1946

FOOT, M. R. D.: *Resistance: An Analysis of European Resistance to Nazism, 1940–1945*. London: Eyre Methuen, 1976. (Includes brief references to events outside Europe.)

FOOT, M. R. D., and LANGLEY, J. M.: *MI 9: The British secret service that fostered escape and evasion 1939–1945 and its American counterpart*. London: The Bodley Head, 1979

FOOTE, Alexander: *Handbook for Spies*. London: Museum Press, 1949

FOURCADE, M.-M.: *Noah's Ark*. London: Allen and Unwin, 1973

GARLINSKI, Josef: *Intercept: the Enigma War*. London: Dent, 1979

GAUCHÉ, Général: *Le Deuxième Bureau au Travail*. Paris: Amiot-Dumont, 1953

GISKES, H. J.: *London Calling North Pole*. London: Kimber, 1953

GOUTARD, Colonel A.: *The Battle of France*. London: Frederick Muller, 1958

GREATOREX, Wilfred: See URQUHART, Major-General R. E.

GROUEFF, Stéphane: *Manhattan Project*. London: Collins, 1967

HARRIS, Marshal of the RAF Sir Arthur: *Bomber Offensive*. London: Collins, 1947

HASWELL, Major Chetwynd J. D.: *The Intelligence and Deception of the D-Day Landings*. London: Batsford, 1979

HAUKELID, Knut: *Skis Against the Atom*. London: Kimber, 1954

HENDERSON, Sir Nevile: *Failure of a Mission: Berlin, 1937–1939*. London: Hodder and Stoughton, 1940

HEYDTE, Baron von der: *Daedalus Returned: Crete 1941*. London: Hutchinson, 1958

HÖHNE, Heinz, and ZOLLING, Hermann: *Network*. London: Secker and Warburg, 1972. Also published as *The General Was A Spy*. London: Pan Books, 1973

IRVING, David: *The Rise and Fall of the Luftwaffe*. London: Weidenfeld and Nicolson, 1974

JACKSON, Robert: *Air War Over France, May–June, 1940*. Shepperton: I. Allan, 1974

JEFFREYS-JONES, R.: *American Espionage: From Secret Service to CIA*. New York/London: The Free Press (Macmillan)/Collier Macmillan, 1977

JONES, F. C.: *Japan's New Order in East Asia*. London: Oxford University Press, 1954

JONES, R. V.: *Most Secret War*. London: Hamish Hamilton, 1978

JORDAN, George Racey (with Richard L. Stokes): *From Major Jordan's Diaries*. New York: Harcourt Brace, 1952. Also Belmont, Massachusetts: Western Islands, 1965

KAHN, David: *The Codebreakers: The Story of Secret Writing*. London: Weidenfeld and Nicolson, 1966

KING HALL, S.: *My Naval Life, 1906–1929*. London: Faber, 1952

KLEIN, B. H. *Germany's Preparations for War*. London: Oxford University Press, 1959

LANGELAAN, George: *Knights of the Floating Silk*. London: Hutchinson, 1959

LANGER, William L.: *Our Vichy Gamble*. New York: Knopf, 1947

LANGLEY, J. M.: See FOOT, M. R. D.

LEVERKUEHN, P.: *German Military Intelligence*. London: Weidenfeld and Nicolson, 1954

LEWIN, Ronald: *Ultra Goes to War*. London: Hutchinson, 1978

LIDDELL HART, B. H.: *The Other Side of the Hill*. London: Cassell, 1951

— (Editor). *The Rommel Papers*. London: Cassell, 1953

— *History of the Second World War*. London: Cassell, 1970

LORD, Walter: *Day of Infamy*. London: Longmans, 1957

McLACHLAN, D.: *Room 39*. London: Weidenfeld and Nicolson, 1968

MARSHALL, Bruce: *The White Rabbit*. [F. F. E. Yeo-Thomas] London: Evans, 1952

MASTERMAN, J. C.: *The Double-Cross System in the War of 1939–1945*. New Haven and London: Yale University Press, 1972

MEAD, Peter: Article, 'Orde Wingate and the Official Historians' in *Journal of Contemporary History*, vol. 14. London and Beverly Hills: SAGE, 1979

MILLAR, George: *Maquis*. London: Heinemann, 1945
— *Horned Pigeon*. London: Heinemann, 1946
MILWARD, A. S.: *The German Economy at War*. London: Athlone Press, 1965
MONTAGU, Ewen: *The Man Who Never Was*. London: Evans, 1953
— *Beyond Top Secret U*. London: Peter Davies, 1977
MORAVEC, Frantisek: *Master of Spies: The Memoirs of General Frantisek Moravec*. London: The Bodley Head, 1975
MORISON, Samuel Eliot: *The Two-Ocean War*. Boston: Little, Brown, 1963
NAVARRE, Henri: *Le Service Renseignements, 1871–1944*. Paris: Plon, 1978
NEAVE, Airey: *Saturday at MI 9*. London: Hodder and Stoughton, 1953
NICHOLAS, Elizabeth: *Death Be Not Proud*. London: Cresset Press, 1946
PAILLOLE, Paul: *Services spéciaux (1935–1945)*. Paris: Robert Laffont, 1975
PINTO, Oreste: *The Spycatcher Omnibus*. London: Hodder and Stoughton, 1962. Includes *Spycatcher* (first published 1955) with *Spycatcher 2* and *Spycatcher 3*.
PRITTIE, T.: *Germans Against Hitler*. London: Hutchinson, 1964
RADO, Sandor: *Codename Dora*. London: Abelard, 1977
ROSKILL, S. W.: *The Navy at War*. London: Collins, 1960
ROTHFELS, Hans: *The German Opposition to Hitler: An Assessment*. London: Wolff, 1961
RYAN, Cornelius: *A Bridge Too Far*. London: Hamish Hamilton, 1974
SANSOM, G. B.: *The Western World and Japan*. London: Cresset Press, 1950
SCHRÖTER, Heinz: *Stalingrad*. London: Michael Joseph, 1958
SCHWARZ, Urs: *American Strategy: A New Perspective*. New York: Doubleday, 1966
SHERWOOD, Robert E.: *The White House Papers of Harry L. Hopkins*. 2 vols. London: Eyre and Spottiswoode, 1948–1949
SHIRER, W.: *The Rise and Fall of the Third Reich*. London: Secker and Warburg, 1960
SLIM, Field-Marshal Sir William: *Defeat into Victory*. London: Cassell, 1956
STEAD, P. J.: *Second Bureau*. London: Evans, 1959
STIMSON, H. L., and BUNDY, McG.: *On Active Service in Peace and War*. New York: Harper, 1947
STOKES, Richard L.: See JORDAN, George Racey
STORRY, G. R.: See DEAKIN, F. W.
STRONG, Maj-Gen. K.: *Intelligence at the Top*. London: Cassell, 1968
SWEET-ESCOTT, Bickham: *Baker Street Irregular*. London: Methuen, 1965
TEMPLEWOOD, Viscount: *Ambassador on Special Mission*. London: Collins, 1946
TREPPER, Leopold: *The Great Game*. London: Michael Joseph, 1977
TREVOR-ROPER, H. R.: *The Last Days of Hitler*. London: Macmillan, 1956
TRUMAN, Harry S.: *Year of Decisions, 1945*. London: Hodder and Stoughton, 1955
TSUJI, Masanobu: *Singapore: The Japanese Version*. London: Constable, 1962
URQUHART, Maj-Gen. R. E. (with Wilfred Greatorex): *Arnhem*. London: 1958
WALLACE, Graham: *RAF Biggin Hill*. London: Putnam, 1957
WARLIMONT, Walter: *Inside Hitler's Headquarters, 1939–1945*. London: Weidenfeld and Nicolson, 1964
WELLES, Sumner: *Seven Major Decisions*. London: Hamish Hamilton, 1951
WERTH, Alexander: *Russia at War, 1941–1945*. London: Barrie and Rockliff, 1964

WHEATLEY, Ronald: *Operation Sea Lion.* Oxford: Oxford University Press, 1958

WINT, Guy: See CALVOCORESSI, Peter

WINTERBOTHAM, F. W.: *Secret and Personal.* London: Kimber, 1969

— *The Ultra Secret.* London: Weidenfeld and Nicolson, 1974

— *The Nazi Connection.* London: Weidenfeld and Nicolson, 1978

WOYTAK, Richard A.: *On the Border of War and Peace.* New York: East European Quarterly, 1979

WU, A. K.: *China and the Soviet Union.* London: Methuen, 1950

YARDLEY, Herbert O.: *The American Black Chamber.* Indianapolis: The Bobbs-Merrill Company, 1931

YOUNG, Desmond: *Rommel.* London: Collins, 1950

YOUNG, Gordon: *Cat with Two Faces.* [Mathilde-Lily Carré] London: Putnam, 1957

ZOLLING, Hermann: See HÖHNE, Heinz

Notes and Sources

Names of authors, and the titles of some books, are given below in abbreviated form. Full data appear in the bibliography.

1   CLOAKS AND DAGGERS

  1 Schwarz, *American Strategy*, 26–28
  2 Hinsley, *British Intelligence*, i, 113
  3 *ibid.*, 186
  4 *ibid.*, 62, 76
  5 *ibid.*, 78–80; *Defence of the United Kingdom*, 77–78
  6 Hinsley, *op. cit.*, 50
  7 *ibid.*, 51
  8 *ibid.*, *loc. cit.*
  9 *ibid.*, 26
10 *ibid.*, 24
11 *ibid.*, 25
12 *ibid.*, *loc. cit.*
13 *ibid.*, 35
14 *ibid.*, 42, 43
15 *ibid.*, 41
16 *ibid.*, 45
17 *ibid.*, 15
18 *ibid.*, *loc. cit.*
19 Jones, *Most Secret War*, 3
20 Foot, *SOE in France*, 1–2
21 *ibid.*, 2
22 *ibid.*, 4

2   BETWEEN THE WARS

  1 Hinsley, *British Intelligence*, i, 16 fn
  2 Largely, but not entirely. For example, between 1907 and 1913 the future Field-Marshal Sir Henry Wilson, while serving successively as Commandant of the Staff College and Director of Military Operations, personally reconnoitred all roads leading from Germany into France and the Low Countries. His forecast of the initial strength of the German armies of the right and centre was more accurate than that made by the Deuxième

Bureau; but neither he nor the French foresaw that the Belgian forts on the Meuse would quickly succumb to plunging fire from outsize howitzers.

3 Dallin, *Soviet Espionage*, *passim*.

4 Yardley, *American Black Chamber*; Kahn, *The Codebreakers*, 359

5 Hinsley, *op. cit.*, 78 fn

6 *ibid.*, *loc. cit.*

7 *Defence of the United Kingdom*, 25–26; Hinsley, *op. cit.*, 49

8 *Defence of the United Kingdom*, 26; Hinsley, *op. cit.*, 49, 78

9 Hinsley, *op. cit.*, 78 fn

10 *ibid.*, 50

11 *Defence of the United Kingdom*, 27

12 *ibid.*, *loc. cit.*; Hinsley, *op. cit.*, 53

13 *Defence of the United Kingdom*, 46. On the outbreak of war the Luftwaffe had 4,161 first-line aircraft (or 3,609 if transport aircraft are excluded).

14 *ibid.*, 77; Hinsley, *op. cit.*, 78

15 *Defence of the United Kingdom*, 29

16 Avon, *Facing the Dictators*, 141

17 *Defence of the United Kingdom*, Chapters II–IV, *passim*; Webster and Frankland, *Strategic Air Offensive Against Germany*, i, *passim*.

18 Hinsley, *op. cit.*, 50

19 *ibid.*, 51

20 Moravec, *Master of Spies*, 77. Hinsley, *op. cit.*, 58, says the first approach was made in February 1936. But Moravec, according to his daughter, did not become Chief of Intelligence until 1937.

21 Moravec, *op. cit.*, 123, 126, 128, 131, 152–53, 182, 185; Hinsley, *op. cit.*, 58

22 Hinsley, *op. cit.*, 311

23 Kahn, *op. cit.*, 14, 30

24 Clark, *Man Who Broke Purple*, 108; Kahn, *The Codebreakers*, 22, says the first complete solution came in August.

25 Hinsley, *op. cit.*, 53–54

26 *ibid.*, 54

27 *ibid.*, 37, 78, 79 and fn, 80

28 Avon, *op. cit.*, 332–33

29 Moravec, *op. cit.*, 87

30 *ibid.*, 123

31 Hinsley, *op. cit.*, 81

32 *ibid.*, *loc. cit.*

33 Moravec, *op. cit.*, 117

34 Avon, *op. cit.*, 173

35 *ibid.*, Appendix D (ii) and (iii) and sources cited

36 *ibid.*, Appendix D (v) and sources cited

37 Hinsley, *op. cit.*, 81

38 *ibid.*, 55–56

39 Henderson, *Failure of a Mission*, 116–17

40 Hinsley, *op. cit.*, 57, 58

41 *ibid.*, 81

42 Moravec, *op. cit.*, 126

43 *ibid.*, *loc. cit.*

44 *ibid.*, 128–29

45 Jodl testified at Nuremberg in 1946 that only five first-class and seven reserve divisions would have been immediately available on the Western Front in September 1938.

46 *Defence of the United Kingdom*, 11

47 *ibid.*, 65

48 Hinsley, *op. cit.*, 78

49 *ibid.*, 75

50 Henderson, *op. cit.*, 152

51 Hinsley, *op. cit.*, 82

52 Henderson, *op. cit.*, 162–64

53 Hinsley, *op. cit.*, 82

54 *ibid.*, *loc. cit.*

55 *ibid.*, *loc. cit.*

56 *ibid.*, *loc. cit.*

57 *ibid.*, 83

58 *ibid.*, *loc. cit.*

59 Moravec, *op. cit.*, 150, 151–53

60 Henderson, *op. cit.*, 183

61 *ibid.*, 204–205

62 Hinsley, *op. cit.*, 84

63 *ibid.*, 83

64 *ibid.*, *loc. cit.*

65 *ibid.*, *loc. cit.*

66 Moravec, *op. cit.*, 182

67 *ibid.*, 183–84

68 *ibid.*, 185

69 Garlinski, *Intercept*, 38; Moravec, *op. cit.*, 118–22

70 Moravec, *op. cit.*, 63–72, 75–76, 106–107, 163–64

71 Bertrand, *Enigma*, 23, says he was in touch with Asché from 1932. Garlinski's highly circumstantial account (*op. cit.*, 14–16, 19, 20–21, 26) puts the first meeting between Bertrand and Asché some time before the end of 1931. Moreover, according to Hinsley (*op. cit.*, 488), the British would seem to have received from the French in 1931 material which must surely have come in the first instance from Asché. Paillole, *Services spéciaux*, 63, also refers. Various accounts of the way in which the Poles achieved their breakthrough are given by Woytak in *On the Border of War and Peace* in an unpublished memorandum by Colonel S. A. Mayer of the Polish intelligence service; and in a number of articles in British, French, German and Polish newspapers and periodicals.

72 Hinsley, *op. cit.*, 488

73 Garlinski, *op. cit.*, 2–3, 19–20

74 *ibid.*, 20

75 *ibid.*, 195

76 *ibid.*, 23–25, 196–98

77 *ibid.*, 37

78 Hinsley, *op. cit.*, 490–91; Garlinski, *op. cit.*, 35

79 Hinsley, *op. cit.*, 490–91

80 Hinsley, *op. cit.*, 491; Garlinski, *op. cit.*, 37

81 Garlinski, *op. cit.*, 37. He says elsewhere (and Bertrand seems also to have believed) that new rotors were added in the summer of 1939; but see Hinsley, *op. cit.*, 492.

82 Bertrand, *op. cit.*, 57; Garlinski, *op. cit.*, 38; Hinsley, *op. cit.*, 491

83 Hinsley, *op. cit.*, 491; Garlinski, *op. cit.*, 38

84 Bertrand, *op. cit.*, 60; Garlinski, *op. cit.*, 45–47; Hinsley, *op. cit.*, 492

85 Hinsley, *op. cit.*, 492

3   THE PHONEY WAR AND AFTER

1 Hinsley, *British Intelligence*, i, 499

2 Masterman, *The Double-Cross System*, 37

3 Also known as Dr Rantzau. Masterman, *op. cit.*, 38

4 He had been threatened with reprisals against a German-domiciled brother if he refused his services. Masterman, *op. cit.*, 40

5 *Defence of the United Kingdom*, 79

6 Hinsley, *op. cit.*, 57 fn

7 *ibid.*, *loc. cit.*

8 *ibid.*, *loc. cit.*

9 Foot, *SOE in France*, 6

10 *ibid.*, 5

11 Hinsley, *op. cit.*, 75, 110; *Defence of the United Kingdom*, 77, 78 and fn

12 Hinsley, *op. cit.*, 100–102

13 *Defence of the United Kingdom*, 81; Hinsley, *op. cit.*, 103, 105

14 Hinsley, *op. cit.*, 103

15 *ibid.*, 105

16 *ibid.*, *loc. cit.*

17 *ibid.*, 108; *Defence of the United Kingdom*, 82; Roskill, *The War at Sea*, i, 75

18 Hinsley, *op. cit.*, 110; Roskill, *op. cit.*, 80

19 Hinsley, *op. cit.*, 107 fn

20 *ibid.*, *loc. cit.*

21 *ibid.*, 108; *Defence of the United Kingdom*, 91–92

22 Garlinski, *op. cit.*, 56–57

23 Hinsley, *op. cit.*, 493. Garlinski, *op. cit.*, 59, names the emissary as Alan Turing, but says he arrived on 17 January 1940 and that the breakthrough was made on the same day. That is the date given in the Mayer memorandum, but clearly it is wrong. The British record shows that the signal encyphered on 28 October must have been read between the middle of December (when the sheets used to read it were completed) and the end of the month (when the emissary returned to England). Bertrand, *op. cit.*, 76–77, implies that the signal was read *on* 28 October, but that too is an evident slip.

24 Hinsley, *op. cit.*, 493

25 *ibid.*, *loc. cit.*

26 *ibid.*, 108

27 The Mayer memorandum. Hinsley, *op. cit.*, 493

28 Hinsley, *op. cit.*, 336

29 *ibid.*, *loc. cit.*; Roskill, *op. cit.*, 131

30 Moravec, *Master of Spies*, 186
31 Hinsley, *op. cit.*, 113
32 Moravec, *op. cit.*, 189
33 Hinsley, *op. cit.*, 114
34 *ibid.*, *loc. cit.*
35 *ibid.*, *loc. cit.*
36 Moravec, *op. cit.*, 186
37 *ibid.*, *loc. cit.*
38 *Defence of the United Kingdom*, 331; Jones, *Most Secret War*, 68–71; Hinsley, *op. cit.*, 100, 308–12
39 Hinsley, *op. cit.*, 99; Jones, *op. cit.*, 64–65
40 See, *e.g.*, Hinsley, *op. cit.*, 95–96
41 Hinsley, *op. cit.*, 97
42 *ibid.*, *loc. cit.*
43 *ibid.*, 91–92
44 Derry, *The Campaign in Norway*, gives the most authoritative of many accounts of the fighting in Norway and the events that led up to it. See also Hinsley, *op. cit.*
45 Roskill, *op. cit.*, 157
46 Hinsley, *op. cit.*, 117
47 *ibid.*, 118, 122
48 *ibid.*, 117
49 *ibid.*, 117–18; *Defence of the United Kingdom*, 83–84
50 Hinsley, *op. cit.*, 120
51 *ibid.*, *loc. cit.*
52 References to the material summarized will be found in the books by Hinsley, Derry and Roskill, already cited.
53 Hinsley, *op. cit.*, 119
54 *ibid.*, *loc. cit.*
55 *ibid.*, 120
56 Roskill, *op. cit.*, 163
57 *ibid.*, 159
58 *ibid.*, *loc. cit.*; Hinsley, *op. cit.*, 122–23
59 Hinsley, *op. cit.*, 123
60 Roskill, *op. cit.*, 159; Hinsley, *op. cit.*, 124. Roskill records (*op. cit.*, 159, 160) that the fleet was brought to one hour's notice for steam on receipt of the substance of the Copenhagen report, and ordered to raise steam when the report from the bomber force was received.
61 Roskill, *op. cit.*, 161
62 *ibid.*, 162
63 Hinsley, *op. cit.*, 124
64 Roskill, *op. cit.*, 160; Hinsley, *op. cit.*, 124
65 Hinsley, *op. cit.*, 125
66 Roskill, *op. cit.*, 173
67 Hinsley, *op. cit.*, 137
68 *ibid.*, 137–38
69 *ibid.*, 138
70 *ibid.*, *loc. cit.*

71 *ibid.*, 138–39
72 *ibid.*, 139
73 *ibid.*, 141
74 *ibid.*, *loc. cit.*
75 This was a marked chart taken from the U-49, sunk by British destroyers near Narvik on 14 April. Roskill, *op. cit.*, 190; Hinsley, *op. cit.*, 140
76 Hinsley, *op. cit.*, 139–40
77 *ibid.*, 139
78 *ibid.*, 139–40
79 *ibid.*, 141
80 *ibid.*, *loc. cit.*
81 *ibid.*, 142
82 *ibid.*, *loc. cit.*; Roskill, *op. cit.*, 198
83 Roskill, *op. cit.*, 196
84 *ibid.*, 197
85 Hinsley, *op. cit.*, 142
86 *ibid.*, *loc. cit.*
87 *ibid.*, *loc. cit.*
88 *ibid.*, 142–43
89 *ibid.*, 109, 494

4   FRANCE AND THE LOW COUNTRIES: 1940

1   Goutard, *Battle of France*, 80
2   Hinsley, *British Intelligence*, i, 133
3   Barker, *Aviator Extraordinary*, 187; Hinsley, *op. cit.*, 136
4   Moravec, *Master of Spies*, 189–90
5   *ibid.*, 190
6   Hinsley, *op. cit.*, 130
7   *ibid.*, 135
8   Gauché, *Deuxième Bureau*, 207
9   Hinsley, *op. cit.*, 131
10 *ibid.*, 131 fn
11 *ibid.*, *loc. cit.*
12 Masterman, *The Double-Cross System*, 36
13 Hinsley, *op. cit.*, 129
14 *ibid.*, *loc. cit.*
15 *ibid.*, 130
16 *i.e.*, 33 field divisions and garrison troops equivalent to 10 divisions, out of a total of 104 British and French divisions. The proportion rises to 46 per cent if we include the 5 divisions of the *Lot suisse*.
17 Goutard, *op. cit.*, 88–89
18 *ibid.*, 83, 97–99
19 *ibid.*, 104
20 *ibid.*, *loc. cit.*
21 *ibid.*, 104–105
22 *ibid.*, 105
23 *ibid.*, *loc. cit.*
24 *ibid.*, *loc. cit.*

25 *ibid.*, 115
26 *ibid.*, 131
27 *ibid.*, 115
28 *ibid.*, 112–13
29 *ibid.*, 37
30 *ibid.*, 175
31 *ibid.*, 176
32 *ibid.*, 165
33 *ibid.*, 170–74
34 *ibid.*, 100–103, 208
35 *ibid.*, 210–12
36 Hinsley, *op. cit.*, 143
37 *ibid.*, 144
38 *ibid.*, *loc. cit.*
39 *ibid.*, 148
40 *ibid.*, 143
41 Ellis, *France and Flanders, 1939–1940*, 148–49
42 Article by Lt.-Gen. Nyssens, cited by Goutard, *op. cit.*, 236 and fn
43 Goutard, *op. cit.*, 224
44 The Defiant, a turret fighter, scored a fugitive success at Dunkirk, but its
    restricted field of fire made it almost useless as a day fighter once its
    limitations became apparent to the Germans. It afterwards proved useful as
    a night fighter.
45 Hinsley, *op. cit.*, 161–62
46 *ibid.*, 162

5   BRITAIN: 1940

1 Hinsley, *British Intelligence*, i, 159
2 *ibid.*, 160
3 *ibid.*, *loc. cit.*
4 *ibid.*, *loc. cit.*
5 *ibid.*, 149
6 *ibid.*, 171
7 Masterman, *The Double-Cross System*, 43
8 Foot, *SOE in France*, 6
9 *ibid.*, 5
10 *ibid.*, 6
11 *ibid.*, 7, 8–9
12 *ibid.*, 8
13 *ibid.*, *loc. cit.*
14 *ibid.*, 10
15 *Defence of the United Kingdom*, 83
16 Wheatley, *Operation Sea Lion*, gives a detailed account of the German
     invasion plan.
17 Hinsley, *op. cit.*, 166
18 *ibid.*, *loc. cit.*
19 *ibid.*, *loc. cit.*
20 *Defence of the United Kingdom*, 103; Hinsley, *op. cit.*, 165

21 Hinsley, *op. cit.*, 166
22 *ibid.*, *loc. cit.*
23 *ibid.*, *loc. cit.*
24 *ibid.*, 166–67
25 Roskill, *The War A: Sea*, i, 250, says that even 24 hours' warning would have been valuable.
26 *ibid.*, 249–51, 253
27 *ibid.*, 260; Hinsley, *op. cit.*, 171
28 Roskill, *op. cit.*, 249
29 *ibid.*, *loc. cit.*
30 Hinsley, *op. cit.*, 169
31 *ibid.*, 170–71
32 *ibid.*, 169
33 *ibid.*, 279
34 *ibid.*, 172; *Defence of the United Kingdom*, 141
35 Hinsley, *op. cit.*, 171–72
36 *ibid.*, 173, 174
37 *ibid.*, 172
38 *Defence of the United Kingdom*, 165–66
39 Oral communication to author
40 Hinsley, *op. cit.*, 177–78
41 *ibid.*, 178
42 *ibid.*, 179
43 *ibid.*, *loc. cit.*
44 *Defence of the United Kingdom*, 184–88, 456
45 Hinsley, *op. cit.*, 179; *Defence of the United Kingdom*, 192
46 Hinsley, *op. cit.*, 178
47 *ibid.*, 183
48 *ibid.*, 184
49 *ibid.*, 183
50 *ibid.*, *loc. cit.*
51 *ibid.*, *loc. cit.*
52 *ibid.*, 184–85; *Defence of the United Kingdom*, 222–23
53 Hinsley, *op. cit.*, 185
54 Masterman, *op. cit.*, 48–50
55 *Defence of the United Kingdom*, 223; Hinsley, *op. cit.*, 185
56 Hinsley, *op. cit.*, 185
57 *ibid.*, *loc. cit.*; *Defence of the United Kingdom*, 223–24
58 *Defence of the United Kingdom*, 465, 466, 467 fn
59 Hinsley, *op. cit.*, 190
60 *ibid.*, 188
61 *ibid.*, 189; *Defence of the United Kingdom*, 227
62 *ibid.*, *loc. cit.*
63 *ibid.*, 190
64 *ibid.*, *loc. cit.*; Roskill, *op. cit.*, 350–51; *Defence of the United Kingdom*, 228–32

6 THE MEDITERRANEAN AND THE NEAR AND MIDDLE EAST: 1939–1941

1 Hinsley, *British Intelligence*, i, 13, 40–41, 191

2 *ibid.*, 195
3 *ibid.*, *loc. cit.*
4 *ibid.*, *loc. cit.*
5 *ibid.*, 193
6 *ibid.*, 196–97
7 *ibid.*, 197, 219–20
8 *ibid.*, 200
9 *ibid.*, 84
10 *ibid.*, 200
11 *ibid.*, 201, 203
12 *ibid.*, 202
13 *ibid.*, *loc. cit.*
14 *ibid.*, 203
15 *ibid.*, 202
16 *ibid.*, 203
17 *ibid.*, 205
18 *Defence of the United Kingdom*, 48, 63
19 Hinsley, *op. cit.*, 204
20 *ibid.*, *loc. cit.*
21 *ibid.*, 200, 204
22 *ibid.*, 204
23 *ibid.*, *loc. cit.*
24 *ibid.*, *loc. cit.*
25 *ibid.*, 51
26 *ibid.*, 208
27 *ibid.*, *loc. cit.*
28 *ibid.*, 205–206
29 *ibid.*, 213
30 *ibid.*, 206
31 *ibid.*, 210
32 Cunningham, *A Sailor's Odyssey*, 203
33 Hinsley, *op. cit.*, 209
34 *ibid.*, *loc. cit.*
35 Roskill, *The War at Sea*, i, 301; Hinsley, *op. cit.*, 211–12
36 Hinsley, *op. cit.*, 212
37 *ibid.*, 276–77
38 *ibid.*, 156
39 *ibid.*, 264
40 *ibid.*, 252
41 *ibid.*, *loc. cit.*
42 *ibid.*, *loc. cit.*
43 *ibid.*, 218
44 *ibid.*, 254
45 *ibid.*, *loc. cit.*
46 *ibid.*, *loc. cit.*
47 *ibid.*, 258, 384, 385
48 *ibid.*, 382–84, 386–88
49 *ibid.*, 177, 300

50 *ibid.*, 300
51 *ibid.*, 301
52 *ibid.*, *loc. cit.*; Singleton report, 21 January 1941
53 Hinsley, *op. cit.*, 302
54 *ibid.*, *loc. cit.*
55 *ibid.*, 303, 304
56 *ibid.*, 304
57 *ibid.*, *loc. cit.*
58 *ibid.*, 259, 357
59 *ibid.*, 358
60 *ibid.*, 357, 359
61 *ibid.*, 359
62 *ibid.*, *loc. cit.*
63 *ibid.*, 363
64 *ibid.*, 363, 389
65 Roskill, *op. cit.*, 424; Hinsley, *op. cit.*, 464 fn
66 Hinsley, *op. cit.*, 404
67 *ibid.*, *loc. cit.*
68 *ibid.*, 404–405; Roskill, *op. cit.*, 424, 427–28. Hinsley points out that Cunningham's decision to take his fleet to sea was made before the Italian cruisers were sighted.
69 Hinsley, *op. cit.*, 364
70 *ibid.*, 369–70
71 *ibid.*, 370
72 *ibid.*, 415
73 *ibid.*, *loc. cit.*
74 *ibid.*, 410, 412
75 *ibid.*, 406, 407, 409
76 *ibid.*, 406–407
77 *ibid.*, 415–16
78 *ibid.*, 416–17
79 *ibid.*, 417
80 *ibid.*, 417
81 *ibid.*, 418. For accounts of the plan and its execution see Playfair, *The Mediterranean and Middle East*, ii, and Heydte, *Daedalus Returned*
82 Churchill, *The Second World War*, iii, 246
83 *ibid.*, 240
84 Hinsley, *op. cit.*, 419
85 *ibid.*, *loc. cit.*
86 *ibid.*, 418
87 *ibid.*, 421
88 *ibid.*, 380
89 *ibid.*, 380–81
90 *ibid.*, 381
91 *ibid.*, 384
92 *ibid.*, *loc. cit.*
93 *ibid.*, 384–85; Roskill, *op. cit.*, 420–22
94 Hinsley, *op. cit.*, 385–86

95 *ibid.*, 386–87
96 *ibid.*, 386
97 *ibid.*, 387
98 *ibid.*, 386
99 *ibid.*, 387
100 *ibid.*, *loc. cit.*
101 *ibid.*, *loc. cit.*
102 *ibid.*, 389–90, 391–92
103 *ibid.*, 389
104 *ibid.*, 389–90
105 *ibid.*, 390–91
106 *ibid.*, 391
107 *ibid.*, *loc. cit.*
108 *ibid.*, 392
109 *ibid.*, *loc. cit.*
110 *ibid.*, 393
111 *ibid.*, 395
112 *ibid.*, *loc. cit.*
113 *ibid.*, *loc. cit.*
114 *ibid.*, 397
115 *ibid.*, 398
116 *ibid.*, 422
117 *ibid.*, *loc. cit.*
118 *ibid.*, *loc. cit.*
119 *ibid.*, *loc. cit.*
120 *ibid.*, 399
121 Playfair, *op. cit.*, 167
122 Gwyer, *Grand Strategy Volume III, Part I*, 90
123 Hinsley, *op. cit.*, 572
124 The account of Crusader given here is based mainly on Playfair, *op. cit.*
125 Liddell Hart, *History*, 185

7 BLITZ AND BLOCKADE
1 Jones, *Most Secret War*, 84–85; Hinsley, *British Intelligence*, i, 552, 556
2 Jones, *op. cit.*, 85; Hinsley, *op. cit.*, 323–24
3 Hinsley, *op. cit.*, 552; Jones, *op. cit.*, 85
4 Jones, *op. cit.*, 87; Hinsley, *op. cit.*, 553
5 Hinsley, *op. cit.*, 552
6 *ibid.*, *loc. cit.*; Jones, *op. cit.*, 92–93. An amended translation substituted 'directed (or set up)' for 'confirmed'.
7 Jones, *op. cit.*, 94
8 *ibid.*, *loc. cit.*
9 Hinsley, *op. cit.*, 553; Jones, *op. cit.*, 95
10 Hinsley, *op. cit.*, 553
11 *ibid.*, *loc. cit.*
12 Jones, *op. cit.*, 100–101
13 Hinsley, *op. cit.*, 553
14 Jones, *op. cit.*, 102–103; Hinsley, *op. cit.*, 553

15 Jones, *op. cit.*, 104; Hinsley, *op. cit.*, 553

16 Hinsley, *op. cit.*, 554

17 Jones, *op. cit.*, 133–34

18 *ibid.*, 127–28; Hinsley, *op. cit.*, 325, 554–56; *Defence of the United Kingdom*, 158

19 Hinsley, *op. cit.*, 556

20 Jones, *op. cit.*, 135; Hinsley, *op. cit.*, 556

21 Personal knowledge

22 Hinsley, *op. cit.*, 326

23 *ibid.*, *loc. cit.*; Jones, *op. cit.*, 135

24 Hinsley, *op. cit.*, 356; Jones, *op. cit.*, 135–36

25 For simplicity, no distinction has been drawn in this drastically compressed account between coarse and fine or between single and multiple beams. This should not be taken to imply that Dr Jones was not aware of the complexity of the system. The director-beam was made up of three beams, two fine and one coarse. It was intersected 50 kilometres short of the target by a coarse warning beam, 20 kilometres short of the target by a fine cross beam, and 5 kilometres short of the target by two fine cross beams. Each of these seven beams operated on a different frequency. The width of the coarse beam was about 4°, that of the fine beams about 0.05°.

26 Hinsley, *op. cit.*, 557

27 *ibid.*, 358; Jones, *op. cit.*, 139

28 *Defence of the United Kingdom*, 494–95

29 Hinsley, *op. cit.*, 316, 528, 537–38

30 *ibid.*, 316, 530

31 *ibid.*, 317, 542; Jones, *op. cit.*, 147

32 Reproduced in Hinsley, *op. cit.*, 539–40

33 Hinsley, *op. cit.*, 317

34 *Defence of the United Kingdom*, 501–502

35 Hinsley, *op. cit.*, 317, 547–48

36 *ibid.*, 318

37 *ibid.*, *loc. cit.*

38 *ibid.*, 535. Dr Jones has stated, however, that he was not told until considerably later that the beams intersected over Coventry

39 *ibid.*, 318; Jones, *op. cit.*, 151–52

40 Hinsley, *op. cit.*, 559–61; Jones, *op. cit.*, 120

41 Jones, *op. cit.*, 120

42 Hinsley, *op. cit.*, 561; Jones, *op. cit.*, 172

43 Hinsley, *op. cit.*, 561

44 Jones, *op. cit.*, 173–75; Hinsley, *op. cit.*, 561

45 Hinsley, *op. cit.*, 561–63; Jones, *op. cit.*, 176–77

46 *Defence of the United Kingdom*, 513; Jones, *op. cit*, 252

47 *Defence of the United Kingdom*, 513–16

48 Jones, *op. cit.*, 397

49 *Defence of the United Kingdom*, 520

50 Jones, *op. cit.*, 121, 189

51 *ibid.*, 122, 189–90

52 *ibid.*, 191–92

53 Hinsley, *op. cit.*, 509

54 Foot, *SOE in France*, 183
55 Jones, *op. cit.*, 236–37; Foot, *op. cit.*, 151
56 Jones, *op. cit.*, 279
57 *ibid.*, *loc. cit.*; Hinsley, *op. cit.*, 278
58 Hinsley, *op. cit.*, 234 fn
59 Webster and Frankland, *Strategic Air Offensive Against Germany*, i, 211
60 Quoted in Jones, *op. cit.*, 183
61 Webster and Frankland, *op. cit.*, Chaps 2 and 3
62 *Defence of the United Kingdom*, 207–208
63 Webster and Frankland, *op. cit.*, 152
64 *ibid.*, 153
65 *ibid.*, 129
66 *ibid.*, 162
67 *ibid.*, 226
68 *ibid.*, 226
69 Hinsley, *op. cit.*, 306
70 *ibid.*, 305; Webster and Frankland, *op. cit.*, 159
71 Hinsley, *op. cit.*, 329
72 Roskill, *The War at Sea*, i, 616, 618
73 Hinsley, *op. cit.*, 330; Roskill, *op. cit.*, 609–611
74 Webster and Frankland, *op. cit.*, 160
75 *ibid.*, *loc. cit.*
76 Hinsley, *op. cit.*, 330
77 *ibid.*, *loc. cit.*
78 Roskill, *op. cit.*, 616
79 Hinsley, *op. cit.*, 337
80 Roskill, *op. cit.*, 341
81 Hinsley, *op. cit.*, 337
82 *ibid.*, 337, 565–69
83 *ibid.*, 337–38; Beesley, *Very Special Intelligence*, 71–72
84 Hinsley, *op. cit.*, 338
85 *ibid.*, 341
86 *ibid.*, 340
87 *ibid.*, 341
88 *ibid.*, *loc. cit.*
89 *ibid.*, 342; Roskill, *op. cit.*, 396
90 Roskill, *op. cit.*, 400
91 *ibid.*, 401
92 Hinsley, *op. cit.*, 342
93 *ibid.*, 344
94 *ibid.*, 343; Roskill, *op. cit.*, 410; Beesley, *op. cit.*, 79–82
95 Hinsley, *op. cit.*, 344; Roskill, *op. cit.*, 411
96 Hinsley, *op. cit.*, 345
97 *ibid.*, 345–46; Roskill, *op. cit.*, 542, 544
98 Hinsley, *op. cit.*, 346
99 Lewin, *Ultra Goes to War*, 209–10
100 Roskill, *The War at Sea*, ii, 485
101 Beesley, *op. cit.*, 93, 118

102 *ibid.*, 118–20
103 *ibid.*, 118–19
104 Roskill, *op. cit.*, 151
105 *ibid.*, 154
106 *ibid.*, *loc. cit.*
107 *ibid.*, 154–55
108 *ibid.*, 155; Wallace, *RAF Biggin Hill*, 242–43; conversation with Group-Captain Beamish, *circa* 1944
109 Roskill, *op. cit.*, 155–56
110 *ibid.*, 156–58
111 *ibid.*, 398–99; Lewin, *op. cit.*, 227
112 Roskill, *op. cit.*, 400
113 Lewin, *op. cit.*, 228–30
114 *ibid.*, 227–28
115 Roskill, *The War at Sea*, iii (1), 88

8   THE EASTERN FRONT

  1 Hinsley, *British Intelligence*, i, 430
  2 Wheatley, *Operation Sea Lion*, 42
  3 *ibid.*, 29 and fn 4, 42; Hinsley, *op. cit.*, 433
  4 Wheatley, *op. cit.*, 29
  5 *ibid.*, 47, 50, 140; Hinsley, *op. cit.*, 433
  6 Churchill, *The Second World War*, ii, 120; Hinsley, *op. cit.*, 430
  7 Churchill, *op. cit.*, 227–28, 643; Hinsley, *op. cit.*, 431
  8 Hinsley, *op. cit.*, 433
  9 *ibid.*, 431–39; Strong, *Intelligence at the Top*, 72–73
 10 Hinsley, *op. cit.*, 438–39, 440
 11 *ibid.*, 445
 12 *ibid.*, 446
 13 *ibid.*, 446–47
 14 *ibid.*, 447
 15 *ibid.*, 454
 16 *ibid.*, 448
 17 *ibid.*, 371, 451
 18 Churchill, *The Second World War*, iii, 319–20
 19 Woodward, *British Foreign Policy*, 605–607
 20 Hinsley, *op. cit.*, 453–54
 21 *ibid.*, 453. Some of their information appears to have come from intercepted landline traffic
 22 Foot, *Resistance*, 188
 23 Woodward, *op. cit.*, 489–98; Hinsley, *op. cit.*, 431–32
 24 The account given here of Sorge's activities is based chiefly on Deakin and Storry, *The Case of Richard Sorge*
 25 F. C. Jones, *Japan's New Order in South-East Asia*, 35
 26 Hinsley, *op. cit.*, 371, 435–36
 27 *ibid.*, 472
 28 *Rise and Fall of the German Air Force* (Air Ministry ACAS (I), 1948), 3
 29 Dallin, *Soviet Espionage*, 75

30 *ibid.*, 93
31 Moravec, *Master of Spies*, 187–88
32 Kahn, *The Codebreakers*, 659
33 Dallin, *op. cit.*, 135–36
34 Hinsley, *op. cit.*, 451–74, 575–76
35 *ibid.*, 455–56
36 *ibid.*, 455
37 *ibid.*, 470–72
38 *ibid.*, 472
39 *ibid.*, 473–74
40 Cited by Werth, *Russia at War*, 139
41 Hinsley, *op. cit.*, 474 (quoting CX/JQ/S/11 of 31 May 1941)
42 *ibid.*, 473, 475
43 *ibid.*, 478
44 *ibid.*, *loc. cit.*
45 *ibid.*, 473–74
46 *ibid.*, 478; Woodward, *op. cit.*, 620
47 Hinsley, *op. cit.*, 478
48 *ibid.*, *loc. cit.*
49 *ibid.*, 478–79
50 Woodward, *op. cit.*, 621
51 *Defence of the United Kingdom*, 294
52 Werth, *op. cit.*, 137–41
53 Hinsley, *op. cit.*, 481
54 *ibid.*, 481–82
55 *ibid.*, 482–83; *Defence of the United Kingdom*, 295–96
56 Dallin, *op. cit.*, gives a detailed account of these developments.
57 Deakin and Storry, *op. cit.*, 231–33
58 Rado, *Codename Dora*, 262–63; Foote, *Handbook for Spies*, 123
59 Foote, *Handbook for Spies*, gives an account of his adventures
60 Schröter, *Stalingrad*, 52–54
61 Roskill, *The War at Sea*, i, 486
62 Sherwood, *White House Papers*, i, 332 ff; Gwyer, *Grand Strategy Volume III, Part I*, 96, 109
63 Gwyer, *op. cit.*, 155–61
64 Roskill, *op. cit.*, 494–95
65 Roskill, *The War at Sea*, ii, 115
66 *ibid.*, 116
67 *ibid.*, 117
68 *ibid.*, 124
69 *ibid.*, 131, 132 and fn
70 *ibid.*, 135
71 *ibid.*, 136
72 *ibid.*, *loc. cit.*
73 *ibid.*, 138
74 *ibid.*, *loc. cit.*
75 *ibid.*, 139
76 *ibid.*, *loc. cit.*

77 *ibid.*, 141
78 *ibid.*, 143 (Table 11)
79 Roskill, *The War at Sea*, iii (Part II), 262
80 Dallin, *op. cit.*, 443–44
81 *ibid.*, 429–30
82 George Racey Jordan (the American officer mentioned in the last sentence of this paragraph) describes the set-up in his book, *From Major Jordan's Diaries*. Major Jordan became a controversial figure when his evidence was used after the war in an attempt to show that Harry Hopkins went out of his way to furnish the Russians with information about the Manhattan Project and with materials associated with nuclear research. Jordan confesses in his book that at one time he confused sulphuric acid with heavy water, and that he had no sure means of knowing whether communications supposed to have emanated from Hopkins did come from that source. But none of this invalidates his factual account of conditions at Great Falls. Dallin, *op. cit.*, 434 fn, refers.
83 Jordan, *From Major Jordan's Diaries*, 35–45
84 Dallin, *op. cit.*, deals at some length with their activities.

9   THE FAR EAST AND THE PACIFIC

 1 F. C. Jones, *Japan's New Order in South-East Asia*, 115
 2 *ibid.*, 195
 3 Jeffreys-Jones, *American Espionage*, 165
 4 Hinsley, *British Intelligence*, i, 312
 5 *ibid.*, *loc. cit.*; Jeffreys-Jones, *op. cit.*, 166
 6 Hinsley, *op. cit.*, 312–13
 7 Jeffreys-Jones, *op. cit.*, 167
 8 *ibid.*, 166
 9 F. C. Jones, *op. cit.*, 263 and fn; Kirby, *The War against Japan*, i, 64, 66
10 Masterman, *The Double-Cross System*, 79–81, 95–96, 196–98
11 F. C. Jones, *op. cit.*, 292
12 *ibid.*, 300
13 *ibid.*, 312–13
14 Morison, *The Two-Ocean War*, 49
15 Kahn, *op. cit.*, 39–40
16 *ibid.*, *loc. cit.*
17 *ibid.*, 32, 88
18 *ibid.*, 48–49, 52
19 *ibid.*, 52
20 *ibid.*, 2–3
21 *ibid.*, 56
22 *ibid.*, 43
23 *ibid.*, 57
24 Text in Kahn, *op. cit.*, 60
25 Lord, *Day of Infamy*, 174
26 *ibid.*, 8; Morison, *The Rising Sun in the Pacific*, 132–33
27 Morison, *Rising Sun*, 138
28 *ibid.*, 100, 125

29 Morison, *Two-Ocean War*, 82
30 Kirby, *op. cit.*, 175
31 *ibid.*, 174–75
32 *ibid.*, 180
33 *ibid.*, 209
34 Morison, *Rising Sun*, 128
35 Morison, *Two-Ocean War*, 80–81
36 Roskill, *The War at Sea*, ii, 11
37 Kirby, *op. cit.*, 13–14
38 *ibid.*, 72
39 Roskill, *op. cit.*, 25
40 *ibid.*, 35; Kahn, *op. cit.*, 565

10   THE DEFEAT OF GERMANY AND HER ALLIES

1 Hinsley, *British Intelligence*, i, 391
2 Playfair, *The Mediterranean and Middle East*, iii, 216
3 Hinsley, *British Intelligence*, ii, 408–409
4 The British lost 1,750 killed, wounded or missing; the Germans 1,859 and the Italians 1,051. (Figures from Playfair, *op. cit.*)
5 For a discussion of American distrust of General de Gaulle see Foot, *SOE in France*, 444
6 Masterman, *The Double-Cross System*, 109–11
7 Roskill, *The War at Sea*, ii, 315
8 Liddell Hart, *History of Second World War*, 320–31
9 Masterman, *op. cit.*, 108, suggests that a cover-plan for the Dieppe operation might have greatly reduced its cost.
10 Masterman, *op. cit.*, 133–38. For a more detailed account see Montagu, *The Man Who Never Was*.
11 Liddell Hart, *op. cit.*, 451
12 Nicholson, *The Canadians in Italy*, 193–94; Liddell Hart, *op. cit.*, 347–58
13 Liddell Hart, *op. cit.*, 458, 460
14 *ibid.*, 460–61
15 Jones, *Most Secret War*, 293
16 *Defence of the United Kingdom*, 340
17 *ibid.*, *loc. cit.*; Jones, *op. cit.*, 332
18 *Defence of the United Kingdom*, 340; Jones, *op. cit.*, 332–33
19 *Defence of the United Kingdom*, 341; Jones, *op. cit.*, 334
20 Oral communication to author
21 *Defence of the United Kingdom*, 343
22 *ibid.*, *loc. cit.*
23 *ibid.*, 344; Jones, *op. cit.*, 340
24 *Defence of the United Kingdom*, 346; Jones, *op. cit.*, 339
25 Jones, *op. cit.*, 350; *Defence of the United Kingdom*, 357
26 Jones, *op. cit.*, 349; *Defence of the United Kingdom*, 357
27 Jones, *op. cit.*, 350–52; *Defence of the United Kingdom*, 357
28 Jones, *op. cit.*, 355–56
29 *ibid.*, 360; *Defence of the United Kingdom*, 357
30 Jones, *op. cit.*, 367; *Defence of the United Kingdom*, 357–58. Constance Babington Smith tells her story in *Evidence in Camera*.

31 *Defence of the United Kingdom*, 360
32 Personal knowledge
33 Masterman, *op. cit.*, 156
34 *ibid.*, 160–62
35 Foreign Armies West Daily Situation Report, 20 April 1944
36 Foreign Armies West Daily Situation Report, 13 May 1944
37 Ellis, *Victory in the West*, 119–20
38 *Rise and Fall of the German Air Force*, 327
39 C-in-C West Weekly Situation Reports, 22 May and 5 June 1944; Ellis, *op. cit.*, 128–29
40 Ellis, *op. cit.*, 129
41 Foot, *SOE in France*, 388
42 *ibid.*, *loc. cit.*
43 Ellis, *op. cit.*, 198
44 Bennett, *Ultra in the West*, 53–58
45 Calvocoressi, *Top Secret Ultra*, 103
46 Personal knowledge
47 Masterman, *op. cit.*, 156–57
48 *ibid.*, 157
49 *Defence of the United Kingdom*, 367
50 *ibid.*, 368
51 *ibid.*, 377
52 *ibid.*, 401–2; Jones, *op. cit.*, 431–32
53 *Defence of the United Kingdom*, 403
54 Jones, *op. cit.*, 441–42
55 *ibid.*, 443–45; *Defence of the United Kingdom*, 401
56 Jones, *op. cit.*, 447–49; *Defence of the United Kingdom*, 403
57 *Defence of the United Kingdom*, 406
58 *ibid.*, *loc. cit.*
59 Stacey, *op. cit.*, 319 (citing SHAEF Weekly Intelligence Summary for week ending 9 September 1944)
60 *ibid.*, 320 (quoting signal of 15 September 1944)
61 Ellis, *op. cit.*, 82–83
62 SHAEF Weekly Intelligence Summary for week ending 16 September 1944; Urquhart, *Arnhem*, 9
63 The allegation appears to have been first made publicly in Pinto, *Spycatcher* (published in Britain in 1955).
64 Letter from Professor Louis de Jong, of the Netherlands State Institute for War Documentation, in *The Times*, 10 January 1981. Stacey, *op. cit.*, 313 and fn, also refers.
65 Army Group B report quoted in Stacey, *op. cit.*, 314
66 *Defence of the United Kingdom*, 409–10
67 *ibid.*, 410
68 *ibid.*, 418 and fn
69 *ibid.*, 417
70 *ibid.*, *loc. cit.*
71 *ibid.*, *loc. cit.*
72 Masterman, *op. cit.*, 179; Jones, *op. cit.*, 420–22

73 Jones, *op. cit.*, 422
74 Masterman, *op. cit.*, 74
75 *Defence of the United Kingdom*, 527
76 Merriam, *The Battle of the Ardennes*, 72–79
77 Liddell Hart, *op. cit.*, 642; Strong, *Intelligence at the Top*, 154
78 Merriam, *op. cit.*, 79
79 Calvocoressi, *op. cit.*, 45–47
80 Merriam, *op. cit.*, 82
81 *ibid.*, 82–84
82 *ibid.*, 82
83 *ibid.*, 83
84 *ibid.*, 87–89
85 *ibid.*, 87 (quoting SHAEF Weekly Intelligence Summaries); Strong, *Intelligence at the Top*, 154–56
86 Strong, *op. cit.*, 156, 157
87 Bradley, *A Soldier's Story*, 466; Merriam, *op. cit.*, III; Liddell Hart, *op. cit.*, 642
88 Lewin, *Ultra Goes to War*, 359–60
89 Strong, *op. cit.*, 187–88
90 Ehrman, *Grand Strategy Volume V*, 384
91 Dulles, *Secret Surrender*, chaps 4–13
92 Masterman, *op. cit.*, 184–85

II THE DEFEAT OF JAPAN

1 Kahn, *The Codebreakers*, 565
2 *ibid.*, 562–63, 565, 567, 568
3 *ibid.*, 569
4 Roskill, *The War at Sea*, ii, 57
5 Kahn, *op. cit.*, 571
6 Morison, *History*, iv, 83, 177–84; *Two-Ocean War*, 151
7 Morison, *History*, iv, 98, 101–102
8 *ibid.*, 103
9 Morison, *History*, v, 12–14
10 Morison, *History*, iv, 284
11 *ibid.*, 281
12 *ibid.*, 282
13 *ibid.*, chaps XII–XIV; vol. v, 16
14 Morison, *History*, v, 19–27; Roskill, *op. cit.*, 223–24
15 Morison, *History*, v, 26; Roskill, *op. cit.*, 224
16 Morison, *History*, 27, 28; Roskill, *op. cit.*, 224
17 Morison, *History*, v, 34
18 *ibid.*, 322 ff
19 Kirby, *The War Against Japan*, ii, 241
20 *ibid.*, 243–45, 309 ff; Mead, 'Orde Wingate and the Official Historians', in *Journal of Contemporary History*, vol. 14 (1979)
21 Kirby, *The War Against Japan*, iii, 127
22 *ibid.*, 191–92
23 *ibid.*, 179

24 It is now generally accepted that this meeting must have taken place on 20 March, not 23 March as stated by Fergusson in his post-war account.

25 Kirby, *op. cit.*, 280–82

26 *ibid.*, 282

27 *ibid.*, 186 and fn

28 Kirby, *The War Against Japan*, ii, 376; Morison, *Two-Ocean War*, 272–73

29 Dexter, *The New Guinea Offensives*, 10–11

30 *ibid.*, 795

31 *ibid.*, *loc. cit.*

32 Ehrman, *Grand Strategy Volume V*, 518; Roskill, *The War at Sea*, iii, Part II, 188

33 According to Dexter, *op. cit.*, 802, Dutch New Guinea had only about two hundred white residents and was described by Dutch officials as 'a colony of a colony'.

34 Dexter, *op. cit.*, 806; Kirby, iii, 423

35 F. C. Jones, *Japan's New Order in East Asia*, 429

36 Ehrman, *Grand Strategy Volume VI*, 300–306; Kirby, v, 175–92; Kahn, *op. cit.*, 610

Index